The Defense Reform Debate

THE DEFENSE REFORM DEBATE

ISSUES AND ANALYSIS

Edited by

Asa A. Clark IV
Peter W. Chiarelli
Jeffrey S. McKitrick
James W. Reed

THE JOHNS HOPKINS UNIVERSITY PRESS
Baltimore and London

The views expressed in this book are those of the authors and do not reflect the official policy or position of the Department of Defense, Department of the Army, or the United States Military Academy.

Chapter 5, by Richard K. Betts, "Dubious Reform: Strategism versus Managerialism," appeared in altered form as "Conventional Strategy: New Critics, Old Choices" in *International Security,* vol. 7 (Spring 1983), © 1983, The MIT Press. Reprinted by permission.

Chapter 8, by Steven L. Canby, was presented at the Woodrow Wilson International Center for Scholars, June 1982. Portions of it have appeared in *International Security Review* (Fall 1982) and *Survival* (May/June 1983).

Major segments of chapter 11, by William J. Perry, have been published in William J. Perry and Cynthia A. Roberts, "Technology's Role in Meeting the Soviet Defense Challenge," *Technology Review,* July 1982, and in "The Nature of the Defense Problem in the 1980s, and the Role of Defense Technology in Meeting the Challenge," in *The Role of Technology in Meeting the Defense Challenges of the 1980s,* The Northeast Asia-U.S. Forum on International Policy, Stanford University, 1981.

Chapter 16, by David C. Jones, appeared as "What's Wrong with Our Defense Establishment," © 1982 by The New York Times Company. Reprinted by permission.

Library of Congress Cataloging in Publication Data
Main entry under title:
The Defense reform debate.

Includes index.
1. United States—Military policy—Addresses, essays, lectures. 2. United States—Armed Forces—Addresses, essays, lectures. 3. United States—Armed Forces—Weapons systems—Addresses, essays, lectures. 4. United States—Armed Forces—Procurement—Addresses, essays, lectures. 5. United States—Armed Forces—Appropriations and expenditures—Addresses, essays, lectures. I. Clark, Asa A.
UA23.D424   1984   355'.0335'.73   83-49196
ISBN 0-8018-3205-5
ISBN 0-8018-3206-3 (pbk.)

CONTENTS

III   DOCTRINAL ISSUES

IV   FORCE STRUCTURE ISSUES

V   MODERNIZATION AND WEAPONS ACQUISITION ISSUES

VI   THE ORGANIZATION OF DEFENSE POLICY MAKING

VII THE OUTLOOK FOR DEFENSE REFORM

FIGURES

TABLES

FOREWORD

The military reform movement is a distinctive but not unprecedented effort to bring about changes in American military doctrine, strategy, weapons, and organization. It is the fourth such effort since World War II. The predecessors of the reformers include the strategists of the 1950s, the systems analysts of the early 1960s, and the arms controllers of the mid-late 1960s and early 1970s. These movements were reactions to perceived deficiencies in American military thinking and performance. The strategists of the 1950s reacted to the perceived American tendency to draw a sharp line between peace and war, between politics (or diplomacy) and the use of military force. The experience of the Korean War, in particular, emphasized the need to relate military force to political purpose; military victory, in and of itself, did not necessarily define the goals that military force should serve. As a result, the strategists developed theories of limited conventional war, of limited nuclear war, of counterforce versus countervalue targeting, and of the ladder of escalation. Their underlying goal was proportionality between political purpose and the use of military force.

The strategists came in large part, although not entirely, out of backgrounds in history and political science. At the beginning of the 1960s a second group of reformers, the systems analysts, emerged. They were, in effect, reacting to the development during the 1950s of a huge permanent military establishment and military-industrial complex and to the high rates of technological change and high levels of technological complexity in the military sphere. Their clearly articulated goal was cost-effectiveness in decision making on weapons and, in some measure, also on strategy, deployments, and tactics. They were concerned with the relation between marginal utility and marginal cost: how to get the most military utility for a given cost or how to achieve a given level of military utility for the least cost. They came largely, although not entirely, out of economics.

The development of substantial Soviet nuclear capabilities stimulated during the 1960s another major strand of defense thinking, focused on arms control. If the United States and the Soviet Union were to avoid endlessly escalating levels of nuclear capabilities, agreements would have to be reached limiting and channeling arms development. The arms controllers saw arms control as the equal partner of defense policy. U.S. security required both the right military policies on what weapons to build and also the right arms control policies to develop mutually acceptable limits on both Soviet and American arms build-ups. The arms controllers came largely, although not entirely, out of the physical sciences.

The military reform movement of the late 1970s shares many characteristics with these earlier efforts to change military policy. Like them, its most active members are largely, although not entirely, civilians. Like its predecessors, it is a reaction to perceived deficiencies in American military policy. The underlying concern of the reformers seems to be with the failure of the United States to adapt its military policies to the overall decline in relative American power in the world. Yet the military reform movement also differs from its predecessors in important ways. Its most active members come from highly varied backgrounds; it is hard to identify any one preeminent disciplinary background or experience. It is also rather hard, except at a most general level, to identify a single, unifying goal of the military reform movement. The strategists wanted to relate military force to political purpose. The systems analysts wanted to increase cost effectiveness in military decision making. The arms controllers wanted to elevate arms control to equality with deterrence in American security policy. What is the comparable overriding goal of the military reformers? It is, obviously, to reform. But to reform what?

The answer would appear to be almost everything. In "The Case for Military Reform," Senator Gary Hart identified the following as reform goals: increases in the defense budget, higher spending on "innovative weapons and programs," "re-examination of basic defense doctrine and concepts," building "smaller, less expensive carriers in much larger numbers," building more "modern diesel-electric submarines . . . hydrofoils and surface effect ships," shifting the emphasis in land warfare doctrine from "attrition dominated by massive firepower" to maneuver, changing the military education and promotion system "to give officers a chance to think about warfare," placing more stress on military history and theory in military schools, "upgrading and revitalizing our military journals," reducing the "administrative load on the officer in the field," shifting from a "bureaucratic model" of organization to a "corporative model" today found only in the Marine Corps, and bringing about (unspecified) changes in the way the armed services make decisions.[1]

One cannot help but be impressed by the scope and diversity of this list. Other reformers would probably come up with equally long and slightly different lists of things that needed to be done, including promotion and rotation policies that will enhance unit cohesion and the desirability of a maritime rather than a continental strategy. The problem is: What do all these proposed changes have in common? Is there any overarching purpose or concept such as the strategists, systems analysts, and arms controllers seemed to have? I must confess that I find it difficult to identify one. Most of the reforms that have been proposed are undoubtedly desirable, and some are urgently needed, but it is hard to see how they fit together and what they add up to.

Two central points in the reform critique, for instance, are the desirability of shifting the emphasis in military doctrine from attrition to maneuver and of shifting the emphasis in military procurement from a smaller number of highly sophisticated (and expensive) weapons to a larger number of proven, less sophisticated (and cheaper) weapons. What relationship exists between these two key elements of the reform program? It is hard to see why maneuver should imply larger numbers of simpler weapons or why highly sophisticated weapons are tied in with an attrition doctrine. If anything, one would think that just the reverse would be true: that a maneuver doctrine would require highly advanced sophisticated weapons for rapid movement and effective command and control, while an attrition doctrine would demand overpowering numbers of simpler, cheaper weapons that one could afford to lose in battle. Indeed, one of the reform arguments against attrition is that it is based on the dubious assumption that in the next war the United States will have precisely the overwhelming superiority in materiel that it had in past wars. But isn't this argument in favor of the reformers' doctrine also an argument against their weapons procurement policies?

The proposals of the reformers are thus heterogeneous and at times possibly contradictory. They do, nonetheless, share one deficiency which is, in fact, their greatest virtue. The reformers almost totally eschew any discussion of nuclear strategy and nuclear weapons. This is, perhaps, their greatest contribution to the discussion of military policy. The central issue of American military policy in the 1980s is how to develop the military capability to support expanded U.S. commitments that now include the Middle East-Persian Gulf in addition to the Western Hemisphere, Japan-Korea, and NATO, during a period that follows two decades of sustained and comprehensive growth in Soviet military power. The reformers have sparked the debate on this issue by directing attention away from the often necessary but also often highly abstract, sterile, and speculative issues concerning strategic forces and their employment to the real-life issues of how to train, equip, organize, and employ the military forces that will, almost certainly, fight real wars in real time in this decade. This concern has appropriately led them into issues concerning doctrine, organization, education, and training that civilians have often neglected in the past.

The reformers have thus tended to avoid the hotter political issues of defense policy that often dominate public attention. They have steered clear of the MX, INF, and the nuclear freeze, and that is a good thing. They have also, however, tended to avoid other highly sensitive political issues that the logic of their analysis almost inevitably at some point will force them to confront. They have not, for instance, gone deeply into the subject of recruitment policy and the trade-offs between technology and manpower. Yet the larger numbers of cheaper tanks, ships, and planes the reformers want will require larger numbers of expensive soldiers, sailors, and airmen to man them. Unless the reformers assume a high and permanent unemployment rate, huge increases in manpower costs may be necessary to implement their procurement proposals. Or do they contemplate reintroduction of some form of selective service? The reformers tend to be rather quiet on these issues.

The reformers may or may not have the right answers for American military policy during the coming decade. As the essays in this book demonstrate clearly, that can be a matter of intense debate. They have, however, surely raised the right questions and have properly focused attention on the most pressing areas of concern in military affairs. For that, all of us interested in military policy should be grateful. There is also no doubt that their zeal, ideas, and contentiousness will result in American military forces better able to meet the challenges of this decade. For that, all American citizens should be grateful.

SAMUEL P. HUNTINGTON

NOTE

1. Sen. Gary Hart, "The Case for Military Reform," *Wall Street Journal*, 23 January 1981.

PREFACE

For two decades the United States Military Academy has sponsored the West Point Senior Conference as an informal seminar to facilitate the open exchange of ideas on a topic of immediate and significant national concern. Topics are chosen based on their current or future impact on United States security planning.

The theme of our twentieth conference was "The 'Military Reform' Debate: Directions for the Defense Establishment for the Remainder of the Century," and was the genesis for this volume. This two-day meeting was organized across three subtopics that have dominated the debate and set the parameters for the discussions: "Future Threats and the Need for Doctrinal Innovation," "The Modernization Debate: Quantity versus Quality," and "The Force Structure Debate: Allocative Implications." Many of the arguments made in the ensuing chapters were first presented at the 1982 conference to an audience composed of prominent advocates of the various positions articulated during the current reform debate. We feel that this publication provides both the interested citizen and the serious student of military studies a balanced volume representing the most current thoughts on this important subject. Additionally, this book should prove to be an important record of one of the more critical defense policy-making periods in our nation's history.

Although an academic institution, West Point's overarching purpose is to train, educate, and inspire officers and cadets to pursue excellence and to cherish integrity as professional army officers. This purpose links West Point directly with the army: as a training source for new and mid-career officers; as a symbol of the professional commitment to "Duty, Honor, Country" for the army; and as an active research resource for the army. West Point has traditionally contributed its faculty talents in service of army concerns; for example, in policy consultation with the army staff, research work with army agencies, and analytical support for army manpower policy. Accordingly, West Point bears a special responsibility to contribute to and participate in continuous and thoughtful examination of issues relating to the army, the military, and American national security in general.

The contents of this publication in no way represent an official policy position of either the United States Military Academy or any other agency of the United States government. It is our hope that this volume will make a contribution to the interest we all have in common—maintaining and enhancing the security of the United States of America.

LIEUTENANT GENERAL WILLARD W. SCOTT, JR.
Superintendent, United States Military Academy

ACKNOWLEDGMENTS

Military reform—a longstanding, but infrequently realized, tradition— aims for the "best" military. This volume is dedicated to that end. There are two reasons for pride that such a volume has been conceived by army officers at West Point. First, this volume testifies to the military's commitment to reform. Second, this research enterprise reflects the academic and professional focus of West Point:

> I must study politics and war, that my sons may have liberty to study mathematics and philosophy, in order to give their children a right to study painting, poetry and music. (John Adams)

We owe much to the members of the Department of Social Sciences and to its head, Colonel Lee Donne Olvey, for their support, encouragement, and assistance as this project progressed through its many stages. Without the professional competence of our outstanding office staff, led by Ms. Barbara Thomas, the journey would have been even longer. Had it not been for the sincere dedication and skill of Ms. Vicky Lilos, the manuscript would still be awaiting final typing. And we would like to give special thanks to Henry Tom, Carol Ehrlich, and the rest of the fine staff at the Johns Hopkins University Press for all their help.

All royalties from this book will be deposited in a fund for faculty research and development at West Point. This was made possible by the willingness of our contributors to donate their time and considerable talents.

Finally, the editors dedicate this book to our wives and children for their patience; and to the soldiers, sailors, airmen, and the nation they serve for whom the continuation of this debate is so critical.

I

STRATEGY OVERVIEW

In his article, tartly entitled "Why We Need More 'Waste, Fraud, and Mismanagement' in the Pentagon," reformer Edward Luttwak condemns critics and reformers alike for what he views as obsessive concern with managerial efficiency in military matters.

> It is the compulsion exercised upon the whole defense structure in the name of efficiency that finally strangles what potential there is for the pursuit of strategic wisdom, operational ingenuity, and tactical art. . . . Why should bookkeeping detract from strategy?[1]

Luttwak continues by decrying reformers' fixation with micro-issues and failure to focus on larger, integrative frameworks for military reform:

> It is the great peculiarity of strategy that its issues can only be understood as a whole, that is, when matters are viewed in the broadest possible perspective.[2]

A reformer himself, Luttwak argues that military reform must begin with articulation of a coherent and comprehensive military strategy, derived from and focused to support U.S. national strategy as the political core of American foreign policy. The reform movement is fundamentally flawed, by this standard, because of its failure to address strategy and strategic issues.

Many rationalize this failure by observing that the problems are simply too difficult. Strategic consensus requires almost unprecedented cooperation, agreement, and coordination among policy makers, strong and dedicated administration leadership, and a commitment by Congress and the American public to support force deployments and resource requirements demanded by such fundamental strategic decisions.

It is imperative that a U.S. military strategy be articulated. Although difficult, this task is not insurmountable. The discussion by Ambassador Komer is presented to spark the reform debate on strategy by arguing for the necessity of a strategic foundation for military reform. Komer also argues the merits of a particular strategy which, in his view, best satisfies U.S. interests and supports future U.S. military policy.

NOTES

1. Edward Luttwak, "Why We Need More 'Waste, Fraud, and Mismanagement' in the Pentagon," *Commentary,* February 1982, p. 20.
2. Ibid., p. 21.

1

STRATEGY AND MILITARY REFORM

Robert W. Komer

Komer points out that reformers, the military, and recent administrations alike have largely ignored the important issues relating to nonnuclear strategy. Reform, says Komer, must address "macro- as well as micro-issues." Although he does not view strategy as a panacea, Komer states that the JCS, as currently organized, is "systemically incapable" of providing the military advice necessary to produce a much-needed unified strategy.

Bureaucracies are by nature conservative in outlook, and military institutions, the archetype of hierarchical bureaucracies, are among the most conservative. Thus, it is not surprising that impulses for change come largely from outside the military itself.[1] Moreover, outside critics can play a particularly important role at a time when, owing to the United States' decline in relative military power and increased vulnerability to nuclear attack, the United States itself is in a less than enviable security position and faces a host of political and economic constraints that make it difficult to meet looming security needs.

To the extent that such critics can organize themselves effectively as a military reform movement, their collective impact can be markedly enhanced. In particular it is doubly encouraging to see congressmen as well as their staffs among movement members, since Congress can be a powerful force for reform. The reformers also rightly concentrate on conventional force issues, the area where most of our money goes but one sadly neglected in our preoccupation with the nuclear calculus.

Thus, it is a pity that the military reform movement seems so amorphous and diffuse that its likely impact will be muted. Unsurprisingly, its members are much better at criticizing than at coming up with realistic alternatives on which action could be taken. Perhaps the only unifying theme among its many adherents is a firm—and understandable—conviction that major changes are needed in our security posture to adapt it more effectively to a changing world. A cynic might call them a gaggle of individualist prima donnas who use "reform" as a rubric for their own particular and widely varying nostrums, rather than seeking a broad-based, coherent approach to the larger issues of national defense.

Indeed, most of the reformers tend to focus primarily on specific micro-issues—hardware choices, doctrines, tactics, force structures, specific quantity versus quality trade-offs, and the like. Only a few of them try to build broad macro-generalizations or to address the broad missions and purposes for which we spend so much these days.[2] As a critic of these critics put it, "They do not see the forest for the trees."[3] Since the military itself is equally prone to this, it is hard to fault the reformers unduly. Nonetheless, as Richard Betts argues, the reform impetus must address "macro- as well as micro-issues." One such larger issue is what strategy we should adopt to achieve our security aims, a subject most reformers tend to neglect. Much of what they loosely call "strategy" turns out, in fact, to be doctrine or tactics.[4] This neglect is doubly regrettable, because recent administrations and their military advisers have tended to ignore many real issues of nonnuclear strategy in all but a rhetorical sense.

THE ROLE OF STRATEGY

After all, the overarching question should be, Reform for what purpose? Here is where strategy comes in. What are the most important security interests that we wish to preserve, and what strategy is best suited to preserve them against the most critical threats? From resolution of these questions should logically flow our doctrine, tactics, force structure, and equipment. In real life, of course, defense planning is far more complex. Strategic options are shaped at least as much by existing posture, tactics, and doctrine as they shape them, and must be designed within a host of other constraints. Indeed, a good working definition of strategy is "choices among constrained options." It cannot be based upon unrealistic hopes converted into assumptions, such as that the Western Europeans could readily defend themselves if only the United States would stop doing it for them. Theoretically this is so; in practice it is a pipe dream.

Nor is strategy a panacea. Especially in a context of constrained resources we must prudently cut the cost to fit the cloth. How to get the greatest capability from what we do invest lies at least as much in the realm of what some reformers condemn as "managerialism" as in that of imaginative strategy. So "strategism" is not an alternative to "managerialism" but an essential complement to it.[5]

Indeed, a valid criticism of what passes for present U.S. military strategy is that it far exceeds our capability to execute it. Here we get into "force sizing," the key link between strategy and programs. Reportedly the Joint Chiefs of Staff believe that nine more carrier battle groups, fourteen more tactical air wings, and nine more army divisions are necessary to carry out the Reagan administration's expansive strategic guidance. This is what the service chiefs mean when they complain about the mismatch between our strategy and our resources. The trouble is that the JCS can only agree on the need for more resources; changing the strategy by choosing among priorities would be unacceptable to one or more services.

Kaufmann describes earlier Pentagon efforts to relate force sizing to contingencies, especially given the perennial JCS concern that a major armed clash of U.S. and Soviet interests would inevitably lead to worldwide war.[6] Hence, in the early sixties we sought forces capable (along with our allies) of coping with a two-and-one-half-war scenario—Europe, the Far East, and a smaller contingency elsewhere. The post-Vietnam decline in U.S. defense efforts led us to capitalize on the Sino-Soviet split by adopting a one-and-one-half-war scenario, dropping the need to cope with Communist China.

However, the fall of the Shah and the Soviet invasion of Afghanistan focused U.S. concern on yet another key theater—the oil-rich Persian Gulf. The Carter Doctrine required the United States to adopt a "one-and-two-half-war" force-sizing scenario—Europe, plus the Persian Gulf, plus Korea-Japan. Now the Reagan administration has adopted an even more ambitious rationale for being able to deal with a full range of global threats. This is certainly the preference of the U.S. Navy, which naturally favors a flexible strategy as best suited to the use of seapower.[7] But clearly, unless we and our allies are prepared to spend a great deal more than presently in sight, something has got to give.

PRIORITIZING OUR STRATEGIC AIMS

In suggesting how best to prioritize our strategic aims, this chapter will start with those U.S. aims or interests deemed most essential to preserve. With these clearly in mind, it is far easier to determine sensible policies, doctrines, tactics, force and equipment mixes, and the like. Aside from deterrence of devastating nuclear attack on our homeland, the United States has an overriding strategic interest in preservation of a satisfactory global balance of power, principally vis-à-vis the only current major threat to that balance—the other superpower. Aside from Henry Kissinger, most Americans do not like to think in terms of a balance of power; it has a ring of European power politics about it. But as Kissinger keeps telling us, it is the most valid basis for ordering our strategic aims.

Here we get into another unfamiliar field, that of geopolitics.[8] Clearly, preventing Soviet domination of three key areas is essential—the industrial agglomeration of Western Europe, Japan, and the Persian Gulf region from which they draw most of the energy that fuels their industry. Accommodation of any one of these areas with Moscow could radically alter the global power balance. In fact, to prevent potentially hostile domination of one of them— Europe—was the underlying strategic rationale for U.S. participation in World Wars I and II.

We must also take into account the geopolitical fact that all three of our regional vital interests lie on the rimland of Eurasia, close to the Soviet heartland and far overseas from the United States. This geographical disadvantage necessarily shapes our conventional strategy (unless we choose to retreat to isolationism). For one thing it compels us to adopt a force projection strategy, which imposes on us greater strategic mobility and logistic burdens than on the Soviets. A counterbalancing advantage is that this limits war damage to the Eurasian continent unless conflict escalates into nuclear exchange (in all four U.S. twentieth-century wars our allies provided the battlefields).

Command of the sea is another sine qua non of any force projection strategy. No one can dispute that maritime superiority is a strategic imperative for the United States. The real issues are how many areas we must dominate simultaneously and what kind and size of navy is optimum for executing this strategy.[9]

To say that Europe, Japan, and the Persian Gulf should logically be the chief objectives of our strategy is not to neglect other lesser or subsidiary objectives. It is simply a matter of putting first things first. Moreover, as is often pointed out, the likelihood of overt Soviet aggression, at least against Europe and Japan, is relatively low. In a nuclear age where both superpowers are careful to avoid clashing directly, conflict is least likely in areas where the lines of superpower interest are most clearly drawn. It is much more likely to break out in the volatile Third World. Witness Korea and Vietnam, two areas where we never expected to have a fight.

This suggests a flexible strategy and a flexible posture to execute it. But we should try to prudently calibrate our strategy for dealing with lesser threats to responses we can afford. Surely this is one of the key strategic lessons of Vietnam. While the loss of Indochinese real estate did not radically alter the balance of power, it certainly cost the United States enormously in terms of our perceived will and ability to cope with larger threats.

Nor can we fall prey to the "likelihood fallacy." At a time of nuclear stalemate and constrained conventional resources, can we afford further major strategic diversions like Vietnam or even Korea if they draw off too many constrained resources from other more vital theaters? To the extent that political realities permit, we should design our strategy and posture to deter or defeat the most critical threats, not necessarily the most likely ones. After all, the likelihood of Soviet aggression against Western Europe or Japan is low precisely because the United States has not only made clear that it would resist but has taken extensive measures to back up its declaratory policy.

RELATED STRATEGIC ISSUES

In a nuclear age, where deterrence must be first priority, a force projection strategy also dictates forward deployments, since forward deployed U.S. forces make clear to any foe that it will be directly engaged from the outset with the United States. They also greatly enhance initial defense. Thus, forward deployment is cheap at the price, especially since the only real economic cost is the utterly marginal differential between what it costs to maintain these forces overseas and back home.

It is often alleged that forward deployments rob us of flexibility, but a closer look suggests that they facilitate quick response, even in other theaters than those to which deployed (for example, our ability to move naval forces expeditiously to the Persian Gulf from the Mediterranean and Western Pacific). Forward basing also reduces strategic lift and logistic requirements. Thus, it is disturbing to find some so-called reformers ignoring these macro-issues, and others even advocating a "bring the boys home" position. What good are better tactics or force structure if we can't get the forces there in timely fashion in the first place?

The reformers tend to neglect the optimum utilization of warning time, so crucial to any responsive strategy—especially one aimed at maximizing deterrence. Another macro-issue to which congressional reformers in particular ought to address themselves is the optimum balance between readiness, modernization, sustainability, and force structure—the four essential pillars on which any responsive conventional posture must be built. The relative priority between readiness and modernization, for example, should depend upon our estimate of the likelihood of major conflict in the turbulent decade ahead. It is worth remembering the British cabinet's infamous "ten-year rule" adopted each year from 1919 to 1932 (the presumption that Britain need not plan on major conflict for the next decade), which undermined British defense preparedness.

COALITION STRATEGY

Even were the United States to abandon any notion that it can any longer afford to be policeman of the world, its vital interests would remain global in nature if for no other reason than that Western Europe, Japan, and the Persian Gulf oil region are widely separated from each other as well as from the United States. It is the Soviet Union that has the strategic advantage of interior lines. Moreover, the United States is far more dependent on overseas trade and resources than is the nearly autarkic Soviet economy.

Consequently, there is no way in which the United States can assure its own security without the collaboration of allies. That the United States has long since recognized this strategic imperative is apparent in the way in which, after two bloody world wars, we definitely abandoned George Washington's policy of "no entangling alliances" in favor of a global network aimed principally at deterring Soviet expansionism.

The sheer growth of Soviet military power, the relative decline of U.S. power, the advent of nuclear stalemate, and the traditional reluctance of democracies to spend adequately on defense in peacetime, all make Americans in the 1980s as dependent on our allies as they are on us. Without their forces, their real estate, and their other contributions, it would be well nigh impossible to preserve our vital interests at any politically acceptable cost. Indeed, at a time when many bemoan our becoming second militarily and losing our technological edge, we still retain one enormous strategic advantage over the USSR: we have many comparatively rich allies, while the USSR has only a handful of poor ones. Most of theirs are a net drain on the Soviet exchequer, whereas most of ours contribute more than it costs us to help defend them.

Yet though we and our allies have long since adopted a collective security policy, we have never taken the next step and adopted an integrated strategy and posture. We are all still gripped by what General David Jones, former chairman of the Joint Chiefs of Staff, calls the "sin of unilateralism." Though coalition war is the historical norm rather than the exception, especially in major conflicts, after each war nations revert to planning and posturing for the next one as if they were going to fight alone. Even NATO, unique in the history of alliances in its peacetime combined command, other coordination machinery, and common programs, is basically just a collection of individually balanced national forces rather than a balanced collective force. The wasteful overlap and duplication in R&D, procurement, training, logistics, and communications is appalling. Since the mismatch between strategy and resources is one of our most serious problems, it is depressing to find most reformers as innocent of ways to tackle this problem as are the official establishments themselves.

ALTERNATIVE OPERATIONAL STRATEGIES

When it comes to operational strategy—what priorities we ought to actually adopt in wartime—at least a few reformers squarely address this issue. Congressman Gingrich and Captain James W. Reed are most clearheaded in urging that the reform impulse be guided by "a clear conception of the Soviet threat, a concern for the process by which we structure the military reform debate, and an appreciation of the political realities that constrain our range of options." Gingrich and Reed frame the issue most clearly, using a British analogy, as being "whether to follow Marlborough's Continental strategy or, alternatively, the elder Pitt's blue water strategy," instead of trying to do both with inadequate resources. They give a series of cogent reasons why the "Continental" strategy must take precedence.[10]

Jeffrey Record, another avowed reform movement member, takes the opposite tack. He sees the "steady and perhaps irreversible disintegration of NATO" as an effective entity for the defense of Europe and the emergence of "a host of new threats to vital U.S. security interests in Southwest Asia and in other areas outside Europe" as dictating abandonment of the conventional wisdom that most U.S. ground forces should be allocated to NATO defense. If our European allies will not contribute adequately to NATO defense, despite their undoubted capacity to do so, then the United States should focus primarily on other threats to our interests, since we cannot do both with the force levels likely to be realistically available. Hence, he calls for withdrawal of U.S. ground forces from Germany, cutting the size of the army, and major expansion of U.S. Navy and Marine forces to carry out "a new global strategy based primarily on seapower and seaborne force projection capabilities and oriented primarily toward non-NATO contingencies."[11]

Whatever one's reaction to the opposing Gingrich and Record theses, both properly pose the key conventional strategic issue facing this nation. Since we cannot realistically meet all the requirements of a potential three-front threat, we should choose between them and form our strategy and force posture accordingly. Here is truly a macro-issue that should influence decisions on force sizing, force structure (for example, light versus heavy forces), and a host of other matters, but which other reformers tend to ignore.

Significantly, however, both Gingrich and Reed and Record tend to view the issue primarily in terms of U.S. strategy and U.S. responses, leaving out the collective contributions that our allies can and should make. Both are guilty of the sin of unilateralism so characteristic of the mainstream establishment they criticize. Gingrich and Reed, however, clearly recognize the larger balance of power and political implications of "losing" Western Europe, whereas Record nowhere bothers to examine these consequences (indeed, he acknowledges that the USSR could take over Persian Gulf oil as well). For example, the disintegration of NATO he forecasts would become a self-fulfilling prophecy were the United States in effect to abandon conventional defense.

While it is desirable to preserve a degree of studied ambiguity about our actual wartime strategy for the sake of deterrence, it is important to look at alternatives that would reduce the likelihood of having to devote major efforts simultaneously to at least three and perhaps additional theaters in the event of a major conventional war. While we must hedge against the possibility of escalation to simultaneous multifront operations, need this be inevitable? Are the Soviets all that likely to see advantage in multiple front operations instead of concentrating on one or two theaters and then shifting to others? One lesson to date of the nuclear age is that it makes superpowers very cautious about expanding conventional conflict, lest it lead to nuclear escalation. In any case, the United States should carefully examine wartime strategic alternatives that could limit the dispersion of constrained resources. The most interesting possibilities may lie in the Far East, where neither China nor Japan is eager to become embroiled in a U.S.-Soviet war.[12]

FLAWS IN A MARITIME STRATEGY

Indeed, the fatal flaw in a maritime supremacy strategy (and posture) is that even were the United States to command all seven seas and use them with impunity, we could not thereby seriously injure the Soviet Union. Nor could we prevent that great heartland power from using its land access to dominate the three key rimland areas of Eurasia (Europe, Japan, and the Persian Gulf), thereby decisively altering the balance of power against us.[13]

The kind of naval posture toward which the dominant carrier admirals, and their articulate leader, Secretary of the Navy John Lehman, are driving is also a classic example of how bad strategy can dictate bad force posture. While command of the seas at times and places of our own choosing is vital to our force projection strategy, do we need fifteen big carrier battle groups for that purpose, as opposed to the twelve that previous secretaries of defense had favored? Moreover, to invest so much of the navy's constrained budget in big carrier battle groups is already proving to be at some cost to antisubmarine warfare capabilities to keep open the sea lanes. And are big carriers the optimum defense against the air threat to convoys, as opposed to land-based air? Even with respect to offensive maritime operations, many "black shoe" admirals contend that proliferation of cruise missiles would enable more effective penetration of heavily defended sea or land targets than would carrier-based air. Thus, even leaving aside questions of carrier vulnerability and capability, there is a serious question of whether we are building the right kind of navy for the strategy we ought to pursue. The only thing not in question is its cost.

Another dubious aspect of a maritime supremacy strategy is its predilection for what has come to be termed "horizontal escalation." That is, instead of first resisting Soviet aggression in areas where the Soviets have an advantage, we should plan to exert countervailing forces elsewhere in areas where we have an advantage, especially where we can capitalize on our superiority at sea. This theory is appealing in principle but all too likely to prove counterproductive in concrete cases. For example, what U.S. response would be optimum should the USSR lunge for Persian Gulf oil? Admittedly, it would be difficult for U.S. retaliation against Cuba or South Yemen to provide adequate compensation for Western loss of vital oil access. Nor would sweeping the Soviets from the seas be adequate recompense for the loss.

Moreover, the Soviets too could escalate against Eurasian targets more vital to us than their offshore satellites are to them. And the risks of nuclear escalation would be brought much closer.[14]

Yet this is precisely the direction in which the Reagan administration is moving, largely by default. Though it talks boldly of an eclectic strategy and force posture, in fact the bulk of its General Purpose Forces spending is going for a costly, carrier-heavy navy designed not primarily for sea control but for offensive force projection against Soviet targets. Suffice it to say that even if its big carrier battle groups could accomplish all that their advocates claim, they could not seriously hurt a land animal like the USSR.[15] Meanwhile, the navy's costs will inevitably rise at the same time the ambitious Reagan defense program is already being cut back sharply by a deficit-conscious Congress.

If, as Secretary of the Navy Lehman claims, his big ship navy, already under contract, will nonetheless be built, then we are liable to end up eventually with dangerously unbalanced forces and a severe "readiness crunch" as readiness programs are sacrificed by Congress to keep funding big ticket procurement items like new carriers (and the B-1 bomber). In effect, regardless of our declaratory strategy, we will be committed to a predominantly maritime one—a recipe for strategic disaster.

LINKING STRATEGY AND REFORM

If the reform movement is to generate the constructive impact it desires, it should address more systematically these larger issues of strategy and posture, which ought to help condition the optimum solutions to the lesser issues the reformers mostly pose. Is preserving a satisfactory global balance of military power the right overall objective? If so, is global unilateralism, to be undergirded by focusing predominantly on a maritime supremacy strategy, the right way to go?[16] Or must we capitalize more effectively on our single greatest strategic advantage over the USSR, which is that we have many more powerful allies than Moscow can count on? If collectively we already outmatch the Soviet bloc in defense inputs, how can we generate more comparable outputs via a rational division of labor and more sensible cooperation? What is the optimum balance among readiness, sustainability, modernization, and force size in a coalition context, given the inevitable resource constraints?

How we resolve these issues in the last analysis will almost surely have more impact on our overall security than whether we build large or small carriers, quantity versus quality tradeoffs, leadership versus managerialism, and the like. These lesser issues are important too, but it is difficult to resolve them without a clearer perspective on what it is we want our forces to do.

Congressman Gingrich and Captain Reed also advise the reform movement wisely when they say that "perhaps more than anything we need to reexamine the process by which we reach for answers to difficult questions of strategy and doctrine." Outside reformers can do a great deal to jog this process, but it will be officialdom that has the final say.

Therefore, the movement might well achieve its greatest impact by pressing vigorously for reform of the institutional system by which decisions are made. From many years of experience at top levels in the process, the author can attest that this process does not work very well. For one thing our military establishment rarely studies the lessons of history (even recent history like Vietnam); it doesn't systematically study strategy even in the senior service schools; and what passes for conventional strategic thinking in our major commands or in the Pentagon is often seriously flawed.

Worse yet, our civilian leadership is more often than not unable to get coherent unified strategic advice from the military institution specifically charged with rendering it. As several secretaries of defense and former chiefs of staff have testified, the Joint Chiefs of Staff machinery is systematically incapable of rendering the military advice they need. As a result we lack a unified strategy. What we have is more like four service strategies with differing emphases and different, often overlapping force structures to execute them. This may well be productive of more waste than any other thing. One has the impression that most avowed members of the reform movement favor JCS reform. They could perform a service by putting it high on their agenda as a practical issue whose time has come.

NOTES

1. There is one major exception, high technology, where the military has systematically organized itself to keep up with the state of the art.

2. Among the chief exceptions are Canby, Luttwak, Record, and Gingrich, who can draw on considerable study and experience. The last two address key issues of strategy in this volume.

3. Trevor Dupuy, "The Pied Pipers of Maneuver Style Warfare," *Armed Forces Journal* (November 1981): 74.

4. The debate over "maneuver strategy" versus "firepower" or "attrition" is essentially a doctrinal debate, though naturally with strategic implications.

5. Richard Betts rather cruelly accuses Edward Luttwak of "strategic romanticism" of this sort in, for example, Luttwak's "Why We Need More 'Waste, Fraud, and Mismanagement' in the Pentagon," *Commentary,* February 1982.

6. William W. Kaufmann, *Planning Conventional Forces, 1950–80* (Washington, D.C.: The Brookings Institution, 1982), p. 6.

7. Kaufmann describes how the navy was never willing to allocate naval forces to specific scenarios in the force-sizing exercises of previous administrations, preferring to rely on "flexibility." Ibid., pp. 11–13.

8. For a compelling update on geopolitics in the contemporary international context,

see Colin S. Gray, *The Geopolitics of the Nuclear Era: Heartlands, Rimlands, and the Technological Revolution* (New York: Crane, Russak & Co., 1977).

9. Adm. Stansfield Turner states this issue most clearly in "The Unobvious Lessons of the Falkland War," *Naval Institute Proceedings* (April 1983): 34–55. See also his "A New Military Strategy," *Foreign Affairs* 61 (Fall 1982): 123–32.

10. See chap. 3, "Guiding the Reform Impulse."

11. See chap. 9, "Implications of a Global Strategy for U.S. Forces."

12. Interestingly, neither Gingrich and Reed nor Record devotes much attention to the northeast Asia theater, including China and Japan.

13. See R. W. Komer, "Maritime Strategy vs. Coalition Defense," *Foreign Affairs* 60 (Summer 1982): 1124–45.

14. Former Secretary of Defense Harold Brown convincingly illustrates the hazards of horizontal escalation at sea in *Thinking about National Security* (Boulder, Colo.: Westview Press, 1983), pp. 172–74.

15. Even Record wants a different kind of navy, oriented primarily toward sea control. See *U.S. Strategy at the Crossroads: Two Views* (Cambridge, Mass.: Institute for Foreign Policy Analysis, 1982), pp. 33–34.

16. This issue should not be simplistically misinterpreted as a navy versus army and air force argument with, as one critic puts its, "all the overtones of a service budget debate with enough strategic fluff to give it respectability" (Col. W. O. Staudenmaier, "One If by Land, Two If by Sea," *Army Magazine* [January 1983]: 37). Of course it has budget implications, but surely the forces that budgets buy should be directed toward some sensible strategic purpose.

II

REFORMING THE DEFENSE ESTABLISHMENT

In the preface to his classic history of World War I, *The Real War, 1914–1918,* Captain B. H. Liddell Hart somewhat sardonically, yet realistically, warned:

> The historian's rightful task is to distill experience as a medicinal warning for future generations, not to distill a drug. Having fulfilled this task to the best of his ability, and honesty, he has fulfilled his purpose. He would be a rash optimist if he believed that the next generation would trouble to absorb the warning. History at least teaches the historian a lesson.

Given the mistakes of those who planned for and led men into the wars that followed, many would argue that Hart's admonition was correct. Foremost among this group today are those that are collectively known as the military reform movement.

Hart's book and the role he and others played in the period between the two world wars are proof that the existence of organized groups critical of military policy is not without precedent. Military reform and the agents it has spawned are as old as the first battle lost.

The performance of the American military in the postwar period has caused some to question the ability of the services to meet future threats. Korea, Vietnam, and the Iranian hostage rescue mission are often cited as examples to support the thesis that recent Pentagon policies have not produced a military capable of winning. Today's reformers are generally critical of established policy and performance in the following areas: strategy, doctrine, force structure, weapons acquisition, and defense organization. What makes this phase of the debate noteworthy is the extent to which the current reformers have begun to build a constituency that includes members of Congress, the military, and even the public.

There are people, including contributors to this anthology, who have been concerned with these same issues for many years and consider themselves reformers. Yet, for various reasons, they do not want to be counted as members of what is commonly known as the "military reform movement." However, they are important participants in the debate and have been a critical element in many of the battles leading to the successes claimed by the reform movement.

The current movement in the United States was sparked in large part by the actions and writings of five individuals: Colonel (Retired) John Boyd, Steven Canby, William S. Lind, Norman Polmar, and Pierre Sprey. Although the modern usage of the term "military reform" was reportedly first coined in a *Wall Street Journal* editorial by Senator Gary Hart (D., Colo.), long before then these five men began working on the specific aspects of the reform movement.

Boyd's work on air-to-air tactics in the 1950s was critical to the movement. From this evolved his theory of air-to-air combat and a period of broad historical research that together yielded his "Patterns of Conflict" briefing. The concepts contained in "Patterns of Conflict" are thought by some, as evidenced by the frequency with which Boyd is cited, to be the intellectual foundation of the reform movement.

Norman Polmar is considered by many to be one of the country's foremost experts on naval affairs. Besides having written numerous books on the subject, Polmar has the distinction of being the only regular columnist in the history of the *Naval Institute Proceedings*.

The first proposals attributable to this most recent of military reform movements came in 1976, with the publication of Senator Robert Taft, Jr.'s (R., Ohio) *White Paper on Defense*. Lind, then a legislative assistant for Taft, and Polmar were the primary authors of this document. Among other things it advocated a large cut in the army to fund a naval build-up of a radically different kind of navy, built around small V/STOL (Vertical/Short Take-Off and Landing) carriers, advanced technology surface warships, and a large diesel and nuclear submarine force.

When Taft was defeated in the 1976 election, Lind went to work for Senator Hart, who soon became a preeminent congressional spokesman for reform. In 1978, a new edition of the *White Paper on Defense* was published. That same year Boyd, Canby, Polmar, Sprey, and Lind began meetings from which emerged three common themes that collectively became the centerpiece for the reform movement. First was the conceptualization of "maneuver warfare" as an alternative to what was seen as the institutionalized doctrine of "firepower and attrition." Second was the common conclusion that weapons acquisition processes were being driven by the latest technology, much of it untested. Reformers questioned the cost-effectiveness of these "gold-plated" systems when compared to cheap, simple, battle-tested weapons. And finally, these reformers highlighted the contradiction between the nature of war and the bureaucratic behavior that had come to dominate the defense establishment.

Hart's 1981 *Wall Street Journal* piece coincided with the creation of the Congressional Military Reform Caucus. Congressman William Whitehurst (R-Virginia), the second-ranking minority member of the House Armed Services Committee, was impressed with Hart's comments and suggested they form a bicameral, bipartisan group to explore the means by which the reformers' ideas could be furthered. In 1983 that caucus includes about fifty members of Congress.

The caucus prides itself in having no designated leader. To associate the group's proposals with any single member of Congress would have the disadvantage of tying the caucus to a political party, ideology, or specific interest group. Thus, the group's goal is to reach consensus, a very difficult task given its bipartisan composition. When the members are united it is normally over only a vaguely defined goal; yet, the caucus's ability to garner membership and support from a broad political spectrum is unusual on Capitol Hill.

Hart, independent of the caucus, recently published what he termed a "military reform budget" that if adopted would operationalize many of the reform group's proposals. Additionally, members of the caucus have indicated that they will begin to address the formulation of strategy and its impact on reform. Although it is impossible to evaluate their effect, if any, on defense policy-making, the mere fact that a bipartisan caucus exists indicates a degree of congressional discontent with "staying the course" in the defense arena.

In chapter 2, Timothy T. Lupfer draws an important distinction between reformers and what he calls "critics" of military policy. He touches on the history of reform while making the point that proposed changes in the military will always encounter resistance. Lupfer insists that contrary to the belief of many reformers, this resistance is not the result of a conspiracy; rather, it arises from the inherent characteristics of the military.

Congressman Newt Gingrich (R., Georgia), a leading member of the reform caucus, joins with James W. Reed, a military officer, to argue against the common and simplistic perception that the current debate is being played out between a largely civilian group of "reformers" arrayed against uniformed defenders of the status quo. They see such conceptions as failing to recognize the degree to which all participants in the debate are united by certain common impulses. While reform is not new, they state that the character of the current debate, in many ways, is without precedent in the evolution of our military thinking.

John M. Oseth steps back from the debate and identifies the main points of contention. He sees the aim of the reformers as nothing less than the top-to-bottom reform of the American military. Rather than entering the debate, Oseth merely identifies and summarizes the principal points of contention and offers an assessment of its ultimate impact.

We conclude this introduction to the military reform debate with an evaluation of the reformist critique. While Richard K. Betts does not entirely discount the value of the reform arguments, he does contend that the reformers fail to demonstrate that their agenda offers unquestionably superior defense for less money.

2

THE CHALLENGE OF MILITARY REFORM

Timothy T. Lupfer

Lupfer argues that perceived resistance to reform is not a result of a conspiracy, but attributable to characteristics inherent in the military. Drawing the distinction between reformers and critics of military matters, he argues that to bridge the gap between criticism and reform one must recognize the obstacles to change and consciously seek to overcome them. He offers a way by which military critics can effectively serve as military reformers.

In fulfilling its unique purpose of applying force in the name of the state, the military must constantly balance two apparently contradictory forces: continuity and change. The need for the proper balance should be acknowledged in any question of military reform. Especially during this century, significant changes in political relationships, economic means, and technology have underscored the need for military forces to adapt to changing conditions. There is also the necessity within this environment of flux, however, to maintain continuity in thinking and in action so that order can be maintained in the chaos of events. Very careful discrimination must be exercised between what ought to be changed and what ought to be preserved, and this discrimination is particularly difficult to achieve in the realm of military matters. One benefit of a responsible approach to military reform will be conscious efforts to discern what should not be changed at a given time, which is just as crucial as identifying what should be changed.

The desire to reform is the intent to make a change for the better, but the best of intentions do not guarantee the desired results. Rather than describe the specific reforms advocated for the American military (these reforms are described in succeeding chapters), this chapter will propose that changes in the military will always encounter resistance. This resistance is not a result of conspiracy; rather, it arises from the inherent characteristics of the military, which spring from

1. the nature of war, the activity toward which all military efforts are ultimately directed;
2. centralized authority: the necessary monopoly that the state maintains over the use of military force;
3. decentralized execution: the dependence upon several participants acting with some autonomy in actual implementation.

These factors make the consummation of reform difficult to achieve, and distinct influences from the present environment (risk of nuclear war, bureaucratic competition) reinforce these general difficulties.

Criticism itself is not reform. To bridge the gap between criticism and successful reform one must recognize the obstacles to change. One must then gain the support of state authority and the cooperation of the active participants in order to implement effective reform. Therefore, today's reform discussions must not stop at the level of argument. Rather, these discussions must dispassionately acknowledge the obstacles to change and realistically seek to overcome them. This chapter will suggest a methodology for achieving this.

It is inherently difficult to change institutions responsible for the conduct of war. War is often likened to other human endeavors such as business or commerce, but the unique attributes of war should not be obscured by such comparisons. For example, to compare war with economic enterprise also reveals essential differences between war and other activities. The dynamism of the economic marketplace is based upon constant activity. Millions of independent decisions and actions create a cumulative economic effect, and the cause-and-effect relationships throughout the process are imperfectly understood. The cumulative effect of American economic activity in our history has been to raise the general material well-being of Americans, and this effect has justifiably been lauded. Yet, within this cumulative improvement, there have been numerous business failures. Defenders of the free market system, however, do not view these failures as an indictment of the system; on the contrary, that these failures can be absorbed in the overall process of cumulative improvement is perhaps the supreme strength of the system.[1] Participants at all levels of economic activity can initiate, take risks, fail, adapt, and recover. Ideally, within such a system creativity can flourish.

Whatever the virtues of the free market system, however, these virtues cannot be transferred directly to military activity. While much of the activity in the free market economy is initiated at various levels by independent actors, any form of government keeps a very tight grip on military activity. The military is a monopoly of the state. Therefore, the best qualities of the American economic system cannot be readily transferred to the military. Because of war's unique characteristics—infrequency of occurrence, tremendous cost, and perpetual uncertainty—the state will always carefully guard its monopoly over the military. The exercise of military power is an attribute of sovereignty. The use of force by the state will be characterized by central planning, close supervision of military means, and tight legal control by the highest authority. These characteristics will occur irrespective of economic, ideological, or cultural factors, and although they might not work effectively when applied to the economy, they are inevitable within the distinct realm of the use of force. Perhaps this explains the apparent inconsistency when a nation thoroughly bungles its national economy by inappropriate state intervention, and yet possesses effective military force and understands its use. The converse is also possible: a nation with a vibrant economy will not automatically be adept in the use of force.

Of the unique characteristics of war, cost is perhaps the most dominant. The awesome expenditure of time and treasure in war and, most importantly, the loss of life make decisions to employ force irreversible. Because of the seriousness of the cost, the decision to use force usually is not entered into lightly. It is an episodic activity of the state. This infrequency makes changes in the use of force difficult, for war lacks the dynamics of constant adjustment, which a free market economic system, for example, possesses. The episodic nature of war breeds uncertainty, for historical evidence is linked to the specific conditions of each occurrence, and direct, personal experience is infrequent. Those who desire to be expert in the use of force spend the greater part of their time and effort in periods of peace trying to anticipate a very uncertain future.

The cost, infrequency, and uncertainty of war generate a natural conservatism that permeates all military activity. The advocate of military reform assumes a great responsibility, since evidence for change must be sufficiently convincing to overcome the understandable caution inherent in the military. The burden of proof in an argument for change clearly rests with the advocate of reform. Many significant military reforms have only been possible in the wake of irrefutable evidence of the need for reform; unfortunately, such evidence often occurs in the form of a military disaster. Several French army reforms of the late eighteenth century, upon which Napoleon eventually capitalized, grew from the humiliation of the battle of Rossbach in 1757 during the Seven Years' War. The Prussian reforms of the early nineteenth century were motivated by the disaster of the battle of Jena in 1806. The inept American mobilization of 1898, irrespective of the fortunate outcome of the Spanish-American War, led to reforms in the early twentieth century. The importance of military readiness became painfully clear to the United States in the beginning of the Korean War.

The question for the United States military today is, Can we reform without a Jena? Can we agree on the necessity for appropriate reform without the painful clarity of failure, which has so often initiated effective military reform? Even if we agree on this necessity, can we effect reform in time? If a reform program is to succeed, it first must have the backing of state authority, and secondly must obtain sufficient backing from members of the military establishment to achieve the necessary collective, or corporate, effort. An advocate of reform without the backing of state authority is only a military critic. Once he gains the authority from the state, he becomes a reformer, but he becomes a *successful* reformer only when he has harnessed the corporate effort of the military establishment. Contrary to popular belief, this collective effort is not achieved by decree alone. State authority can initiate change but cannot consummate it. A reform will only be accepted if a sufficient body of active participants will see it through (possess the will) and are able to see it through (possess the means).

It is instructive to note that not all military thinkers have become military reformers. The examples of two famous theorists, Carl von Clausewitz and Sir Basil H. Liddell Hart, demonstrate the necessity of gaining state authority to achieve reform. The examples of these two men also provide a useful comparison of careers, for Clausewitz was a professional soldier, while Liddell Hart wrote the majority of his works after he had left active service.

Clausewitz's influence on military thinking has been profound, but his reputation is posthumous. His life was one of great frustration. Clausewitz belonged to a group of patriotic officers of the Prussian army who advocated broad political and military reforms for Prussia, in the hope of expanding the base of talent from which Prussia could draw for its benefit and security. These reform ideas posed a threat to the tight control exercised by the king of Prussia and the nobility, a control often exercised in the absence of much talent, as the Jena campaign so graphically illustrated. As a soldier, Clausewitz experienced the dilemma of owing obedience to a king whose bad judgment threatened the safety of his own country. In 1812, the king of Prussia became an ally of Napoleon and provided a Prussian contingent to support the French invasion of Russia. The Prussian officer reformers were appalled, for they had argued against any cooperation with Napoleon. The depth of Clausewitz's feeling was so great that he resigned his Prussian commission to serve with the Russian army against Napoleon and, therefore, against the king of Prussia.

Napoleon's Russian campaign was a disaster. Prussia subsequently broke with France and joined in an alliance with the Russians. Napoleon was finally defeated in 1814 and 1815. That the judgment of Clausewitz, now back in Prussian uniform for the final battles against Napoleon, had been proven correct did him no good in his relations with the king of Prussia. Once the danger of Napoleon had receded, reaction against the reformers and their ideas (the most lasting idea would be the general staff system) set in. For the rest of his career, Clausewitz usually occupied military positions of little direct importance to the army. During this period of frustration, Clausewitz directed his energies inwardly. He expressed his ideas on paper, but the effort was introspective. His ideas, published after his death in *On War*, have had a great influence, not during Clausewitz's lifetime, but upon posterity.[2]

Sir Basil H. Liddell Hart enjoyed much greater public recognition during his long lifetime than did Clausewitz, but like Clausewitz, he experienced great frustration in failing to have his ideas accepted by the highest authority. Liddell Hart was deeply affected by his participation as a company grade officer in World War I. Throughout his life, he was convinced that there was a better way to employ force than to rely on the massive, mechanical slaughters of the western front. Liddell Hart left the British army in 1924 for reasons of health and became a military correspondent. He was a prolific and beautifully expressive writer, and he soon gained a wide reputation. In contrast to the introspective work of Clausewitz, Liddell Hart's works were for a large public audience. Despite his reputation, though, his goal of military reform remained elusive. Liddell Hart was primarily a critic and a pundit. Although he exerted influence on British government defense policy in the late 1930s, with the advent of World War II, and particularly of Winston Churchill, Liddell Hart's influence became negligible. As British historian Brian Bond has written, during Britain's greatest struggle Liddell Hart "was offered no official appointment . . . and remained very much an outsider."[3]

Liddell Hart's example demonstrates the difficulties in going from critic to reformer. In a nation where expression is relatively free, there will be no shortage of critics. But because of the necessary state monopoly on the use of force, participation at levels of authority which affect military policy is limited. The critic thrives on argument; the reformer succeeds only where there is some form of reconciliation and cooperation, so necessary to implement reform. Liddell Hart's criticisms seemed at times to be for the benefit of argument only. While he was always eloquent, he was sometimes inconsistent (stressing mechanization for offense in the 1920s, but stating the primacy of the defense in the 1930s) and often hasty and inaccurate in his criticisms (particularly his condemnation of Clausewitz in *The Ghost of Napoleon*). It is also very questionable if his direct influence on British defense policy in the late 1930s was beneficial.

This distinction between the critic and the reformer is not intended to decry the role of the critic. That role is essential in reminding those in authority of the need for sound judgment and clear thinking. As Brian Bond remarks in his assessment of the utility of Liddell Hart's concept of the Indirect Approach, "There was a great deal to be said for encouraging a new generation of officers to think for themselves."[4] The distinction between critics and reformers is made, however, to distinguish between the indirect influence of the critic and the direct influence of the successful reformer on the military establishment.

Clausewitz became introspective, Liddell Hart became more stridently critical. Neither achieved the authority to enact lasting reform. Even if one succeeds in acquiring the authority of the state, that alone does not guarantee success. The desired change must also permeate the large military institution. Although the state carefully guards its authority with respect to the use of force, the institutions of the military execute the desires of the state in a decentralized manner. Decree does not ensure compliance. The resistance of military institutions to change is not satisfactorily explained by references to the alleged stubbornness of people in uniform; rather, it probably arises from the personal accountability, the professional ethic of being answerable for actions where stakes are so high, and results so uncertain. The military is a skeptical audience, and this applies as much to attempts to change the military from within as it does to attempts from outside. Although a critic can be bold in his individualism, the reformer, whether civilian or military, must recognize that the active support of the military establishment is essential to effect change.

An interesting example of cosmetic changes versus effective change in the military at the tactical level was provided in World War I in 1917. On the French side, a new commander in chief of French forces on the western front, Robert Nivelle, planned a great offensive for April. Exclaiming "I have the formula," he trained his army in methods which he thought would make it unbeatable. He was intolerant of skepticism and he ignored contradictory evidence. On the German side, new defensive tactics were adopted which were the product of a more careful use of evidence from the field. Rather than relying on rigid formulas, the Germans tended to rely on general principles, derived from experience and applied tactically with a fair amount of initiative left to the field commanders. Despite the stereotype of Germans as robots, in the 1917 campaigns they were more alert than were the Allies to the value of soliciting evidence from the field and allowing subordinate commands to exercise independent judgment within the bounds of practical doctrine. This realistic cast of mind contributed to German tactical success in 1917, while Nivelle's dogmatic attitude and superficial concepts caused a failure which nearly took France out of the war.

The size of military organizations and the decentralized nature of military activity create an inevitable problem of digesting any change. Time is required to exploit fully the potential of any reform. Historically, changes in training, doctrine, and education have invariably required considerable investments of time to achieve the desired effect. Perhaps it is overlooked that the difficulties of digestion also apply to changes in technology. Modernizing equipment is centrally directed and controllable, and this may create the temptation to believe that changing equipment is the fastest method of effecting change in the military. Evidence suggests, however, that the desired effect of a technological change is often more elusive than was originally anticipated.

A particularly instructive example is that of the mitrailleuse, the wonder weapon of Napoleon III. Prior to the Franco-Prussian War of 1870–71, Napoleon III had recognized the potential importance of this new multibarrel weapon, which could generate a great volume of fire in a short period of time. He directed that this weapon be developed secretly, and he placed great hope on its success. When the war with Prussia broke out, the mitrailleuse was available, but few French soldiers knew of it, let alone how to operate it or, most importantly, how to employ it. This weapon had no effect on the outcome of the war.[5] Technological creativity at the drawing board or at the prototype stage does not, by itself, make any military more effective, as, in another example, Germany's misplaced technological inventiveness in World War II showed. It is axiomatic that technology has made significant changes, especially in this century, but it is not axiomatic that a military institution can, or must, accommodate every change. Time must be allowed in order to exploit the capability of a given system. Because even changes in technology require a sufficient digestion period, discrimination must be exercised in making changes based on new technology.

Despite the inherent difficulties of changing the military and the uncertainty of our times, a recognition of these difficulties should not dilute the importance of reform. For something so costly and so serious, a better way must always be sought, but it must be sought with the understanding of the limits of change.

How should necessary reforms be agreed upon, so that debate will not become a terminal illness? I believe that the two basic ingredients in the discussion of any reforms must be concern for evidence and recognition of accountability.

Proposals for reform and the resulting counterarguments are essentially judgments about what major factors affect military performance. Sound judgments can only be achieved if a considerable effort is devoted to examination of evidence. We Americans must look at our past military experiences and our present capabilities with a dispassionate and a ruthlessly honest scrutiny. We must maintain the same rigorous standards in examining the military capabilities of other nations. In our analyses, articles of faith must give way to evidence. The necessary corporate effort to achieve change for the better will not be attained until we first share a collective opinion about the facts surrounding a specific military problem. Once this agreement is reached, we must then attempt to identify the dominant cause-and-effect relationships that are suggested by the evidence. In this way the influences of factors such as morale, training, and technology can be identified. By proceeding from an evaluation of the evidence to a tracing of cause-and-effect relationships, the final state is attained: making a judgment that will guide change. But no consensus about change will be reached without agreement in the first two stages, that of evidence and cause/effect relationships.[6] Therefore, I suggest that we begin with a very deliberate effort at the first level, that of agreeing upon the evidence that relates to the problem under discussion.

The factor that can drive the process to the level of responsible judgments, rather than having the activity remain mere argument over evidence and cause/effect, is a sense of personal accountability, that is, being answerable for one's proposals. Accepting responsibility for the possible results of one's ideas reveals a recognition of the seriousness of the endeavor and the acceptance of the accompanying risks. A sense of accountability separates the potential reformer from the perpetual critic. If all participants in discussions of military reform are willing to assume responsibility, should their judgments become policy, for the results of what they advocate, the caliber of reform debate will be high.

No one should aspire to change the military who does not recognize the inherent difficulties involved. No one should advocate a concept that is so esoteric that only he can comprehend it. No army should purchase a weapon that is allergic to mud, rain, or abuse. Implementation of change is a difficult process. Accountability for one's recommendations for change must be accepted with the full knowledge that a large organization is involved and that direct personal control over every facet of implementation is impossible. In other words, when judgments become policy, eventual success will involve a large number of participants, many acting independently. Accountability for one's reform recommendations must be assumed despite the lack of total control of implementation. To accept that risk requires a healthy confidence in one's ideas and not a small amount of courage.

Accountability must apply to all who wish to participate seriously in defense, to the Clausewitzes in uniform as well as to the Liddell Harts in civilian clothes. Accountability must be applied to the professional military, so that rapid turnover in assignments does not free someone from the results of his judgments in a given job. The turbulence of the personnel system cannot be allowed to create a "here today, gone tomorrow" attitude, which weakens accountability. The higher authority one possesses in the military, the greater is the possibility that one's influence will extend over time, often beyond the tenure of office. Those who aspire to exercise higher authority must possess the imagination to recognize how their influence—and hence their accountability—extends into the future.

Accountability must also be applied to the civilian voices of reform, both those within the defense establishment and those on the periphery. Think tanks should not be paid handsome sums of money for the volume of their advice; they should be paid according to the value of their advice. The anonymity of the business suit should not foster the "here today, gone tomorrow" attitude either. Memories should not be so short as to forget who advocated what, and what the military still finds itself living with, even after administrations have changed.

Despite arguments about the lethality of weapons, the real killer on the battlefield is superficial judgment. It is also the ultimate wrecker of strategy. The damage is self-inflicted. In the serious business of military reform, a sense of being answerable for the effects of one's proposals should add more depth to the quality of thought, while reducing the traffic in shallow concepts. With greater sensitivity to accountability on the part of all participants, reform discussions can be enhanced in the following manner:

1. Ideas will not be limited to a catch-phrase. Terms will be defined with precision, evidence will be sought, and thoughtful analysis will proceed. Emphasis will be on implementing a change, not marketing an expression.
2. Weapons developments will be evaluated, not according to drawing board scenarios, but fully exposed to the ravages of Murphy's Law.
3. The collective nature of the military endeavor will be recognized, diminishing the cult of the personality, which too often characterizes arguments for change.
4. Recognition of the seriousness of change in the military will reduce tendencies toward whimsical or trendy change. Balance will be maintained. The need for agencies of continuity, such as military discipline and tradition, will not be ignored.

The military is both always difficult to change and always in need of change for the better. True change for the better can only be achieved through appreciation of the inherent limitations in changing the military, clarity in presenting change, and a willingness to accept the consequences. Perhaps this approach can help us rise above our national penchant for loving argument for its own sake. Let us not drive future Clausewitzes to isolation or future Liddell Harts to bitter criticism. Let us instead attempt to rise above adversary relationships, harness our talents, accept responsibility for the results, and produce the corporate effort necessary to achieve success.

NOTES

1. While I admire the flexibility and creativity of American economic activity, I feel it is not wise to consider national defense activity in the same terms. In our justifiable enthusiasm for our economic system, we Americans must guard against the tendency to apply business techniques too hastily to military problems.
2. The life of Clausewitz is thoroughly examined in Peter Paret's *Clausewitz and the State* (New York: Oxford University Press, Clarendon Press, 1976).

3. Brian Bond, *Liddell Hart: A Study of His Military Thought* (New Brusnwick, N.J.: Rutgers University Press, 1976), p. 119. A passage on p. 106 summarizes Liddell Hart's influence in the late 1930s: "It is ironic to reflect that he probably exerted more influence in Britain on the shaping of policy and strategy through his doctrine of limited liability than on the development of armoured forces, with which his name is often more linked."

4. Ibid., p. 59. It is important to note that few military theorists have enjoyed a direct and lasting influence in their lifetime. Perhaps the best example of such success in American history is Alfred Thayer Mahan.

5. Michael Howard, *The Franco-Prussian War* (New York: Granada Publishing, 1979), p. 36.

6. This method of analysis is taken from Clausewitz, *On War,* translated by Michael Howard and Peter Paret, (Princeton: Princeton University Press, 1976), pp. 156–69.

3

GUIDING THE
REFORM IMPULSE

Newt Gingrich and James W. Reed

Gingrich and Reed argue that simplistic conceptions of reform ignore many of the important nuances presented by the participants in the military reform debate. Warning that identifying the right questions must precede the search for answers, they outline an overarching strategic framework to guide military policy making.

To many observers the current debate concerning the future course of our defense establishment appears to pit two diametrically opposed schools of thought against each other. While the arguments from each camp are undeniably complex and sometimes overlapping, a common perception persists that the debate is being played out between an alliance of largely civilian "reformers" arrayed against uniformed defenders of the status quo. The variegated arguments of the former group are seen to revolve around a simple proposition: certain fundamental changes in our defense policy will permit us to do better for less cost. Military professionals, in contrast, are portrayed as rejecting the reformist challenge, arguing instead that only marginal improvements are required to maximize our defense capabilities.

Such simplistic conceptions ignore many important nuances in the arguments being presented at both ends of the spectrum. More importantly, however, this popular view fails to recognize the degree to which all of the participants in this debate are united by certain common impulses.

In many respects the character of the so-called military reform debate is without precedent in the evolution of our military thinking. What underlies the debate on all sides is a presumption that the habits and behaviors that led us to success over at least the last forty years are not likely to lead us to anything but disaster over the next forty years. We find ourselves asking questions not only about the lessons to be drawn from our military past but also about the very relevance of that past to our efforts to confront future challenges to our security. We see today concurrent efforts in our society to wrestle with problems we have never faced before as a nation. Coping with a century or more of protracted conflict is not a part of our national experience, and we are having to learn slowly how to survive in that kind of environment.

In an article entitled "The American Military Experience: History and Learning," John Shy set out what he perceives to be several deeply implanted and powerfully reinforced attitudes derived from our military heritage. They include

1. a deep respect for the kind of military prowess that has become so closely bound up with the very definition of American nationhood;
2. a concept of military security expressed not in relative but in absolute terms; and
3. an extraordinary optimism about what, when necessary, can be achieved by the exertion of American military force.[1]

Shy's point was to suggest how such uniquely ingrained aspects of our military experience led us to a war in Vietnam that could not be won in a manner consistent with our historical legacy. The broader point for our purposes, however, is that two parallel trends have shaken the very foundations of our collective subconscious concerning the nature of the American military experience. The first of these is the evolution of a world that knows neither absolute war nor absolute peace; the second is a growing sense of unease with the efficacy of the American military establishment in the aftermath of the Vietnam experience and even, in the minds of some, such discrete failures as the Iranian hostage rescue attempt.

In this sense, all of us have had certain widely shared assumptions undermined by our recent history; and to the degree those asumptions or attitudes have been shaken, we are all, civilian and military alike, united by similar desires to alter some aspects of our defense apparatus. All of us share in the reformist impulse. But seemingly cast adrift with few, if any, historical landmarks, we find ourselves searching for new points of reference by which to chart the future course of our defense establishment.

In the sections that follow, we describe certain principles that we believe ought to guide the ongoing debate over how to improve our nation's defenses; and in that context we suggest the overarching strategic framework from which, we argue, our defense policies must be derived.

THE SALIENCE OF THE SOVIET CHALLENGE

Without a clear conception of the nature of our military dilemma, we can hope to discover effective solutions only accidently. Intellectual honesty requires us all to recognize that, on balance, were we to factor out the Soviet threat, we possess military capabilities at least adequate to the task in any conflict likely to confront us.

In a Falklands-type crisis, we are still the dominant power on this planet; if you compare the assets we could have brought to bear with the assets marshaled by the British, one can appreciate the scale of difference in terms of power projection. If one considers possible threats to the Middle Eastern oil fields, our military capabilities become suspect only to the degree Soviet intervention is deemed likely.

This is not to assert that improvements cannot be made in our military posture. We need better doctrine for coping with low-intensity conflict; we need to devise a doctrine for utilizing proxies in the Third World. It is clear that we have never fully understood the challenge of the non-West as it seeks to develop on its own terms. Nor have we ever been comfortable with the concept of no war and no peace in regions where our interests were threatened by dictatorial regimes.

Nonetheless, on balance, we are in pretty good shape against anyone except the Russians. While our response might not always be the most cost-effective, given the requisite political decisions and national resolve, the systems we currently possess are at least adequate to deal with any contingency aside from the Soviet threat. Were we to somehow exclude the Soviet empire from our calculus, the debate would essentially take place at the margins of our military capability.

The grim reality is, however, that we do confront a Russian empire, and it is a threat to our very survival. Sun Tzu warned us in 500 B.C., "Know your enemy and the battle is half won; know yourself and the battle is yours." The fact is that we have avoided taking the Soviets seriously despite the inflation of threats for narrow bureaucratic purposes. Even worse, we have avoided examining ourselves with candor, preferring instead to imagine ourselves as we would like to be rather than as we really are.

Let us first examine the character of the Soviet challenge. The simple reality is that the Russian empire is a failure in all its essential aspects except the military. The Soviets have the capability to win militarily because they have consistently displayed a willingness to devote a preponderance of human and economic resources to achieve military success. The Russians take history more seriously than we do. They pursue lines of doctrinal debate more rigorously than we have. Most importantly, they marshal vastly greater quantities of men and materiel toward their military goals. And the lesson for us is, as Lord Nelson once noted, that numbers annihilate.

In contrast to the Soviets, Americans collectively have tended to behave irresponsibly with respect to security. Many congressmen vote too little money, avoid tough decisions, and focus on micromanagement; and their aides are frequently even worse. Congressmen and their aides then blame "stupid generals" and "greedy contractors." Decrying the lack of resources, many generals and admirals often give misleading answers, sometimes shade the facts to suit their narrow goals, and ultimately blame the reality they face on "stupid congressmen." Many contractors are narrow, myopic, and greedy in their manipulation of both the Pentagon and the Congress.

Most dangerous of all, many in the press refuse to take war or the Soviet challenge seriously, opting instead for patterns of investigative reporting that emphasize scandals or cost overruns. As a result we fail to educate the American people, and that ultimately may prove to be our greatest crisis. In a free society the press serves as our nervous system; if it does not function well, we literally cannot talk to ourselves or accurately interpret our environment. No democracy can survive for very long if it consistently deludes itself about the nature of the reality it faces.

All of this, then, raises the question, How should we view the Soviets? What is the reality of the Soviet challenge? Some answers to these questions are provided in Edward Drea's insightful analysis of the battle at Nomonhan between the Soviets and the Japanese in the early days of World War II.[2] Drea begins the account at a place called Changkufeng along the Manchurian coast; it was here that the Soviets administered the Japanese a bloody and brutal lesson on the difficulties of confronting a combined arms force with light infantry. This and other early skirmishes gave rise to a fierce debate within the Japanese Imperial Army over how best to deal with the Soviet challenge. Acutely aware of the constraints under which they operated, the Japanese knew they would never be in a position to take on the Soviets on their adversary's terms. Large armored forces and mobile warfare were luxuries the Japanese army could not afford.

From such introspection the Japanese drew the conclusion that they could fight outnumbered and win if they took full advantage of such intangibles as the Japanese fighting spirit. Armed with a tactical doctrine that emphasized offensive action, the Japanese would substitute willpower and inventiveness for material resources.

All this was to culminate in 1939 in a two-and-a-half-month battle at Nomonhan. Following an initial Japanese victory, the Russians responded precisely as they had earlier at Changkufeng: they simply heaped on more resources. Stalin's guidance to General Zhukov, his premier armor officer, was, simply, "You can have whatever resources you need. You will have total use of the Trans-Siberian Railway. Just tell me what you want." And not long thereafter three hundred thousand Russian troops armed with all that they could possibly need arrived to take on the Japanese forces. Ultimately, the Japanese tactical doctrine proved insufficiently flexible. Electing to assume a defensive posture designed to wear down the Soviet forces as a prelude to offensive action, the Japanese forces were simply annihilated by the overwhelming Russian forces.

From this account, Drea extracted the following conclusion:

> While the overwhelming Soviet qualitative and quantitative materiel superiority ultimately defeated the Japanese at Nomonhan, the defeat cannot be ascribed to materiel deficiencies alone. A tactical doctrine designed for infantrymen that stressed offensive action to achieve a quick victory was pitted against a doctrine which emphasized combined arms and protracted warfare. The Japanese decision to fight a war of attrition against the superior Soviet Red Army was, in retrospect, a mistake. . . . Only the decision of a battle exposes what later generations regard as self-evident truths.[3]

What lessons does Nomonhan offer us? To be sure, the many participants in our debate will undoubtedly draw differing and perhaps even contradictory interpretations of the Nomonhan example. But one inescapable conclusion must register upon us all: there is a point beyond which tinkering with doctrine, even wholesale revisions of doctrine, becomes irrelevant. At some ill-defined threshold the cold reality of numbers intrudes and the side with vastly superior military resources ultimately prevails.

ASKING THE RIGHT QUESTIONS

Coming to grips with the nature of the Soviet threat is only the first step we must take in enhancing our defense posture. Responding effectively to that threat requires that we make intelligent choices concerning our strategy, doctrine, and force structure; but to make the right choices we need first to ask the right questions.

More than ever before, we need to be concerned with optimal solutions to our military problems. The scale of the Soviet threat, when combined with inevitable constraints on our resources, ill affords us the luxury of muddling through as has often been our habit in the past. In his masterful study of American generalship during World War II, Russell Weigley cogently identified our problem as "unimaginative caution," an unwillingness, born of our material plentitude, to make clear-cut doctrinal choices. Compelling as they are, his comments merit quoting at some length.

> The American army lacked a clear conception of war. It had resolved neither upon a doctrine of winning the war by way of the direct application of superior power, in the manner of U. S. Grant, nor upon a doctrine of winning by means of superior mobility and facility in maneuver in the manner of the indirect approach of the British military critic B. H. Liddell Hart. In the end, the American army rumbled to victory because it had enough material resources to spare that it could exhaust

the enemy's resources even without adequately focusing its own power for a decisive, head-on battle of annihilation, or exploiting its mobility in behalf of a consistent strategy of indirect approach. . . . That preponderance of material resources, however, cannot be counted on again.[4]

Americans have often displayed a disconcerting tendency to avoid thinking about problems that seem intractable. But Americans now find themselves in a position in which we must make some fundamental choices. We must choose between a land-based or a maritime strategy; between a doctrine premised on mobility or one based on attrition; between heavy and light forces. Too frequently, however, we analyze such decisions with biased data and resist changes in our time-honored solutions to problems. Note that these are traits not just of the military but, rather, are broader cultural traits that seem to be part of American society. Each of us works well within our own niche, but we tend to suboptimize so that we win at our particular game, only to lose as a nation at a holistic level.

Perhaps more than anything we need to reexamine the process by which we reach for answers to difficult questions of strategy and doctrine. In this concern for the process of discovery, participants in the military reform debate would do well to adhere to a process that John R. Platt, a physicist, labeled "strong inference."[5] Simply stated, Platt's concept of strong inference entails the rigorous application of inductive logic to problem solving. It combines (1) a willingness to explore multiple alternatives simultaneously with (2) a willingness (eagerness) to disprove a particular hypothesis. Platt's words have more than passing relevance to the participants in this debate.

> The conflict and exclusion of alternatives that is necessary to sharp inductive inference has been all too often a conflict between men, each with his single Ruling Theory. But whenever each man begins to have multiple hypotheses, it becomes purely a conflict between ideas. It becomes much easier then for each of us to aim every day at conclusive disproofs—at *strong inference*—without either reluctance or combativeness. In fact, when there are multiple hypotheses which are not anyone's "personal property" and when there are crucial experiments to test them, the daily life in the laboratory takes on an interest and excitement it never had.[6]

The process of making the critical choices that face us must begin by identifying the pivotal questions. What are the questions worth a million dollars to answer? In searching out answers to these questions we must ask, What are the multiple alternatives we should explore? And in formulating our alternatives, we must ensure that they are susceptible to disconfirmation; we must ask, What test could disprove this particular approach? The obligation falls upon us all to structure our proposals with sufficient content, clarity, and specificity that they lend themselves to empirical analysis. As Platt cautions us, progress does not result from "proving" that any particular approach is the correct one. Rather, we advance by successively reducing the uncertainty that faces us, that is, by proving which approaches are the wrong ones and discarding them.

All of this should cause us to ask, How can we get good answers to the questions we raise? To this at least two responses readily appear, both involving little more than modification of some current attitudes. First, the quality of the military reform debate hinges on the willingness of all the participants to examine each other's arguments with open-mindedness and intellectual honesty. Too often we have seen instances of one side knowingly distorting the position of the other or displaying a degree of arrogance that is unproductive. Second, we are more likely to arrive at good answers if we learn to view our maneuvers at least as much as an opportunity to test new ideas as an occasion to practice old habits. In this sense, the Army's effort to establish the 9th Infantry Division as a "test bed" is a major step in the right direction.

In short, the task that faces us is to structure the reform debate in such a manner that it becomes a conflict of ideas, not of men. If it becomes simply a fight between reformers and conservatives, both will lose. In the end we will have a military that successfully repudiates reform but will probably not defeat the Soviets. Or we will see reformers win the publicity battle in the *Washington Post* only to lose the next war.

The importance of asking the right questions as a prelude to arriving at the right answers cannot be understated. In part because they failed to ask the right questions, the British failed to have the right doctrine in 1914 and again in 1939. The Germans may have had the right doctrine, but they had the wrong strategy in 1914 and 1939. And each paid for their failures with their blood.

WAR AS POLITICS

History provides us with innumerable and sorrowful examples of societies that lost sight of the subtle relationship between war and politics. Clausewitz admonished us that war and politics are inextricably entwined as different aspects of the same continuum. In part owing to the democratic character of our society, Americans have too often honored that maxim in the breach.

Democratic societies have never been comfortable with the use of war as a political instrument. The need to be responsive to the popular will causes leaders in a democratic society to maintain a studied detachment from situations in which a measured application of military force might usefully serve political ends; or, alternatively, such leaders are pressed toward an all-out commitment of military forces in a way that political objectives become obscured. When democracies go to war, means have a way of becoming ends.[7]

Simply stated, war is a form of political activity that occurs in a political milieu. Politics defines both the objectives toward which military force must be directed and the constraints under which it must operate. Decisions about strategy, doctrine, or force structure cannot be made on "strictly military" terms alone; in fact, by definition, such terms do not exist. This requires a sensitivity to both the domestic and the international political context in which military decisions are made.

It was, in part, because Mao Tse-tung's strategy in the 1930s and 1940s was rooted in an astute understanding of China's political culture that his forces were ultimately to prevail over the Kuomingtang. The British and French use of military force in the Suez in 1956 was a failure on political, not military, terms. Dulles's nuclear strategy of "massive retaliation" was eventually discredited because it proved to be out of touch with the political realities of the time.

These are but a few examples that illustrate the link between war and politics. What they tell us is that the military reform debate cannot take place in a political vacuum. At every level, the choices we make will be judged rational only to the degree they serve our political ends and reflect political realities.

TOWARD A RATIONAL STRATEGY

These, then, are the principles that should guide the reform impulse: a clear conception of the Soviet threat, a concern for the process by which we structure the military reform debate, and an appreciation of the political realities that constrain our range of options.

But how is the military reform debate to be informed by these guidelines? What relevance does such broad counsel have to the intricacies of these ongoing deliberations?

Quite simply, Nomonhan offers us at once the most frightening and yet the most realistic model of our future There is no reason to believe that the Russian state has changed in any important respect. The Russians understand the reality of the world they live in. They have assimilated the lessons of a thousand years of living at the center of Eurasia, and they are willing to pay the costs to survive. And as a general rule of history, societies that are willing to pay the costs to survive prevail over those that are not.

We see as well in Nomonhan the importance of searching out the pivotal question to be asked. Nomonhan is but one of the many examples illustrating that questions of strategy take primacy over questions of doctrine. While focusing on issues of doctrine, the Japanese missed the central question: Could any doctrine, however astute, defeat the Soviet masses? Clearly, there are times when the military or political realities facing a nation should cause it to choose a strategy that does not entail the use of force.

It is on the issue of grand strategy, however, that our three principles most clearly converge. We currently find ourselves at a fork in the road in terms of choosing a grand strategy. Our problems are magnified by the fact that to date we have yet to commit ourselves forthrightly to one path or the other. Our current defense plans attempt to travel both simultaneously. At issue, to use the British analogy, is whether to follow Marlborough's Continental strategy or, alternatively, the elder Pitt's blue water strategy. On the surface, the issue is a relatively straightforward one; at least in theory, either strategy offers prospects for success, and persuasive arguments have been advanced by advocates on each side.

Choosing wisely between these two grand strategies requires that we be mindful of the guidelines we have argued here. The question then becomes, Given the character of the Soviet threat, what political goals must our grand strategy be designed to serve? It is here that proposals for a maritime strategy—that we reduce our land-based presence in Europe and Asia and focus our efforts on the navy and strategic nuclear forces—fail essentially for five reasons.

First, to opt for a maritime strategy would be to abandon five hundred million relatively free people, and that would be tantamount to a denial of the democratic values we purport to represent. Second, it would lead rapidly to the Finlandization of those peoples on the periphery of the Soviet empire. The Japanese are not going to become more militant because we pull out, nor are the Germans going to resurrect the Wehrmacht and dominate Europe. Out of their own self-interests our allies would have little choice but to accommodate themselves to the Soviet Union as best they could.

Third, we ought to be honest with ourselves about the perceptions we would foster by choosing to follow a maritime strategy. One cannot "sort of withdraw" but really stay. Irrespective of our underlying intentions, the signal that would go out from a maritime strategy would be one of weakened American resolve and recognition that we, in fact, are the eventual losers, the Soviets the eventual winners. One need only to recall the Carthaginian struggles to see what happens when people decide that their former allies are not going to make it: they accommodate with astonishing alacrity.

A fourth flaw in the maritime strategy is that it fails to anticipate the likely Soviet response. Were we to withdraw from the Eurasian continent and concede the contest for dominance on land, that clearly would free substantial Soviet resources that are currently devoted to fighting a war on land. And there is precious little evidence to suggest the Soviets would then redirect those resources into consumer goods. More likely, it seems to us, the Soviets would channel that same 5 or 6 percent of their GNP into head-on competition in those areas in which we had elected to concentrate. That is a consequence to which too little attention has been paid.

Lastly, a withdrawal from head-on competition with the Soviet Union would deal a crushing blow to the morale and élan of the American people. America exists essentially as a figment of its collective imagination. We are, in fact, a dream, not a nationality, not even a geographic point. To shy away from competition with our adversaries would be to depreciate our sense of self-respect and deflate the character of that dream. And it is only as long as we perpetuate that dream that we stay together as a nation.

So it is because our military strategy operates in a political milieu that we must confront the massive Soviet military forces with a land-based strategy oriented to the Eurasian continent. At the same time, recognition of the political imperative that underlies a land-based strategy tends to narrow the range of choices we have in terms of doctrine and force structure. Simply stated, the United States is not currently in a position to conduct a serious land-based defense on the Eurasian periphery. Our forces are too small, too poorly equipped, and backed by too few reserves. A national commitment to stay in Eurasia, therefore, compels us to abide by three prescriptions.

First, we must build dramatically larger reserve and national guard forces. We simply lack the manpower resources to stay the course in a lengthy conventional war against the Soviets.[8] And given the nature of the Soviet threat, there is no reason to think that the Soviets would allow us to win a short conventional war. True staying power will inevitably require universal military training or, at a minimum, an extension of the draft.

Second, we need to improve vastly our conventional forces, especially in Europe. How to go about that is clearly a contentious point between the so-called reformers and nonreformers. In essence, though, much of the debate is a function of the scale of production. Should we field smaller military forces equipped with weapons on the frontiers of our technology? Or should we opt for larger forces, albeit less exotically equipped? A realistic appraisal of our budgetary constraints suggests that we cannot afford to pay large sums to achieve small additional increments in weapons capabilities. Rather, we need to build less expensive equipment in much greater quantities; we need a commitment to standardize and mass produce once again on a very large scale.

Third, we must adopt a forward defense in Europe, that is, an Israeli-style territorial defense which avers that collateral damage will occur on the *enemy*'s territory. To that end, the army's evolving AirLand Battle doctrine, incorporating many aspects of maneuver doctrine, offers the prospect of a serious defense of Europe. The application of this doctrine will require that we commit substantial amounts of relatively inexpensive infantry to the defense of built-up areas and rugged terrain, thus freeing our maneuver units to exploit opportunities for offensive action. We must learn to defend cheaply and be expensive on the attack.

In implementing the necessary reforms in our strategy, doctrine, and force structure we must recognize that they will require changes not just in the military but changes as well in American society, politics, industry, academe, and the news media. The most successful and most often referred-to reforms, those of the Prussian military, came not only out of defeat but were fundamentally societal reforms, not military. They were based on a clear understanding of the nature of an emerging nationalist people and were rooted in a willingness to change the state and the entire incentive system of that society, not just in a willingness to engage in a different style of training or a different method of promotion.

As one surveys the level of ferment engendered in the military reform debate, there is reason to be optimistic that ultimately we will succeed in making the right choices. Clearly the military is listening. More importantly, though, the military as an institution has displayed a willingness to ask tough questions and engage in serious debate within and without. Irrespective of the outcome, that alone is cause for optimism.

What is at stake in all of this is literally the possibility that freedom as we know it may not be here thirty years from now. Given the gravity of the issues involved, Americans can ill afford not to invest great intellect and energy toward correctly answering the questions our reformist impulses have spawned. All Americans in all walks of life have an obligation to demand of their news media, elected leadership, and military professionals the open mind and clear thinking necessary to survive.

NOTES

1. John W. Shy, "The American Military Experience: History and Learning," *Journal of Interdisciplinary History* 1, no. 1 (February 1971): 205–28.

2. Edward J. Drea, *Nomonhan: Japanese-Soviet Tactical Combat, 1939,* Leavenworth Papers, no. 2 (Fort Leavenworth, Kans.: U.S. Army Command and General Staff College, January 1981).

3. Ibid., p. 90.

4. Russell F. Weigley, *Eisenhower's Lieutenants* (Bloomington: Indiana University Press, 1981), p. 729.

5. John R. Platt, *The Step to Man* (New York: John Wiley & Sons, 1966), pp. 19–36.

6. Ibid., pp. 28–29.

7. Fred Ikle, *Every War Must End* (New York: Columbia University Press, 1971).

8. See Kenneth J. Coffey, *Strategic Implications of the All-Volunteer Force* (Chapel Hill: University of North Carolina Press, 1979).

4

AN OVERVIEW
OF THE REFORM DEBATE

John M. Oseth

Oseth surveys the arguments and identifies the major contentious issues.
He concludes by providing some comments on how the debate can be
improved in the future.

In the last several years an important—and at times profoundly divisive—
debate has emerged about the quality of American military forces or, more
specifically, about our ability to use military force successfully in contingencies below the threshold of strategic nuclear war. In an uncertain world such
concerns are understandable, of course, and in a pluralistic political system
we must expect a certain amount of continuing, unreconciled contention even
on matters pertaining to the system's defense. The challenge for policy making will always be to choose among competing points of view, and in that
sense this "military reform" debate is nothing new. But in other respects the
critique at its center is noteworthy, if not truly distinctive, particularly with
regard to its genesis and its purpose.

The debate has been generated and sustained by a surprisingly small group
of "outsider" critics; a dogged knot of dissenters poised against the Pentagon
and its allies among attentive publics. Working from initially isolated out-
posts of expertise on the periphery of the official defense establishment, they
have tenaciously and with a growing sense of solidarity captured significant
media attention, cultivated substantial support in the Congress, and kept
mainstream policy postures on the defensive with increasingly coherent

attacks on the state of American preparedness for war. In the process they have been transformed from guerrilla fighters caught up in skirmishing tactics to mainforce regulars seeking stand-up engagements with the "establishment" in all available arenas. Their aim, in the large, is nothing less than top-to-bottom reform of the American military. In that sense they are avowedly revolutionary in vision and purpose. Their critique has become, quite self-consciously, a movement.

Their names and voluminous writings are well known—Edward Luttwak, Jeffrey Record, James Fallows, William Lind, Pierre Sprey, and Stephen Canby are among the most prominent. Their number includes strategists, weapons and force structure specialists, journalists, and defense analysts and former defense officials in the major universities and think tanks. They find recruits, as well, among members of Congress seeking to set sensible directions for the defense establishment in this decade and the next. Their efforts in the Congress, in fact, sparked formation of a bipartisan "Defense Reform Caucus," an increasingly formalized group of senators and congressmen united in their concern about the nation's defense posture. In the arena of public debate, some reform arguments have overtaken and eclipsed the efforts of those within the military services who have worked for some time on similarly motivated, but usually more modest, changes.

As this military reform debate takes shape across a wider and wider spectrum of issues, it becomes more and more important to step back from the controversy and assess the dimensions of the powerful critique at its core—to see where it reaches and why. The aim of this article is to do just that: to survey the debate and identify the main points of contention, to assess what seems ultimately to be at stake, and to provide some thoughts on how the discourse might be sharpened in the future. The intent is not to enter the debate but to summarize its main points and thereby to begin to define its ultimate impact.[1] For the sake of synthesis and simplicity, reform movements are categorized here according to their main points, not according to schools of thought associated with particular critics.

"PATTERNS OF CONFLICT" AND THE AMERICAN STYLE OF WARFARE

Although the reform movement has earlier antecedents, most reformers agree that its theoretical foundations have been made most visible in the widely noted "patterns of conflict" study by former air force colonel John Boyd.[2] That study—really an attempt to identify the main ingredients of successful military operations via a survey of military history—has been used by many reformers for many purposes. But, for most, the conceptualization of contrasting "maneuver" and "attrition" styles of warfare is central, and much discussion has focused on these terms. Attrition warfare, which critics say characterizes the American approach to combat now and in much of the past, has as its overarching purpose the physical destruction of enemy forces by application of massive strength and firepower. On the battlefield it uses *attrition* massed troop formations as a bludgeon, seeking by straightforward, frontal attacks to batter the enemy away from advantageous terrain in physical, firepower-oriented engagements. Ultimately, it relies for its success on lengthy mobilization periods prior to combat and on ultimate preponderance in military resources.

maneuver The maneuver approach, by contrast, is more sensitive to the human and psychological factors in combat. It is oriented to the enemy's will to resist and to the command and control mechanisms the enemy needs in order to wage war successfully both on the battlefield and at higher echelons. It seeks the enemy's defeat—not his destruction or obliteration—by flexible and unpredictable movement of forces and firepower. It applies strength to enemy weaknesses as opportunities arise or are created, disrupting and confusing enemy leaders, ultimately dissolving their units' cohesion and undercutting their operational effectiveness.

In the reformers' view, each of these approaches to war begins with its own way of thinking: a pervading mindset about combat, about expected enemies, and about the capabilities of one's own military forces. The critics' main concern stems from their belief that America's military force structure, operational doctrine, and weapons acquisition policies have been shaped mainly by the attrition perspective, while the nation has lost the material preponderance, the strength of numbers, and the assurance of mobilization time needed to make attrition warfare work. They also believe that forces organized, outfitted, and trained for attrition warfare may be hopelessly incapacitated and even irrelevant for many other kinds of military contingencies. As a result, they fear that the military establishment is now poorly prepared to defend the nation and its vital interests abroad, and they argue that truly fundamental changes are necessary in order to correct the most central disabilities.

American preparations to deal with possible Soviet aggression in Europe have been attacked on both counts: reformers believe that the military services—and their civilian leaders—have prepared wrongly for that contingency, because of the attrition approach, and at the same time they also argue that the narrow focus on Europe has undercut American capability to respond to military contingencies in other areas of the world. The Army, it is argued, has resigned itself to fighting basically a linear defense in Europe with relatively rigid techniques, with too little operational discretion vested in tactical commanders, and with heavy forces that can move quickly on the battlefield but have little strategic mobility. Reformers find evidence of this approach in all aspects of Army preparations. Even map symbology is said to be symptomatic of larger rigidity: boundaries outlining battle areas are seen not simply as control measures for planners and commanders, but as unnecessary and unwise constraints on subordinate leaders' operational initiative and battle-field flexibility. Air Force views on the uses of air power are also criticized heavily, especially the emphasis on deep interdiction missions intended to disrupt supply and reinforcement routes. Many reformers, concerned about supporting maneuver warfare in the clash of ground forces, hold that the air force should be primarily concerned with close air support missions and capabilities.

In the end, then, reformers point to two primary disabilities attributable to the attrition mindset: *strategic* immobility resulting from development of heavy forces designed for one kind of tactics and one kind of battleground; and *tactical* rigidity resulting from obsession with linear defense of terrain and excessive intrusion on tactical commanders' discretion. As a result, it is argued, the United States cannot send forces to Europe with the mechanical wherewithal or the strength of numbers needed to fight successfully. Those forces that do enter that battle (or any other) will not be prepared mentally, logistically, or operationally to fight a maneuver war, which the reformers argue can be the only successful formula under current conditions of Soviet numerical preponderance.

This argument has sparked pointed objections and rejoinders from defense analysts and government officials alike. No one is wholly satisfied with the status quo, of course, nor does anyone oppose the idea of reform. Few outside the movement, however, have been satisfied that the current reform critique has captured all the available wisdom.

Many hold that reformers have done their cause a great disservice by failing to identify and clarify the most significant empirical referents of the "maneuver" notion. As used in discussions about operational doctrine, it has seemed much too ethereal and platitudinous. And important questions still need answers—for instance: What levels of warfare—strategic, grand tactical (or operational), or tactical, or all three—does the maneuver concept address? What specifically does it mean at each level? How exactly, at each level embraced, does it relate to, rearrange, or refocus the principles of war understood by all military leaders?

Other observers have argued that the central terms "maneuver" and "attrition," though counterpoised in the reform literature, are not dichotomous even in concept. Each contains ideas useful to battlefield commanders in a variety of combat situations. In this view the two styles are best understood not as mutually exclusive, but as alternative blendings of the same operational techniques, or as the polar extremes of a hypothetical spectrum along which are arrayed various operational mixes of firepower and movement. As so conceived they amount to nothing more than a repackaging of ideas about war familiar to any soldier or serious student of military affairs—a repackaging that constructs overstated and oversimplified central contrasts by artifice. Some argue more specifically that the historical examples used by reformers to support the attrition/maneuver typologies, and to attribute the attrition style to the United States, have been chosen arbitrarily or have been incorrectly categorized as indicative of one style or the other. Others hold that reformers do not understand—and therefore are unduly concerned about—current military doctrine, force structure, and equipment policies. Still others hold that they do not give sufficient credit to the military for moving upon its own initiative in the directions now advocated as reform. The army's newly-revised capstone manual of tactics (Field Manual 100-5, *Operations*) is frequently cited as an example of discernible movement toward the approach that reformers prefer.

Another recurring observation about the maneuver versus attrition debate is that it has tended to dwell on attitudinal and doctrinal matters but has not been particularly helpful on other reform issues. Even for those observers who understand and accept maneuver as the correct approach to thinking about war, it is not clear what kinds of equipment and forces would be best suited to put that approach into practice. Cost and other resource implications are not self-evident, either, and this distresses many who have been otherwise receptive to reform analyses and proposals.

Finally, it has been apparent to some observers that critics of America's overall military posture, and particularly of U.S. preparedness for war in Europe, have not taken sufficient account of the political considerations that have shaped the missions assigned U.S. forces. Reform proposals that make sense in an unconstrained academic or think tank setting may be unrealistic and unhelpful in the context of current political commitments and guidance. These political realities in Europe orient the military from the outset to a particular theater-wide mission and strategic objective: defend if attacked, and restore the border. Measures taken or planned by our forces to prepare to accomplish that mission and achieve that objective might seem to some observers less flexible or maneuver-like than if the mission were to attack eastward into East Germany and ultimately into the Soviet Union. At all levels of warfare and preparation for warfare, commanders and planners will take bearings from their mission, not from prepackaged notions of how war in general is conducted. Criticism of an alleged preexisting mindset, or of the peacetime choices commanders make concerning operational techniques appropriate to their assigned tasks, is misplaced if it does not also address the national policy that undergirds and shapes ensuing military preparations.

Though not everyone has been satisfied with the central ideas and orientations of the reform movement, there is much agreement that the maneuver-attrition debate, with all its faults, had served several useful purposes. Many defense officials and analysts value the reformers' emphasis on the study of military history, though they may also feel that the movement has not used military history well. All seem to approve, additionally, of the institutional introspection that has resulted from reformist criticism. This can go far to counteract any tendencies toward bureaucratic inertia, lethargy, and self-satisfaction. Also valuable, many think, is the maneuverists' skepticism about doctrinal recipes for battle: their criticism of operational dogmas, which may deaden commanders' imagination and initiative by rewarding conformity on the one hand and by making the struggle to innovate professionally risky on the other.

A further benefit of reform analyses has been an increased sensitivity to the possibilities for disjunction among the several services on doctrinal and other matters. These divergencies—each service preparing in its own way for war—can make thoroughgoing reform quite difficult, especially in the view of those who argue that we lack a joint military decision-making structure that can impose needed changes on recalcitrant services.

It would seem, indeed, that reform proposals that have cross-service implications or effects would do well to devote more attention to devising better mechanisms for cross-service decision and coordination. Recent proposals to revise the Joint Chiefs of Staff system are thus most pertinent to reformers' concerns, though they have not yet been fully incorporated into the movement.

But perhaps the most telling observation that can be made about the maneuver-attrition element of the debate is this: it has been not so much a critique of mindsets about war as a questioning of the competence of this nation's military officer corps. Seen in this light, maneuver advocates (or attrition opponents) really argue, in the end, for tactical excellence and for an officer corps capable of drawing upon a full repertoire of combat techniques, resources, and behaviors in order to perform diverse battlefield missions. The reform challenge, then, is not to choose one combat style or dogma over another, but to develop officers' ability to select the right maneuver and firepower, to make the right choices, in specific combat contexts. Effective fighting is the goal; what is therefore required is an officer corps astute, professional, and even learned enough to exercise judgment and use resources wisely in pursuit of varied tactical missions. If required to defend, well-prepared, competent, and confident unit leaders will then choose those techniques and resources appropriate to defensive operations on the given battlefield and against the given enemy. When seizing an opportunity to attack, they may select a different mix of available techniques and resources appropriate to offensive operations. The reformers, however, are profoundly skeptical about the ability of today's officer corps to make those choices well. And as so understood, the reform movement's criticisms are focused as much on the quality of military leadership as on anything else.

This may explain, in fact, the occasionally heated nature of rejoinders from some military participants in the debate. It may also go far toward explaining why the reformers have had such difficulty in even gaining a hearing for their views in some corners of the Defense Department. To be sure, several important themes of criticism challenge assumptions, beliefs, and practices that are at the center of several services' *raison d'être*. Navy leadership can be expected to react badly when aircraft carriers and paraphernalia associated with power projection missions are questioned by anyone. Similarly, air force leadership will hardly view with equanimity any proposals that would curtail activities—such as long-range interdiction—that have become part of the service's institutional essence. But at another level, senior military personnel, regardless of service, as well as their civilian superiors, may well have found in the reform critique an indictment of their performance as leaders, and of their ability to perform as leaders in the future. That perception hardly conduces to open, reasoned communication, yet it is an inevitable one, given the substance of the critique. A major challenge for all concerned with addressing reform issues will be to find a way to work through this sense of personal and professional—apart from institutional—affront.

THE CENTRALITY OF LEADERSHIP: THE CAPSTONE "PEOPLE" ISSUE

In the final analysis, then, maneuverists question the ability of troop commanders to make the right tactical decisions in combat, and the capacity of military leaders to outfit and train the services properly in peacetime. Much of the reform movement has attempted to describe the dimensions and origins of that problem. Not unexpectedly, the effort has produced varied analyses. But in the end, even for observers impressed by the general thrust of the critique, it has not been clear what specific steps should be taken to help the services develop leaders having the experience, personal qualities, and intellectual capacity to execute maneuver war. What has emerged from debate on this point is a heightened awareness of the reformers' unease about the quality of command at all levels in all services, without specific guidelines about how exactly to do better. Let us look a bit closer at this reform position.

A prominent thesis argues that the military services, for one reason or another, do not develop creative, inventive leaders capable of the truly independent and innovative thinking that will be required on future battlefields. Nor have the services taken sufficient care to foster an ethic of professionalism infused and animated by a spirit of service to the nation as a whole. There is much mythology, reformers argue, about selfless military devotion to national duty. In practice, however, other concerns are more often controlling.

A cluster of observations (offered mainly but not exclusively by civilians) has depicted an officer corps whose individual personalities and aggregate spirit have been shaped importantly by the narrow and divisive service interests evident on the national level, by competitive, careerist concerns, by a dehumanizing and risk-minimizing managerial ethic that tends to identify failure with deviation from an expected (if not explicitly mandated) norm, and by the certain knowledge that there is safety (and career progression) in conformity and much personal risk in innovation. Because the services have not understood that maneuver war can be the only successful formula for the American military, they have not structured rating, promotion, and command selection systems to identify officers with the personal qualities necessary for maneuver-style battle. Rating systems provide no safety valve for innovators who fail or lose ground because of deviation from the expected, well-trodden (and therefore easier) course. Superiors do not know how to differentiate between malcontents and true pathfinders. Indeed, they do not try to do so because the actions of both kinds of officers may jeopardize the superiors' own reputation and ratings. More importantly, some have argued, promotion and command selection boards, staffed by senior officers produced by the system, tend to select those who have made the system work, regardless of its incongruities, not those who have the intellectual capacity to evaluate the system objectively and the personal strength to press for change. Over time, the accumulated, institutionalized wisdom about the path to advancement and command in all services is that one must adjust, cooperate, and accommodate within given system boundaries. Reformers argue, however, that the services need leadership at all levels that can transcend boundaries and operate comfortably in a context of uncertainty, without more specific guidance than a mission statement, and with loyalty only to the goal of defending the nation sensibly and well.

There has been some argument, more specifically, that officer career patterns are not designed to develop the type of accomplished troop leaders sought by many reformers. In the army, for instance, the requirement for officers to become expert in two separate specialties, one of which may have little relation to mainstream soldiering skills, is viewed by some as an unjustifiable and harmful professional distraction. More generally, some note that the officer education system does little to inculcate a sense that a true professional is one who studies his discipline, who understands the lessons of its history and struggles to adapt it to the future in light of those lessons. Instead, rather than esteeming scholarship and erudition in military officers, the services tend to regard these qualities as irrelevant to more pressing everyday concerns. The result is a profession of arms that is appallingly illiterate in military history and ignorant of the national and international affairs that determine its destiny and ought to inform its development.

Some argue that the military establishment suffers from an even more insidious disability: a reflexive instinct for institutional self-protection and concern for self-advancement which reformers say is evident at all levels from service staffs in the Pentagon to fire-teams and gun crews in line units. Old and recurring stories about false unit readiness reports, devious unit training and evaluation practices, and rigged equipment tests seem inevitably to find their way into current critiques. Though many in the reform movement know the limits of anecdotal evidence of this sort, some also believe that the cumulation of such evidence must inevitably be taken to indicate

weakened and untrustworthy leadership, compromised performance standards, and military capabilities of questionable quality measured by any standard. At the national level, some reformers are convinced that narrow concern
for self-preservation accounts for the services' failure to acknowledge and
respond to reform critiques (though the marines, and to a lesser extent the
army, are sometimes complimented for their openness to suggestions).

As noted earlier, specific prescriptions for improvement have been few, in
part because the diagnosis is controversial, and debate at that level has left
little time for elaborate explication of solutions. Reformers tend to approve,
however, of recent army moves toward lengthened command tours and the
British-style regimental system, finding much in both developments that can
improve unit cohesion, leader-subordinate relationships, and ultimately battlefield performance. Many further hold that formal officer education must
be improved, in two ways in particular: (1) expanded study of military
history, and (2) more testing of ideas and exercising of practical skills in
combat simulations, war games, and tactical training. While there have been
significant advances in theses areas at the several war colleges and in major
command headquarters, critics note that these advances have been made only
recently, and that they come much too late in an officer's career to redress
central deficiencies.

FORCE STRUCTURE:
WHAT KINDS OF FORCES,
HOW MANY, AND FOR WHAT?

Reformers' arguments about the nature of maneuver-style war, and about
the doctrine, leadership, and organizational wherewithal required to fight it,
have led them to be severely critical of America's current military force
structure. At bottom, their concerns have revolved around relatively simple
questions, though their analyses can be extraordinarily complex. What kinds
of forces should the United States maintain? How large should they be, and
what capabilities ought they to have? Should they be "heavy"—armored and
mechanized—or—"light," or some combination of both? Even when the key
questions are asked at this level of generality, there has been much debate
about fundamental choices.

In an important sense we should not be surprised about this. Questions
about force structure are, at bottom, questions about expected threats and
missions. In answering them one must inevitably seek guidance from some
prior description of the relevant world, from preferred and trusted assessments of threats, and from strategic imperatives thought to be derived from
those assessments. All participants in the reform debate have their own views
on these matters, and few are in total agreement. Thus, arguments about
force structure have deeply rooted origins in contrasting world views. As
many have noted, America cannot really come to grips with the most funda-

mental force structure issues unless a coherent strategic outlook is made explicit as guidance for military force designers.

To be sure, the vicissitudes of the American political process may well be such that any strategic postures adopted at the national level cannot capture consensus support. But even with the prospect of wholesale administrative changes every four years, and even with the pulling and hauling of bureaucratic policy making characteristic of the American system, some critics feel that our political leadership can do better at devising grand strategy and at making it explicit as the driving factor in force design. Thus, clarification of controlling world views has been seen by some as a critical first step in rationalizing America's military force structure.

At the same time, however, clarification of strategy will by no means answer all questions about force structure, nor can it solve all dilemmas. America, with worldwide interests and commitments, needs large and diverse military capabilities. No clarified world view can relieve the United States of that burden. The United States needs flexible forces capable of insertion into diverse potential contingencies worldwide. But how should those forces be composed and organized in order to obtain the requisite flexibility? Once discussion reaches that point, little agreement is found.

For some reformers, furthermore, America's resource constraints transform the force design problem into an even broader and more complicated foreign policy challenge. Even with more liberal defense spending in the Reagan administration, America must attend to national security needs in a context of limited resources and with a focus on efficiency. For many, this inescapable reality mandates an attempt to expand the security contributions of America's allies around the world, to enlist their increased support as vigorous members of a total force structure. The Far East, Middle East, and Europe are areas in which some would seek, indeed demand, significant augmentation of U.S. efforts by contributions from allies whose security interests are at risk there.

But by any standard the dominant focus of force structure debate in the reform movement has been America's own force posture. What can America do with her own national resources to improve defense preparedness? Discussion here has revolved around the problem of choosing between—or mixing—heavy and light forces.

The heavy-versus-light policy dilemma has been outlined by reform arguments as follows: because of U.S. strategic concerns worldwide, and especially in Southwest Asia and other areas where U.S. and allied forces are not now deployed, the United States needs highly capable forces with great strategic mobility. Yet once in place abroad these forces must have great tactical mobility as well, to deal with Soviet (and conceivably other) armored forces. The first need, strategic mobility, favors light forces, or at least forces lighter than those in much of present U.S. ground force structure. The second need, tactical mobility, argues for more heavy forces—mechanized and armored troops and weapons that can move quickly and with some degree of safety and protection on the battlefield. Several reformers have fiercely criticized a decade and more of perceived policy emphasis on heavy forces, especially in the army. In their view, that long-term focus has reduced the overall strategic mobility of U.S. forces, as strategic lift capacity has been far outpaced by the increase in heavy forces. And, they argue, it has also diminished if not thoroughly vitiated the utility of most ground forces for conflict contingencies outside scenarios of superpower confrontation.

But there has been great difficulty in many quarters with the heavy-light debate as it has emerged from reform councils. Some observers have objected, most basically, to an artificial, dichotomous counterpoising of those terms. They hold that heavy and light, like maneuver and attrition, are better understood as hypothetical poles at the ends of a spectrum of mixed mobility and firepower capabilities. As used in much of the reform argument, it is thus suggested, these terms are not useful analytical tools, since most of reality is found toward the center of that conceptual spectrum. Others note that the terms need much clarification when used to describe actual U.S. military structure, since there are many different types of light forces: standard infantry, air assault, airborne infantry, Ranger and Special Forces, to name only army elements. (Marine infantry units significantly expand the calculus.) Each varies significantly in organic transport and firepower, yet the heavy-light debate frequently proceeds at a high level of generality, neglecting critical differences and unrealistically treating different units as if they shared equally in the same list of advantages and disadvantages. Such analytical oversimplification, it is argued, obscures more than it can illuminate, and is of little use to decision makers facing the challenge of improving actual forces-in-being.

It has been further pointed out that reform critiques could be improved by clearer specification of what is being compared by the terms heavy and light. Do they compare different components of U.S. forces? Or are they used to compare U.S. forces to those of anticipated enemies? If the latter, then a more differentiated perspective may be required than has been offered to date. Some potential adversaries having nominally heavy forces, mechanized or armored, may in fact be no match for certain well-equipped, yet relatively fast-moving, U.S. light forces.

Another theme of discussion has explored the potential of new technology to bridge the putative chasm between heavy and light. The army's "high technology test bed" experiment in the 9th Infantry Division has been applauded by many who believe that technology will help develop multicapable forces transcending heavy and light analytical categories. These forces are likely to be quite expensive, however, and not available until far in the future. Some reformers are therefore quick to point out that technology will be no panacea for a force structure they see as badly misshapen.

Finally, there is an identifiable undercurrent of opinion—inside and outside the movement—which holds that we must avoid the temptation to disaggregate America's worldwide interests into specific conflict scenarios, and then to tailor specific forces for each one. America cannot avoid the implications of diverse and worldwide commitments. Her forces, in the aggregate, must be prepared for all of them, yet that preparedness can be undercut by dissecting it into discrete segments, each with its own allocated force posture. The managerial mentality, some have noted, will always resist vagueness in description of force design objectives. But its search for more precision must not be allowed to create a total force that is a composite of discrete functional capabilities without organizational or functional coherence.

Some observers make a related point: that force designers must not be mesmerized by the magic of technology and organizational theory, which may seem alluring tools to cope with a complex and diverse reality. Pursuit of either to its extremes may result in forces that are incongruent with the requirements of the real world. There can be no retreat from the effort to understand the world, and possible future wars. But since there will never be perfect understanding, and since uncertainty about future missions cannot be wished or managed out of the calculus, it is doubly important to concentrate on the truly fundamental building blocks of good armies and successful military campaigns: unit cohesion and sound leadership. These can go far toward making any force structure an adequate one.

EQUIPPING THE FORCES: CRITERIA AND COSTS OF EXCELLENCE

Everyone wants to equip U.S. forces with excellent, effective weapons and equipment. But there are clearly divergent views about what constitutes excellence or effectiveness in the case of particular weapons and equipment systems. Two disputes in particular have been central: disagreements about the correctness of data offered to demonstrate quality, and disagreements about the kinds of data which do in fact demonstrate quality.

Arguments about the correctness of data have been the easiest to resolve. Careful designing of tests and painstaking scrutiny of results can reliably establish, for instance, the accuracy of Maverick missiles, or the target-identification capabilities of pilots during periods of limited visibility. But disputes about the appropriateness of effectiveness criteria have been more intractable, since they touch upon broader issues of force design, tactical doctrine, and visions of future war and future enemies. Judgments about combat effectiveness necessarily depend in the end on beliefs about the nature of combat and about how to wage war successfully. Maneuverists' views of weapons and materiel are products of the maneuverist image of war. The reformers' concern, most simply stated, is that the concept of "quality" now governing weapons procurement policies has been informed by a mistaken vision of what future war will require.

Several sets of questions illustrate the kinds of issues that remain unresolved in the reform debate: Is the army's new main battle tank a good piece of equipment because, among other things, it has a turbine engine that propels it at speeds up to 45 miles per hour? Or is that same tank a bad piece of equipment because, among other things, it is so heavy that it cannot be moved by strategic lift in any significant quantities? Or is it a bad piece of equipment because, when in place on any battleground, it uses large amounts of fuel and has other special logistical requirements? How are such questions answered? At what point in the design and procurement process are the answers developed? What are the ultimate perceptions and beliefs about the world and about combat that drive the acquisition process? Were such perceptions and beliefs articulated in this case? If so, are we still comfortable with them? To what extent are they shared among all services whose efforts and equipment must combine to fight the same battle?

There is surprisingly little convergence on questions such as these, and it is evident that several interrelated factors have complicated the analysis and evaluation problem in general.

1. Different perceptions of individual service roles, and of appropriate battlefield doctrine, generate different views concerning the demands that will be placed on equipment and thus concerning the things equipment must be able to do. In the air force, for instance, belief in the deep interdiction role produces quite different arguments about equipment than does focus on the close-air-support role. In the army, belief in the operational primacy of armored ground forces fighting in blitzkrieg style on the "modern" European battlefield will lead to acquisition of equipment far different than if concern were focused on other combat contingencies.

2. Many observers, whether reformers or not, are suspicious of technology and of "advances" trumpeted as technological improvements. Where others applaud leaps in technology, they see increases in complexity and vulnerability to breakdown. The believer in technology points to vastly increased operational capability, but the skeptic fears that fancy equipment will work less frequently or will be beyond the capacity of the ordinary person to understand and use well.

3. Perception of proper criteria can be influenced by loyalty to the observer's own branch of service, corporation, or legislative constituency. Arguments about the effectiveness of weapons, then, may disguise the promotion of narrow, parochial interests having little or nothing to do with quality.

4. For some observers, high end-item and operating costs of weapons systems and other materiel items mean, ironically, diminished effectiveness, even when all can agree that the items in question are good ones. In an environment of constrained resources, it is argued, having costly (and therefore hard to replenish or replace) equipment actually reduces the amount of training done on that equipment, which inevitably detracts from the ability to use the equipment effectively in combat. Thus, systems that appeal to some as high-quality improvements worth

significant extra cost become, in a resource-constrained military, essentially useless showcase paraphernalia.

There is, it must quickly be noted, no substantial argument in favor of avoiding all these problems by acquiring huge quantities of older and simpler weapons. But the fear of runaway technology is recurrent: we must not make sophisticated weapons simply because we have the technological capability to do so. Weapons development must serve functional needs identified for foreseeable battlefields. Some overarching concept of purpose and function must rule the development and acquisition process.

Finally, some observers argue that Americans can do more in the weapons arena to maximize the "total force" potential of alliances. They suggest that there are foreign-made weapons systems which, if purchased by the United States, would be comparable to products of our own design and manufacture, but available at a lower price and at an earlier date. There are, of course, well-recognized impediments to foreign procurement by U.S. defense authorities: extensive bureaucratic procedures and finely-drawn U.S. military specifications are not the least of these. But some believe that we can and should explore the economies of scale in defense production from a "total allied force" perspective.

THE JOINT CHIEFS OF STAFF: WHETHER AND WHITHER REFORM?

Proposals for reorganization or revision of the JCS system have generated divisive discussion both inside and outside military circles. Though the cogency of this point may be arguable, those who favor reform often note that the United States has not "won" a war since the creation of the Department of Defense and the JCS. They argue more specifically that because of the JCS unanimity practice, our present military decision-making structure produces lowest-common-denominator "committee" decisions reflecting self-serving, service-oriented bargains, not sound coherent military judgment. Proposed reforms range from an American general staff manned by select general staff officers to less sweeping changes intended to fine-tune our existing system.

The most conservative responses to these proposals illustrate three general positions. The first contends that the reformers have not yet provided compelling evidence that there is anything seriously wrong with our present system. The second argues that reform will destroy the very desirable redundancy and competition that exist in our present system. The third line of argument holds that the reformers fail to see that their proposals push centralization well beyond its natural limits of efficiency.

In between those poles of debate several more general themes of discussion have emerged. First, there seems much agreement that although JCS reform has not been made a mainstream military reform issue, some sort of change is essential to the success of most of the reform program. Reform proposals often cut across service boundaries, yet there is no structural mechanism (since the JCS is held to be disabled by the unanimity practice) for hammering out and if necessary imposing cross-service positions and perspectives *within* the services. Individual officers and services may see much merit in many reform proposals, but they simply cannot put them into effect unilaterally. A second point is related: many reform proposals that move at a micro-level (debates about weapons-system choices, force structure composition, and so forth) reflect larger propositions, at a macro-level, about the nature of the world, about assessments of threats, and about consequent defense requirements. As noted earlier, these often unarticulated strategic perspectives are at the heart of the military reform debate. Proposals for change really require an explicit adoption of fundamental propositions about the world. But there is no structural mechanism, if some critics are to be believed, for producing that unambiguous national declaration, nor even for developing a unified defense establishment perspective, undiluted by interservice bargains, that would help shape that declaration.

A third theme holds that the finest, most rational decision-making structure cannot perform to expectations if it does not have the highest quality people within it. Reform of national-level structure, then, while perhaps necessary, will not in itself be enough. The structure must be staffed by military persons familiar with service problems and interests, comfortable with and competent in broad questions of strategic outlook and purpose, and sensitive to the nature and demands of the national political process. Some participants in the debate have questioned whether the military services can develop such persons, but others argue forcefully that they can, if shown how and why.

A fourth theme deals with the ultimate expectations of those who argue for JCS structural reform. Such arguments, it has been pointed out, seem to spring from a desire to affect the outcome of very large choices about societal purposes, directions, and allocation of resources. In such matters the "military perspective" can never be more than one competitor in a classic political contest held in the arena of national public debate. If structural reformers expect more, say some observers, they are bound to be disappointed.

THE FUTURE: A STRATEGY
FOR ADVOCATES OF CHANGE

The debate engendered by the military reform critique has frequently been acrimonious, with radical denunciations contending against entrenched and equally unyielding defenses of the status quo. In a sense, this is understandable, if regrettable. The stakes in the debate are high, and so, inevitably, are the associated passions.

In such circumstances it would be unrealistic to hope for substantive convergence on all the issues outlined here. But even if some contention must inevitably remain, there is no reason why participants in the debate cannot find more common ground than has been discovered to date. After all, in spite of the distractions of polarized rhetoric, they all are united in their desire to ensure that U.S. military forces can fight effectively wherever they may be committed in defense of the national interest. To be sure, agreement about that goal cannot settle all disputes about instrumental means. But as a beacon on the horizon of argument it can remind all of a common directional orientation and of the need to find the straight-line distance from here to there.

As discussion proceeds, and as awareness of the dimensions and import of the reform critique continues to increase, those who press for change from outside the military establishment might profitably devote attention to several points of argumentative strategy. The first deals with the single-service analytical focus chosen by some reformers, and the narrowly drawn critiques that result from their inquiries. Critics who concern themselves solely with the policies or programs of individual services, and who therefore focus mainly on micro-level problems, risk ignoring macro-factors at joint service levels (and higher) that account for those service policies and programs. The army's weapons design and force structuring policies, for instance, have roots in decisions made (or not made) at the level of national strategy. Reform-minded observers must drive their analyses to that level, and give their evaluations coherence in those terms, in order to address the most fundamental issues.

Further, there are three other tasks that might enlarge the reformers' ultimate contribution to enhancement of national defense capabilities.

First, it would be of some practical benefit for them to find resonance and congruence with the work of analysts and planners within the military. Then, having demonstrated their relevance to those ongoing developmental efforts, reformers should try to show how their approaches and perspectives appreciably improve those internal efforts. And finally, at the most general level of argument, all who advocate reform must make a persuasive case that their proposals should be given attention and even priority in a vastly overworked and overloaded defense policy process. Though these practical advisories are derived from truly fundamental maxims of policy advocacy, outsider critics have seemed to honor them more in the breach than in the observance, at great cost to their cause.

The first task would involve identifying the forces working for change within the military establishment, and then capitalizing on the reform momentum they have generated. This requires, of course, a certain sensitivity to the internal dynamics of the services' self-evaluation processes. It also requires ample, but certainly not disabling, doses of patience, realism, and modesty in outlook and expectations. Radical departures may well be achievable over the long haul, but in the short run effective advocates must establish intermediate goals that can move the establishment incrementally toward desired ends.

Not all outside reformers have neglected the services' self-generated momentum for change. Some advocates of the maneuver style of warfare, for instance, have been well attuned to kindred doctrinal developments in the military, especially in the marines and army. But even in these cases, there has been a tendency for discourse to dissolve into disputes over attribution of credit for the changes; the reformers insisting that their efforts are responsible, the military insisting that the reforms have been internally generated. And, at some distance from these exchanges, many prominent outside observers continue to view the military establishment as uniformly and obtusely conservative, steadfastly resisting all change.

In fact, there has been a good deal of ferment within the military on all issues now composing the reform program. Dissatisfaction with the post-Vietnam doctrinal focus on the European battlefield, skepticism about the fascination with fancy technology, and suspicion of the claims made on behalf of improved management techniques, all characteristic of the present reform movement, were also evident years ago in the military. Reformers might well have obtained a more receptive hearing at the outset if they had understood that. Now, as the military establishment scrutinizes the reform movement, the critics themselves might study the present dynamics of change in the military and seek convergence with compatible elements of it. This is not a recipe for compromise or cooptation. It is simply good sense, given the congruence of final goals in both camps.

Since the outside scrutiny proceeds essentially alongside the services' own internal self-assessment, it must also be able to show how reform perspectives can advance or refine the ongoing search for better policy, beyond what the services' internal dynamics can offer. Not only, then, should reformers seek to discover resonance with internal reform efforts, but they should also demonstrate how they can improve them. It is not enough to formulate or repackage familiar ideas. Insights must be shown to be new and useful, not simply clever, and the burden of proof is on the reformers.

It has been noted earlier, for instance, that advocates of maneuver concepts have been challenged by military men who contend they need no instruction on those ideas. And it is no wonder; as I write I have before me several issues of the *Infantry Journal* published in 1939. Their pages are literally filled with the notions now advanced by maneuverists as new perspectives on the essence of combat.[3] The point here is simply that the military has heard this part of reform perspective before, and already believes much of it. The real challenge for critics is not to explain these familiar ideas more elaborately, but to show how the "new" analysis takes the old wisdom farther, or refines it, or reveals significant and unwise departures from it.

Finally, having shown resonance and congruence with internal pressures for change, and having demonstrated how their analysis enhances the services' own approaches, reformers must be prepared to compete vigorously in the national policy process. The wisdom of their proposals will not be self-evident. Interests outside the defense establishment will seek a quite different allocation of national resources than some reformers would prefer. And within the establishment, reform proposals must compete for a place on the national agenda with other issues and programs also claiming high priority. The relevant audience is potentially huge, and advocacy must ultimately attempt to reach all its elements—in industry, in the universities, in the public at large, and even among America's allies abroad.

Reformers of all types must be able to show that their analysis and advocacy has identified the most critical, meaningful choices, and that they offer the most insightful advice on how to choose. They must prepare, in the end, for politics, not just for the lecture hall. And they must set aside the solitary grandeur and arrogance of radical chic in favor of the practical struggle to communicate and persuade. If they do not, they will probably fail, and it may be that the loss will be the nation's more than their own.

NOTES

1. In preparing this overview the author has benefited from having observed and taken part in discussions held during the conference that generated this volume. The author has, further, reviewed discussion summaries prepared by round-table rapporteurs at the conference, and these have been most useful in identifying the main points of contention.

2. Mr. Boyd, now a defense consultant, has not yet published his study in book or article form. His findings and conclusions, presented in an oral briefing, have been made widely available within the defense establishment, however.

3. Two articles are of special interest, both written by the then-chief of infantry, Maj. Gen. George A. Lynch: "The Tactics of the New Infantry Regiment," *Infantry Journal* 46 (March–April 1939): 98; and "Firepower . . . Manpower . . . Maneuver," *Infantry Journal* 46 (November–December 1939): 498.

5

DUBIOUS REFORM: STRATEGISM VERSUS MANAGERIALISM

Richard K. Betts

Although Betts describes the reform movement as "polymorphous and often discordant," he accepts reform criticisms of "business as usual" defense planning. He indicts many reformist critiques as poorly developed and many reform proposals as rationalizations, supported mainly by hyperbole. Rejecting both micro-management and strategism as panaceas for defense ills, Betts charges reformers to raise the practical and intellectual content of the debate.

The American military's conventional strategy and force structure are now subject to more scrutiny than at any time since the early 1960s. The passing of U.S. nuclear superiority—no longer cushioned as it was in the early 1970s by hopes for detente or success in Mutual and Balanced Force Reductions negotiations—has raised the salience of conventional defense for the West. Hawks who fear Soviet intentions and doves who seek a rationale for a nuclear no-first-use policy are united in the search for more credible conventional deterrence. Recent increases in military spending and reinvigoration of forward commitments, however, have not been matched by a clear official articulation of whether or how strategic concepts might be revised. The Reagan administration has placed more emphasis on naval power but has not presented a compelling plan for improving the ability of land forces to fulfill their primary missions. All the aircraft carriers in the world would not stop the Soviet army from overrunning Europe.

This combination of change in the importance of conventional strategy and continuity in official conceptions has left a large opening for critical analysts outside the Defense Department. The so-called military reform movement has seized prominence in the debate, but the movement is polymorphous and often discordant. One thing reformists agree on is the inadequacy of "business as usual" approaches to defense. As the first section of this chapter will suggest, there is much merit in such criticism, especially when it highlights the astrategic quality of standard analyses oriented to calculating the "balance" of military power.

To an unfortunate degree, however, some reformist critiques have resorted to hyperbole, overlooked dilemmas, and focused on stark conceptual alternatives that rarely stand up to the practical requirements of fielding a large, variegated force committed to meet multiple contingencies. Those who focus on innovation in strategy sometimes confuse heuristic arguments with policy prescriptions, because they suffer from insensitivity to political constraints (or simple disdain for them). Some who focus on technology point out the costs of undisciplined sophistication but go overboard, and many of them implicitly foster the dangerously alluring illusion of a military "free lunch"— better defense for less money. Valuable as these gadflies have been, it is time to step back and subject such critics to criticism and to admit the unedifying but real merits of some conventional wisdom. But first it is useful to explore an area where conventional analyses of conventional forces are weakest.

ASSESSMENT OF THREAT
AND MYTHS OF THE "BALANCE"

Modern intelligence-gathering methods permit a historically unprecedented degree of accuracy in determining the quantities and physical qualities of enemy military forces. Yet analysis is too often abused and debate degraded by epistemological errors. The crudest and most common is comparison of particular elements abstracted from integrated capability as a whole—for example, comparison of numbers of tanks without reference to antitank weapons; numbers of artillery tubes without reference to tactical aircraft that may be used for similar missions; numbers of ships without consideration of tonnage and unit capability; numbers of nuclear warheads without attention to yield; or defense expenditure totals of the superpowers without mention of the overall totals of the two alliance systems. This approach can lead to a meaningless inductive basis for defining requirements. Desirable forces are simply aggregated, which offers no basis for planning because available resources—except at the margins—are determined deductively from the political balance between visceral mood about the threat and pressures against increased taxation, deficits, or reductions in domestic programs. The crucial defense budget debates in Washington hinge on the desirable percentage of change for the aggregate budget; this is not a measure calibrated to the actual military balance.

To provide a more useful estimate of requirements, given the pressures against potentially endless aggregation, the most relevant, albeit difficult, form of analysis is net assessment: comparison of the full panoply of capabilities available to both sides in a prospective encounter. Relative power, not absolute power, is the only meaningful measure of the adequacy of a conventional force. Too much of what passes for criticism in security debates glosses over this obvious point. For example, those doves who simply decry the precipitous increase in Third World military expenditures, or the record growth in U.S. defense spending in the Carter and Reagan administrations, do not demonstrate that either phenomenon is wasteful or dangerous. Data on absolute levels of military investment do not show that Third World countries have bought more than they need to defend against local enemies, or that U.S. expenditures will produce more than would be needed to defend against Soviet attacks, or that the world would be more peaceful if there were less total military spending but greater imbalances in relative capabilities. At the other extreme those hawks who, for example, simply point to the massive growth in Soviet naval capabilities do not demonstrate that this causes Western maritime inferiority (as opposed to diminished superiority), because they ignore the earlier baseline. The Soviet naval buildup proceeded from next to nothing in blue-water operational capability. The quantitative balance, however, does not speak for itself. Geographic asymmetries give Soviet and American naval forces different missions. The military significance of whatever balance obtains varies widely depending on objectives and strategy.

Much of what passes for net assessment, however, is a narrow focus on static orders of battle—the observable and quantifiable constituents such as manpower and equipment—or dynamic simulations of combat engagement. The numerous subjective or intangible factors such as campaign strategy, operational doctrine, training, morale, or command competence receive shorter shrift, yet these factors (unless materiel imbalance is overwhelming) almost always do more to determine the outcome of battle than the number of troops and distribution of weapons. This point is illustrated by the German campaigns of World War II, the Israelis in 1956 and especially 1967, and, most recently, the South Atlantic War, in which a numerically inferior force of British marines with little fire support quickly rolled up the well-entrenched Argentinian garrison on the Falkland/Malvinas Islands.

The reason for the tendency to focus on the more visible balance of forces is akin to "the principle of the drunkard's search." Although it is Procrustean, concentrating on what is clear and quantifiable rather than what is murky and uncertain *appears* to allow more rigor and confidence in the estimate. Moreover, despite its limitations, the quantitative balance must remain an important element in discussion because it is the closest thing we have to a simple index of relative power. Much discussion has to rely on shorthand measurements. But shorthand calculations imprison the relevance of estimates within narrow assumptions about specific operational missions that may not correspond to actual priorities in war. This problem is aggravated by the fact that major wars are usually fought with new technologies untested in previous large-scale combat. Consider this assessment of the relative import of battleships and aircraft carriers written by a naval officer on the eve of Pearl Harbor:

> The power of aviation is increasing, but . . . the strength of the battle line is still the decisive factor. . . . a battleship would begin an engagement with about 1,200 heavy projectiles; it would require 1,200 bombing planes to carry in a single flight 1,200 1-ton bombs, which are comparable in destructive power. As planes improve this ratio will decrease, but when planes can carry 3 1-ton bombs it will still take 400 planes to equal a single battleship in hitting power for the destruction of an engagement.[1]

For attacking coastal targets on land, this assessment of the battleship's advantage was quite reasonable; it was simply irrelevant to the more critical decisive battles at sea in 1942.

More comprehensive assessments are necessarily more complex and scenario-dependent. While scenarios clarify issues at the micro-level, they confuse them at the macro-level; overall strategy must handle multiple scenarios, and the hypothetical permutations and combinations are endless. The problem with holding subjective variables in abeyance is that estimates of the quantifiable balance can easily provide analytical ammunition for both sides in U.S. defense debates, because either can temper the significance of the balance by appealing selectively to other considerations. Those who debunk alarmist views of the Soviet threat can point to areas of overwhelming U.S. advantage, such as in long-range logistical capacity and power projection forces for intervention in Third World regions. Despite dramatic growth in Soviet projection forces, the Russians would still have only weak options for contesting Western military action in Latin America, Africa, and the Pacific Basin. Opponents can counter that in parts of the Middle East—a more likely and important scene of confrontation—the USSR's geographic proximity neutralizes U.S. superiority in airlift, sealift, and aircraft carrier striking power.

Those who see Warsaw Pact power in central Europe as overwhelming point to the large disparity in ground forces that would exist even after NATO mobilization, but opponents cite mitigating factors: improbable cohesion of the Eastern alliance, questionable skill levels and esprit among Soviet troops, long mobilization (and hence longer warning time) necessary to mount an attack with more than fifty or sixty divisions, and the military advantage of a defensive posture, which allows NATO units to hold off larger numbers of offensive forces. Assuming that NATO mobilizes and reinforces, force-to-space ratios make it difficult for the Soviets to funnel enough divisions into narrow sectors to achieve breakthrough.[2]   The pessimists can counter by citing asymmetries in the vulnerability of rear areas that favor the Warsaw Pact,[3] severe doubts about the political capability of NATO to reach a decision for mobilization in response to warning, lack of sufficient operational reserves to contain a penetration, and the strategic advantage of the initiative for the attacker (the option to focus effort, to exploit deception and innovative plans, and to choose the timing, locale, and mode of engagement), which may neutralize the tactical advantage of the defense.[4]

At a very simple level of analysis, assessments of the balance are the least unsatisfactory indicator of which side has the advantage because the quantitative data are firmer than the data on intangible factors. Serious investigation, however, should take such assessments as the starting point for analysis, not as the answer to what capabilities are adequate for defense. Otherwise, evaluations must rest on the dubious assumption of the equivalence of imponderables (that is, that the various advantages in subjective factors are about evenly distributed between the two sides and cancel each other out). Or, even more riskily, the U.S. assessment would have to assume that most of the subjective variables favor the West. Given the huge uncertainties about these questions, however, the only way to hedge in a direction that minimizes risk is to compensate for the unknowns by overinsurance in the quantitative elements, to provide a cushion against bad luck or unexpectedly high enemy competence. This is the solution that Moscow appears to have chosen in regard to the area of highest military priority for both superpowers—the central front in Europe.

American planners, therefore, must either accept higher risk (by resting on one of the above assumptions) than the Soviets do, or they must arrive at a more complex assessment of how the more intangible factors weigh in the balance. As examples of the difficulty in reaching definitive judgments about the subjective issues I will briefly mention some considerations in regard to one: the relative advantages of tactical defensive operations and strategic initiative for the attacker.[5] Uncertainty about coalition solidarity in wartime probably favors NATO. But even if just one or two countries in the Western alliance—for example, Belgium or the Netherlands—opt out of mobilization, critical difficulties in covering the front would arise. Moreover, because Soviet troops account for a large majority of Pact forces and are more heavily equipped than many NATO units, with surprise they might outnumber and outgun the West even if they attacked alone after incomplete mobilization. But their advantage would not be sufficient to overcome a reinforced and entrenched defense (that is, a NATO front line augmented by U.S. POMCUS[6] divisions that had time to deploy and prepare fortified positions during the warning period) unless the Soviets used uncharacteristically bold and innovative tactics. Therefore NATO's greatest vulnerabilities are probably (1) political indecision in response to warning indicators that could delay alert and coordination of the defense (especially if several "cry wolf" false alerts in a gradually evolving crisis dulled sensitivity); (2) an adventurous

Soviet attack plan that, for example, launched air strikes well before the ground offensive was ready, in order to disrupt the U.S. airlift, interdict sea ports, wreck POMCUS depots, and short-circuit Western communications; and (3) deceptions that could mask the main axes of Soviet advance, preventing NATO's limited mobile reserves from moving efficiently to the critical sectors.

Judging by most historical precedents, the first vulnerability is quite plausible. The second is not thoroughly consistent with what is known of Soviet doctrine, which stresses careful preparation and mass, and condemns adventurism (although the doctrine does also emphasize surprise), but it is certainly conceivable. The third is unlikely, given the technical capabilities of modern intelligence surveillance mechanisms, unless there is a combination of bad weather and novel Soviet means of spoofing. In any case, the position of initiative gives the Soviets more options for resolving the uncertainties on preferred terms, for setting the conditions of engagement and focusing an attack on NATO's weak points, if they are willing to take high risks and mount operations in ways unheralded by previous evidence in their military writings and exercises. Any decision to resort to war, though, presupposes radical action. Thus, some elements in this collection of uncertainties favor NATO, and some Moscow. Which way they tilt overall depends largely on faith, though the net result probably favors the USSR. A sterile assessment based on the quantifiable balance of forces, however, provides no answers about the effect of these considerations on the question of which side would achieve its objectives in war.

If the balance were the problem, the solution is simple: deploy more weapons and manpower until it is even, or favors the West. Some doves, focusing on NATO strengths and Soviet weaknesses, believe this could be done with modest increments of investment. Hawks believe the increments would have to be massive. The latter thus have a greater incentive to increase power by changes in strategy and tactics.

STRATEGIC ROMANTICISM

The importance of subjective factors and initiative has been recognized by reformist critics. Until recently, civilian contributions to conventional strategy have been much sparser than to nuclear strategy (largely because palpable experience with the former made clear its daunting complexity, while the purely hypothetical nature of nuclear strategy made it seem susceptible to analysis by logical deduction). Civilian analyses of conventional forces rarely ventured beyond the static balance. The most eloquent figure in the new school is Edward Luttwak, who has performed a great service by brutally exposing the sterile, ahistorical, and mechanistic quality of much American defense analysis.[7] The exposé, however, sometimes goes too far and is limited by its own monomania. Strategic thinking is implicitly conveyed as an autonomous art that should direct defense planning, unhobbled by managerialists. As Luttwak waxes at one point, "the Way of Strategy is not given to all."[8] The criticism reveals severe debilities—such as the simplistic focus on "the balance"—but then often caricatures and misconstrues the dominance of economists, systems analysts, and astrategical micro-managers in U.S. defense planning, and it promotes an almost mystical apotheosis of strategy as a vocation.

The attack on managerial methodologies confuses principle and practice and fails to grapple with the problem of opportunity cost. The function of systems analysis is to estimate investment tradeoffs, allowing the most effective mix of combat power to be obtained from the aggregate resources available—which are always finite. Eliot Cohen attacks systems analysis for its pretentiousness in claiming to determine "how much is enough" for defense.[9] This critique has some validity for the 1960s, but is exaggerated. First, it takes too seriously the claims of early practitioners. Even in the McNamara period, despite official declarations to the contrary, the defense budget ceiling was set independently, according to general predispositions about threat and competing budgetary demands. In an ingenious exposition Arnold Kanter reveals that arbitrary financial constraints, civilian controls, and outcomes actually differed far less between the 1950s and 1960s than folklore maintains.[10] The real utility of systems analysis is to highlight tradeoffs deductively, within the expenditure ceiling.

Second, Cohen overestimates the influence of systems analysts. Even in the heyday of the 1960s it is difficult to find many programs whose fate was primarily determined by the "Whiz Kids." At best their judgments were usually only one of several competing inputs to decision, and most of the time they were less influential than the advice of other interest groups. (The most prominent example of a program that was warped by McNamara's approach—the TFX/F-111 fighter project—actually contradicts another of Cohen's criticisms, that systems analysis ignores the incalculable advantages of versatility in a weapon and promotes single-mission systems. The TFX fiasco was due in large part to systems analysts' pressure to widen the capability of the plane.) Even if the criticisms are valid for the 1960s, before systems analysis was reined in, how instructive is it to beat a horse that has been dead for fifteen years?

Third, the wrongheaded quests for narrow efficiencies that the critics lament are regrettable, but are only examples of bad cost-effectiveness calculation. And the criticism does not offer any forthright definition of which alternate mode of assessment guarantees fewer bad decisions, other than the experience and intuition of professional soldiers. There is no clear evidence that the overall force structures developed before or after the period when the role of systems analysis was greatest were "better" in terms of the match between available resources and effective power than those of the 1960s. If seasoned strategists have made proportionally fewer unwise program trade-offs within a finite budget than the McNamara regime did, the fact remains to be demonstrated. The clear examples are those that add extra capabilities rather than those that explicitly give one up to gain another—in short, cases where hard choices could be avoided.

The alternative to crude economic reductionism is not to do without such calculations. Rather, it is to make them better or, as the critics imply, to do them intuitively, or by another name ("strategic thinking"), or by default. Like Tartuffe, who was surprised to find that he had been speaking prose all his life, strategists who make choices between alternatives (rather than simply adding all desirable capabilities together) practice systems analysis without realizing it.

This point is obscured by some of the critics' assertion that efficiency and military effectiveness are contradictory. This is true only when "efficiency" is defined quite narrowly. The elementary economic reality of opportunity cost means that for each inefficient program, some other useful element of combat power is foregone. Luttwak cites the strategic benefit of inefficient production in a hypothetical case[11]—and in this case he may be correct—but does not state what other capability he wants to give up for that benefit. The real logic of this line of criticism is an argument for a higher resource ceiling, to allow acquisition of more of all sorts of things. This may be a valid goal, but it is a separate issue from how to determine choices within a constrained budget. Resource ceilings are determined by vague senses of threat and acceptable risk, not by strategy; rather, strategy must put the available resources to work in the best combination of outputs. Visionary strategists who gloss over opportunity cost have a usefulness as limited as that of mechanistic managers who don't understand the vagaries of war. Rather than flagellate inept systems analysts, critics aiming to change policy might more profitably link their strategic thought to the corpus of serious organization theory that explains the impediments to rational action by complex institutions. But while managerialists can be criticized for not having read Xenophon, Clausewitz, or Douhet, those who venerate strategy give no indication that they have read Cyert, March, or Simon. Thus, they are subject to the same joke told about the analytic propensities of the professional fraternity they criticize: two professional economists are marooned on a desert island (in the days before flip-tops) and find a can of beer. When one asks, "What shall we do?" the other cogitates and says, "First, assume a can opener."

In railing against managerialism, systems analysis, and the "bookkeeping" approach to defense policy, critics have implicitly enshrined bold and creative strategic thought as an independent solution, and strategy as the factor to which other constraints must be adapted. Luttwak argues, "Only a fully strategical appraisal can yield a valid answer. Beginning at the level of *national* strategy, one must proceed level by level to the intended theater strategies, to the operational methods . . . all the way down to the tactics of specific forces in particular situations."[12] This sort of pure "strategism" is heuristically valuable but is a prescription for thought, not policy. Like the focus on quantitative balance assessments, it neglects critical mitigating factors. Foremost are political constraints that are essential (rooted in the U.S. Constitution), not peripheral. In a nation that has never faced imminent extinction or unambiguous threats, one cannot expect the polity to adapt to strategy; rather, strategy must adapt to the polity. The polity must respond to threats if it is to survive, but the mode of response—the strategy—will be pushed, pulled, and squeezed by competing theories and interests. Coherence may emerge if the process is well managed, but it will always be suboptimal according to the logic of any particular philosopher king. *Apolitical strategy is no improvement over astrategic economics.*

Strategic innovation depends on the social and political milieu. The German blitzkrieg was attributable not just to the genius of Manstein and Guderian or the superior tradition and ethos of the German army; the army originally resisted the 1940 Manstein Plan as too adventurous, and it was Hitler's direct personal intervention that made its implementation possible. The Prussian military reforms of earlier times were also societal reforms.[13] Napoleon's genius would have had less effect on military history were it not for the *levée en masse* made possible by the French Revolution. Do current critics propose a cultural revolution or constitutional change to make radical reform possible? If so, what sort, and how is it to be brought about? Despite critics' frequent invocation of the need to consider nontechnical and social factors, little attention at best is given to these questions, aside from exhortations to take the Soviet threat more seriously, and when there is it sometimes takes the counterproductive form of sneering at the effeteness of American society.

Realistic strategic analysis must be interdisciplinary, not a field in its own right. Focusing on military genius in concepts as the key to strategy, and implicitly viewing resource management or political constraints as distractions, is neither empirically realistic nor normatively legitimate. Doing so makes criticism either curmudgeonlike or wistfully romantic. Romance may be a necessary condition for an ideal marriage, but it is not a sufficient one; strategism may be a necessary contribution to improvement of American defense, but it is also insufficient.

In strictly military terms, pure strategism rejects modernity almost as much as it embraces it. The conventional forces of today's superpowers are too complex and their commitments too diverse and contradictory to allow full subordination of strategy to genius in campaign planning. Just as the theories of Adam Smith or Karl Marx, intellectually powerful as they are, can no longer sufficiently explain the functioning of postindustrial technocratic economies, neither Clausewitz nor Jomini can sufficiently guide modern strategy. Changes in technology, logistics, and costs per unit of combat capability make management as vital as leadership and bookkeeping as vital as inventiveness in operational concepts. Because the West is in the defensive and reactive position, it must emphasize its ability to conduct a long war more than Moscow (only an offensive or preemptive doctrine is conducive to banking on a short conflict, and such a change is still foreclosed by United States and—even more—allied public opinion). And because the United States itself is blessed by large buffers of water, it is cursed by huge mobility requirements if it is to aid its allies. Thus, logistics is more central to American strategy than to that of most other great powers in history. Logistics requires efficient management more than anything. There is an old joke that amateurs talk strategy and professionals talk logistics. This is unfair, but efficient logistics for modern forces requires the sort of systems analysis "bookkeeping" at which critics sneer.[14] Consider the trade-offs that have to be calculated in integrating "intrinsic" logistics (elements inherent in hardware design) with "extrinsic" alternatives deriving from "processes of support structure."[15]

Napoleon faced awesome logistical challenges, but they were simpler to grasp intellectually—involving mainly food, a few types of ammunition, and (with limited exceptions) campaigns that were less than intercontinental—than those that face U.S. planners today. Even Patton and MacArthur had less complexity to manage than today's SACEUR or CINCPAC who deals with force structures dependent on a raft of high-technology weapons, communication systems, and phased global mobility operations. The increased salience of managerial concerns is less an aberration of national style than a reflection of the secular trends in modern technology and potential geographic scope of war that have driven up the tail-to-teeth ratio in force structures. Smaller military establishments such as Israel's can escape some of this complexity, or larger ones like the USSR's can drown it with less efficient mass, but the United States can do neither. For American planning, management that deprecates strategy is sterile, and strategy that deprecates management is helpless.

One basic problem in disparaging the U.S. emphasis on managerial skill and techniques is that making strategy the independent variable implies that force structure and weaponry can be dependent variables, developed to fit strategy. This is proper in principle but has been infeasible in practice. Modern weapons have long lead times from conception to deployment (five to fifteen years), and changes in force structures tend to proceed glacially because adaptability varies inversely with complexity. Luttwak and others recognize this and are not naive about tailoring weaponry to doctrine. And of course it is possible to go further in that direction. Innovative attempts such as the army's "High Technology Test Bed"[16] are desirable experiments, although more ambitious projects such as the "Concepts-Based Requirements System"—attempting to direct technological development to doctrine for battles in the year 2000[17]—seem too much like an exercise in planning with a crystal ball. Modern technology has too much of a life of its own to be pressed into service on that time-scale without sacrificing potential benefits (through doctrinal adaptation) from scientific serendipity.[18]

A more fundamental problem obstructs strategism. For the United States since World War II, changes in strategy—or, less charitably, strategic fads—often outpace changes in both weaponry and force structure. For example, Western deterrence before the Korean War rested almost entirely on the U.S. Strategic Air Command. Soon, however, NATO shifted to planning for serious conventional defense—the Lisbon meeting in 1952 decided on force goals of ninety divisions and 9,000 aircraft to be reached by 1954. But less than two years later, the Eisenhower administration's "New Look" shifted to the massive retaliation strategy, which pushed the army toward reorganization around the assumption of tactical nuclear war (recall the Pentomic Division). Scarcely later than this alteration had shaken down, the Kennedy flexible response strategy shifted back to prolonged conventional operations. As the Vietnam War wound down, the army was driven to reemphasize the NATO mission and the heavy force structure appropriate for it. No sooner had this reorientation solidified than anxiety about the Persian Gulf and the need for a Rapid Deployment Force (RDF) compelled attention to novel structures and lighter equipment. By the time the RDF finally becomes viable it is not unlikely that change in strategic priorities or in perceived threats will be working in another direction. Whatever ideal Pattonesque strategist critics have in mind will have to engage novel threats with forces determined largely by criteria other than those of the strategy of the moment.

Practitioners of strategism can respond by saying, "Exactly! That's the problem. American defense is incoherent because leaders don't know what they want." The problem, however, cannot be solved by better military education or appointment of officials with a more subtle flair for the "Way of Strategy." Nor is the problem simply cultural (which would make it irremediable, since only disaster can bend a liberal culture to military requirements). It is, however, almost as deeply rooted as culture. The problem lies in the juncture between the American political system and the ambiguity of conventional military requirements for a superpower in a world of both nuclear risks and changing commitments. Ambiguity fosters diverse notions of deterrence and defensive options, while democratic politics makes the dominance of any view ebb and flow. Only if U.S. administrations had the duration and consistency of the Soviet Politburo, or if Americans really saw their survival as being tenuous, could there be much more persistent congruence between U.S. strategy and force structure, and thus more room for subtle tuning of doctrine and tactics to strategic guidance.

One solution for bringing strategy and structure into alignment in this context is to emphasize flexibility in structure through long-range mobility and versatility in weaponry. This requires maximal efficiency in resource allocation and calculation of tradeoffs between technical alternatives, because versatility goes hand-in-hand with sophistication and cost, and transport investments are made at a cost to combat equipment. As with logistics, efficient calculations require the cost-effectiveness methodologies and management systems that are denigrated as "bookkeeping," because calculations in this realm are more scientific than artful.

Critics can counter that there is another alternative—to emulate the Russian solution by developing new prototypes in greater numbers, with more frequency, so choices can be made more often and forces modernized steadily rather than episodically. Some argue that the Soviet approach successfully subordinates weapons acquisition to doctrine.[19] Or there is the option to compensate quantitatively with higher force levels, avoiding risky choices in trying to squeeze the best from each defense dollar, relying rather on an investment cushion of size and diversity. Because of geography, however, the Soviets do not need to divert resources from combat formations to long-range mobility and logistics to the same extent as the United States. So even with equal spending direct U.S. combat power would be less. In any case, the solution of washing out uncertainties through higher military expenditures runs into the basic problem with strategism—it is less practicable (in peacetime) in a democracy than in an autocracy.

As a source of power potential the West's economic superiority is more than offset by the East's administrative superiority, even discounting the recent weakness of capitalist economies and the specter of global financial crisis. The Soviet system can subordinate competing demands to strategy, and has been able to produce steady, long-term increases in military investment. Because U.S. defense budget changes are determined more by broad swings in public and congressional mood than by consistent strategic planning, they fluctuate much more. Even under circumstances most propitious for raising defense spending—the election of a hawkish president in 1980—it is clear that U.S. defense budgets will not rise to levels that would establish conventional superiority or parity in Europe. It does no good for critics to argue that cost is not a barrier because we spent a far larger proportion of the GNP on defense in the 1950s (this was before the revolution in welfare and entitlement program budgets) or the 1960s (when the economy expanded fast enough to increase both guns and butter). If Ronald Reagan cannot succeed in exacting more than incremental military increases from the polity, no administration will, short of an epochal crisis.

It would be naively fatalistic to assume that this condition is immutable. But it is only realistic to recognize that domestic politics determines military options far more than expert strategic analysis does. Until pro-defense critics offer a pathbreaking domestic strategy to secure more solid and enduring support for defense allocations, all the military strategic genius in the world will be scarcely more relevant to policy than any other sort of wishful academic philosophy, and scarcely more helpful than concentrated managerial efforts to maximize effective use of available resources.

Despite its limitations, strategism still performs a vital role as an irritant in defense debate, goading leaders to remember that good management is a necessary but not sufficient condition for military planning. The ideal solution would be to mold the defense planning process so that the distinct levels of analysis could be coherently combined. Democracy in a generic sense does not preclude this, but the unique character of American democracy makes it quite difficult. The essence of the Constitution is the dispersion of power and turnover of leadership, whereas coherent planning requires both concentration and consistency of authority. A more integrated military staff system that reduced the centrifugal influence of the separate services would help. Indeed, the reason that systems analysis in the Office of the Secretary of Defense burgeoned in the 1960s was that there was no comparable center of integrative analysis within the military. Were the United States to have a genuine and effective general staff, there would be less need and less excuse for concentrating assessment of cross-service trade-offs in the hands of civilian managers (although given the competitive balance of power between the separate services, special pleading would persist and some autonomous civilian analytical discipline would still be helpful). General staff types of organizational solutions, however, have often been proposed but have traditionally been anathema to Congress, which normally prefers to constrain the executive by dividing it and to deal directly with the separate services. The putative fear of a Man on Horseback, used as an excuse for precluding a general staff, is more a rationale for maintaining legislative clout than for protecting the nation. Recently the climate in Congress has become markedly more receptive to reform and centralization of the JCS system, but the proposals considered stop short of a full-blown general staff system.

DOCTRINAL FETISHISM

The American political system and the complexity of modern technology and military organization conspire to make force composition only loosely responsive to specific strategies. The only clear way to reverse this trend is to attack it like the Gordian knot—by frontal assault on fundamental trends and assumptions in military planning and weapons production. Two groups of iconoclasts have visibly promoted such approaches since the late 1970s. But the danger to guard against in the Gordian knot approach is being left with what Alexander had after he cut the knot—a loose bunch of string no more useful than the original mess.

One group deals in terms of operational doctrine, arguing that ground and air operations should be oriented much more to the canons of maneuver and agility than to the emphasis on firepower and attrition that they charge has governed American doctrine. They have argued that such reorientation is the only way to reconcile the constraints that limit the size of Western forces with hope for successful conventional defense against Soviet hordes. Maneuverist critics often couple their doctrinal diagnosis with assertions that the U.S.

military has a steady record of operational failure ever since the Inchon landing of 1950. This hyperbolic combination exaggerates both the merits of maneuver and the obtuseness of American commanders. Few of the critics bother to point out that MacArthur, the strategist they revere, caused a debacle at the Yalu when the propensity for high risks that had yielded success at Inchon produced the longest retreat in U.S. military history. The larger strategic disappointments in Korea and Vietnam were not due to doctrinal deficiences half so much as to political constraints against escalation and the inherent disadvantages of a status quo power in unconventional war. Tactics in Vietnam, in fact, *were* dominated by maneuver (insofar as maneuver involves movement—a definition some reformists quarrel with, though unconvincingly as I will argue below). Airmobile warfare, "vertical envelopment" by helicopters, was a remarkable innovation and became the staple of ground operations. The only way maneuver might have been sweeping and decisive was through an invasion of North Vietnam, which would have been as reckless and irresponsible as the policy of prosecuting more limited war in the South. Military leaders can be criticized for not resigning in the face of political constraints which, though proper, precluded sensible strategy and made lasting military success improbable, and for not appreciating the inappropriateness of conventional forces for an unconventional revolutionary war, but it is inaccurate to charge them with not utilizing maneuver to the degree that was operationally feasible.

Here again the intellectual vulnerability of the critics derives from addressing strategy and doctrine autonomously, without clarifying the political context and constraints that govern them, and also from fuzzy definitions of doctrinal concepts. There are indications that maneuverist criticisms have been taken to heart in the army's latest revision of its basic operations manual, FM 100-5.[20] Some skeptical observers, however, view the change as largely cosmetic ("more or less multiplying the number of times the word 'maneuver' appears by two," as one suggested to me), half meant to coopt the critics. The problem is that contrasting firepower and maneuver is a bit like contrasting hitting and fielding in baseball—both are necessary components for success. One can be emphasized over the other only by a matter of degree, and in an integrated campaign the emphasis in the mix may not appear very stark. This problem is underlined by the appreciable limitations of maneuver doctrine for defensive operations, especially on the central front in Europe. (Given the vagaries of terrain in Germany and the extent to which a mobile defense would have to surrender the advantages of prepared positions, Mearsheimer argues that such a change in doctrine would increase risks and ease the Soviets' tasks. McKitrick also points out that maneuver requires more fuel and less ammunition than defensive operations, but the logistics for moving fuel on the battlefield are more difficult than for ammunition.)[21] There are also substantial arguments for the case that revolutionary technological developments linking data collection and transmission to new types of ordnance will make firepower a far more dominant factor on the European battlefield of the near future.[22]

There is also an implicit question about whether full exploitation of maneuver at the operational level would not imply a generally more offensive strategy. The army's new AirLand Battle 2000 concept is explicit about application of firepower—emphasis on interdiction and second-echelon targeting—but, at least in public explanations, the novel forms of maneuver envisioned seem to be primarily tactical. Could grander-scale emphasis on maneuver logically be separated from plans for very deep and sustained counterattacks into East Germany and Czechoslovakia? Samuel Huntington has advocated such a revision of conventional deterrence strategy.[23] This aim would probably require substantial increases in NATO force levels (though Huntington believes reorganization and reorientation might suffice), and it would certainly require a diplomatic coup. The consensus holding NATO together, especially today as political strains within the alliance have intensified, is the sacred premise that the organization is purely defensive. It is true that there is no inconsistency between defensive policy and offensive military strategy. The Soviets and Israelis have recognized this very clearly. However, it is hard to see how even very adept diplomacy could convince NATO governments, let alone fractious European publics, that this notion is anything but revolutionary and frightful.

Most of the pro-maneuver critics have skirted this issue—although recommendations to increase the NATO teeth-to-tail ratio and ape Soviet emphasis on short-war capabilities would seem, logically, to imply decisive offense, since nothing else could militarily bring the war to a conclusion before the tail collapsed. Perhaps it is not necessary to resolve the issue, especially if political impediments might be finessed by masking strategic implications with discussion in tactical terms. When it comes to elucidation of the maneuver critique at even this more limited level, however, the prescriptions turn out to be quite vague. When army spokesmen maintain that maneuver has been a vital element in doctrine all along, some critics resort to very expansive definitions of the concept, arguing that maneuver is more than "movement."[24] When defenders of more traditional approaches try to pin down the critics, they are faced with arguments that seem to identify maneuver with unspecified sorts of creativity, excellence, or any sort of sensible ingenuity in command.

> Operations and tactics follow no formulas. . . . The real defeat is the organizational/mental/systemic breakdown caused by the enemy's realization that the situation is beyond his control. . . . maneuver warfare is not a new formula, but a replacement for formulas. . . . since we cannot offer a formula, a certain degree of abstraction is necessary. . . . our goal is not a commander with a mental "checklist," but one with what the Germans call "a feeling in the tips of his fingers" . . . a thought process rooted in a *Gestalt* . . . mental reference points, not rules. . . . The key to success is less often a brilliant plan than the ability to innovate rapidly under severe pressure . . . agility.[25]

This sort of slippery abstraction could be a prologue to reformed doctrine, but it is far short of a prescription. *Mystique is no substitute for formulas.* All the preceding desiderata tell a commander is that he should be smart, quick, and ready to take advantage of opportunities in whatever undefined way is appropriate. Who could quarrel with that? At such a level of discussion the critique is immune to refutation.

If maneuverists claim I focus only on the tactical aspects of the concept, I can only amplify my points about the grander notions they mention. First, they are too vague and negative to buttress clear operational prescriptions. Second, the positive aspects glamorize themselves by hiding under the misnomer of "maneuver," when what is really meant is simply "initiative," "speed," "creativity," or "appropriate behavior" (the example of Israeli frontal assault on trenches as "maneuver warfare" illustrates the terminological absurdity).[26] Third, assertions about how actual practice contradicts these notions, or can be turned toward them, are presented without substantiation or depth. For example, the charge that promotion patterns favor "managers" and discriminate against "combat leaders" is completely undocumented; it would (at least for the army) be arguable at best for the pre-Vietnam period, and then to a very circumscribed degree,[27] and it is the reverse of most observers' impression of promotion patterns over the past decade and a half. The simplistic bifurcation of organizational styles into "bureaucratic" and "socialized" ignores most literature on the subject and avoids practical issues of how large institutions function and change. It is hard to escape the feeling that romanticism intrudes here too, that the solution envisioned is some exhilarating combination of brilliant, confident, adventurous commanders, jut-jawed, scarves flowing in the wind, backed by organically bonded troops singing the *Panzerlied,* elbowing aside wimpy military bureaucrats. Granted, the maneuverists have more than this in mind, and some have put their case more carefully and convincingly, but too often their case has been made by assertion rather than by rigorous analysis, and the prescription for how to get from here to there rests on sweeping exhortation more than on prosaic but operationalizable formulas.

The maneuver advocates have performed a valuable service by pushing debate beyond assessment of the static balance and refocusing attention on operational doctrine and the need to find ways of grabbing back the initiative in an engagement rather than resting on reactive defensive concepts. But they have done so by functioning as one pole in a dialectic, not by providing a synthesis. The useful impact of their service will be a nuance rather than a revolution.

VOODOO TECHNOLOGIES

Another group of critics has helped the defense debate by focusing attention on the counterproductive aspects of reliance on complex technology and on the dangers of sacrificing quantity to quality in weapons deployments. By insisting on incorporation of the maximal technical capability available in new weapons—particularly tactical aircraft and tanks—U.S. force structure has developed to the point that it has a small number of weapons, but those weapons are sometimes so sophisticated that they spend much of their time being repaired instead of standing ready for combat. Moreover, past experience and recent exercises have suggested that in many likely combat scenarios the most sophisticated aircraft subsystems could not be brought to bear, and numbers (rather than individual capability) would dominate the battle.[28]

The solution suggested by some is, if not Luddite, at least reactionary: emphasis on simpler technology to reduce procurement costs (allowing more weapons to be deployed) and to reduce maintenance loads (allowing greater readiness). The defenders of the status quo point out that this course—for example, abandoning the state-of-the-art F-15—would deprive the U.S. fighter force of nightfighting and all-weather capability, while enemy armies "move forward under darkness and bad weather."[29] Moreover, the Soviets have not only greater numbers but now equivalent quality as well in many of the systems that U.S. weapons would have to engage.[30] Finally, some of the critics have based parts of their case on analytical sleight-of-hand. For example, one prominent reformer persisted in presenting briefings that contrasted the readiness rates of brand-new M1 tanks and F-15 fighters with older systems, to demonstrate the fragility of the new systems; he also emphasized the alleged superiority of the lower-cost F-16 to the F-14, F-15, and F-18 by presenting a graph of their respective acceleration capabilities.[31] A more rigorous presentation would emphasize that readiness rates are always lower at the beginning of a new weapon's deployment than after it has been broken in,[32] and that acceleration is not necessarily the most crucial index of aircraft capability.

Even if the critics were correct in the assertion that in practice less sophisticated systems are as effective as the most advanced, they overlook a crucial barrier to substituting large numbers of cheap aircraft or tanks for expensive ones. James Fallows, for instance, presents data purporting to show that because an F-5 costs only one-fourth as much as an F-15 and can fly 2.5 sorties for each one by an F-15, the same dollar investment could produce an F-5 force that could put ten times as many planes in the air per day as an F-15 force.[33] This overlooks the elementary difference between unit flyaway cost and system life-cycle cost—especially the huge increase in manpower requirements attached to the larger F-5 force (not to mention the comparably greater fuel requirement). This is the principal reason that the Soviet Union faces a less agonizing quality/quantity tradeoff than the United States. As former under secretary of defense William Perry notes:

> The United States spends more than half of its defense budget on manpower while the Soviets—with twice the manpower—spend only a fourth of theirs on manpower. As a result, they can devote half of their budget to equipment procurement

while we devote a less than a quarter of ours to equipment. . . . even with equal defense budgets, the Soviets can—and do—*spend twice as much on equipment procurement* as the United States.[34]

Countercritics such as Perry argue that technology is not synonymous with complexity (the real bête noire), and that exploitation of the right technological advantages, such as micro-electronics (which have not all risen in cost the way other producers have), is the best hope for offsetting Soviet advantages in manpower and numbers of weapons.[35] And air force leaders attack the critics' glorification of simple systems with examples such as the destruction of the Thanh Hoa Bridge in North Vietnam. During the 1960s 873 sorties were mounted against the target, with eleven planes lost, but the bridge did not go down. When bombing was renewed in 1972 eight planes with laser bombs knocked the bridge down in one mission with no losses. Moreover, the choice between simple and sophisticated systems is not dichotomous; the logical solution is a high-low mix, combining for a force structure of balanced capability and cost. Thus, critics should remember that F-15s constitute only about 20 percent of the air force's complement of fighters.

These countercriticisms naturally face problems too. Precision-guided munitions (PGMs) may be wonderful for attacking bridges, but their revolutionary implications across the board are more ambiguous. Antitank guided munitions, at least those in the current generation, such as TOW and Dragon, are likely to be far less effective under combat conditions—where the soldier launching the PGM must expose himself for an extended time to guide it to target, and where terrain and countermeasures may vitiate accuracy—than in laboratory tests.[36] Nonetheless, some reformers are often reactionary in their preference for older weapons systems, such as the 106-mm recoilless rifle. Though it requires less exposure, it cannot engage tanks before they come within range to shoot back, as TOW can. The real solution is Hellfire, a "fire-and-forget" PGM now in development—in short, yet more advanced technology. PGMs are also not unalloyed defensive weapons; they can be put to good use in offensive operations. What empirical evidence exists is mixed. The Egyptians used PGMs to decimate the 190th Israeli Armored Brigade on 9 October 1973. "The real instruction of the Middle East War," however, ". . . is not to be drawn from the early slaughter of a single unsupported, and incautious, Israeli tank brigade. The true lessons may be extracted from the knowledge that, of the approximately 3,000 Arab and Israeli tanks destroyed or damaged . . . at least 80 percent were knocked out by other tanks."[37] And terrain and climate in the Sinai are more conducive to PGM accuracy than in Central Europe.

American planning has also not succeeded well in disciplining the pursuit of a high-low aircraft mix. The F-18, for example, was originally conceived as a low-cost complement to the F-14 and F-15. In the course of development, however, the F-18's cost advantage disappeared (although its mission versatility grew). The systems analysts who attack such results, and who are attacked by strategists as petty "bookkeepers," do well to hold planners' feet to the managerial fire.

CONCLUSION

This chapter's insistence on the complexity of defense planning is perforce conservative in its implications. Both the intellectual power and the policy weakness of reformist critiques lie in their simplicity and the clarity of their theoretical premises. Because the purpose of the theory is to simplify, any theory's implications for policy can be made vulnerable by focusing on whatever complexities it does not encompass. Analysis has to treat critical variables and hold other factors constant, so any policy conclusion can be shaken by pointing out that some of the constants are really variables. This chapter does this to critics, which is a bit unfair because it is always easier to debunk an intellectual position than to prescribe a more viable policy position. But it is no more unfair than what the most provocative critics have done to conventional wisdom.

Some amounts of strategic innovation and technological reform are vital, but more as gyroscopic adjustments than as guides to fundamental redirection of policy. Because conventional wisdom does not offer a sufficient solution does not mean that it has less to offer than unconventional criticism. The overall size of U.S. forces (that is, their comparative smallness) is more the source of difficulties than is their structure or doctrine. The essential problems for U.S. strategy lie in immutable geography and only marginally tractable politics. Geography makes the U.S. homeland more secure than the Soviet Union, but reverses this where defense of allies and conflict in crucial third areas is concerned. Washington must inevitably sacrifice combat power to logistics more than Moscow, so combat force levels are limited by support force structure. Political, social, and economic constraints further inhibit overall force size by limiting military manpower, which reinforced the orientation to qualitative solutions by technological substitution. Both better strategy and better management could ameliorate these problems but not solve them. Reformist critics will do more to translate acute thought into feasible action if they become less polemical and categorical and slightly more forgiving of "business-as-usual" conventional wisdom.

NOTES

1. Capt. W. D. Puleston, USN, *The Armed Forces of the Pacific: A Comparison of the Military Power of the United States and Japan* (New Haven: Yale University Press, 1941), pp. 178–79. On "the drunkard's search" see Abraham Kaplan, *The Conduct of Inquiry* (San Francisco: Chandler Publishing Co., 1964), pp. 11, 17–18. The metaphor

refers to the old joke about the drunkard who looks for his lost house key under a street light, not because that is the place in which he had dropped it, but because the light was better there.

2. John J. Mearsheimer, "Why the Soviets Can't Win Quickly in Central Europe," *International Security* 7, no. 1 (Summer 1982): 26–29.

3. Robert Shishko, *The European Conventional Balance: A Primer,* Paper P-6707 (Santa Monica Calif.: Rand Corporation, November 1981), p. 21.

4. Richard K. Betts, *Surprise Attack: Lessons for Defense Planning* (Washington, D.C.: Brookings Institution, 1982), pp. 9–10, 12–16.

5. Part of the following draws on ibid., pp. 170–88, 199–207.

6. Prepositioned Overseas Materiel Configured to Unit Sets. These are equipment stocks in depots in Germany, to which divisions can be airlifted from the continental United States. Without prepositioned equipment, the units would have to move by sea, which takes much longer.

7. Examples of Luttwak's arguments are "On the Meaning of Strategy . . . for the United States in the 1980s," in *National Security in the 1980s: From Weakness to Strength,* ed. W. Scott Thompson (San Francisco: Institute for Contemporary Studies, 1980); and "Why We Need More 'Waste, Fraud, and Mismanagement' in the Pentagon," *Commentary* 73 (February 1982).

8. Luttwak, "Why We Need More 'Waste, Fraud, and Mismanagement,'" p. 25.

9. Eliot Cohen, "Systems Paralysis," *American Spectator* 13 (November 1980).

10. Arnold Kanter, *Defense Politics: A Budgetary Perspective* (Chicago: University of Chicago Press, 1979), pp. 74–78, 82–93. The premier example of quasi-memoir accounts that inflate the role of systems analysis is Alain Enthoven and K. Wayne Smith, *How Much Is Enough?* (New York: Harper & Row, 1971).

11. Luttwak, "Why We Need More 'Waste, Fraud, and Mismanagement,'" p. 22.

12. Ibid., p. 20 (emphasis in original).

13. I am indebted to Barry Posen and Congressman Newt Gingrich for reminding me of these points.

14. Attempts at excessive calibration of logistical operations in the fog of war are of course unrealistic. See Martin Van Creveld, *Supplying War: Logistics from Wallenstein to Patton* (New York: Cambridge University Press, 1977), pp. 202–10, and Betts, *Surprise Attack,* pp. 185–87. That sort of unrealism, however, is only pseudoefficiency, not an argument against the importance of management.

15. Col. Elbridge P. Eaton, USAF, "Let's Get Serious about Total Life Cycle Costs," *Defense Management Journal* 13, no. 1 (January 1977): 3.

16. The "High Technology Test Bed" was described by Lt. Col. Huba Wass de Czege at the conference that generated this volume.

17. Ibid.

18. Richard K. Betts, "Innovation, Assessment, and Decision," in *Cruise Missiles: Technology, Strategy, Politics,* ed. Richard K. Betts (Washington, D.C.: Brookings Institution, 1981), p. 9.

19. Col. Richard G. Head, USAF, "Technology and the Military Balance," *Foreign Affairs* 56 (April 1978). Critics also argue that the Russians manage to develop and deploy several new types for each one the U.S. does—for example, T62, T64, T72, (and almost T80) tanks during the ten years it took to turn out the U.S. M1. Maj. Jeffrey McKitrick maintains, however, that this difference is overrated. During this period "the M60 was upgraded to the M60A1, M60A2, and M60A3 with design improvements in engines,

ammunition, suspension systems, range-finding equipment, and night-fighting equipment resulting at each step in a tank with greater capabilities than its predecessor. Further the three 'new' Soviet tanks . . . were not always different tanks. The T62 was basically the same tank as the older T55 except for the main gun. The T64 was new, but the T72 follow-on was again basically the same as its predecessor." Debunking the horror stories about cost overruns for the M1, McKitrick reports that the Army's director of weapons systems says the price of the M1 at the time of deployment, with inflation discounted, was within 5 percent of the first projection. "A Military Look at Military Reform," *Comparative Strategy* 4, no. 1 (January 1983).

20. See Lt. Col. Huba Wass de Czege and Lt. Col. L. D. Holder, "The New FM 100–5," *Military Review* 62, no. 7 (July 1982): 53–70.

21. John J. Mearsheimer, "Maneuver, Mobile Defense, and the NATO Central Front," *International Security* 6, no. 3 (Winter 1981/1982): 123–43; McKitrick, "A Military Look at Military Reform."

22. Neville Brown, "The Changing Face of Non-Nuclear War," *Survival* 24, no. 5 (September/October 1972): 211–13.

23. Samuel P. Huntington, "The Renewal of Strategy," *The Strategic Imperative: New Policies for American Security,* ed. Samuel P. Huntington (Cambridge, Mass.: Ballinger Publishing Co., 1982).

24. See chap. 6, William S. Lind, "The Case of Maneuver Doctrine."

25. Ibid. There are more reasonable and refined conceptualizations of maneuver. See Edward Luttwak's correspondence and my reply in *International Security* 8, no. 1 (Summer 1983): 140–62.

26. Lind, "Case for Maneuver Doctrine."

27. See Morris Janowitz, *The Professional Soldier,* 2d ed. (New York: Free Press, 1971) on "adaptive" vs. "prescribed" careers, and Richard K. Betts, *Soldiers, Statesmen, and Cold War Crises* (Cambridge: Harvard University Press, 1977), chaps. 2–3.

28. See for example James Fallows, *National Defense* (New York: Vintage Books, 1981), chap. 3, and Michael I. Handel, "Numbers Do Count: The Question of Quality versus Quantity," *Journal of Strategic Studies* 4, no. 3 (September 1981): 225–60.

29. Brig. Gen. Robert Rosenberg, quoted in Edgard Ulsamer, "We Can't Afford to Lose the Technological Edge," *Air Force* (February 1982): 92.

30. Handel's critique emphasizes this point.

31. See chap. 12, Pierre Sprey, "The Case for Better and Cheaper Weapons."

32. For example, see Leonard Famiglietti, "Ready-to-Go Rate Climbing as TAC Fine-Tunes Its F-15s," *Air Force Times,* 8 March 1982, p. 14.

33. Fallows, *National Defense,* pp. 42–43.

34. William Perry, "Fallows' Fallacies," *International Security* 6, no. 4 (Spring 1982): 175 (emphasis in original).

35. Ibid., pp. 181–82.

36. See Fallows, *National Defense,* pp. 22–24. and Michael Handel's forthcoming monograph on PGMs.

37. Staff Study, "The Military Balance," *Strengthening Deterrence: NATO and the Credibility of Western Defense in the 1980s,* ed. Kenneth Rush et al. (Cambridge, Mass.: Ballinger Publishing Co., for the Atlantic Council, n.d.), p. 129.

III

DOCTRINAL ISSUES

It is a curious paradox that while the doctrinal dimensions of the military reform critique arguably form the conceptual centerpiece of the widening debate, doctrine has formed a less visible component of the public debate. Several factors seems to account for this. First, perhaps more so than with other aspects of the reform debate, the controversy over doctrine is relatively arcane and, thus, excludes those not totally familiar with the techniques by which militaries ply their art. Second, in contrast to force structure or weapons procurement issues, arguments for doctrinal reform are less easily translated into terms that capture the public's attention. One cannot demonstrate with clarity, for example, that a particular approach to doctrine would result in a net savings of dollars. Lastly, many observers, including many military professionals, have only a hazy understanding of what doctrine is or why doctrinal questions are central to so many aspects of military policy.

What, then, is doctrine? What does (or should) doctrine do for a military service? In a very real sense these questions probe at the very essence of the controversy over doctrine, and more refined answers must be postponed until the reader is thoroughly acquainted with the chapters that make up part III. As a prelude, however, it seems useful to attempt at least a first-order definition. Simply stated, doctrine can be viewed as a set of authoritative guidelines for the conduct of war. As such, doctrine is important in that it prescribes not merely how a war is to be fought; ideally, it determines as well the organizational structure of an armed service and the procurement of weapons designed to implement that doctrine. One seasoned military professional offered this view:

Doctrine provides a military organization with a common language, a common purpose, and a unity of effort. Doctrine influences, to a major degree, strategic thinking as well as the development of weapons, organization, training and tactics. Doctrine is the cement that binds a military organization into an effective fighting unit.[1]

In the current debate over doctrine, the reformers charge that the American army's traditional approach to warfare has been characterized by what they describe as a "firepower-attrition" doctrine. That is, the central theme of the army's battlefield doctrine, so the argument goes, has been the physical destruction of the enemy's forces through the application of overwhelmingly superior amounts of firepower. Since the army can no longer afford the luxury of such materiel largesse when matched against our principal potential adversary, the reformers advocate a different approach to combat. Their preferred doctrinal alternative, "maneuver warfare," strives to outwit an opponent through what Liddell Hart called the "indirect approach"; the aim of maneuver warfare is the psychological defeat of one's opponent as much as his physical destruction. The following chapter by William S. Lind exemplifies the reformist critique of the army's doctrine.

In a subsequent chapter Huba Wass de Czege responds to the reformer allegations, first, by arguing that many reformers have not well understood the army's earlier doctrine. More importantly, while conceding that the army's previous doctrine was flawed in important ways, Wass de Czege maintains that the army's current doctrine has evolved to incorporate the essence of maneuver warfare to a degree not yet acknowledged by the reformers. He points out that the army's newly developed doctrine, AirLand Battle, is organized around principles consistent with maneuver warfare: initiative, agility, and synchronization.

In contrasting the chapters by Lind and Wass de Czege, the reader is likely to be struck initially by the apparent similarity in the arguments of each. Both authors accept the view that the precepts of maneuver warfare represent a distinctly more intelligent approach to combat than the firepower-attrition paradigm. Despite the similarities, real, though subtle, distinctions can be drawn between the argument made here. In the first instance, the authors diverge on the question of how thoroughly the army has adopted (or should adopt) the tenets of maneuver warfare.

More fundamentally, however, the tone, if not the literal substance, of the chapters by Lind and Wass de Czege may well represent altogether different views on the very nature of doctrine and the question of what doctrine should do for a military organization. Lind states that "doctrine is a way of thinking . . . not what to think, but how to think." Alternatively, Wass de Czege argues that "doctrine must tell soldiers today how to fight tomorrow. . . ." Indeed, this "how to think" versus "how to do" dichotomy appears to underlie the whole of the doctrinal debate. This distinction has important implications to which we shall return in a concluding chapter.

Finally, while the chapters in part III focus almost exclusively on the army's doctrine, it is worth recalling that the arguments made here have important cross-service applicability. In focusing on the army's current doctrine, both authors offer arguments which, since they truly represent propositions concerning the American military's overall approach to warfare, are easily extrapolated to apply across each branch of our armed services. Clearly, the tactical doctrines of each service have little in common. (Mastering the tactics of ground force combat teaches one little about the techniques of a fighter pilot.) Nonetheless, to the degree that doctrinal discussions properly inform our thinking about the operational level of warfare, the ensuing chapters have a relevance that extends beyond the boundaries of any single service.

NOTE

1. Gen. George H. Decker, "Doctrine: The Cement That Binds," *Army* 2 (February 1961): 60.

6

THE CASE FOR MANEUVER DOCTRINE

William S. Lind

Lind sees the army and the marines in transition between "firepower and attrition" doctrine and maneuver warfare. Because the latter involves more than doctrine, Lind questions whether the armed forces will make the institutional changes necessary to implement maneuver warfare precepts.

During the 1970s, maneuver warfare became a significant new issue and part of the national defense debate. The purpose of this chapter is to explain what maneuver warfare is, how it translates into army doctrine, and what its adoption as doctrine would mean for the army as an institution.

Thanks to the debate engendered by the 1976 edition of FM 100–5, *Operations* (the army's fundamental doctrinal publication), the army has been studying maneuver warfare. Some maneuver warfare concepts have already been incorporated into the AirLand Battle doctrine and the 1982 version of FM 100–5.

The practice, as distinguished from the theory, of maneuver warfare is not entirely new to the American army. While maneuver warfare practitioners have been and remain a minority, some of America's foremost generals, including Winfield Scott, Stonewall Jackson, George S. Patton, and Douglas MacArthur, were masters of maneuver. A number of commanders in today's army understand it and use it, sometimes very successfully, in exercises.

The issue facing the army today is not, however, whether some officers will understand maneuver warfare; a few always have. Rather, it is whether or not maneuver warfare will be adopted as the army's doctrine, and beyond that whether it will be institutionalized—that is, whether the army will be organized, trained, educated, equipped, and structured for maneuver warfare. As we shall see, maneuver warfare cannot simply be doctrine. It must either become the central idea around which all else revolves or remain an abstract notion to which we may pay lip service in doctrinal publications, but which we cannot perform with consistency on the battlefield.

THE ALTERNATIVES: MANEUVER WARFARE VERSUS FIREPOWER/ATTRITION

Before the army can make the choice, it must understand exactly what maneuver warfare is. The term "maneuver warfare" has itself created some of the confusion. After all, doesn't all warfare involve fire and maneuver? Isn't maneuver just another word for movement? How can there be such a thing as "maneuver warfare"?

Maneuver warfare and firepower-attrition represent alternative ways of thinking about the nature of war. Firepower-attrition is warfare on the model of the battle of Verdun in World War I, a mutual casualty-inflicting and absorbing contest where the goal is a favorable exchange rate. The conflict is more physical than mental. Questions concerning "what to do" receive greater doctrinal and training attention than questions of "how to think." Operational art—the evaluation of the implications of battles for campaign and strategic objectives—is ignored. Efforts focus on the tactical level, with objectives usually defined in terms of terrain. Defenses tend to be linear ("forward defense"), attacks frontal, battles set-piece, and movements preplanned. "Maneuver" really means "movement," and movement is used primarily to position firepower so as to inflict maximum casualties.

In contrast, maneuver war is warfare on the model of Genghis Khan, the German blitzkrieg, and almost all Israeli campaigns. The goal is destruction of the enemy's cohesion, not piece-by-piece physical destruction. The objective is as much the enemy's mind as his body. Efforts focus on the operational rather than the technical level. Operations and tactics follow no formulas, although objectives are generally defined in terms of shattering the enemy force. Depending upon the opponent and other circumstances, defenses often are organized in depth, with strong reserves; attacks are concentrated against enemy weaknesses; battles are fluid; and the focus of effort changes constantly as the situation develops. Firepower is generally a servant of maneuver, used to create openings in enemy defenses and, when necessary, to annihilate the remnants of hostile forces after their cohesion has been shattered.

A key to understanding maneuver warfare is to realize that not all movement is maneuver. Maneuver is *relational* movement. Maneuver is not simply a matter of moving or even of moving rapidly. Maneuver means moving and acting consistently more rapidly than the opponent, and more rapidly than his expectations.

Recently, the concepts behind maneuver war have been elucidated, organized, and expanded into an overall theory of conflict. This theory was developed by Colonel John Boyd, a retired air force officer, and is appropriately known as the "Boyd Theory." Boyd has observed that in any conflict situation, all parties go through repeated cycles of observation-orientation-decision-action. The potentially victorious party is the one with an observation-orientation-decision-action cycle consistently quicker than his opponent's (including the time required to transition from one cycle to another). As the faster party repeatedly cycles inside his opponent, the opponent finds he is losing control of the situation. Because of his longer cycle time, the opponent's reaction is facing a later action than the one it was intended to oppose, and is irrelevant. Instead of achieving convergence, he finds himself facing ever-widening divergence. At some point, he realizes there is nothing he can do to control the situation or turn it to his advantage. At that point, he has lost. Often, he suffers mental breakdown in the form of panic or passivity and is defeated before he is destroyed physically.

The Boyd Theory is the background for maneuver warfare doctrine. In maneuver warfare the physical destruction of the enemy is not the decision but the denouement. The real defeat is the organizational/mental/systemic breakdown caused by the enemy's realization that the situation is beyond his control, which is in turn a product of our ability consistently to cut inside the time of his observation-orientation-decision-action cycle.

History can add to the understanding of maneuver warfare that the Boyd Theory gives us. Maneuver warfare is not new: it is threaded through the writings of Sun Tzu, it enabled Thebes to defeat Sparta, and it kept Byzantium alive for a millennium. But in the West in this century, it was rediscovered, developed, and institutionalized by the German army, and it is to the Germans we must turn if we are to flesh out our picture of what it is.

In 1914, the tactics of the major Continental armies had many common elements. Chief among these was an overriding concern with the maintenance of the line in the attack and the defense. This concern resulted in other common practices: control was tight, with subordinate units expected to act only on orders; reserves were committed where the enemy was strongest; the axis of advance was determined early in an operation at higher levels of command and was seldom shifted; and forces tended to be spread over broad frontages, at least at the tactical level. The goal, at the tactical as well as the operational level, was to destroy the enemy physically in battle.

With the onset of trench warfare, both the Central Powers and the Allies were forced to look for new ideas in order to break the deadlock of the trenches and restore movement. The Allies, who had a preponderance of both manpower and materiel, chose a firepower/attrition approach. Infantry tactics changed relatively little. What did change was the quantity of artillery support the infantry received. Artillery preparations lasted for days and consumed trainloads of shells. The Germans called the new allied style *Materialschlacht,* a battle of materiel. The French summed it up with the phrase, "The artillery conquers, the infantry occupies."

The Allied approach failed to restore movement. The Germans changed their defensive tactics to deal with the Allied bombardments, and their lines held. But the massive quantity of artillery did inflict heavy casualties on the Germans. Although this was not their purpose, the Allies perpetuated a static war of attrition, a war in which their superior numbers would eventually prevail.

Most Germans realized they could not win a *Materialschlacht.* If they failed to re-create a war of movement, they could not fall back on a war of attrition with much hope of success (as proven at Verdun). They needed a radically new approach. That approach was maneuver warfare.

Maneuver warfare meant revising and, indeed, reversing most of the tactical practices of 1914. The basic objective shifted: no longer was it to kill the enemy soldier or destroy the enemy's piece of equipment. Rather, it was to take the enemy unit, as a whole, out of play.[1] The emphasis on linearity was gradually abandoned. New elastic defensive tactics allowed the enemy to penetrate, letting his own momentum combine with positional elements in the defense to pull his cohesion apart. The enemy was then shattered with a strong counterattack into his flank or rear. On the offense, the goal was to flow around enemy front-line units and get into rear areas. Storm units sought to create gaps in the enemy's defenses and to draw main units through the gaps. Control was radically decentralized, with subordinate units expected to act on their own initiative; reserves were committed where the enemy was weakest, not strongest; the axis of advance shifted constantly in response to the discovery of gaps in the enemy's defenses; and assaults were on very narrow frontages, with the main strength reserved for exploitation. On both the offense and the defense, the goal was to shatter the enemy's cohesion by creating unexpected and dangerous situations faster than he could cope with them.[2]

These new tactics were highly successful. Unlike the Allied tactics, they did restore movement to the battlefield. In the Kaiser's Offensive of spring 1918, the new "Von Hutier tactics" almost won the war for Germany. German errors on the strategic level, the exhausted physical condition of the German army, a highly competent French general staff, and, perhaps most important, a mobility differential favoring the Allies on the operational level (the Germans had to move forward on foot through difficult terrain with horse-drawn artillery and logistics, while the Allies could shift reserves laterally by rail) prevented Germany from turning tactical success into strategic victory.

But the Germans had found something new. By 1918, blitzkrieg was conceptually complete. It lacked only the mechanized forces of 1939 to succeed operationally and strategically (forces that reversed the mobility differential that had favored the Allies in 1918). When asked why so many of the best Panzer generals of the Second World War had been light infantry commanders in the First, General Hermann Balck responded, "Because it was the same." Maneuver warfare had been rediscovered.

While an understanding of the evolution of German tactics during the First World War is very helpful in understanding maneuver warfare, it can easily lead to some dangerous misconceptions. Some critics say that maneuver warfare is just a different tactical formula. Instead of attacking frontally, the attack is made into the enemy's flank and rear. Instead of defending a rigid line, maneuver warfare allows the enemy to penetrate; then a counterattack is made, and he is encircled. From this oversimplified perspective, that is all that maneuver warfare means.

Flank attacks and elastic defenses, such as those used by the Germans, are techniques very likely to be employed in maneuver warfare. But they are not formulas for maneuver warfare, since maneuver warfare replaces reliance on formulas with unpredictable selections of battle techniques. In maneuver warfare, the object is to shatter the enemy's organizational and mental cohesion by creating unexpected and dangerous situations more rapidly than he can deal with them. If our actions are formulistic, they will be predictable. If we are predictable, we will seldom be able to create situations unexpected by the enemy.

Maneuver warfare, correctly understood, offers hope to an army that must expect to fight outnumbered. Against physically superior forces, an attrition contest can have only one outcome. But maneuver warfare makes physical size and strength less important. A large and powerful, but slower and more clumsy, force can fall victim to a small force adept at maneuver warfare, as history has often shown.

MANEUVER WARFARE DOCTRINE

If the American army wants to adopt maneuver warfare, what should it do? The first step is to adopt maneuver warfare as its doctrine. Doctrine is an approved set of guidelines for the conduct of war. In the U.S. Army, doctrine is expressed in field manuals, TRADOC publications, and the content of courses in the army's schools. Changing those publications and courses to reflect maneuver warfare concepts is obviously central to the adoption of maneuver doctrine, and it is not accidental that maneuver warfare advocates have concentrated their efforts on revising FM 100–5 to reflect their ideas.

However, there is a preliminary step that must be taken if changes in doctrine are to be meaningful. Before we can have a maneuver warfare doctrine, we must have effective doctrine. Currently, however, we have doctrine only in an academic sense. We have doctrinal manuals, such as FM

100–5, that have been approved by the responsible agencies and commanders. Officially, they are doctrine. But in fact, in terms of their influence on the thinking of officers in the field, these manuals are not effective. Not all commanders have even read the official doctrine; fewer really understand it. Each tends to do, in practice, whatever he best understands: the old linear or mobile defense, a cavalry-style offense, the active defense, or even maneuver warfare. Each battalion, brigade, and division has its own approach, depending on the individual commander. Doctrine remains a suggestion at best, and often simply an unknown.

Does this mean we need to force everyone to do the same things and act the same way to have effective doctrine? Not at all. In maneuver warfare, doctrine is a way of thinking that is shared throughout the officer corps. It is not a checklist of rules and recipes, or even a shared grasp of techniques (though the latter is certainly useful). It is not *what* to think, but *how* to think. Historically, the Wehrmacht prominently displayed this shared way of thinking. Confident that those operating above, below, and beside him understood what he was doing and why, a commander in the Wehrmacht was able to seize the initiative and act boldly; he knew that leaders at every level would act to exploit the opportunities he created or to protect him if he encountered unforeseen difficulties. Doctrine understood in this way is an important part of the foundation for the trust among officers that must characterize any maneuver warfare army.

How does maneuver warfare translate into doctrine at the tactical level? Like current doctrine, it deals with techniques. Techniques in the form of both individual skills (for example, using a weapon) and unit skills are crucial on the battlefield.

But maneuver doctrine also seeks to develop creativity and originality in selecting and combining techniques. An officer must be able to put his specific situation into context, to see how the situation looks through his opponent's eyes, to have some idea about the enemy commander's thought process. He must understand how to think through his own situation.

This is perhaps the hardest part of maneuver warfare doctrine to explain clearly, because the goal is not a commander with a mental checklist, but one with what the Germans call "a feeling in the tips of his fingers" for his situation and the opportunities inherent in it. Seeing these opportunities is a thought process rooted in a *Gestalt*—in seeing something as an entity—not in analysis by checklist.

Study of military history can be of great assistance in developing this ability; but such study must not be a search for precise analogies, for there are none. Its focus must be not the actions, but the thought processes of successful commanders. The goal is not knowledge, but understanding; not what to think, but how to think. As General Hermann Balck said:

> Therefore, one of the first principles has to be: There can be no fixed schemes. Every scheme, every pattern is wrong. No two situations are identical. That is

why the study of military history can be extremely dangerous. . . . No one thinks of becoming a great painter simply by imitating Michelangelo. Similarly, you can't become a great military leader just by imitating so-and-so.[3]

Beyond studying history, three doctrinal "filters" or guideposts can help commanders in the process of selecting and combining techniques:

Mission-type orders. The commander does not expect or attempt to control every action of his subordinates, nor does he attempt to foresee and plan for every event that will take place. Rather, he determines his intent—what he wants to have happen to the enemy. He makes certain this intent is consistent with the intent of his superiors, and he communicates it clearly to his subordinates.

As the action develops, he supports and expands the local successes of his subordinates, committing his reserve where he perceives the enemy weakest and the chance for success greatest. At times, he will issue detailed orders in order to do this. But in general, he will trust his subordinates' abilities to make the best decisions as to how to achieve his intent—what techniques to select for their particular unit—within the framework of his guidance and support. In effect, he tells them what result he wants and leaves it up to them to obtain it.

The search for enemy surfaces and gaps. Maneuver warfare seeks to avoid enemy strengths (surfaces) and throw maximum strength against enemy weaknesses (gaps). This can result in something very much like the German tactics of 1918, or it can lead to very different combinations of techniques. An illustration may be helpful. In the 1950s, the Israelis developed effective tactics against Arab fortified positions. They attacked frontally, got into the trenchworks, and engaged the enemy in hand-to-hand combat. This may not sound like maneuver warfare, but it was. The Israelis had identified a specific weakness of their opponent. The Arabs' lack of social cohesion outside the family made it very difficult for the Arab soldier to show initiative, and he had no reason to expect support from those around him. When faced with a melee in the trenches, the Arabs' cohesion came apart as each soldier looked out only for himself. The Israeli techniques were very different from those of the Germans in 1918, but the process of tactical thought was the same.

We must understand surfaces and gaps on a macro-, not just a micro-level. The micro-level is useful technique but unless it is relevant to the specific opponent, it is a formula. The techniques that take advantage of the weaknesses of one opponent will run head-on into a different opponent's strengths. In maneuver warfare, techniques must be selected and combined in relation to the specific opponent.

Focus of effort. This is the German concept of *Schwerpunkt,* the conceptual focus of effort which each subordinate commander uses to link his actions, through the intent of his superior, to the actions of those around him. It is the "glue" that permits mission orders to allow initiative without losing unity of effort.

Can we now understand more clearly what maneuver doctrine means on the hierarchical level? Imagine yourself a brigade commander. You have just conducted a successful attack. You have collapsed the enemy line of resistance, pocketing one enemy battalion, sending a second plus the enemy reserve fleeing in disorder. You pass the encircled enemy battalion off to a division reserve unit to contain or reduce. You advance until you meet the enemy's second defense line.

Now you must again think, "What are my tactics here?" You look at the new situation and ask, "What techniques can I employ?" That is, given the factors of mission, enemy, terrain, troops available (METT), time, the availability of supporting arms, and so forth, what is the full range of options open to me? Put your situation in context—how have successful commanders thought through situations like this in the past? Consider your three "filters": What intent does my superior have, and what intent do I communicate to my subordinates? What are the specific strengths and weaknesses of this enemy in this place? Among the units available to me, on which do I focus my effort?

The answers to these questions are a set of actions, a combination of techniques. But tactics include the whole thought process, not just the actions. Unless you see tactics as the whole process, you are likely to be reduced to formulas, to techniques applied by the book.

The same thought processes are appropriate at the operational and strategic levels. In each case, the commander must grapple, through the fog and friction of battle, with the questions, "How do I shatter the enemy's cohesion? How do I take him out of play? How do I avoid his strengths and hit his weaknesses?" Because the situation constantly changes, there can be no long-term plan. Field Marshal von Moltke's rule was, "No planning past D + 1." Actions must change constantly as the situation changes. The key to success is less often a brilliant plan than the ability to innovate rapidly under severe pressure. In Boyd's words, variety and rapidity are the most important qualities. Together they are the basis of maneuver doctrine: agility.

How do we obtain agility? The answer to this question has broad implications for the U.S. Army in the 1980s. Agility is a very difficult quality for any institution, military or civilian, to achieve. It can only be achieved with consistency if everything in the army's structure and behavior is designed to create and foster it. That is, maneuver warfare doctrine must be supported by an infrastructure appropriate to maneuver warfare.

BEYOND DOCTRINE: INSTITUTIONALIZING MANEUVER WARFARE

If we want to design the army as an institution to be supportive of and consistent with maneuver warfare, what must we do? Major changes are needed in a number of areas. I will look at four of them here: soldier issues, officer education and promotion, organization, and institutional structure.[4]

Soldier Issues. Maneuver warfare is characterized by uncertainty, confusion, and rapid change. These characteristics are perceived by the troops as well as by officers. If units are to remain effective in the face of uncertainty and rapid change, they must be cohesive; that is, the troops must be sufficiently comforted by the unit's internal situation that they are not panicked or frightened into passivity by external circumstances.

How is unit cohesion created? The first and most important element is personnel stability. Troops must remain with those immediately around them—their fire team and squad, perhaps their platoon—long enough for strong psychosocial bonds to form. They must serve long enough with the same platoon, company, and perhaps even battalion NCOs and officers so they know and trust them.

General Edward C. Meyer's initiatives to strengthen unit cohesion in the army are of vital importance for maneuver warfare. The personnel policies we have been following, with their high rate of personnel turnover, make maneuver warfare impossible. Indeed, they may make all but the most rudimentary forms of firepower/attrition warfare impossible. Without cohesion, no unit can be expected to fight well, and without units that can fight effectively, no style of warfare is likely to succeed.

However, stability of personnel assignments alone will not create dependably high levels of cohesion. Another important element is the troops' perceptions of their NCOs and officers. If they know their NCOs and officers, but perceive them to be self-serving, careerist, tactically incompetent, disinterested in or even afraid of their men, or simply bad leaders, cohesion will not develop. Many armies have had stability of personnel assignments, but because quality was lacking in the NCO corps or among the junior officers, they broke and ran or at least remained largely passive in combat. While the American army can feel confident in the quality of its junior officers, a professional NCO corps is also necessary for the successful implementation of maneuver warfare.

Finally, it should be noted that cohesion alone is not enough. Three other factors must be mentioned briefly: quality in combat units, esprit, and morale. The combat units must receive quality people, both officers and enlisted personnel. They cannot be dumping grounds for those with too few brains or too little self-discipline to qualify for the technical services. They need esprit: pride in their unit, branch, specialty, and service. And they need good morale, that elusive element which is influenced by everything from the quality of the battalion mess hall through the way civilian society values (or fails to value) its soldiers. Only units with cohesion, quality, esprit, and high morale can hope to remain effective in warfare, especially maneuver warfare.

Officer Education and Promotion. What qualities do we need in our officers if they are to practice maneuver warfare? First, we must realize that understanding maneuver warfare is one thing, practicing it is something quite different. Practice depends upon understanding, but it requires more than that. It requires officers who can see the options in the situation facing them, including subtle options. It requires officers capable of assuming heavy responsibilities and taking great risks. It requires boldness and imagination and an ability to innovate. It demands men who can lead effectively under very difficult circumstances.

Does today's army foster and reward officers with these qualities? It is not clear that it does so. Too often, the rewards seem to go not to the imaginative and the risk takers, but to those who follow all the rules, to the risk avoiders and the courtiers, to the managers and the bureaucrats. Bureaucratic qualities, rather than battlefield qualities, appear to be the tickets for career success.

What do we need to do differently? First, we need to change the type of people we promote. This probably cannot be done by changing the details of the promotion system—the promotion board structure, the performance evaluations, and so forth. Instead, it will require a careful effort to put those who do exhibit and value battlefield qualities on the promotion boards and to instruct them to promote others like themselves (a natural tendency for promotion boards in any case). Character must become the first criterion in promotion; it is the sine qua non of success on the battlefield.

Second, we need to reform the basic structure of the officer corps. Space precludes discussing this in detail, but three basic changes are needed:

1. We need to eliminate "up or out," to decrease the fixation on getting promoted.

2. We need to separate grade and pay, so the officer who does not strive for higher rank can still support his family adequately. This would provide the means for eliminating the up or out policy.

3. We need a substantial reduction in the size of the officer corps at the general and field grade levels. Having excessive levels of senior officers breeds bureaucratic behavior.

These steps will decrease careerism, permitting officers to do their jobs instead of punching tickets in the drive for promotion. And, with a smaller officer corps, those on promotion boards will have a better chance of knowing the people they are considering.

Third, we need to revamp the military education system. Officers with knowledge but without strong character are hopeless in terms of maneuver warfare; they will never be able to do it. But officers with character and without knowledge are wasted potential; they may eventually learn maneuver warfare, but the lesson is likely to be expensive, since it will be gained by personal combat experience.

The basis for understanding maneuver warfare is the study of military theory and history—not electrical engineering, or management, or foreign policy. We need to refocus the curricula of all defense schools, from West Point through the War College, on the theory and history of war. Military history should be studied not to develop models to be applied to contemporary situations but, rather, to develop an understanding of the thought processes of commanders. That is, given a particular set of circumstances, how did the commander analyze the situation facing him in order to determine his course of action? The case study approach may be the best method by which to teach military history. If we give our officers a solid background in military history, they will have an important tool with which to put their battlefield situations in context, to see their options and to develop an instinct for shaping the battle to take advantage of the enemy's weakness.

Organization. Maneuver warfare offers the potential of a substantial improvement in teeth-to-tail ratios, yielding two to three times more combat units. Why? In firepower/attrition warfare, the support system is structured on the assumption that at any given time, most units are on line, engaged with the enemy in a heavy exchange of fire. Accordingly, the unit must be able to sustain itself. In contrast, the assumption in maneuver warfare is that at any given time, most units are not decisively engaged—that is, they retain freedom of action and movement. The ability to sustain itself can be less, because support is channeled to those units that are engaged. This assumption is the key to the much higher Soviet teeth-to-tail ratio and can clearly be seen in the structure of their support system. With it, we can obtain a significantly greater number of combat units without an overall increase in personnel strength.

Institutional Structure. This is the single most important and most difficult change required for maneuver warfare. There are two basic models for hierarchical organizations: the bureaucratic and the socialized. The bureaucratic model has become the standard American model in the business world, the government, and the military, where three of the four services have adopted it (the Marine Corps is a partial exception).

In bureaucratic organizations, individuals focus on doing their jobs, which are defined in narrow "in-box, out-box" terms. The bureaucrat is discouraged from focusing on the overall purpose of his organization. Since he still needs some reference points, he tends to develop two: the first is personal career success, and the second is an identification of what is most important with what takes most of his time. Since most of his time is taken by intrainstitutional considerations—the shop next door, the people immediately below him, the people immediately above him, the competing program, branch, service, and so on—he comes to make decisions based on these considerations.

The socialized organization, in contrast, attempts to convince all those within it to adopt the organization's external goals and purposes as their personal goals and values. This model is exemplified by such organizations as Toyota and IBM. Socialization of the work force creates a counterweight to the tendency to give internal considerations dominance in the decision-making process. Throughout the organization, socialized individuals will question a decision that is comfortable institutionally, but dysfunctional externally. Further, they will show initiative in achieving the organization's goals, rather than merely waiting for directions—the Japanese quality control circles are a case in point.

A good example of the behavior of a socialized organization was given by a Japanese professor in a talk at Stanford. He told a story about a bank in San Francisco which had been failing and was bought out by a Japanese bank. The new owners sent in Japanese management. The American employees said, "Tell us what to do differently." The Japanese, in response, explained the values and goals of their bank. The Americans said, "Fine, but tell us what to do." The Japanese continued patiently to explain the values and goals of the bank.

The Americans were initially confused, and productivity fell further. But eventually they came to understand that they were to use their individual intelligence, imagination, and creativity to do everything they could—beyond as well as within their jobs—to advance the goals and values of the bank. Productivity rose rapidly, the bank became one of the more successful in the city.

Why is the difference between a socialized and a bureaucratized organization important for maneuver warfare? Because *only* a socialized organization can conduct maneuver warfare. Maneuver warfare requires a very high degree of internal agility, with actions focused entirely on the external environment. A bureaucratic institution, focused on the need to prevent change from upsetting comfortable internal arrangements, does not have this ability. This is, in fact, the bottom line of America's military weakness today: the contradiction between the nature of warfare and the inherent behavior patterns of bureaucracies. It means we face a massive task: the resocialization of the U.S. Army, Navy, and Air Force, and the strengthening of socialization in the Marine Corps, which faces increasing tendencies toward bureaucratization. Without this change, larger defense budgets, maneuver warfare, and anything else is unlikely to do much good.

CONCLUSION

How, then, should the U.S. armed forces regard maneuver warfare doctrine? First, maneuver warfare doctrine is a promise, not a threat, to all whose primary interest is winning in combat. Its principal promise is obvious: it has been, historically, the most effective means for a force to fight outnumbered and win. That alone should be enough to ensure its welcome in the army. But that is not the only promise. Maneuver warfare offers a substantial increase in the number of combat units without the need for additional expensive manpower. It offers to make expertise in war central to an officer's profession. And it offers the officer corps a powerful weapon against the stultifying blanket of bureaucracy that has become such a prominent part of life in the army and in the other services. Most officers seem disheartened and discouraged by the constant misdirection of their time and energy into internal concerns, and away from the things needed to succeed in combat. With the adoption of maneuver warfare, officers will be able to do more than gripe about bureaucracy. They will be able to point out that bureaucratic behavior is fundamentally contradictory to the army's doctrine. And they can point this out to civilian authorities and systems analysts as well as to their own bureaucrats.

Second, maneuver warfare is not a minor change for the army. It is not just a matter of rewriting some field manuals. It is a call for fundamental change in almost every aspect of the army's life. We cannot restrict maneuver warfare to doctrine and expect it to be of more than academic significance. Having a maneuver doctrine is one thing; being able to practice maneuver warfare consistently on the battlefield is very much more.

The challenge is enormous. So is the opportunity. Can it really be done? That is a question only the officer corps can answer. While civilians may have a role to play, fundamental reform can only come about if those inside the institution work for it. Whether the American officer corps is willing to undertake the task remains to be seen.

But the omens are auspicious. A growing number of officers, especially junior and field grade officers, are sufficiently disgusted with bureaucracy, careerism, and inadequate professionalism that they are challenging "business as usual." And the bureaucracy, including its civilian and congressional components, is beginning to feel the pressure. Voices in Congress are beginning to join voices within the officer corps in demanding reform. The combination is potentially a powerful one—powerful enough, perhaps, to change the way the army and the other services think and behave as institutions.

And that, at the most fundamental level, is the task.

NOTES

1. Gen. Hermann Balck, Conversation with author, 1981.

2. For an excellent discussion of changes in German tactics in World War I, see Capt. Timothy T. Lupfer, *The Dynamics of Doctrine: The Changes in German Tactical Doctrine during the First World War,* Leavenworth Papers, no. 4 (Fort Leavenworth, Kans.: U.S. Army Command and General Staff College, July 1981).

3. Translation of taped conversation with Gen. Hermann Balck, 13 April 1974, Battelle Columbus Laboratories, Columbus, Ohio, p. 42.

4. For a thorough treatment of institutionalization, see Martin van Creveld, *Fighting Power: German and U.S. Army Performance, 1939–45* (Westport, Conn.: Greenwood Press, 1983).

7

ARMY DOCTRINAL REFORM

Huba Wass de Czege

Wass de Czege rejects the dichotomy drawn by reformers between fire-power-based attrition warfare and maneuver warfare. Rather, the real world lies between these doctrinal poles. He goes on to summarize the key concepts that form the basis of the AirLand Battle doctrine.

A heated debate over how the U.S. Army should fight, and about its doctrine, has gone on outside the service for several years. But it is impossible to segregate a discussion of doctrine from other matters central to how an army fights. These include the purposes of the army, its equipment, its soldiers, the existence of external threats, the nature of modern combat, society at large, technological advances, and so on.

The army's internal and external critics have made the following charges:

1. The army's doctrine is basically flawed. The preferred method of combat consists of direct, stereotyped frontal engagements oriented against enemy strength and is tailored to whittle the enemy down to size by destroying his fighting men and machines. They call this "attrition warfare."[1]
2. Defensive tactics consist of a "fall back by ranks." There appears to be too little doctrinal difference between delay and defense, and many defending units in the field are apparently unwilling to accept decisive engagement.[2]
3. The active defense is a "zero-defects" defense, but it must be executed by imperfect soldiers and commanders. It is reactive, surrendering the initiative,

and is intended to be a safe solution. Its flawed application of principles makes it a risky method of defense.[3]

4. Officers tend to cultivate managerial skills over leadership and fighting skills. The study of military history and military theory takes a low priority. Army officers, critics charge, are hidebound bureaucrats wedded to archaic methods.[4]

5. Training exercises consist of stylistic and unimaginative applications of "doctrinally approved" methods.[5]

6. The army compensates for its lack of imagination in fighting methods by relying on high technology to build sophisticated weapons systems that will reduce the gaining of victory to a simple engineering problem.[6]

This could be viewed as an alarming list of indictments. As I will show, the army's record in these areas is better than the critics may assert. Some critics are better theoreticians than most soldiers, but what the theoreticians say must wash through the sluice of practical experience and meet a full range of real world problems before the true nuggets can be recognized. That, in fact, is occurring.

THE DOCTRINE DEBATE

Much of this specific criticism fits under the rubric of the maneuver/attrition warfare debate in one way or another. Many critics suggest that U.S. forces should adopt simpler weapons and a maneuver-oriented doctrine. Such doctrine, they state, is best executed by using numerous, inexpensive, simple, and small fighting formations armed with equally numerous and inexpensive fighting systems that are simple to operate and maintain.[7] While elegant in their theoretical simplicity, such prescriptions in many cases result from oversimplifications of battlefield realities and must be carefully analyzed.

The prescriptions for wholesale adoption of maneuver warfare are compelling in theory. For example, most maneuver warfare advocates make Colonel John Boyd's decision cycle theories,[8] in a very stripped down form, central to their concept of a successful style of warfare.

> The commander with the faster (observation-orientation-decision-action) cycle will eventually win, because he is already doing something different by the time the enemy gets to the action part of his cycle. The enemy's action becomes irrelevant. If one side is consistently faster, the margin of irrelevance keeps growing, until the enemy either panics or becomes passive. At that point, he has lost.[9]

This simplified interpretation of Colonel Boyd's theories is based on three questionable assumptions. First, that contemporary professional armies are so lacking in resiliency that they are easily susceptible to psychological disorientation and collapse. The Germans learned in World War II that the

Russian soldier does not always become "passive." The Soviet army at the tactical level may be very resistant to maneuver-induced collapse. At this level the discipline, routinized training, battle drill, and strict adherence to plans may require shock and violent firepower to destroy the elements of the formation. Second, purposeful ambiguity and the creation of false images on the battlefield to disorient and collapse an enemy require that the enemy be sophisticated enough to recognize the images but not too sophisticated to see through them. To make it the sole basis of a doctrine of warfare is a risky and dangerous game. Opponents seldom perceive messages as we think they do. Finally, with this focus on rapid operation of the decision cycle, the maneuver warfare proponent neglects the impact of numbers in warfare. At some point, numbers do count.

While these methods are conceivable, they are difficult for skilled, professional ground forces to execute, and much more so for an army with a large reserve force. The historical antidotes for inexperience in the ranks have been increased control, direct methods, and greater reliance on firepower.[10] However, surprise, deception, and the purposeful creation of ambiguity through speed of action and efficient, decisive command and control are readily recognized as elements of military excellence. Colonel Boyd, an experienced fighter pilot and long-time student of war, fully recognizes these limitations. He deals at length with what Clausewitz called the friction of war and readily recognizes the role of other variables in war.

Several critics charge that the U.S. Army espouses firepower-based attrition warfare—a methodical chewing up of the enemy's strength, which they say is reminiscent of Grant's battles in Northern Virginia against Robert E. Lee, and they claim exclusive advocacy for the opposing theory of maneuver warfare. This is a false dichotomy. It is difficult to make a case for attrition warfare and against maneuver, and few soldiers have done so. While the tactics of positional warfare have succeeded at times, no one in the military has made a case against Jackson's conduct of the Valley Campaign or Grant's generalship in the Vicksburg campaign. The brilliant maneuvers of Patton, Sherman, and MacArthur are as much a part of our tradition as the stubborn positional operations of Lee, Bradley, and Ridgeway.[11]

The critics have created two uniformly unreal, but academically convenient, polar cases. The real world lies between. Often conditions dictate which end of the spectrum is most appropriate for success. General Grant's Vicksburg campaign is lauded by many historians as the most daring example of maneuver warfare during that war. Yet he ground his way to Appomattox Courthouse because that seemed more appropriate to the Army of the Potomac and the conditions he found in that campaign. Those operations, when viewed from the strategic level, complemented Sherman's maneuver through the Confederate heartland. Sherman was acting under Grant's overall command. Even MacArthur was forced into occasional vicious head-on assaults, as in the taking of Buna and Gona in New Guinea. Clearly the traditional factors of mission, enemy, terrain, troops available, and time dictate the most appropriate course in war.

Often the conditions that set the terms for the conduct of operations are beyond the purely military realm. Such was the case in Eisenhower's broad-front campaign following the Normandy invasion. It was politically unwise to allow either Montgomery or Patton to strike the decisive blow. Alliance politics are often overriding factors. This is particularly true of the defense of West Germany today. In a recent war game and seminar, even General Hermann Balck, who is famous for his fluid operations on the Russian front in World War II, had to admit that the conditions applicable to the defense of the Fulda Gap in West Germany were vastly different from those on the steppes in the Soviet Union.[12] While there is little room for maneuver in West Germany, it is politically impossible to suggest that we create maneuver space by launching preemptive attacks into East Germany.

If the advocates of a maneuver doctrine suffer from oversimplified perceptions, so too do those who look mainly to modern technology to solve problems of warfare. Modern technologists offer hope of finding weapons that will make war simpler and more manageable. They propose solutions that depend on weapons that will kill the enemy more quickly, in greater numbers, and at less risk—simply translating ideas associated with strategic violence into the tactical realm. While such notions may be attractive to deterrence- and defense-oriented constituencies, they overemphasize the mechanized aspects of war—the "servicing of targets" and the application of firepower. The mechanical aspects of war are readily quantifiable and can be effectively used to justify hardware requirements. The intangibles in war—maneuver, leadership, courage—are grossly underplayed and are not well understood by many of these who help shape modern fighting systems. The dynamics of one-on-one engagements are relatively simple; however, the dynamics of battles and campaigns require a sophisticated level of understanding often lacking in our governments. While the effects of firepower are often of paramount importance in deciding engagements, maneuver becomes increasingly important in battles and campaigns, and the object ultimately becomes the will of the enemy and not his piece-by-piece destruction.

Those who do not understand the role of maneuver, and who have become confused by the vague prescriptions of modern-day maneuver warfare advocates, would do well to read the more definitive prescriptions of J. F. C. Fuller, B. H. Liddell Hart, and F. O. Miksche.[13] By translating their ideas and historical descriptions into current contexts, the real essence of maneuver warfare can be better understood and applied. Application need not, and should not, be modeled after the World War II blitzkrieg experience. Rather, it should be an application of principles adapted to current and future weapons and circumstances appropriate to the American character. Certainly the blitzkrieg tactics described by these authors worked in 1939 and 1940 and occasionally thereafter. It is also clear that they failed in 1941 when Operation Barbarossa ran out of steam in the depths of Russia.[14] Furthermore, the conditions of modern war resulting from more powerful weapons accurate at greater ranges, including tactical, nuclear, and chemical weapons, more kinds of chemical weapons, and more sophisticated means of acquiring targets will demand new solutions. To wholly adopt the 1939 Wehrmacht approach to war, as some critics suggest, would be somewhat like resurrecting the horse cavalry.

The German Wehrmacht of the 1930s did not invent the blitzkrieg; instead, they adapted it to their time. The idea central to blitzkrieg was described by Sun Tzu about 500 B.C. "Rapidity is the essence of war; take advantage of the enemy's unreadiness, make your way by unexpected routes, and attack unguarded spots."[15] It was practiced by military leaders who never read Sun Tzu—Alexander the Great, Hannibal, Genghis Khan, Julius Caesar, Frederick the Great, Napoleon, and others. When the idea was borrowed by Zhukov and Patton, it had to be adapted to the circumstances of the Russian and American armies.

IN SEARCH OF THE "RIGHT" DOCTRINE

The question is, "What is the right doctrine for the U.S. army today?" This simple question requires a complex answer. This doctrine must tell soldiers today how to fight tomorrow with weapons designed yesterday against enemies we must presume under conditions that are difficult to imagine to achieve purposes of a shifting national strategy in an environment of rapid technological change, scant resources, and other murky variables. And as Michael Howard reminds us;

> I am tempted indeed to declare dogmatically that whatever doctrine the Armed Forces are working on now, they have got it wrong. I am also tempted to declare that it does not matter that they have got it wrong. What does matter is their capacity to get it right quickly when the moment arrives.[16]

But to get it right quickly means that is must be nearly right to begin with. This places an additional burden of responsibility on an army facing the possibility of having to fight a very short war indeed.

Sound doctrine is often the least expensive and most effective way to increase an army's fighting effectiveness. However, to increase effectiveness, a successful army's doctrine must do several things. First, it must not depart radically from principles of combat which have stood the test of time from ancient history to the present. Next, it must exploit the potentialities of the existing materiel and human components of the army. It should not demand things of soldiers which are difficult to execute in training and impossible to do in war. Finally, it must provide direction for change. That is, doctrine must at least keep pace with the changing technology of war; ideally, it should anticipate technological change.

The U.S. Army's doctrine has undergone major changes since the Vietnam War. Current doctrinal reform began soon after our withdrawal from Vietnam as the U.S. Army turned its attention away from its previous counterinsurgency, jungle warfare orientation and refocused its attention on the defense of our NATO allies. About that time the 1973 October War was fought, and many new concepts and weapons were used for the first time. All this caused the army to greatly revise operational doctrine. This doctrine, expressed in the 1976 edition of FM 100–5, pointed the way for the modernization of hardware and force structure that is currently in progress. It also touched off the extensive debate that continues today.

The 1976 manual reoriented the army to the problems of war against a major power; it familiarized U.S. leaders with Soviet tactics; and it made us consider problems we had been able to ignore in Vietnam—particularly the problems of air defense, electronic warfare, chemical defense, logistics, and fighting when outnumbered. It also built on a foundation of tactical lessons learned in Vietnam—for example, close coordination between infantry, artillery, helicopter gunships, and air force close air support; and, most significantly, tactical mobility at the speed of the helicopter in a form of warfare without secure flanks.

The 1976 doctrine was the result of a rapid shift in doctrinal emphasis resulting from new priorities and the realization of new conditions. The great concern of the army's leadership was to realign our doctrinal priorities quickly. Extensive studies were conducted using computer simulations and systems analysis techniques that were coming into use to assist in understanding the problems of modern war. The evolution and refinement of concepts of fighting continued even as the 1976 doctrine was printed. The "active defense" concept evolved into the "central battle" concept, which was followed by the "integrated battle" and "extended battle" in turn. In 1979, as these ideas were maturing, the army leadership decided to revise FM 100–5. During the extensive revision process, which lasted from that time until the publication of the manual in August 1982, the army pushed out, refined, and merged these ideas into the AirLand Battle concept of today. The new manual reflects a new consensus on how the army should fight. It would be helpful to enumerate the major internal concerns and assessments that shaped the final product.

The basic question of why this doctrine changed can be answered simply: army commanders became convinced as a result of their field training and war games that they would be unable to defeat the Soviets using the doctrine of 1976. These commanders believed that even if they could beat the leading Soviet echelons using the "active defense," the initial battles would render their units ineffective while leaving Soviet follow-on forces intact with complete freedom of action. The doctrine allowed the enemy complete freedom of maneuver beyond the line of contact because it ignored the use of operational level interdiction by Warsaw Pact follow-on echelons.

It was clear to the authors of the new FM 100–5 that there needed to be a recognition of some real constraints and new conditions. The first of these was that war was fought by people and not by machines. Further, people would behave as people have always behaved throughout the history of battle.[17] This constraint resulted in the important realization that optimizing the effectiveness of weapons does not always optimize the effectiveness of soldiers.

The second important realization was that the chaos of the next battlefield will make centralized control of subordinates always difficult, sometimes impossible. This led to the incorporation of a doctrine of command and control which features decentralization of decisions by the use of mission orders similar to that used by the Wehrmacht early in World War II. This style of leadership is called *Auftragstaktik* by the Germans.

Third, a constant in the pattern of successful doctrines of the past was the thorough integration of tools of battle. This also became a focal point of the revision. The theory of combined arms was given greater treatment than in any previous U.S. Army doctrine.

Fourth, a real constraint, which was recognized in the revision of FM 100–5, is that which logistics places on operations. Current logistics concepts and organizations were not flexible enough to support fast-paced operations in great depth. They were optimized for operations that fall back on lines of support. While this constraint is never adequately dealt with, the manual does at least address the issue and points to further necessary work in this area.

Fifth, the authors used the following propositions as a basic operating premise: if we are to operate more flexibly and more effectively, our leaders will have more need for principles and less need for cookbook formulas. Therefore, rigid forms and formulas are done away with in the new manual; instead, it articulates the most important principles by which our army will fight. The idea is that members of the profession must understand a common set of principles. Tactical solutions are derived from these principles and from thoroughly understood processes and techniques that are laid out in subordinate manuals.

Sixth, U.S. Army doctrine cannot be theater-specific; it must be adaptable to operations anywhere in the world. General Meyer's remark about "the most important war for the U.S. being in Europe while the most likely wars are elsewhere," is to the point here.[18] We must be able to fight effectively in either case. A doctrine based solely on European requirements would place us at a disadvantage when called on to fight in another area.

Seventh, the proliferation of nuclear weapons, and the spread of the technology which makes them potentially available to any nation in the world, forces us to anticipate operations in a nuclear environment. Since chemical weapons are widely available and have been used in recent conflicts, it is also imperative that army forces plan and train to fight under chemical warfare conditions. The 1976 doctrine largely discounted the impact of possible sudden employment of tactical nuclear weapons by either or both sides, as well as the enemy's probable employment of chemical weapons. The effects of tactical nuclear weapons, besides causing inestimable shock, would make the "active defense" tactic of "thickening the battlefield" unworkable. The new doctrine had to address the conduct of operations so that nuclear or chemical fire support could be added or deleted as necessary. Army units must also design their operations flexibly so that enemy initiation of nuclear or chemical fires cannot by itself decide the battle.

This presents us with an unavoidable dilemma. Under purely conventional conditions, concentration of forces is necessary to win, and extreme dispersion risks defeat in detail; this same concentration vastly increases the likelihood of defeat when the enemy has nuclear weapons. Mobility, good operations security, and precise timing of dispersion and concentration offset the risk of defeat by nuclear fire and make possible the concentration necessary to win. The actual planning and control of such operations will obviously require training of a very high order in staffs and units. The authors of the new manual grappled with this problem but could not offer an easy answer. Nonetheless, this problem was exposed and considerations for overcoming it were offered.

The final impetus for change in doctrine comes from the near term introduction of new systems which increase our mobility and firepower, as well as enhancing our command and control, surveillance, and target acquisition capabilities. The MI tank, M2 and M3 fighting vehicles, and the Advanced Attack Helicopter are among the weapons in this group. New sensors and longer-range artillery weapons are also influencing the way we will fight. The new manual needed to integrate the capabilities of these new systems into its operational concept. As laser and directed energy weapons appear and sensor capabilities improve, the doctrine of 1982 must ease their integration into the force structure and facilitate transition to doctrine being formulated for the year 2000.

THE NEW DOCTRINE

The new FM 100–5, *Operations,* published in August 1982, lays the theoretical base for all other manuals and becomes the basis for service school curricula. It represents a major but natural evolutionary change in doctrine and a culmination of our post-Vietnam reorientation. Its publication will inevitably stimulate fresh discussions of our operational thinking in the field, in the service schools, and outside the army. The new doctrine will play a central role in defining a new American approach to war. Although the manual differs from the previous FM 100–5, it does not represent revolutionary change when viewed against the doctrinal traditions of the U.S. Army. Instead, it retains many of the themes of the old manual, modifies some of the best ideas of our older doctrine, and presents a comprehensive view of modern warfare which accommodates our newest technical capabilities and worldwide commitments. It is keyed to the perceived vulnerabilities and characteristics of the Soviet Army. The term used in FM 100–5 to describe this doctrine is "AirLand Battle." It is worthwhile to summarize its content here.

AirLand Battle doctrine has a number of distinctive features. It takes a nonlinear view of battle and enlarges the geographical area of conflict, stressing unified air and ground operations throughout a theater. It distinguishes the operational level of war—the conduct of campaigns at the corps and higher levels—from the tactical level. It recognizes the nonquantifiable elements of combat power, especially that of maneuver, which is now accorded the same importance as firepower. It acknowledges the importance of nuclear and chemical weapons and of electronic warfare and details their effects on operations. And, most importantly, it keeps the human element prominently in the foreground.

THE THEORETICAL BASIS OF U.S. ARMY DOCTRINE

The conduct of the AirLand Battle is based on the broad operational concept of securing the initiative as early as possible and exercising it aggressively to defeat the enemy. Every weapon, asset, and combat multiplier[19] is employed to gain the initiative and use it to throw the enemy off balance with a powerful blow from an unexpected direction and then to follow up rapidly to prevent his recovery. This operational concept applies to any type of force operating anywhere in the world, whether it is attacking or defending.

The key principles of the AirLand Battle doctrine are the use of indirect approaches; the maintenance of the initiative through speed and violence; flexibility and reliance on the initiative of junior leaders; clear definition of objectives, concepts of operations, and the main effort; and attack on the enemy in depth. Wherever it is possible, the enemy will be defeated by destruction of critical units or facilities rather than through overall attrition. This is particularly true about the operational level. At the tactical level, attrition and the substitution of massed fire for massed soldiers occasionally play an important role in facilitating decisive maneuver at the operational level. Quick decisions are preferred at both operational and tactical levels (especially in offensive operations), but the emphasis on the first battle, which was so powerful in the past FM 100–5, has been diminished, and greater importance has been accorded to extended operations.

The theoretical content of the manual is drawn from the lessons of history, the writings of the great military theorists, and the army's historic approach to operations.[20] Examination of these sources led to a reevaluation of the stress formerly placed on simple force ratios. The manual now gives equal emphasis to both the tangible and intangible aspects of combat. The human element—the soldiers's training, courage, and leadership—figures more heavily than any other single element in the new operations manual's picture of battle.

The combat power that decides battles is described as a combination of factors that changes over time, even during the course of battle. It is not an absolute equation. Training, leadership, morale, and psychological shock are as much a part of combat power as the number of units and weapons on the battlefield.

The operational concept of FM 100–5 is the central idea of the manual. Success in battle requires that *initiative, depth, agility,* and *synchronization* characterize our thinking and our operations. These terms apply at all levels of command and at both the tactical and operational levels of war.

AirLand Battle doctrine identifies *initiative,* the ability to set the terms of battle by action, as the greatest advantage in war. This recognition orients the new FM 100–5 more strongly than the previous manual toward offensive operations and maneuver. Whether U.S. forces are attacking or defending, they are expected to seize and preserve the initiative to hasten the enemy's defeat and prevent his recovery. Independent action will have to compensate for lapses in command and control communications caused by the effects of electronic warfare, the destruction of friendly forces and headquarters, or the "fog of war." The chief doctrinal corollaries of initiative are the requirements for well-defined, thoroughly understood objectives and aggressive, independent action by subordinates to accomplish the mission.

Depth in the AirLand Battle refers to time, space, and resources. Combat will extend throughout the operational area, with actions in depth influencing the outcome of the battle between committed forces. Rear area protection and the deep battle against the enemy's uncommitted forces and support facilities are the operational aspects of the battle in depth. Equally, the commander's provisions for continuous operations represent depth in the AirLand Battle. His readiness to carry the battle into new areas, to fight and support for an extended period of time, to continue his operations if the enemy resorts to nuclear weapons, and to convert battlefield successes into campaign advantages can determine the overall success of the force.

Agility means acting faster than the enemy to exploit his weaknesses and frustrate his plans. It implies a constant effort to pit friendly strengths against enemy weaknesses. The use of maneuver to concentrate friendly strength in vulnerable areas and the employment of tactics which exploit friendly technical, human, or geographical advantages, while avoiding enemy strengths, are operational applications of agility. Good intelligence, imaginative planning, flexible operational techniques, and responsive tactical units are indispensable in achieving superior agility. FM 100–5's renewed emphasis on mission orders, initiative, maneuver, and the rapid exploitation of fleeting advantages are all intended to foster agility.

Synchronization aims to maintain the synergistic effect of the combined arms team as necessary to sustain the momentum of the force. It requires that no effort be wasted initially or as operations develop. A designated main effort must be supported by every means necessary and maintained or shifted as the battle progresses or the campaign matures. This is necessary to insure synchronization. In nonlinear combat, where the situation can change quickly, maneuver units from company to corps must be able to support their main efforts continually and modify or shift them as the situation changes.

Battlefield application of the operational concept requires a more specific set of guidelines. Seven "imperatives of modern combat" combine the operational concept and the principles of war to provide general guidance for field commanders. The imperatives embody notions long familiar to successful armies of the past.

"Unity of effort" addresses the necessity to harness every force and capability to attainment of the mission. Air, ground, and naval forces must cooperate fully. Elements of the ground force must understand the overall objectives of operations and know their own parts and those of their neighbors if they are to fight effectively. This requires the use of mission orders and the application of mission-oriented tactics. Three principles of war—"objective," "unity of command," and "economy of force"—are the theoretical supports for this imperative.

"Directing friendly strength against enemy weaknesses" means looking for, attacking, and exploiting the enemy's soft spots and vulnerabilities. Two principles of war—"maneuver" and "surprise"—and Liddell Hart's concept of the "indirect approach" support this imperative.

"Designate and sustain the main effort" means that one unit within a force makes the main effort and becomes the focal point for combat, combat support, and combat service support efforts. Agility derives in part from the ability to shift this main effort as appropriate during battle. "Objective," "economy of force," and "mass" are the principles of war underlying this imperative.

"Sustaining the fight" implies combined arms cooperation as well as those supporting activities that are necessary to maintain the tempo of combat throughout the course of a battle or campaign to its successful conclusion.

"Move fast, strike hard, and finish rapidly" expresses the need to act quickly and violently to reach a decision and to avoid becoming a target for enemy counterattack or counterfire. While such action has always characterized successful operations, the potential lethality of the modern battlefield makes this doubly important.

The "effective use of terrain and weather" is basic to successful operations. Skillful use of these natural elements enhances our combat power and reduces that of the enemy.

"Protect the force" refers to a wide range of actions inherent in successful military operations. In its general form, the imperative applies to activities as diverse as security, counterintelligence, maintaining morale and unit cohesion, proper medical care, and rear area protection. The purpose of protecting the force is to preserve a force's fighting strength so that maximum combat power will be available at the decisive time and place and throughout the course of a campaign.

To highlight the unique characteristics of large unit operations, the manual distinguishes the operational level of war between the familiar divisions of military strategy and tactics. The disposition of corps and divisions, selection of objectives or directions of operations, and actions taken to weaken or outmaneuver the enemy and exploit tactical gains are all part of the art of war at the operational level. While the principles of war are appropriate to all levels of war, applying them involves a different perspective for each.

THE THEORETICAL BASIS
FOR DEEP ATTACKS

Whether attacking or defending, a timely and well-executed deep attack against enemy forces not yet in contact is an important element of operations. This is not a new discovery. U.S., German, and Israeli campaign plans have historically made use of long-range interdiction to gain local battlefield advantages.[21]

To date, the deep battle of interdiction against forces in the enemy's rear area has attracted more attention than any other feature of the AirLand Battle. In-depth attack on enemy forces is an integral part of doctrine and requires careful attention to insure that plans for the deep battle are realistic, complete, and firmly linked to the commander's central concept of an operation. Improved sensors, long-range weapons, and a more responsive intelligence distribution system are assets that can be used to great advantage in the deep battle. The purpose of deep attack in the AirLand Battle is to complement the central concept of operation. It is neither a sideshow nor an optional activity without importance to the outcome of battle; it is an inseparable part of a unified plan of operation.

The aim of the deep battle is to disrupt the enemy's timing, to block critical junctions, to defeat his plan, and to create opportunities for offensive action—"windows of opportunity"—that allow us to defeat him in detail. It is a critical adjunct of maneuver. The deep battle is based on thorough intelligence and knowledge of the battlefield, the availability of timely intelligence from organic and higher-level intelligence sources, the identification of high-value targets, and the synchronization of organic and supporting means of attack. Corps is the focal point for intelligence collection and distribution in the deep battle. However, deep-battle planning and execution are just as important at division and lower levels.[22]

At the present time, our primary strike assets for deep attack are air and artillery interdiction. Conventional and unconventional military forces can also be used to interdict enemy movement in depth and, while tactical electronic warfare systems do not have the range to hit deep targets, they can be of some use in freeing artillery units for use in the deep battle. Deception also plays a part in delaying, disrupting, and diverting an enemy and frustrating his plans for commitment of follow-on forces.

While some may suggest that it would be ideal to destroy enemy following forces with deep attack—to whittle him down to size—that is not possible with our currently limited assets, nor will it be possible in the future.

What *is* possible is to delay, disrupt, or divert selected enemy forces by attacking elements of that force, or chokepoints in the terrain, and thus to achieve the desired effect. But these efforts must be directed toward a specific goal (Clausewitz's center of gravity) if an actual tactical or operational advantage is to be obtained.

Commanders will fight the enemy in an *area of influence* designated by the next higher level of command. This area normally encompasses enemy forces whose actions can affect the unit's close-in battle. Commanders simultaneously monitor activity beyond and adjacent to their areas of influence in what is called the *area of interest*. The area of interest includes territory that contains enemy units capable of affecting future operations. It is nothing more than the enlarged perspective of successful commanders of the past. It merely institutionalizes intelligence requirements and is the basis for information flows about the enemy. It allows higher-level staffs to quickly identify which of their subordinate units need to know what.

Operations facilitated by deep attack can take several general forms. The first is attack by fire to disrupt enemy forces in depth in a particular sector and delay their arrival in the battle area so that enemy forces in contact can be isolated and defeated. Deception, offensive electronic warfare, artillery fires, and air force battlefield air interdiction may all be used singly or in combination to disrupt the enemy's timing in this form of deep attack.

The second form is to attack enemy forces in depth with fire, thereby preventing them from intervening in the close-in battle while we maneuver against the flanks or rear of enemy forces in contact. In the defense the object may be to prevent enemy forces in depth from interfering with a friendly counterattack force for a specific period of time rather than simply to prevent such forces from reinforcing committed enemy units. In the attack the object may be to interdict a relieving enemy force, thus allowing the attacker to secure some deep objective or to maneuver to the rear of defending forces without interference for a specific period of time.

The third form is more complex and more difficult to achieve. It requires engaging follow-on echelons with both firepower and maneuver forces while the close-in battle is being fought. In the attack this may mean using air force attack aircraft, attack helicopters, electronic warfare measures, and a ground maneuver force to assault reinforcing or counterattacking enemy forces in order to allow the main effort to go against deeper and more decisive objectives. In the defense this may mean dispatching a similar force to defeat follow-on enemy forces so that the main effort can transition from defense to attack. This form of attack depends upon the impact of combined arms action to achieve its effects, and will require close coordination between army air and ground maneuver forces, artillery, electronic warfare, and air force battlefield air interdiction missions.

In all cases, deep attack seeks to destroy or neutralize a particular type of enemy target which by its very nature poses a threat or which by its elimination provides an advantage. An example of the first would be an enemy nuclear-capable weapons system within range of the friendly force. An example of the latter would be the destruction of enemy bridges when the enemy is threatening a river crossing. The key notion behind any of the forms of deep attack is to focus very narrowly on the purpose to be achieved and to attack elements of the target array which will yield the highest payoff. In the new doctrine, the procedure for doing this is called target value analysis.

THE THEORETICAL BASIS
FOR OFFENSIVE AND DEFENSIVE COMBAT

The major division of offense and defense has been modified to conform with the manual's operational concept. The most noticeable effect of this revision has been a shift away from formulas or prescriptions. Commanders will have far more latitude in the design of their operations and will be expected to fit their plans to particular situations with less specific guidance. The absence of recipes for attack and defense will doubtlessly draw some criticism; but since successful operations have never been a matter of automatic processes, the replacement of step-by-step methods with broad principles is a realistic and healthy development.

While the types of offensive operations have not changed, the manual attaches greater importance to speed and violence of operations, the seeking of soft spots, flexible shifting of the main effort, and prompt transition to exploitation. The creation of a fluid situation in which the attacker can maintain the initiative and completely destroy the coherence of the enemy defense is the goal of the attack. Continuation of the attack for as long as it takes to defeat the enemy is expected and requires considerable flexibility in the use of supporting and reserve units.

The attack should resemble the expanding torrent described by Liddell Hart;[23] that is, it should move quickly, follow reconnaissance units or successful probes through gaps in enemy defenses, and shift its strength rapidly to widen penetrations and reinforce its successes. The attacker tries to carry the battle deep into the enemy rear to break down the enemy's defenses before he can react.

Momentum takes on added significance in this dynamic doctrine. The enemy must never be permitted to recover from the shock of the initial assault, never given the time to identify the main effort, and above all never afforded the opportunity to mass his forces or supporting fire against our main effort. To deny the enemy this critical reaction time, we must capitalize on opportunities and act faster than he does.

An offensive effort is designed to produce the fastest possible attainment of the commander's objective. All else supports that effort. Deep attacks, supporting attacks, and the size, composition, and placement of reserves are all designed to facilitate the success of the main attack. Airborne, air assault, amphibious, or unconventional warfare operations can also be used to contribute to the rapid success of the main attack.

The synchronization required by the operational concept extends beyond the disposition of maneuver forces in offensive operations. Conventional, nuclear, and chemical fire support is used to protect flanks, to attack deep targets, and to support maneuver forces. Offensive air support must be carefully planned to provide the proper mix of close air support and battlefield interdiction needed for the specific operation. Enemy command posts, logistics installations, bridges, and defiles are frequently identified as high-value targets for deep attack by air. Synchronization also includes allocating the bulk of combat service support forces to support the main attack.

Doctrinal emphasis on maneuver and the offensive demands that army units learn to use terrain as effectively in the attack as they do in the defense. Our attacking units must seek attack avenues which are indirect and support rapid, concealed movement along their entire length. Commanders must stress the use of obstacles to protect flanks and train subordinates to avoid or breach enemy obstacles quickly if they must. A good avenue of approach should also permit the deployment of combat support and combat service support elements that are committed to the attack. Alternate axes should be identified in advance, and plans made to activate them by oral order if movement on the primary route is slowed. Momentum is the key requirement; the attacker cannot stop to make plans in the middle of his operation.

When nuclear or chemical weapons are used, maneuver schemes must consider their effects. These weapons can sometimes allow small maneuver units to accomplish missions that would otherwise require larger forces. Rubble, residual radiation, and trees blown down by a nuclear strike— friendly or enemy—may cause the redirection of an attacking force.

The potential use of nuclear weapons by the enemy makes massing of forces particularly risky. Attacks will have to be conducted by forces that mass suddenly, penetrate rapidly, and disperse quickly to avoid presenting a lucrative target. While sudden massing, violent attack, and quick dispersion have been characteristic of successful large-force offensive actions since World War II, the contemporary nuclear-potential battlefield makes it even more critical to survival and victory.

The changes in defensive doctrine reflect the fact that no war has ever been won by a passive or purely reactive defense. Although we are likely to begin the next war on the defensive, our defensive doctrine should have but one aim: to turn the tables on an attacking enemy and assume the initiative ourselves. The character of the U.S. defense will be an increased level of resistance and early, opportunistic local counterattacks to halt the enemy, followed by transition to the offensive as soon as possible.

Previous doctrine was predicated on two notions. One was that what counted in the defense was the number of weapons systems sited forward to "service enemy targets." This idea supported the common conclusion that few elements should be retained in reserve. The other related notion was that the enemy attack is best defeated by massing lightly-engaged elements from either flank of a threatened penetration against the front of the enemy's main attack to achieve at least the ratio of one defender for every three attackers. The lopsided ratio is offset by the advantage of firing from carefully prepared defensive positions and the shock effect of coordinated fire falling on a moving attacker. This all sounded very logical and was borne out by computer-simulated tests. But officers in the field, commanding real soldiers, reflecting on the precision required of these tactics on a rubble-strewn battlefield, and considering the problems of possible chemical attack and of residual radiation and trees blown down by enemy nuclear weapons, were not comfortable with this scheme.

With regard to the first notion, they judged that what was important was not how many weapons were up initially, but how many they could ultimately get into the fight. The difficulties of disengaging against even light enemy reconnaissance screens or an enemy secondary attack, and then traversing even rehearsed alternate routes to preplanned battle positions in the path of the enemy main attack, gave them pause.

The second notion also gave them concern. It seemed that a rather narrow view was taken of the defender's advantages. Knowing the ground also gives the advantage of being able to set up decisive counterattacks into the enemy's flanks along preplanned and reconnoitered avenues after the enemy has been allowed to extend himself into the defensive zone. This additional advantage of the defender allowed him to seek out the enemy's weakness rather than his strength. A corollary to these notions was that in a nuclear environment it may be easier to attack forward through enemy secondary efforts at the forward edge of the battle area (FEBA) and into the flank and rear of his main attack. These notions were encouraged by the development of more accurate sensors. Procedures for deep attack on follow-on forces also would make such tactics more workable. Also, many field commanders were prepared to take risks to win.

AirLand Battle doctrine describes the defense as a mixture of static and dynamic elements—in reality, a combination of offensive and defensive action. The commander's concept of defense is based on a thorough analysis of the factors of mission, enemy, terrain, and troops available[24] and can be visualized as a combination of static and dynamic elements falling along the continuum between wholly static and completely dynamic operations.

No single form or technique is prescribed by FM 100–5. Each defensive battle will be designed for the specific situation facing the unit. Some defensive missions may dictate retention of terrain, others may allow the defender to focus strictly on the defeat of the enemy force. The commander may conduct his defense in the depth of the main battle area (MBA) or near the forward edge of the battle area (FEBA) depending on his mission, his forces, the terrain, and the overall concept for defense specified by higher levels of command.

One-third or more of a force's maneuver strength may be held in reserve in the defense. This figure is only a guideline, not a requirement. The actual size of the reserve will depend on the commander's concept and, again, the mission, nature of the enemy, troops available for defense, and the nature of the terrain in the sector. The doctrine gives preference to employing the reserve to strike a decisive blow, rather than to restoring some initial line of defense or reinforcing committed forces. This decisive blow may well be struck forward of the main battle area.

The covering force mission has been broadened. Large covering forces may be assigned to fight defensive actions forward of the main battle area, while lighter security forces may be used in lieu of covering forces. Such forces would only be required to give the main defending force advance warning of the enemy's approach. The role of the covering force or security force will derive from the commander's overall plan.

Whatever the case, the covering force will rarely withdraw on line. It will give ground where it is forced to, often leaving some elements forward. By remaining forward, troops of the covering force prevent the enemy from applying equal pressure all along the front of the main battle area, allow the commander to fight one major defensive battle at a time, and offer opportunities to observe, interdict, and attack enemy flanks.

This new doctrine also makes a clearer distinction between defense and delay. Defending units are prepared to accept decisive engagements. While delaying units may be required to accept decisive engagement to achieve the required delay, their actions are dictated by the assigned mission and should avoid decisive engagement when they can. They may also be called on to attack in order to achieve the necessary degree of delay. The doctrine now increases the emphasis on the use of strongpoints. Although strongpoints may become surrounded, they serve to disrupt the enemy's attack and can be used to set him up for defeat by a counterattacking force.

The new FM 100–5 has adopted Clausewitz's philosophy for the defense: "The ideal defense is a shield of blows."[25] It makes use of all available resources and avoids stereotyped patterns by calling for bold, flexible, offensively oriented defenses organized to meet the requirements of the mission, the attacking enemy, the nature of the defending troops, and the terrain in the defensive sector.

CONCLUSION

In execution, the AirLand Battle means nothing more (or less) than fighting "smart," using every element of combat power from psychological operations to nuclear weapons (when released by the National Command Authority) to defeat the enemy. The new FM 100-5 represents an innovative general approach to fighting at both the tactical and operational levels which provides for the coordinated employment of all arms, all services, and all means of support. It relates today's dynamic technology to today's soldiers and leaders through forward-looking ideas about fighting based on time-tested principles. It provides the parameters within which technology should be pursued. Subordinate manuals will add appropriate detail to the general philosophy of FM 100-5, but the keystone operations manual will have special value in disseminating broad ideas—especially in linking air and ground efforts more closely, defining the relationship of battles to campaigns, and providing a framework for force development and materiel procurement in the future. The basic idea quoted earlier from Sun Tzu—that "rapidity is the essence of war," so that one should take advantage of the enemy's unreadiness and move by unexpected routes and attack unguarded spots—is captured in the army's new operational concept and thus fits the pattern for the doctrines of successful armies of the past.

NOTES

1. The following articles are representative of this point of view: Col. Wayne Downing, "U.S. Army Operations Doctrine," *Military Review* 61, no. 1 (June 1981): 64–73; Edward N. Luttwak, "The American Style of Warfare and the Military Balance," *Survival* 21, no. 2 (March–April 1979): 57–60; William S. Lind, "Some Doctrinal Questions for the United States Army," *Military Review* 57, no. 3 (March 1977): 54–65; William S. Lind, "Defining Maneuver Warfare for the Marine Corps," *Marine Corps Gazette* (March 1980): 55–58; Steven L. Canby, "NATO Defense: The Problem Is Not More Money," in *American Security Policy and Policy-Making,* ed. Robert Harkavy and Edward Kolodziej (Lexington, Ky.: Lexington Books, 1980), pp. 85–99; Steven L. Canby, "Mutual Forces Reductions: A Military Perspective," *International Security* 2, no. 3 (Winter 1978): 122–35; Steven L. Canby, NATO: Reassessing the Conventional Wisdoms," *Survival* 18, no. 4 (July–August 1977): 164–68.

2. See articles by Paul Bracken, "Urban Sprawl and NATO Defense," *Survival* 18, no. 6 (November–December 1976): 254–60 and Lt. Col. Barry R. McCaffrey, "Infantry on the High-Intensity Battlefield of Central Europe," *Military Review* 18, no. 1 (January 1978): 3–6.

3. Maj. Richard H. Sinnreich, "Tactical Doctrine or Dogma," *Army* 29, no. 9 (September 1979): 16–19.

4. See Lind, Luttwak, and Canby articles mentioned in n.1 above.

5. Ibid.

6. Ibid.

7. Ibid.

8. Col. John Boyd, "The Patterns of Conflict," a four-hour presentation, unpublished.

9. Sen. Gary Hart, "What's Wrong with the Military," *New York Times Magazine,* 14 February 1982, 19.

10. Examples of this phenomenon include Kasserine Pass for the U.S. Army, the growth of the Soviet Army in World War II, and the decline of the German Army in World War II.

11. A good discussion of mobility and power, the mixed legacies of the American army, can be found in Russell Weigley's *Eisenhower's Lieutenants: The Campaign of France and Germany, 1944–1945.* The history of that campaign also illustrates the competition of the two legacies. There were a number of commanders of corps and armies who understood maneuver, most notably Patton, Collins, Van Fleet, and Truscott. There were also those who did not. Both kinds of commanders exist in the U.S. Army today.

12. BDM Corporation, *Generals Balck and von Mellenthin on Tactics: Implications for NATO Military Doctrine* (Washington, D.C.: BDM Corporation, 1980).

13. While all three authors were prolific writers, the following books are recommended: J. F. C. Fuller's *Armored Warfare,* B. H. Liddell Hart's *Strategy,* and F. O. Miksche's *Attack: A Study of Blitzkrieg Tactics.*

14. A good discussion of this topic can be found in Martin van Creveld's *Supplying War* (New York: Cambridge University Press, 1977). The author discusses the failure of the logistical system to keep pace with the tempo of operations and the impact of bypassed Russian units who failed to collapse in the wake of the blitzkrieg.

15. Sun Tzu, "On the Art of War," *Roots of Strategy,* ed. Brig. Gen. T. R. Phillips (Harrisburg, Pa.: Military Service Publishing Co., 1940), p. 52.

16. Michael Howard, "Military Science in an Age of Peace," *RUSI Quarterly* 119, no. 1 (March 1974): 7.

17. In addition to more recent writings on this subject including Martin van Creveld's "Fighting Power: German Military Performance, 1914–1945," paper submitted to the Office of Net Assessment, Department of Defense, December 1980, the authors of the new FM 100–5 were heavily influenced by Ardant DuPicq's *Battle Studies* (New York: Macmillan Co., 1921), Marshall Maurice De Saxe's *Reveries on War,* trans. Brig. Gen. T. R. Phillips (Harrisburg, Pa.: Military Service Publishing Co., 1944), Brig. Gen. S. L. A. Marshall's *Men against Fire* (New York: William Morrow & Co., 1947), and John Keegan's *The Face of Battle* (New York: Vintage Books, 1977).

18. Edward C. Meyer, former chief of staff of the army, has frequently made this point in public.

19. Combat multipliers refer to supporting assets which, when deployed in conjunction with combat forces, augment the disruptive and destructive effects of these forces on

the enemy; for example, electronic warfare, minefields and obstacles, smoke and battlefield deception, intelligence gathering, closely coordinated attack helicopter and close air support aviation, advanced fire control mechanisms, and sophisticated fire support coordination techniques.

20. Specifically, the manual draws heavily on the writings of Sun Tzu, Clausewitz, Fuller, Liddell Hart, Miksche, and Willoughby. The American commanders whose operations were most closely examined were Sherman, Jackson, Lee, Patton, MacArthur, and Clarke.

21. Historical examples are numerous. They include air and land interdiction operations in the modern period such as the Israeli closure of the Mitla Pass behind the Egyptian army in 1967 and the air interdiction of German reserve routes during the Third Army's breakthrough in Operation COBRA. In earlier wars, actions in depth have often been critical to the success of battles and campaigns. The cavalry operations of Nathan Bedford Forrest and Benjamin Arierson are particularly noteworthy.

22. Donn A. Starry, "Extending the Battlefield," *Military Review* 61, no. 3 (March 1981): 31–50. W. R. Richardson, "Winning on the Extended Battlefield," *Army* 35 (June 1981): 35–42.

23. B. H. Liddell Hart in *A Perspective on Infantry,* ed. J. A. English (New York: Praeger Publishers, 1981), pp. 41–49.

24. Clyde J. Tate and L. D. Holder, "New Doctrine for the Defense," *Military Review* 61, no. 3 (March 1981): 2–9.

25. Clausewitz, *On War,* trans. M. Howard and P. Paret (Princeton, N.J.: Princeton University Press, 1976), p. 357.

IV

FORCE STRUCTURE ISSUES

When asked his prescription for military success, General Nathan Bedford Forrest replied, "Get there fustest with the mostest." While this is a conceptually powerful formulation, it leaves unanswered the question, the "mostest" of what kind of forces? It also leaves unanswered what those forces do when they get there.

The latter question was examined in the preceding section on Doctrinal Issues. The question of what type of forces are necessary is the focus of this section on Force Structure Issues. Steven Canby, Jeffrey Record, and John Mayer discuss the forces the United States *should* have based in terms of the considerations they consider to be most critical. Although they address, to a degree, the problem of what the United States *can* have—subject to budgetary, resource, and bureaucratic constraints—that question is explored more fully in subsequent sections.

Force structure issues did not arise with the military reform debate: they are defense issues that have consistently been addressed in the past. At times the focus was on interservice mix, such as the debate and decision to create an independent air force. At other times the focus was on intraservice mix, such as the interwar debate over the proper role of the tank. And at times the debate has concerned itself with the proper strategy and its implications for both inter- and intraservice mix, as was the case with the shift from massive retaliation to flexible response.

The military reform movement focuses on force structure for rather pragmatic reasons. The kind of force available acts as a a constraint in implementing other types of reform (for example, maneuver warfare). Further, the other reform areas (for example, weapons acquisition) have direct implications for the force structure. So, while not new, force structure issues assume great significance in the context of the entire military reform debate.

What are the considerations that determine what our force structure should be? The authors maintain that there are at least three. First is geographic location. In what parts of the world do U.S. interests lie? Certainly the answer to that helps determine the force structure necessary to meet those interests. Record maintains that although U.S. interests in Europe remain high, other parts of the world, particularly southwest Asia, have become so important to U.S. interests that they dictate a restructuring of U.S. forces to meet those interests. Canby, in contrast, defines the "centers of gravity" in "global power politics" as Europe and northeast Asia. Canby's assumption is that the United States is a global power and must have an interest in these key places. The United States, therefore, should restructure its forces to meet those interests. Mayer is the most implicit of the authors on this consideration. He assumes that U.S. interests focus on a variety of areas, including Europe and southwest Asia, and proposes a force structure to meet those interests. For the authors of all three chapters, the consideration of geographic location, whether made explicitly or implicitly, acts as a determinant of necessary force structure. And in all three chapters it is held that the United States has interests overseas, although the authors differ as to exactly where those interests lie and what the priority is among those interests.

The second consideration used to determine the appropriate force structure is the perceived threat to those interests. If the United States has interests overseas, but there is no perceived threat to those interests, there is obviously then no necessity to design a force to safeguard them. Canby and Mayer deal primarily with a Soviet-style, armor-heavy, military threat to those areas as being the most serious in terms of consequences, but Mayer goes somewhat beyond this in a brief discussion of the threat that insurgencies can pose to U.S. global interests. Record sees the most likely threat as insurgencies or local conflict.

The third consideration used to determine an appropriate force structure is what capability the United States has to meet the perceived threats to its national interests. Given that the United States has interests overseas that may be threatened, what capabilities do U.S. forces need to counter that threat? This question has two major components. First, how quickly can U.S. forces be deployed overseas (getting there "fustest")? Second, what battlefield capability will those forces have (getting there with the "mostest")? Having the "mostest" means having forces that can get to a contested battlefield, that have the proper battlefield capabilities, and that can be logistically sustained in battle for a period of time.

On the face of it, answers to these two questions seem to cut against each other. Those forces that strategically are the most deployable are light infantry, since they have little heavy equipment (for example, tanks) to be deployed with them. But for that same reason, light infantry also seems to have the least battlefield capability. Conversely, armored forces would seem to have the greatest battlefield capability against armored threats, but are the most difficult to deploy overseas in a timely manner because of their heavy equipment.

Use of the three considerations then allows for determination of the proper interservice and intraservice mix. Interservice mix deals with the proper balance among the services. Should the United States rely on a larger navy and a smaller army, for example, or a larger army and a smaller navy?

Intraservice mix deals with the balance of types of forces within each service. Should the army have more light or heavy forces? Should the navy have more, smaller ships or fewer, large ships?

Canby's view of U.S. interests and the threat to those interests results in a recommended shift in the interservice mix (greater allocation of resources to ground forces) and a shift in the intraservice mix (emphasis on a type of light infantry which he calls *Jaeger* infantry). Canby further argues that the Jaeger infantry is strategically more deployable than current heavy forces, more capable than current infantry on the battlefield, and is more useful in counterinsurgencies than current U.S. forces.

Record agrees that the United States has interests in Europe, but feels that the European countries have the economic and technological wherewithal to provide for the greater part of their own ground defense. This would then free U.S. resources for protecting the recently heightened interests the United States has in other parts of the world, particularly southwest Asia. Because the United States does not have peacetime military access to the countries in southwest Asia, Record argues that the United States should shift its intraservice mix to focus more on naval forces (for strategic deployability and sustainability) and Marine Corps units (for battlefield insertion capability). His intraservice mix emphasis for the navy is on the surface fleet, where he calls for 600–800 ships. He calls for smaller ships in order to meet the necessary naval force level. His intraservice mix for the Marine Corps would place armor and heavy equipment on ships in the Indian Ocean for use in that area.

Mayer's view of U.S. interests and threats to those interests leads him to conclude that the United States does not currently have an adequate number of battlefield-capable forces, since of the total twenty-eight army and marine divisions in the active and reserve force, only thirteen are heavy. Consequently, his intraservice mix calls for a conversion of light divisions to heavy divisions to meet the threat, leaving only three light divisions. He points out that with fast sealift, one heavy division can get to the Persian Gulf faster than two light divisions can get there by air. Once on the ground, that division will have more than twice the battlefield capability of a light division. Further, Mayer maintains that the additional battlefield mobility of armor and mechanized divisions is necessary if the forces are to conduct the new maneuver warfare being proposed. The implications of this "levying-up" in the army and marines for interservice mix are not made explicit by Mayer. Nonetheless it is clear that he would place greater emphasis on strategic sealift capabilities over strategic airlift.

All three authors have different views on what it takes to "get there fustest with the mostest." Those views flow quite naturally from their perspectives on where the forces are going, what threats they might face on arrival, and what they need to meet those threats. Whether one force structure is better than another depends in great part on the assessment made of those three considerations.

8

MILITARY REFORM
AND THE ART OF WAR

Steven L. Canby

Canby maintains that the United States and its allies are militarily inferior to the threats they face in Europe and northeast Asia. He argues this inferiority stems not from inadequate men and money in peacetime but from inadequate military organization and doctrine. Proposals that do not address these fundamentals will not solve the problem. The author cites four possible solutions. Among these is light (*Jaeger*) infantry for intervention and for complementing NATO's existing tank fleets.

Despite high costs, the ongoing defense build-up ironically is accomplishing little; upon its completion, the West will still be distinctly inferior in NATO, Korea, and southwest Asia and will be little better off at sea. The build-up is oriented to input, not output. Nonetheless, using familiar strategy and tactics abroad, the United States and its allies could obtain global military superiority within present budgetary and manpower allocations. In terms of policy, achieving military superiority at present costs would eliminate the need for large outyear budgetary increases with concomitant deficit financing and confrontational posturing vis-à-vis the USSR to justify those costs. Only with military reform are military strength and supply-side economic revitalization compatible national goals.

Defense spending is not a good measure of military prowess and capability. It is merely a measure of input and the burden upon a society. In Europe, little Finland is a competent military power, yet its population is five million and it spends only 1.5 percent of a small GNP on defense. Similarly, neutral Sweden is a respected high-technology air and naval power. Yet Sweden is smaller in population and GNP than Holland or Belgium and spends only a slightly larger percentage of its GNP for defense. Swedish military forces are almost as large as those of West Germany; both spend the same percentage of their GNP on defense. Indeed, the phenomenon can be generalized: the Warsaw Pact spends less on defense than NATO and has no more personnel under arms in peacetime, yet it has many more combat forces and is significantly stronger.

The Reagan administration's Five-Year Defense Plan calls for a real increase of 43 percent from 1982 to 1987,[1] yet it does not improve the Western military position. In NATO and Korea the same inadequate conditions remain. For the Middle East, a rapid projection RDJTF may be deployable, but its tactical methods remain flawed and prone to debacle in difficult terrain. At sea very little will have changed. Additional Nimitz-class task forces remain vulnerable and do not eliminate the real threat to the surface navy, namely, long-range antiship missiles launched from submarines and bombers. Carriers in general do not have great value vis-à-vis the USSR. More carriers are not needed against the Soviet surface fleet, nor is horizontal escalation a viable strategy. Since NATO is weak, the strategy is dangerously counterproductive; if NATO were strong, it would not be needed.

From the perspective of grand strategy, the centers of gravity in global power politics are Europe and northeast Asia. With Western conventional superiority in central Europe and a balance in Korea, the Russians would have neither spare forces nor incentive for overt military action elsewhere, such as the Persian Gulf. They may still support covert action and wars of revolution; these, however, are won by political-military technique and do not require large expenditures.

In this article, neither nuclear weapons nor the clearly favorable policy implications of new-found military superiority are addressed. All military strategies must admittedly be considered against the backdrop of nuclear weapons and deterrence; however, nuclear weapons are mutually threatening and mutually unusable. Unless one side obtains a dramatic strategic advantage, the only usable forces are conventional. For the United States, strong conventional forces can minimize the stress on and rhetoric about nuclear forces, as well as add an additional measure of conventional deterrence. In this article "military superiority" is defined as a condition of strategic parity and conventional superiority.

I

Conventional parity is widely believed to be unattainable vis-à-vis the USSR. Yet it is strange that a country that is still backward in many respects should be militarily superior to the great countries of Europe, Asia, and

COMPARISON OF NATO AND WARSAW PACT
TOTAL DEFENSE COSTS

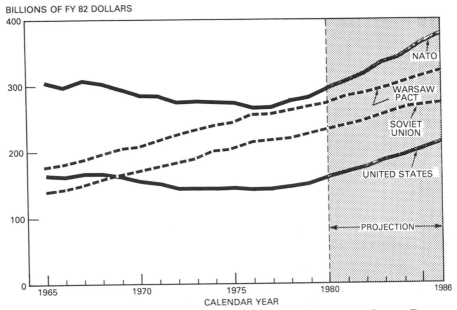

Figure 1. Comparison of NATO and Warsaw Pact total defense costs. (*Source:* Department of Defense, *Annual Report FY 1982*, C–12.)

North America combined. In population, industrial wealth, and technology the free world allies are far superior.

Nor is it a question of resources devoted to military pursuits. NATO (fig. 1) has always outspent the Warsaw Pact. Using the CIA methodology, which calculates the costs of Soviet forces at U.S. prices (including manpower), NATO in 1980 outspent the Warsaw Pact by 10 percent in dollars (and at least 25 percent more in rubles).[2]

In peacetime strength, NATO is slightly ahead (4.93 to 4.78 million).[3] On the NATO central front, adding France, NATO has nearly 200,000 more men in its air and ground forces. *Yet, as graphically displayed in table 8.1, the Warsaw Pact, with fewer personnel, deploys more than twice the weapons and combat strength!*

Western military inferiority is due, not to inadequate resources, but to a lack of combat forces and to a tactical and operational passivity stemming from a doctrine emphasizing positional defense of linear lines with firepower. This is true in Europe, in Korea, and for the RDJTF.* For example, the last-named requires more than 50,000 army troops to field one division; yet in Afghanistan the Soviets field five roughly equivalent divisions from a total

*The Rapid Deployment Joint Task Force has been officially designated CENTCOM, or the U.S. Central Command.

Table 8.1. NATO's Changing Military Balance, Central Front, In-Place Weapons

Weapons	1960	1970	1980
Tanks			
Pact	11,700	13,350	18,000
NATO	3,885	5,745	6,200
Armored vehicles			
Pact	8,400	14,400	18,000
NATO	5,500	13,000	14,400
Antitank weapons			
Pact	1,700	3,300	7,400
NATO	1,900	3,300	5,000
Artillery pieces			
Pact	4,750	5,150	6,500
NATO	1,600	2,000	2,300
Air defense weapons			
Pact	4,700	4,400	5,000
NATO	1,000	1,900	2,300
Aircraft			
Pact	2,800	2,850	3,200
NATO	1,850	1,550	1,420

Source: Phillip A. Karber, *The Central European Arms Race, 1949–1980.* © 1980 by the BDM Corporation.

strength of 90,000. These are issues of doctrine and organization. They are not caused by lack of resources, nor will they be resolved by more spending, complex technology, standardization, or marginal improvements. The solution requires structural realignment.

II

NATO. The U.S. objective in NATO has traditionally been a conventional balance in order to obviate the need to resort to nuclear weapons. The Europeans, however, are primarily interested in deterrence. Their strategy has been to ensure that U.S. strategic weapons remain coupled to the defense of Europe. They argue that a conventional force balance is too expensive, unnecessary given U.S. strategic strength, and contradictory to their preferred strategy of deterrence. Theater nuclear forces fit into their scheme only as a connecting device; they abhor anything more than their symbolic and token use. Their policy has been to commit the U.S. to the defense of Europe in every possible way. Initiatives for both conventional and tactical nuclear forces are evaluated by their ability to enmesh the United States, not their military worth.

NATO's military problem is conceptually quite simple. NATO needs more divisions—two to three times more. Forces of this magnitude cannot be financed or manned by budgetary increases of 3 percent per year. Nor can they be financed by the putative savings from standardization; nor can the lack of numbers be offset by greater interoperability, superior technology, and tactical airpower. Savings from equipment standardization have not materialized; even under nonexistent ideal conditions, savings could only amount to 2 to 3 percent annually from economies in production, with another 2 to 3 percent from pooled research and development.[4]

Rationalization, standardization, and interoperability (RSI) and greater technological complexity do not come to grips with NATO's military problem. The RSI issues are low cost, but they have also absorbed and distracted top management attention from the real issues. Technological complexity has numerous drawbacks. First, it is expensive, diverting funds from the more pressing need to equip reserve formations. Second, much of what is advocated is undesirable; for instance, good armored tactics are highly decentralized and are ruined by centralized command and control, however sophisticated the sensors, communications, and data processing. Third, many technological solutions are not robust and can easily be countered. They assume a passive, predictable enemy. Fourth, the quest for quality over quantity is self-defeating. If NATO's organizational deficiency allows the Pact to attain twice the combat units from the same number of people, then according to the Lanchesterian Formula, which underlies so much of modern war gaming and force planning, Western technology has to be four times better than the Soviets!* Unfortunately, the attempt to maintain technological superiority in mature technologies yields diminishing returns and increasing relative costs. Invariably this leads to repeated cuts in force structure to pay for ever-more-expensive equipment and a worsening spiral of ever-increasing demand on technology to offset reduced force levels.

It is, of course, a political reality that NATO must have a forward defense. Moreover, because any viable strategy must emphasize deterrence, forward defense must be done in a manner that emphasizes Alliance commitment and resolve, that of the United States in particular. The initial defense must therefore be some form of cordon defense. Yet without strong reserves, a cordon defense is not militarily viable. An attacker can probe his way through

---

*The Lanchesterian Formula refers to a model of combat attrition as a function of force ratios. The most common variant, the square law, postulates that combat losses for a side are a constant multiplied by the combat power of the other side. Based on a set of differential equations, this model serves as the basis for many war-gaming simulations. Many challenge the validity of Lanchesterian models, however, because the predicted loss exchange ratios and battle outcomes are too sensitive to opposing sides' force ratios. In fact, these critics argue, battle outcomes historically are remarkably insensitive to force ratios. Leadership, morale, training, and luck may count for as much.

(the new Soviet method) or concentrate and smash his way through (the old Soviet method). Once through, the remaining forces along the cordon are enveloped and further organized defense preempted.

NATO's military inferiority is due purely to inadequate combat numbers. NATO lacks the numbers to provide for both forward forces and operational reserves, the latter of which must be mechanized. Exactly how NATO expands its forces, their tactical quality, and the split between on-line forces and operational reserves are details. There are at least four different solutions, all of which can be reached within present costs. None of them depends on U.S. ground forces, technological complexity, or standardization.

The defense of Western Europe cannot depend on U.S. ground forces. The United States can supply only a small part of total Alliance requirements. These could become instrumental in a real conventional defense only if the Europeans themselves increase their own reinforcement capability. But in that case, European NATO could field more than enough divisions for its own defense, and do so quickly and relatively cheaply.

The expanded forces must come from mobilized reserve formations, but these need not all be high-grade armored units or capable of being instantly mobilized. Although the specific combination depends on the solutions posited, it must be based on three principles. First, forward elements must be strong enough to defend secondary sectors while sidestepping major thrusts. This provides a forward screen for masking reserve movements and secure terrain shoulders for counterattacking deep against the flanks and rear of the Soviet thrust columns, into the weakly held spaces between them, and into the GDR itself. Second, operational reserves must be large, armored, of high quality, and available within days of any attack. Third, peacetime forces must be of sufficient size and readiness to guard against a preemptive surprise attack by the nineteen Soviet divisions in East Germany and several of the nine in Czechoslovakia and Hungary, and to provide a training base of sufficient size for generating mobilizable reserves. In addition, large tank reserves must be garrisoned and held back from the border to protect them from surprise heliborne attack and to provide operational flexibilty in confused and chaotic circumstances.

The trained manpower for large numbers of Western European reserve formations already exists. Its organization into equipped and structured units has been inhibited by the low priority accorded reserves by the Anglo-Americans, by SHAPE's (Supreme Headquarters Allied Powers Europe) fear that anything less than expensive standing forces would lead countries to cheat on their commitments, and by the European emphasis on deterrence. Most reservists lack meaningful assignments. Newly released conscripts are generally assigned to low-priority local security units or to replacement pools as individual replacements for sustaining the standing forces in combat. Only recently—in a program significantly slowed by the NATO Long-Term Defense Program (LTDP)—have a few been organized in the traditional continental manner of structured units capable of being quickly mobilized for combat (which is the Soviet practice).

There are at least four ways of structuring reservists. One solution is territorial defense. In one variant, NATO's standing armored forces can be concentrated in operational reserves while the forward space—two-thirds of which is fortuitously close terrain (urban, forest, and mountain)—is defended by light territorial infantry operating fluidly in forests and defending statically the many stone villages and towns dotting the German countryside.[5] These units are cheap to equip and easy to mobilize. Tactically, territorials must be considered auxiliaries, capable of defending against regular forces only in close terrain (45 percent of the total West German landscape). Operationally, territorial defense (and the defense of built-up areas athwart major Soviet thrusts) can only serve as adjuncts to the main regular forces. Territorial forces by themselves cannot be decisive, and often they will not inflict serious losses on the enemy. Their importance is the leverage they allow in the deployment of NATO's expensive standing forces.

In the past, territorial defense has been politically unacceptable to the Germans. It undercut the German preference for deterrence by substituting Germans for allied soldiers. In the last several years it has become politically respectable, corresponding to growing German doubts about America.

A second similar solution using regular forces in lieu of territorials is the *Jaeger* (forest) infantry approach for complementing and supplementing expensive armored forces. In this scheme, mobilized light infantry will occupy and control the many small forests and villages dotting the German countryside, and high quality, active-duty Jaeger brigades will control and limit movement through the extensive tracts of close terrain covering most of the East-West border.

Control of small forests prevents the enemy from unexpectedly outflanking defending tank reserves. Villages, for their part, make a natural checkerboard of mutually supporting, readily fortified strong points from which fire, antitank in particular, can dominate the open spaces. Large forests can be used to channel enemy movement, shred mechanized forces moving through them, and shield and mask concentrated operational reserves.

Operationally, light infantry contributes to the overall armored battle in five ways.

1. It screens the front and sidesteps main thrusts.
2. It relieves armored forces for concentration into operational reserves.
3. It strips out the reconnaissance elements and breaks down the synergism of the attacking combined arms teams.
4. It channels the attack into narrow thrust vectors.
5. It sets up and masks the tank counterattack into the deep flank of the enemy thrust vector.

In addition, with so much light infantry available, the tank-mechanized infantry ratio can be changed from the present 50:50 to 75:25.

This solution is cheap. It attains conventional parity by an (infantry) shield and (tank) thrust approach, which maximizes the defensive value of German terrain while minimizing the required size and therefore offensive potential inherent in tank reserves. It is the solution the Germans themselves are moving toward.[6] In the recent restructuring of the *Bundeswehr* from thirty-three to thirty-six brigades, two (cadre) battalions of light infantry were added to each of the eleven German armored divisions, and fifteen (cadre) regiments of light infantry were to be formed in the non-NATO committed Territorial Army. In addition, of the roughly twenty-four high-quality Jaeger brigades required, most (nine French, four German, five British, and one Belgian) are already in existence, though the French, Belgian, and three British units are not NATO-deployed. Equally significant (see the section on southwest Asia and Third World Intervention below), if the RDJTF and American infantry were properly structured, there would be a corps-sized force of true light infantry to draw from.[7]

A third solution is restructuring. In recent years, the British, French, and Germans have restructured their forces to obtain greater combat power and lower tail-to-teeth ratios. Nevertheless, all NATO countries still have much larger tail-to-teeth ratios than comparable Soviet formations of equivalent combat strength. The United States has the largest, West Germany the smallest. Restructuring continues this stripping-out process. Streamlining NATO forces by revising longstanding practices serves two goals. First, it releases manpower, in this particular case to form active-duty cadres for mobilizable divisions. Second, it makes forces more suitable for maneuver warfare.

The potential of this solution can be seen in the following calculation. Assuming Western divisional slices can be squeezed down to 20,000 (Erickson calculates the equivalent Soviet figure at 16,000),[8] NATO plus French divisions on the Continent could be configured from thirty-three to seventy-five divisions (using the same readiness categories and distribution of readiness as the Soviet army).[9] The main cost is additional divisional equipment, of which perhaps a third already exists in prepositioned and in sustaining war replacement stocks.[10]

A fourth solution, which can be combined with restructuring, is a new modified cadre system developed by the Dutch (termed RIM for *Rechtstreeks Instromend Mobilisable*). RIM matches reserve battalions with identical active battalions. The Dutch innovation is that rather than assigning former conscripts to equipment-holding or cadre units, structured active units are placed *in toto* on "leave," complete with equipment. Accordingly, all the relationships that personnel develop with each other and their equipment are retained, and the period is short enough for skills to remain high. Dutch conscripts serve thirty-six months (sixteen active and twenty reserve) in the same company with the same cadre doing the same job. (Comparable turnover in U.S. companies is 80–100 percent per year and largely explains the consistently better performance of Dutch conscripts against American volunteers in the various NATO competitions).

The Dutch innovation yields mobilizable combat battalions equal in quality to active battalions at 20 percent of their cost.[11] This is a dominant mobilization system for field forces. By reducing the size of the required cadre, costs are lower than for comparable cadre systems. No additional demands are placed on the citizenry for refresher training. Units can be mobilized as rapidly as those of any reserve system. Units are effective almost immediately after their assembly, as compared to the normal cadre system, which always requires some integration of reservists and familiarization of personnel. Reservists are restricted in their movements for twenty months after their active duty; however, this is not onerous because most European army units are recruited from their garrison regions.

After their RIM duty reservists can be be grouped with normal equipment-holding cadres to form yet additional reserve divisions. These cannot be of the same quality as the RIM units without extensive refresher training. But their lower quality is suitable for the close terrain tasks described above after mobilization. The costs of these units is estimated by the Dutch Ministry of Defense at half the cost of RIM units.

By using the RIM system, the continental Europeans could triple their division count for about a 30 percent increase in army costs (or less if combined with restructuring). This means an increase from twenty-five to seventy-five U.S. division equivalents in German, French, Dutch, and Belgian forces. Half this increase would consist of high-quality mechanized formations; half would consist of low-quality truck-borne infantry performing secondary but still essential tasks. Since the budgetary ratio within the European military is 50:30:20 for ground, air, and naval forces, respectively, a 30 percent increase in army budgets equates with a 15 percent increase in overall defense budgets.

For this 15 percent increase in continental European budgets, NATO would obtain a real conventional defense with strong forward forces and large operational reserves. The (German) political imperative of forward defense would be satisfied, the American commitment would remain, and the emphasis on theater nuclear weapons could be much reduced. Most important, in addition to continued deterrence by U.S. strategic weapons (deterrence by threat), there would now be conventional deterrence (deterrence by denial). Seventy-five Continental divisions plus another fifteen divisions from restructured American, British, and Canadian contingents would give NATO almost as many divisions as the Warsaw Pact.[12]

Of the four constructs outlined, the cheapest are territorial defense and mobilized light infantry. These would give NATO a true defensive capability with only limited offensive capability. The restructuring and RIM constructs would give NATO military superiority in conventional forces. The Warsaw Pact is powerful because of the sheer number of its divisions and the flexibility inherent in numbers. Ninety divisions also give NATO the power and flexibility of numbers. Once the numbers are in relative balance, there are four factors likely to swing superiority to the West. First, Warsaw Pact forces are vulnerable to defeat in detail. NATO's ninety divisions are concentrated; the Warsaw Pact's are widely strung out and cannot be readily focused in central Europe. In recognition of this reality and the increasing importance of preemptive attack, Group Soviet Forces Germany has become the cutting edge and decisive element of any Soviet offensive. The second strategic echelon in the Western military districts has become a follow-up and consolidation force, in the mold of the German foot infantry of 1939–1941.[13] Second, there is a cultural X factor still pertinent today that gives Western nations and armies a vitality missing elsewhere. This is reflected in the inferiority complex of the Russians toward the West, the Germans in particular. Third, the Soviets are very sensitive to German military prowess. Soviet flexibility is preprogrammed, and Soviet units tend to unravel when presented with unexpected situations. This is the forte of the Germans, who emphasize the unexpected in deep flank and rear counterattacks. Finally, the Warsaw Pact, and perhaps even the USSR itself, may lack the political stability to withstand the pressures of a protracted conflict or the appearances of a military defeat. If, for instance, West German divisions would appear in apparent strength deep in the GDR, there is no way of knowing whether the East Germans would switch sides. This could collapse the Soviets' front and lead to a military debacle.

The price for military superiority in Europe using these constructs is $9 billion, or a 15 percent increase in the level of Continental spending.[14] Even this amount need not be spent if there were a division of labor and partial specialization among Alliance members. Specifically, with a budgetary split of 50:30:20 for ground, air, and sea, respectively, the four Continental countries could, at no cost to themselves, triple their divisional count by increasing ground allocations 30 percent and correspondingly reducing air and sea allocations 30 percent. These, in turn, could be offset across the Alliance at no additional cost, yielding nearly a threefold increase in divisions with no loss in relevant air and naval capabilities.

In tactical air forces, the combined inventory of the Continental countries is 1,350 combat aircraft.[15] A 30 percent reduction is 400 aircraft, which could be replaced from the United States, resulting in no loss in overall air capability if the aircraft are stationed in Europe. Of a total U.S. inventory of 5,500 combat aircraft, roughly 2,000 are deployed to Europe.[16] The balance of 3,500 aircraft are not. Forty percent of these are navy and marine. These aircraft may initially be needed for a war at sea; thereafter they have little relevance to a conflict with the USSR. Nor can the full strength of the U.S. Air Force be deployed to Europe, due to secondary commitments, homeland training requirements and, most important, the limited supporting (beddown) capacity in Western Europe itself. Consequently, if a war in central Europe were to last only several weeks, nearly two-thirds of U.S. tactical airpower would not have been brought to bear, a force more than double that of the Continental air forces.

For naval forces and airlift, tripling the Continental divisions implies a much reduced dependence on the "arsenal of democracy" and the need for airlift and sea lane protection forces. There is little need for large-scale movements of troops and supplies to Europe for short wars or in the first months of a protracted war. The threat to sea lanes will be much reduced by the time these might be needed, significantly reducing NATO requirements for frigates and destroyers.

The airlift question has two parts. With more Continental divisions, there is less need for airlifting U.S. ground forces. Second, restructuring U.S. forces can improve the plan for deploying ten divisions into the theater in ten days. One approach is changing from the existing structure of two corps and five divisions to a structure of three corps and eleven streamlined divisions. The eleven divisions would be structured for rapidly fleshing out in wartime and would equate to seven unreinforced division equivalents against a surprise attack.

This procedure would improve the plan by one division, allow faster deployment into combat, reduce airlift requirements substantially, and credit the LTDP's three divisional sets of additional prepositioned U.S. equipment to the Europeans for their expanded division count. Organizationally, this procedure reduces the size of companies but increases their number from three to four per battalion. All equipment would be prepositioned with the parent battalion in Germany, but personnel of the fourth company plus part of the battalion overhead would be assigned to a division based in the United States.[17]

In short, NATO is not inherently militarily inferior to the Warsaw Pact. NATO can attain a military balance, and it can do so in a nonprovocative manner without increasing European costs and slightly decreasing U.S. costs, and in a manner that adds a conventional deterrent to an existing, if tenuous, nuclear deterrent. In addition, should deterrence fail and war occur, the nature of thrust and counterthrust tactics now to be used by NATO as well as the Pact is a style of war which does not lead to widespread civil destruction—as shown by Germany's French campaign of 1940 and Patton's thrust through France in 1944.

Northeast Asia. Northeast Asia, where three major powers converge, is the second region of global military importance. Its fulcrum is the Republic of South Korea (ROK). In contrast to the United States' NATO allies, the Republic of Korea takes defense very seriously indeed. Its best manpower is drafted, and the ROK military has become highly proficient by American technical standards. Unfortunately there has been a breakdown in the theory and art of war. It is as if a wand had been waved over the Korean battlefront and everything frozen for thirty years. Little has changed, despite the fact that foreign analysts have severely criticized the tactics used by the United Nations forces in that conflict.[18] Yet these are the tactics still in use in Korea (as well as those planned for the RDJTF in southwest Asia).

South Korea has a population double that of the North and a GNP four times larger. Yet militarily the South has always been the weaker, even when its military forces were larger. With 700,000 men the North has fifty-eight divisions; the South with 520,000 has only twenty-five roughly equivalent divisions. This is, of course, characteristic of U.S.-model forces everywhere.

This deficiency is worsened by the ROK's deployment and operating doctrine. Strategically, ROK forces are dispersed laterally across a mountainous peninsula in cordon fashion, which violates the Clausewitzian precept.[19] The defender is everywhere weak and his reserves compartmented. Any concentration leads to a breakthrough and roll-up of the flanks, often leading to a collapse of the line and, given the terrain, a military debacle. (This is the basis for Clausewitz's contention that the attacker, not the defender, has the advantage in mountains.)

Tactically, ROK forces are deployed in battalion strong points on forward slopes of hills against an enemy known to be strong in heavy, pulverizing artillery. Forward forces will either be smashed in place or corridors opened for penetration. When a penetration occurs, ROK reserves occupy positional blocking positions. Since there is no longer a continuous line of mutually supporting positions, advancing North Korean light infantry can flow around them, causing a collapse of the reserve positions as well, even though the attacker is often minimally supported with artillery. The North Koreans have forty-two brigades of light infantry, exclusive of light infantry organic to each of thirty-five regular infantry divisions.

Finally, the ROK Army deploys the reserve regiment of each forward division in peacetime along the DMZ to stop peacetime infiltration. A significant fraction of forward forces and the entire immediate reserve is thus vulnerable to a pouncing surprise attack, possibly compromising the main defense as a whole.

These vulnerabilities are familiar from the western front between 1914 and 1918. The Germans solved them with new tactics in 1917–1918.[20] By contrast, the inferior Allied solution was ever greater firepower, just as the United States has tried in the last decade in Korea, first by greater application of artillery and close air support, and now by sophisticated technology as well.[21] Technology may indeed offset poor military practice and organization. But it is cheaper, simpler, and more logical to remove the malpractices in the first place.

The cordon deployment is a political imperative and can be accepted without unduly biasing the defense. The main requirements are to outpost and patrol the forward zone, place main defenses on rear slopes and crew-served weapons in heavily fortified, cross-firing positions, and strip out most riflemen from forward positions to form local light infantry reserves for immediate counterattacks. In addition, by deploying forward forces in this static manner, the division slice can be significantly reduced and large numbers of operational reserves formed, some of which must be light infantry to counter the North's use of this infantry.[22]

With the South's malpractices corrected, the North has little chance of succeeding in a surprise attack and none in a long conflict. There is little opportunity for deploying tanks down the corridors to Seoul; they remain, as in 1950, mere distractions for the light infantry and a force that can apply a subsequent coup de grace against a collapsed defense.

A military balance in Korea requires no additional resources. Indeed, some can be saved by deemphasizing heavy firepower and antitank weaponry. Politically, the doctrinal revisions would be a signal to the North: it is no longer feasible to attack except by bruising frontal assaults. This is a form of war the North with its inferior population and industry cannot win. For the United States it also suggests that U.S. ground forces are militarily superfluous, while their deterrent value could be replaced by greater air and naval forces, which could be militarily very useful in the overall global equation.

Southwest Asia (and Third World Intervention). The Persian Gulf is a region of serious military concern for Western security. The concerns in Europe and northeast Asia are military power and regional and global military balance. In the Persian Gulf, the concern is qualitatively different. It concerns the flow of a single commodity: oil. This oil is not needed for fighting or winning a war vis-à-vis the USSR. It is needed for the economic well-being and sociopolitical stability of the Western world. Its flow can be interrupted by overt or covert action; it can also be interrupted without any connivance on the part of the USSR.

Regardless of whether there were any Soviet threat to the Persian Gulf, an effective intervention force, larger and more capable than those of the British and French, would be in the U.S. interest. Among the intervention scenarios, the most demanding in terms of resources is a Soviet trans-Iran invasion to the Persian Gulf. If accompanied by a preemptive *fait accompli,* it is also among the most demanding in terms of time.

Deterrence is much simpler and cheaper—if it can be accomplished. Vertical escalation to nuclear weapons is possible, but always raises the issue of credibility. The possibility of horizontal escalation has been raised as a major justification for expanding the fleet to 600 ships, including two additional carrier task forces. It is, however, an infeasible proposition as long as NATO and Korea are militarily vulnerable. Deterrence by the mere existence of a stronger NATO, in particular a militarily superior NATO, is very credible. Its very existence in the center of Europe is likely to deter overt Soviet adventurism in the Gulf.

Even if deterrence were not fully effective, a strong NATO would increase Turkish confidence and reduce its reticence about basing Western air forces in eastern Anatolia. Basing there, and possibly in western air forces in western Pakistan as well, reduces the possibility of a preemptive Soviet airborne attack.

It can, of course, be argued that the Soviets could still invade to the Gulf and that the United States still requires a countering RDJTF. Even so, it can be shown that the programmed force is excessively large, and therefore difficult to insert and sustain, and that it would be downright dangerous to deploy. The programmed force is driven by a tactical construct designed for flatlands warfare and is completely invalid in high mountain warfare. Its weakness was displayed in Italy in World War II and more starkly in Korea in 1950, in the early defeats of arriving U.S. forces and later at the Yalu River against battle-tested American forces. The deficiency was poignantly captured by S. L. A. Marshall in *The River and the Gauntlet.*[23] The crux of the problem is that the American infantry fights positionally. Its flanks are extended linearly in order to protect them, and this requires large numbers of additional units. Further, because units fight positionally, and therefore are tactically and operationally passive, heavy reliance is placed on firepower, artillery, and tactical air support in particular. This requires a very large tail. The end result is a huge total force, much of whose combat function is merely to prevent outflanking and whose supporting function is to sustain an addiction to heavy firepower.

There is an alternative tactical construct. It is the construct used in Alpine warfare: Jaeger infantry. And light infantry, including heliborne raid infantry, can complement and partially substitute for armor on the high plateau deserts of Baluchistan.

The tank is not a direct threat to infantry in mountains; the threats are artillery and envelopment. Positional infantry on forward slopes (as, for instance, is the case in Korea today) is readily smashed by artillery and enveloped by armor if the close terrain is not extensive, and by light infantry if it is extensive. Mountain infantry stops the tank by positioning tank-stopping obstacles in defiles behind forward positions; it protects itself from frontal assault by choice of location and from artillery by rear-slope defenses. The bulk of a mountain force is deployed to protect the flanks of the blocking subunit from envelopment by counterattack. The basis of allocation is a brigade for a major road axis and its tributaries, two battalions for a lesser road axis. Across the mountain and desert barriers of southern Iran there are but nine major and minor axes. In this form of defense, the dominating elements are terrain, tactics, relative tempo of operations, and troop conditioning; not force size, weight, and firepower, which are the criteria of the present tactical construct.

Logistically, mountain infantry is considerably easier to support than regular infantry. For strategic movement, the overall force is smaller and units are individually lighter in weight. For tactical resupply, requirements by unit are less than half those of normal infantry. this is principally because terrain limits motorization and the usefulness of tanks and artillery. Fuel and ammunition for tanks and artillery normally account for 70 percent by weight of division supplies. Mountain infantry, by contrast, relies on physically conditioned troops for tactical movement; on the shock rather than the sustained

Table 8.2. Comparative Strengths of Jaeger and Standard Infantry/Persian Gulf Scenario

RDJTF Characteristics	Standard Infantry	Jaeger Infantry
Size, ground	Greater than 250,000	Approximately 100,000
Size, all services	Greater than 325,000	Approximately 150,000
Trans-Iran scenario	Delay	Destroy
Preemptive *fait accompli* scenario	Not designed for capability	Capable
Regional aggression scenario (Iran vs. Kuwait)	Capable	Capable
Internal security scenario	Not designed for capability	Capable
Initial weight, normalized	One	One-third
Sustained requirements, normalized	One	One-fourth
Number of brigades	Twenty	Twelve: Nine mountain infantry Two armored cavalry One armored
Operational availability	Constrained by inadequate air and sea lift	Eighteen months required for organizing and training new units

many Third World areas, they have the ability to perform large-scale security effect of firepower; and on low munitions-consuming (by weight) mortars, machine guns, snipers, and grenades. Equally important, because mountain infantry deploys in an elongated manner along a road axis as opposed to the lateral dispersion perpendicular to it of normal infantry, resupply is easier.

The Jaeger construct is a much-tested method of combat in mountains. The present RDJTF construct of standard infantry is not; it was designed for warfare in open flatlands. Its use in mountainous terrain has been limited and distinctly inauspicious.

A comparison of the characteristics of a Persian Gulf-oriented RDJTF based on the Jaeger and standard infantry constructs, shown in table 8.2, indicates that the Jaeger construct is preferable in all regards to the present standard infantry approach. It leads to reduced airlift and overseas basing requirements and a fourfold relative increase in infantry line combat strength because of its inherently smaller tail. Jaeger infantry is the solution to the U.S. military problem in many areas. Jaegers are useful as commandos and as precursors for main forces, they are militarily superior to heavy forces in tasks, and, of course, they are useful in Europe as well. Most important, the Jaeger infantry substitutes technique for size. Size alone is not sufficient in wars of insurgency, and can lead to debacles in environmentally hostile mountains and deserts.

Naval Forces. The surface fleet, the carrier task force in particular, receives the lion's share of the current U.S. Five-Year Defense Plan. In expanding from twelve to fifteen large carrier task forces, three or four large carriers and their associated escorts will have to be constructed, each costing (with their air wings) $17 billion in procurement alone. Yet nowhere is there an articulated strategy for naval operations; what is termed strategy is a mere collection of justifications for more ships.

The navy justifies its carriers in many ways. The two central difficulties are that it requires three to maintain one on station, and each has a total offensive punch of but three air squadrons of thirty to thirty-eight A-6s and A-7s. Everything else, including some of the A-6s and A-7s, protects the task force. In the navy's formative days, cheap planes fought expensive ships. It now has expensive planes to protect an expensive fleet built to support only the planes, while many of that service's offensive functions have atrophied. In other words, the navy has fallen into the trap of being a system operating within itself and of itself, with little regard for external utility. Until the navy breaks out of this trap, its usefulness as an instrument for applying power (as opposed to merely symbolizing interest) will be limited: too much effort and too many aircraft are devoted to protecting its own base.

In the public debate, the roles and usefulness of the carrier task force are too readily presumed. The carrier is not useful for attacking the Soviet land mass, nor for supporting NATO with air power, at least on the central front. Carriers can project a mere handful of offensive aircraft, and the aircrafts' own base is far too vulnerable. For the NATO flanks, the carriers are often justified for their symbolic presence; but if they move out of the Mediterranean and Norwegian seas when the shooting starts, their impact will be more destabilizing than beneficial.

The large carrier is generally justified in two roles: the war at sea and force projection ashore. In the first, the large carrier is undoubtedly effective against hostile surface forces. It is also very expensive, as well as having a serious vulnerability and a major operational limitation. The fleet is vulnerable to the so-called D-Day shootout, whereby in a crisis the Soviet squadron hugs the American fleet and, in conjunction with antiship missiles from Backfire bombers and submarines, disables the carrier and therefore the usefulness of the entire fleet before aircraft can respond and the task force can obtain adequate standoff distance. Subsequently, it remains vulnerable to submarines and to massed raids by aircraft equipped with antiship missiles.

The operational limitation is inherent in the limited numbers of carriers and the limited range of naval aviation. At any one time, the navy can put to sea only four to six carriers on a sustained basis. Soviet naval squadrons will be in many locations, some of which will be out of reach of carrier aviation or sheltered by land-based air defense. Land-based long-range maritime aviation assisted by satellite surveillance can find and target these ships. If the U.S. fleet, with its air defense fighters and specialized air defense ships, is vulnerable to the Backfire, Soviet ships may be even more vulnerable. A long-range maritime air force, though much discussed, has remained undeveloped because of the division of roles and missions between the navy and air force.

The major mission that only carrier task forces can perform is force projection ashore, both air defense of the objective and ground attack. Unfortunately, while the mission is loudly proclaimed, the navy is in fact only moderately capable of the first task and almost completely incapable of the second, except against minor powers, in which case major forces are not needed. The problem is threefold: aircraft type, inadequate numbers, and flying distance. The carrier air wing is designed for the surface war at sea and air defense of the task force itself. The carrier's twenty-four F-14s are designed for long-range standoff air defense. They are too expensive for dogfighting and notoriously weak in that role. The thirty to thirty-eight A-6s and A-7s are effective against high-contrast targets, but they are too sophisticated for ground attack. They fly too fast to find (low-contrast) ground forces, which blend into the background. This limits them to (civil) counter-value targets and to interdiction which, other than air base attack, often has little military value.

Lack of numbers is inherent in limited deck space, large and costly aircraft, and the many competing aircraft requirements. The latter (ASW and electronic warfare and early warning) account for twenty-six of the eighty-six aircraft in a typical air wing.[24]

Finally, there is distance. In a hostile environment the fleet tends to stand off from shore for its own safety, lowering sortie rates, payloads, and response times. Distance is particularly acute should the Soviets attempt a *coup de main* in the northern Persian Gulf. The fleet normally sails some 1,000 kilometers, at the extreme range of unrefueled F-14s. If a preemptive attack were accompanied by Backfires (which may only feint), the fleet would likely move further to sea for safety, thereby forgoing the national mission of preventing an airborne *fait accompli.*

These deficiencies are not solved, or indeed even recognized, in the navy program. Wide distribution of antiship missiles can help somewhat to reduce demands on the carrier air wing in order to free attack sorties for power projection ashore. It does not solve the problems of distance and aircraft type and numbers in general. This requires Harriers, or better yet, new aircraft—small dogfighters and small cross-section low-wing loaded aircraft—onboard additional, less valuable carriers (recommissioned or new, small or large). As an adjunct squadron, it could be escorted by smaller, less capable ships, all of which would be under the protection of the main large carrier fleet. In addition, of course, the adjunct squadron is a suitable proxy for the main fleet during crises, as well as for the sea-control mission in other contexts.

The notion of adjunct complements has application too for attack submarines. The navy has ninety-one nuclear attack subs, five old diesels, and no modern diesel-electric, so popular abroad. Their cost is but a fifth of the cost and crew of an SSN-688. Yet in some circumstances they are more effective, and their combination can provide a powerful synergism in certain seas.

The Falkland Islands conflict has made explicit what many have long suspected: large, seagoing, force projection ships are asymmetrically vulnerable against antiship missiles and submarines. The nation is not well served by new ship construction in order to continue present operational methods and deployments. New methods and different ships are required. At the same time, these must complement existing investments and, where possible, add new tactical combinations.

Tactical Air Forces. The problem facing those in charge of tactical aviation (including attack helicopters) is whether value is commensurate with costs, which are slightly more than half the cost of general purpose forces. In contrast, for strategic air forces the great issue is not cost effectiveness but strategy. Strategy belongs to the overall combined arms force, of which tactical air forces are but a part, land or sea. Tactical air forces in this regard are much like artillery on land and destroyers at sea.

The long-unresolved analytical questions are the air-ground trade-off and the choice of missions. Implicit in this quest is an imbalance between value and costs. All air forces are expensive. However, U.S. air power has become so expensive and reliant on electronics that even the NATO European air forces have serious misgivings.[25] From their perspective, U.S. tactical air is unduly expensive and operationally susceptible to spoofing and other countermeasures. There is a balance between tactics and technology. In this regard it is worth noting that the Israeli feat against the SAM missiles in the Bekaa Valley had little to do with state-of-the-art technology and a lot to do with tactical insight and interservice coordination.

To the extent that these issues are valid, tactical airpower can be made significantly cheaper. The facets addressed here, however, are different. The most important is recognition of the economic principle of comparative advantage (macro division of labor). Each "dollar" of replacement of European air forces from the pool of non-NATO committed U.S. air assets buys five dollars worth of in-place ground forces (mobilized, to be sure).

A second facet is the type of air force needed in support of RDJTF operations. These require high performance air defense fighters, but the workhorse is the light fighter (which the U.S. Air Force adamantly opposes, and so it has none) capable of bouncing nap-of-the-earth flying helicopters and attacking low-contrast infan ry in difficult terrain or confused situations characteristic of Third World contingencies. (Some analysts believe that because modern technology is reducing aircraft radar signature and upgrading guns, light fighters are the ground support fighters of the future in more general conflict.)

A third facet is excessive waste in numbers and quality of personnel in manning U.S. air forces. Sophisticated equipment is maintained by intelligent but unskilled apprentices and journeymen in lieu of older and fewer master craftsmen. In this way the personnel system ensures poor infantry and high-cost maintenance.

Saving Money as Well. The Western military problem is not a question of resources, but is one of strategy, tactical construct, and organization. There is no requirement for additional U.S. or European active forces. However, the Europeans must organize their trained reservists into equipped and structured divisions. Western requirements elsewhere are primarily for light forces, complemented by rather small amounts of armor and suitably supported by tactical air power.

The navy needs more ships, but these are smaller, and over the long run can largely be financed by normal ship construction allocations. The air force, partly at the expense of its preferences for sophisticated fighter-bombers capable of quasi-strategic bombing and for highly orchestrated air operations, needs to give greater emphasis to antihelicopter air defense and to ground attack. Both tasks require larger numbers of new-technology (low visibility, high power to weight, airframe and gun) small aircraft capable of operating from simple airstrips. The army and marines need better combat units obtainable by revised tactical concepts and personnel practices. Through better use of reserves and sharply reduced tail-to-teeth ratios, total manpower can be reduced while still adding more divisions.

CONCLUSIONS

United States and Western military inferiority is purely self-inflicted. It is a case of dated doctrine causing too few combat units, misuse of technology and manpower, and poor strategy and integration with allies. It is *structural* waste many, many times larger than the familiar forms of "fraud, waste, and abuse." It is the waste of Shumpeterian economics, not the marginalia that passes for analysis in the Pentagon.

NOTES

1. Department of Defense, *Annual Report to the Congress: FY 1983* (Washington, D.C.: Government Printing Office, January 1982), pp. 1–4.

2. F. Holzman, "Soviet Military Spending." *International Security* (Spring 1982).

3. *The Military Balance, 1981–1982* (London: International Institute for Strategic Studies), p. 112. General Jones cites the comparison at 5.9 to 5.3 million in favor of the Warsaw Pact. This number, however, includes paramilitary forces. JCS, *Military Posture for FY 1983,* January 1982, p. 5. *The Military Balance* figures are 5.9 versus 4.7 million in the Warsaw Pact's favor.

4. Standardized tactics, which are sometimes also listed as a NATO goal, are difficult to attain and less desirable than they may appear. Tactical success requires diversity of repertoires and quickness of action, objectives that often run counter to the ponderousness inherent in standardization and some forms of interoperability. In practice, standardized army tactics lead to lowest common denominator tactics and a new weakening of NATO.

5. For an elaboration of this thesis, see Steven L. Canby, "Territorial Defense in Central Europe," *Armed Forces and Society* (Fall 1980): 51–67.

6. For an elaboration of infantry for complementing the tank, see Maj. Gen. Franz Uhle-Wettler, *Gefechtsfeld Mitteleuropa: Gefahr der Untertechnisierung von Streikräften* (Munich: Bernard & Graefe Verlag), 1980. The author is indebted to Gen. Franz-Joseph Schulze for the Jaeger construct. This theme is developed in S. Canby, *Classic Light Infantry and the Defense of Europe,* (Washington, D.C.: C&L Associates, September 1982).

7. To survive on the modern battlefield, infantry must be armored or use light infantry tactics. In recognition of this reality, as of 1982 the central northern Europeans have phased out the regular line infantry still predominant in the U.S. force structure. Line infantry of the World War I and II variety depends on extended, linear, positional defenses and rely on heavy firepower. This infantry is deemed suitable for deployment anywhere. Jaeger infantry by contrast is suitable for deployment only in close terrain. It survives by stealth and fights by stalking tactics. It is also suitable for city fighting and as special-purpose commandos in open terrain. In the latter role, they were the precursing elements in the German offensives of 1918, which broke through, in open terrain, the densely packed and firepower-supported Allied defenses and almost restored movement and maneuver in that war.

8. *Soviet-Warsaw Pact Force Levels,* Report 76–2 (Washington, D.C.: United States Strategic Institute, 1976), p. 33.

9. For the details of restructuring and the forming of reserve divisions, see Steven L. Canby, *The Alliance and Europe: Part IV; Military Doctrine and Technology,* Adelphi Papers, no. 109 (London: Institute for Strategic Studies, Winter 1974/1975). French forces are included in these calculations both because of changes in several underlying assumptions and because of their necessity in the conventional defense of Europe. France withdrew from the military side of the alliance because, given the widespread belief of NATO's inherent conventional weakness, an independent nuclear force was believed necessary to increase the credibility of a nuclear response and to help control the decision to initiate it. The validity of this proposition has eroded with the loss of American strategic superiority. In addition, France has a policy of maintaining relative balance with Germany; more West German divisions mean more French divisions too.

10. NATO practice has been to sustain in combat a fixed number of standing divisions with reserve equipment and individual replacements. The contrasting Soviet approach—formerly practiced by the Continental countries themselves—is to structure both into mobilizable divisions.

11. Dutch estimates include first line equipment, facilities, and civilian maintenance

personnel numbering 1.5 percent of unit strength. The regular army officer and NCO cadre numbering 7 percent of unit strength are mostly excluded. During the leave period they are assigned to schools, staffs, and other overhead activities of a peacetime military.

12. In Eastern Europe, there are 30 stationed Soviet divisions and 39 (nominal) Warsaw Pact divisions. In all of European Russia there are 58 divisions, less the Leningrad Military District whose forces are purportedly earmarked for the far north. This totals 127 divisions. *Military Balance, 1981–1982*.

13. Based on detailed conversations with John Erickson and Christopher Donnelly of the Soviet Studies Centre at Sandhurst. In addition, both argue the Soviets no longer use wave attacks, and the echeloning of Soviet forces presumed by American technologists has been drastically changed. For an elaboration of these themes, see S. Canby, *NATO Corps Battle Tactics* (Washington, D.C.: C&L Associates, November 1978).

14. Fifteen percent is the steady-state increase and assumes amortization of equipment. A quick buildup implies a corresponding temporary increase above 15 percent, and less later. In addition, tripling divisions does not imply tripling ammunition stocks because of an implied shift in the deployment of the divisions (most at any point in time are in reserve) and because artillery would be more for suppression and shock than destruction. However, this is separate from the shortfall in the total days of available supply, where the Europeans have a serious deficit.

15. *Military Balance, 1981–1982*.

16. Department of Defense, *Annual Report: FY 1982*, (Washington, D.C.: Government Printing Office, January 1981), p. 72.

17. This concept is explained in detail in Canby, *The Alliance and Europe*, pp. 21–22. See also n. 10.

18. For two well-regarded books from Germany and the United Kingdom, see Uhle-Wettler, *Gefechtsfeld Mitteleuropa: Gefahr der Untertechnisierung von Streitkräften;* and Col. (Ret.) J. R. Alford, *Mobile Defence: The Pervasive Myth: A Historical Investigation* (London: Kings College, 1978).

19. *On War,* trans. Col. J. J. Graham (London: Kegan Paul, Trench, Trübner & Co., 1911), 2:234–62.

20. For an excellent account, see Timothy T. Lupfer, *The Dynamics of Doctrine: The Changes in German Tactical Doctrine during the First World War,* Leavenworth Papers, no. 4 (Ft. Leavenworth, Kans.: U.S. Army Command and General Staff College, July 1981).

21. See for instance, D. Cotter and N. Wikner, "Korea: Force Imbalances and Remedies," *Strategic Review* (Spring 1982): 63–70.

22. For a detailed discussion of these themes, see S. Canby and E. Luttwak, *Notes on the Defense of Korea* (Washington, D.C.: C&L Associates, December 1981).

23. Row, New York, 1953. Other excellent accounts are Uhle-Wettler, *Gefechtsfeld Mitteleuropa: Gefahr der Untertechnisierung von Streitkräften;* Alford, *Mobile Defence;* and T. R. Fehrenbach, *This Kind of War* (New York: Macmillan Co., 1963).

24. Department of Defense, *Annual Report: FY 1982* (Washington, D.C.: Government Printing Office, January 1981), p. 174.

25. For a discussion, see Steven L. Canby, "Tactical Airpower in Armored Warfare: The Divergence within NATO," *Air University Review* (April 1979); and "The Interdiction Mission—An Overview," *Military Review* (July 1979).

9

IMPLICATIONS
OF A GLOBAL STRATEGY
FOR U.S. FORCES

Jeffrey Record

Record argues that two changes in the strategic environment, the disintegration of NATO and the emergence of new threats to U.S. interests in southwest Asia, dictate a change in U.S. force structure. He advocates a draw down of U.S. ground forces in Europe and an expansion of naval and marine forces in order to meet the new strategic requirements facing the United States in the Persian Gulf and elsewhere in the Third World. Record maintains that the emphasis must be on smaller, less expensive ships if the necessary expansion is to be accomplished.

This chapter addresses the issue of heavy versus light ground forces within the broad context of present and future U.S. strategy. The proper amount and mix of heavy and light forces cannot be determined in the absence of a clear idea of where and whom the United States may have to fight. Consequently, this chapter examines the changing international environment confronting the United States and, based on this strategic assessment, argues the value of a U.S. force structure sufficiently flexible, adaptable, capable, and sustainable to support U.S. global strategy in the face of diverse and dynamic threats. Adaptability to the profound changes currently occurring in the locus and character of the designated threat is essential to the maintenance of an effective fighting force. Although this discussion focuses primarily on the army at the outset, force structure arguments presented encompass all U.S. armed forces.

CURRENT U.S. FORCE STRUCTURE AND RATIONALE

Existing active-duty U.S. Army combat forces are organized around sixteen divisions, ten of which are armored or mechanized infantry formations. Airborne, air-mobile, and dismounted infantry divisions make up the rest. The army's predominant investment in heavy forces is the product of a thirty-year planning focus on preparation for combat in central Europe against heavy, first-line Soviet ground forces, and a somewhat belated recognition that such preparation requires a significant investment in tactical mobility as well as firepower. All army divisions deployed in Europe today are armored or mechanized infantry units, as are most U.S.-based army divisions slated to reinforce Europe. The army's light divisions, although theoretically available for commitment to a war in Europe, remain for the most part deployed in or oriented toward areas outside NATO, where the character of potential military challenges and natural operating environments often combine to decrease the need for and utility of the kind of heavy forces essential to the prosecution of high-intensity land warfare in Europe. Foot-mobile infantry units are as likely to be of as little value against Soviet armor on the North German Plain as were armored units in Southeast Asia.

Of significance is the fact that in its primary planning focus on Europe, a focus that reached its apogee in the latter half of the 1970s with the conversion of some light divisions to heavy divisions, the army managed in large measure to offset the principal deficiency of heavy ground forces—their comparative strategic immobility. Politically secure peacetime access ashore in Europe has afforded the army enormous operational and logistical advantages. By stationing divisions in Europe, and by prepositioning additional sets of equipment there for NATO-slated divisions in the United States, the army has been able to sustain increases in tactical mobility at minimal expense to strategic mobility.

In sum, the army's present mix of heavy and light forces is justifiable as long as Europe remains the central focus of U.S. force planning, and as long as U.S. military forces enjoy the advantages of prepositioning on the continent.

THE CHANGING STRATEGIC ENVIRONMENT

However, two seminal events are now unfolding in the strategic environment, both of which contain profound implications for U.S. Army planning and force structure, especially the present ratio of heavy to light ground forces. The first event is the steady and perhaps irreversible disintegration of NATO as an instrument of collective security capable of mustering an adequate forward defense of Western Europe. The second is the emergence of a host of new threats to vital U.S. security interests in southwest Asia and in other areas outside Europe where the United States does not enjoy politically secure military access ashore. The combination of these two developments requires a fundamental reappraisal of the wisdom of continuing to allocate the bulk of U.S. ground forces to contingencies involving major sustained inland combat against Soviet forces in Europe.

CHANGES WITHIN NATO

An independent and democratic Europe is, to be sure, vital to the political and economic well-being of the United States. America could physically survive an extension of the Soviet empire into Western Europe, but probably only at the price of becoming a garrison state, economically regimented and lacking civil liberties. Nevertheless, precisely because the United States cannot defend Europe by itself, the American commitment to Europe's defense cannot be regarded—and never has been—as unlimited or eternal. It must of necessity be conditional, like all U.S. defense commitments overseas. What our NATO allies do dictates in the final analysis what the United States can or cannot do.

A major portion of the U.S. defense budget and approximately one-half of its active-duty general purpose forces continue to be allocated to Europe's defense. Bearing these strategic and structural opportunity costs would be both politically and militarily warranted if that investment produced the desired result—a credible defense of Europe. The United States, however, has never been in a position to defend the Continent alone. As in 1917–1918 and 1943–1945, the United States must rely on militarily powerful local allies that are no less willing to make necessary sacrifices for the common defense. In the absence of requisite allied sacrifices, the presence in Europe of 337,000 U.S. soldiers, sailors, and airmen cannot be justified, since they would have little alternative to immediate capitulation in the face of a full-scale Soviet invasion.

It is the collective muscle of U.S. and allied forces that makes possible a successful defense of Europe, and it is for this reason that allied military behavior in peacetime—crudely measurable by such indicators as force levels, national defense expenditures, and compliance with specific defense initiatives adopted by the Alliance as a whole—is properly regarded as a test of NATO's integrity as a collective security organization.

By almost any standard of peacetime military performance, key European allies—notably Germany and the Low Countries, where most U.S. forces in Europe are stationed—are failing to do their part for the common defense. Facing on their very doorstep a hostile force build-up unparalleled in peacetime, Germany, the Netherlands, and, to a lesser extent, Belgium, often behave as if nothing militarily consequential has happened in the world since the 1950s, when the West ruled the seas and enjoyed a crushing nuclear superiority over the Soviet Union. Economically robust and fully recovered from the ravages of World War II, they still devote to their own defense a far smaller portion of their national wealth than does the United States, whose borders are not menaced by a Group of Soviet Forces Canada or Group of Soviet Forces Mexico.

During the past decade the United States has accounted for 65 percent of the total national defense expenditures of NATO states and has maintained 45 percent of the Alliance's total active-duty military personnel, even though the American GNP and population represent but 45 and 38 percent, respectively, of NATO's as a whole. Allied national defense expenditure per capita in 1980 ranged from $71 to $410, compared to $644 for the United States. The United States currently devotes 5.9 percent of its GNP to defense, a share slated to rise to over 7.4 percent by the middle 1980s. In contrast is the 3.7, 3.4, and 3.3 percent allocated, respectively, by Germany, the Netherlands, and Belgium, the three NATO members lying astride the North German Plain, long regarded as the main corridor of a potential Soviet invasion.

The United States also maintains more active-duty men under arms as a percentage of the national population than most of its allies in Europe. America's soldier/citizen ratio of 1/107 is considerably higher than, for example, Germany's 1/125, the Netherlands' 1/138, and Great Britain's 1/163. Thus, whatever the deficiencies of the U.S. All-Volunteer Force (and they are legion), it nevertheless commands a significantly larger claim on America's human resources than, for example, does the *Bundeswehr* in Germany, where the AVF often has been criticized as an example of U.S. unwillingness to make the necessary social sacrifices for the common defense. If just Germany, the Netherlands, and Great Britain were to match the U.S. soldier/ citizen ratio, NATO would be endowed with over 310,000 additional active-duty military personnel, a number far exceeding the strength of the U.S. Army Europe. Such an increase in military manpower is certainly obtainable, given the demographic resources of Western Europe.

Europe's substantial national reserve forces, if adequately equipped, could provide a substitute for active-duty U.S. forces withheld in the United States as reinforcements for NATO. Germany and the Low Countries alone maintain ground force reserves totaling over one million men, a figure surpassing the active-duty end strength of the whole U.S. Army. It is difficult to justify the retention of American active forces in the continental United States to reinforce NATO, instead of equipping existing European reserve forces to accomplish the same mission.

The most disturbing manifestation of Europe's relative military abdication, however, is the failure of prominent allies to implement specific defense initiatives to which they have pledged themselves in good faith. In May 1977, for example, the members of NATO agreed to increase annually their respective national defense budgets by 3 percent over and above inflation for a period of five years. Real increases were (and still are) long overdue, following a decade of declining real Western military spending in the face of steady annual real Soviet growth averaging 4–5 percent per year. To date, however, few members of NATO have consistently attained this modest goal.

A second and no less critical military initiative, adopted by the Alliance as a whole in December 1979, also is being torpedoed by lack of allied resolve. In that year, in response to European requests, NATO agreed to modernize its long-range theater forces through deployment in Europe, beginning in 1983, of 572 new long-range nuclear missiles. The Long-Range Theater Nuclear Force (LRTNF) modernization program is a necessary if incomplete response to the Soviet Union's continuing deployment of new SS-20 missiles and Backfire bombers targeted against Europe.

Yet as with the 3 percent spending agreement, no sooner had the ink of allied signatures begun to dry when some began to back away. Subjected to intense pressure by Moscow and by powerful domestic constituencies that regard the United States as a greater threat to international peace and stability than the Soviet Union, the Netherlands has more or less reneged on its pledge to accept its share of the missiles, and Belgium and Germany have attached a host of political conditions to their final acceptance that will be difficult to satisfy. Worse still, Germany and the BENELUX states, as the price of their "compliance" with the modernization program, succeeded in goading the United States into premature negotiations with the Soviet Union on theater nuclear forces, negotiations that can lead to nothing but trouble for NATO as long as Moscow perceives within the Alliance a lack of political resolve to deploy the new missiles, the first of which was not available until December 1983. The result could well be a European failure to follow through on a program whose implementation is widely regarded as an acid test of political cohesion within NATO.

The precise meaning of all this for the United States cannot be gauged with certainty. At this point, however, two things do seem clear. First, a credible forward defense of Europe cannot be sustained in the absence of a significant change in the present military behavior of key allies. Continued abdication of their military responsibilities to the common defense—an abdication exemplified by persistent irresolution on defense spending, theater nuclear force modernization, and other security issues—compromises NATO's *raison d'être,* irrespective of the level of U.S. investment in Europe's defense. It is noteworthy that despite faltering allied performance in recent years, U.S. troop strength in Germany alone has been augmented since 1966 by 35,000 men, an increase of over 16 percent. Second, the military behavior of Germany and the BENELUX states is unlikely to change, because it reflects fundamental political and social undercurrents in Western Europe that appear to be inexorable.

The disintegration of NATO as an effective instrument for the forward defense of Europe is nowhere more evident than in the plummeting credibility of the Alliance's declared strategy of flexible response and forward defense. The strategy of flexible response, formally adopted in 1967, was predicated on the assumption that NATO's pronounced strategic and theater nuclear superiority over the Soviet Union was sufficient in and of itself to deter a Warsaw Pact invasion of Europe. NATO's chronic inferiority in conventional forces deployed in or readily available for combat in Europe was deemed tolerable, since nuclear superiority permitted the Alliance to escalate a conflict across the nuclear threshold to the disadvantage and ultimate defeat of the Pact.

During the past decade and a half, however, the Soviet Union, in a comprehensive military buildup unprecedented in peacetime, has managed to eliminate NATO's nuclear superiority at both the strategic and theater levels, while at the same time expanding its traditional preponderance in conventional forces. Taking advantage of America's preoccupation with Indochina and the subsequent erosion of U.S. military resolve, and playing upon Germany's faith in *Ostpolitik* as the harbinger of a lasting era of good feelings between East and West, the Soviet Union set out in the late 1960s and early 1970s to undermine NATO's military integrity.

Moscow has clearly succeeded. By attaining strategic nuclear parity with the United States, the Soviet Union has irreparably compromised the credibility of U.S. strategic forces as a deterrent to an attack on Europe alone; by creating theater nuclear forces that are now palpably superior to NATO's, the Soviet Union has demolished the utility of NATO's TNF as a means of coupling the U.S. strategic deterrent to Europe's defense and as an instrument of defeating a massive nonnuclear invasion; and by actually enhancing its longstanding superiority over NATO in conventional forces—through deployment of additional forces in Eastern Europe and the progressive elimination of the West's qualitative advantages in conventional arms—the Soviet Union has diminished what were always rather tenuous prospects for successful forward defense.

NATO's loss of strategic nuclear superiority, which many observers regarded as inevitable, was not in and of itself fatal to flexible response. Had the demise of strategic superiority been attended by retention of theater nuclear advantage and by creation of conventional defenses unambiguously capable of mounting an effective forward defense of Germany, the basic integrity of NATO's strategy could have been preserved. During the 1970s, however, the Alliance chose to live for the most part off the aging theater nuclear capital generated in the late 1950s and early 1960s; and despite mounting evidence that the Soviet Union was mustering in Eastern Europe the capacity for an unreinforced conventional blitzkrieg (thereby eliminating the degree of warning time so essential for a successful forward defense), NATO's conventional defenses were allowed to decay.

Thus, as NATO enters the 1980s, it confronts a military environment characterized by strategic nuclear parity, growing theater nuclear inferiority, and unstinting deterioration in the conventional force balance. It is a military environment that probably precludes a successful forward defense and thus diminishes credibility of the Alliance's declared strategy.

This grim picture can be altered only through a substantial conventional rearmament on the part of NATO Europe, especially Germany, whose admission to NATO in 1955 ultimately created the stringent conventional force requirements associated with forward defense. The magnitude of the Soviet theater nuclear and conventional force buildup west of the Urals demand a rearmament program of a scope far exceeding that contemplated in the Alliance's modest Long-Term Defense Plan and Long-Range Theater Nuclear Force Modernization program.

Unfortunately, perfunctory and cosmetic responses to the Soviet buildup are likely to characterize the behavior of Germany and the BENELUX states for the foreseeable future. The issue is not one of resources, but rather a growing political incapacity to address, much less sustain, new military initiatives entailing major budgetary sacrifices or possible provocation of the Soviet Union. Although small in size, antinuclear and proneutralist activist groups have successfully tapped the anxieties, fears, and uncertainties of the larger public to create strong domestic political constituencies throughout Western Europe that oppose increased defense spending.

The burgeoning influence of these forces on state policy is profound and is likely to continue unchecked. It accounts for allies who want equidistance from the two superpowers, who want defense (but not too much of it), who are more afraid of American sanctions than of events in Poland, who are more apprehensive about American than Soviet missiles, who want to be allies and mediators at the same time. It accounts for the Netherlands' refusal to accept its share of ground-launched cruise missiles slated for deployment under the LRTNF modernization program. It also accounts for Germany's behavior during the Polish crisis in December 1981.

The strategic implications of NATO's disintegration are profound. It is important to note that any future U.S. military moves designed to accommodate the new strategic imperatives in Europe are likely to be driven as much by public and congressional opinion as by military necessity. Certain political realities on this side of the Atlantic seem to have escaped the attention of many Europeans. The first is that although Europe is America's first line of defense, it is hardly the only line of defense.

The second is that the commitment of the Congress and the American people to NATO is not, and never has been, regarded as unlimited and everlasting. The postwar deployment to Europe of large U.S. ground and tactical air forces was in large measure justified as an interim commitment pending prostrated Europe's full economic and military recovery. If Europe's political tolerance for long-overdue military measures in response to expanding Soviet military power is declining, so, too, is the American taxpayer's tolerance for guaranteeing the security of allies who act as if their security were no longer jeopardized.

Finally, it is essential for Europeans to understand that American isolationism, at least in its classic garb of resistance to security entanglements in Europe that could involve the United States in war, is not dead but only dormant. Signs of its potential re-eruption are already apparent within the American foreign policy establishment and on Capitol Hill, where prospects of legislatively mandated U.S. troop withdrawals from Europe are being seriously discussed for the first time since the early 1970s.

CHANGE OUTSIDE NATO

The second major force of change stems from the intersection of supply and demand patterns for global resources and the dynamic politics of Third World regimes, particularly those in southwest Asia.

If the existing scope and character of the U.S. military presence in Europe—especially ground forces allocated to Germany's forward defense—can no longer be strategically or politically justified, demands on U.S. military power outside Europe have expanded sharply in recent years and are likely to remain unabated for at least the foreseeable future.

These new demands derive from growing U.S. dependence on fossil fuels and other critical raw materials in increasingly unstable areas of the world where the United States does not, as in Europe, enjoy politically secure military access ashore in peacetime. Such demands argue strongly not only for a shift in the geographic focus of postwar U.S. force planning but also for fundamental alterations in U.S. strategy and force structure, especially the army's.

When NATO was founded in 1949, the United States was comparatively self-sufficient in energy and most important raw materials; and where it was not, the United States, largely through the medium of friendly colonial empires, enjoyed secure and more or less uninterrupted access to overseas deposits at reasonable prices. By the 1970s, however, the United States had become vitally dependent on overseas sources of oil and a host of critical metals and minerals, secure access to which had been gravely jeopardized by three seminal developments.

The first was the collapse of Europe's colonial empires in the 1950s and early 1960s and the emergence of a plethora of weak, largely unstable, and often warring states incapable of providing the requisite political stability associated with the West's traditionally untrammeled access to their raw materials. Nowhere in the Third World today is this instability more pronounced than in the greater Persian Gulf region—the locus of over one-half of the world's proven oil reserves.

The second development was the steady recession of Western military power outside the North Atlantic area that paralleled the demise of colonialism. That recession was highlighted by Great Britain's decision in the late 1960s to withdraw all but token forces deployed "east of Suez," and by the concomitant decline in the U.S. military presence in the Third World in the wake of the Vietnam War. It was accompanied by a contraction in the size of the U.S. fleet, despite the emergence of a powerful blue-water Soviet navy sustained by ever-expanding Soviet access to far-flung naval bases and facilities.

Indeed, the third and in some respects most ominous development threatening U.S. access to vital overseas raw materials has been the relentless establishment of Soviet military power and influence in critical areas vacated by the West. An excellent case in point is Indochina, where Soviet utilization of U.S.-constructed naval facilities at Danang and Cam Ranh Bay has led to the establishment of a permanent, hostile naval presence in the South China Sea, astride one of the West's critical sea lines of communication to the Persian Gulf.

This is not to suggest that American misfortunes in the Third World are attributable solely to Soviet perfidy or that Soviet aggression, overt or via surrogates, is the principal threat to the West's economic lines of communication with the Third World. The Soviet Union did not overthrow the Shah of Iran, seize Mecca's Grand Mosque, start the present war between Iraq and Iran, or assassinate Anwar Sadat—events that have had a profoundly adverse effect on America's strategic position in the critical Persian Gulf region.

The threat of overt Soviet aggression in the Third World cannot, however, be cavalierly dismissed. The Soviet invasion of Afghanistan in December 1979 demonstrated both a capability and a willingness to employ military power directly against a benign Third World state in a manner that poses a distinct menace to American interests outside the NATO treaty area. Given the political turmoil in neighboring Iran and a history of unflagging Russian imperial designs on that country, the Soviet occupation of Afghanistan threatens to compromise defense of the entire structure of Western interests in the Persian Gulf and southwest Asia.

Whether Soviet forces will advance beyond Afghanistan remains a matter of speculation. Possible targets of a Soviet invasion, such as Iran or Pakistan, present innumerable political and logistical problems. Even in the more feasible scenarios of a lightning employment of limited Soviet airborne military force to assist local pro-Soviet factions or to preempt the arrival of U.S. forces, the price to the USSR most likely far exceeds perceived benefits.

Deterrence of overt Soviet aggression in areas of the Third World adjacent to the USSR imposes enormous demands on U.S. military power. The direct employment of Soviet forces there, however, cannot be regarded as the most likely to materialize of the myriad threats now confronting uninterrupted U.S. access to essential overseas oil and minerals. It is a comparatively unlikely threat, if for no other reason than the success the Kremlin has enjoyed to date in gaining power and influence in the Third World indirectly, via local or imported surrogate forces.

More immediate threats abound, including wars among resource-rich Third World countries, and terrorism, rebellion, or revolution within such countries. The disruptive impact of local conflicts is manifest in the continuing war between Iraq and Iran, which has virtually paralyzed oil production in Iran.

The most pressing threat to Western economic interests outside the North

Atlantic area, however, is the internal overthrow of regimes friendly to the West, either by Soviet-sponsored subversion or by purely indigenous forces hostile to the United States. Examples of governments resulting from Soviet-sponsored or sustained internal revolutions are the Qaddafi regime in Libya, the Neto regime in Angola, the Mengistu regime in Ethiopia, and the Frelimo government in Mozambique. All of these countries are positioned along critical Western maritime lines of communication with the Third World and have provided the Soviet Union varying degrees of military access to their territory.

That a national revolution unsupported by the Soviet Union can be just as detrimental to Western security interests as those that have taken place in Africa with Soviet and Cuban assistance has been evident in Iran. In fact, the collapse of the Shah underlines a central reality that the United States cannot afford to ignore in devising responses to its threatened interests outside the NATO area: the turmoil that has engulfed the non-Western world since the demise of colonialism is attributable for the most part to indigenous political, social, and economic factors over which neither the United States nor the Soviet Union has any immediate influence, much less control. While there is no doubt that the Soviet Union has sought to exploit that turmoil for its own purposes, and in so doing has contributed to instability, it would be a serious mistake to view Soviet policies in the Third World as the principal cause of instability.

Poverty, corruption, autocratic rule, excessively rapid economic development in a backward social and religious environment, gross maldistribution of wealth, inequitable ownership of land—these are the ultimate enemies of American interests in the non-Western world. As such, the problem of internal aggression, supported or not by outside forces, is less susceptible to purely military solutions than the problems of direct Soviet aggression and transnational aggression committed by a Soviet client state. To the degree that the use of U.S. forces is appropriate for supporting U.S. interests in the Third World, these forces must be sufficiently flexible and capable of reacting to threats outside the central NATO area, and even outside the southwest Asia region.

THE RDF: THE WRONG ANSWER
TO THE WRONG PROBLEM

In fairness it must be acknowledged that our defense planners have shown heightened awareness of the threats we face outside the NATO treaty area. In the wake of the Soviet invasion of Afghanistan, the Carter administration created the Rapid Deployment Force (RDF). Designed for contingencies in southwest Asia, the RDF has two rationales: deterring overt Soviet aggression in the Persian Gulf and preserving uninterrupted access to Persian Gulf oil. Although the Reagan administration has endorsed the RDF, it has been no more successful than its predecessors in overcoming the major obstacles confronting the effective application of U.S. military power in the logistically remote Persian Gulf. These obstacles include inadequacies in the size and structure of the forces available, the lack of politically secure military access ashore in peacetime, and a dearth of strategic air and sealift assets.

In the belief that a massive Soviet armored thrust into Iran constitutes the "worst case" scenario, RDF contingency planners have oriented the character and capabilities of the RDF around two dubious assumptions: first, that the RDF should be structured to deter and defeat an overt Soviet military aggression; and second, that any intervention force with such capabilities would be more than able to defeat what are perceived to be less demanding non-Soviet threats to Persian Gulf oil. This faulty assessment had led us to the wrong answer to the wrong problem.

Far more likely and immediate threats face the United States in the Persian Gulf. Recent events there have conclusively demonstrated that U.S. interests in the region are more immediately jeopardized by indigenous revolutionary upheavals and local wars than by Soviet aggression. It moreover defies logic to assume, as the Pentagon appears to, that a massive, firepower-oriented, logistically cumbersome, and land-dependent intervention force of the type now being created in the RDF would also be effective against lesser, more diffuse, and more pressing threats. In this regard, it would seem that little has been learned from America's military engagement in Indochina. A heavy force structure designed to deal with Soviet armor in open country is not necessarily capable of defeating regional adversaries practicing a different style of warfare in rugged terrain.

But irrespective of the assumptions one makes about the threats we face, one cannot escape the conclusion that the RDF is ill-prepared to deal with any contingency in a region as logistically remote as southwest Asia.

First, secure military access ashore in the Persian Gulf is essential for the RDF as it is currently organized, certainly in contingencies entailing a prolonged land campaign. To get ashore, the present RDF must have access to ports, airfields, and other reception facilities. To stay ashore, it requires continued access to proximate logistical support bases. Neither is available to the RDF in the Gulf region.

With the exception of the tiny atoll of Diego Garcia, some 2,500 miles from the Strait of Hormuz, the United States possesses no military bases in that vast area of the world stretching from Turkey to the Philippines. Nor are prospects favorable to the United States for establishing regional naval or air base facilities.

The political sensitivity of potential host nations to a permanent U.S. military presence on their own soil is certainly understandable and is manifest in their refusal to permit the peacetime stationing of any operationally significant U.S. forces on their territory. Such a presence would confirm radical Arab criticism of the conservative Gulf states as stooges of Western imperialism and thereby increase prospects for internal unrest and revolution. Cognizant of the political barriers to the establishment of a permanent U.S. military presence ashore in the Gulf region, defense planners have tried to gain contingent rights of access to selected facilities in times of crisis. Agreements along these lines have been concluded with Kenya, Somalia, and Oman; and Egypt has agreed to permit contingent U.S. force utilization of facilities at Cairo West Airport and the Red Sea port at Ras Banas.

Yet simply having the promise of access to facilities on a contingency basis is no substitute for U.S.-controlled and -operated bases that are not subject to the political calculations of host governments. The same internal political considerations that deny the United States a permanent military presence ashore in the region could well be invoked to deny the United States access to facilities in the event of a crisis, irrespective of the agreements that have been negotiated. During the October War of 1973, the United States was denied overflight rights by NATO allies, countries usually regarded as more reliable than nontreaty U.S. "friends" in the Gulf.

Even were military access in the Gulf not a problem, the combat commitment of any sizable U.S. force in the region would automatically weaken the defense of other critical U.S. interests elsewhere in the world. The decision, reaffirmed by the Reagan administration, to rely on existing military units for the RDF, almost all of which are already earmarked for NATO and the Far East, serves to widen the gap between U.S. commitments abroad and U.S. capabilities to defend them that was substantial even before Afghanistan. Barring a return to conscription in the United States or a major redistribution of military labor within NATO, U.S. force planners will be compelled, as they are today, to rely on forces unable to meet the demands of a worldwide war, including concurrent reinforcement of Europe and deployment to southwest Asia.

Compounding the problems of uncertain access and insufficient force is an inability to move forces that are available to the Gulf in a timely fashion. This problem derives from the RDF's heavy reliance on units stationed in the United States and a persistent shortfall in strategic sea- and airlift capabilities. Ongoing programs to enhance strategic mobility include (1) the procurement of additional strategic transport and tanker/cargo aircraft; (2) prepositioning afloat in the Indian Ocean, aboard twelve specialized maritime prepositioning ships (MPS), of an entire Marine Corps division's worth of equipment and thirty days' worth of food, fuel, and ammunition; and (3) purchase of eight commercial SL-7 fast deployment logistics ships. Additionally, a Near-Term Prepositioned Ship (NTPS) force has already been deployed to the Indian Ocean, consisting of eighteen ships containing equipment, supplies, fuel, and water sufficient to support a Marine Amphibious Brigade of about twelve thousand men and to sustain several USAF fighter squadrons. With the exception of the NTPS force, however, none of these mobility enhancement programs will be realized for at least several years.

The problems of uncertain access and insufficient force ought to have impelled the Pentagon toward (1) either larger force levels or a reduction in forces allocated to non-Gulf contingencies, and (2) the creation of an instrument of intervention based primarily on on-station seapower and supplemented by robust amphibious assault and other forcible-entry capabilities. An RDF of this kind could be maintained on the scene without political entanglements and would be comparatively free of logistical reliance on unstable host governments.

In sum, the RDF represents a laudable attempt to create a force capable of responding to threats outside the central NATO region. However, this effort is crippled by critical deficiencies: inadequate forces for effective penetration and sustainability, forward basing facilities, and strategic mobility. Because the resultant strategy/force mismatch cannot be resolved through higher spending rates to finance new and expanded force structures, the solution to these mismatches lies in revising and reallocating existing force structures.

A FORCE STRUCTURE PROPOSAL

The manifest disintegration of NATO as a viable collective security organization warranting the present commitment of U.S. ground forces to Europe's forward defense, and the rise of demanding new threats to vital American security interests outside the North Atlantic area, for which many residual U.S. forces are inadequate in both size and character, argue strongly for fundamental alterations in postwar American strategy and force structure. Such a strategy and force structure would be predicated on recognition of the following realities:

1. The United States cannot fulfill its present commitment to Europe's forward defense and at the same time meet the new strategic demands confronting it outside the North Atlantic area.
2. A major expansion in present U.S. force levels is neither feasible nor warranted.
3. An effective forward defense of NATO Europe is in any event no longer possible in the absence of a reversal of present political and cultural trends in Germany and the Low Countries.
4. The principal condition governing the application of U.S. military power in most places outside the North Atlantic area is the absence of politically secure military access ashore in peacetime.

In combination these realities would seem to call for the following fundamental changes in American strategy and force structure:

1. withdrawal of U.S. nonnuclear ground forces from Germany and attendant alterations in the U.S. Army's size and force structure, including expanded investment in light forces at the expense of heavy forces;
2. a major expansion in U.S. naval power and seaborne force projection capabilities;

3. creation of a new global strategy based primarily on sea power and seaborne force projection capabilities and oriented primarily toward non-NATO contingencies.

PROPOSED CHANGES
IN ARMY FORCE STRUCTURE

If a forward nonnuclear land-based defense of NATO is no longer politically feasible, irrespective of the presence of U.S. ground forces in Germany, then those forces should be removed; and if the United States is to abandon its ground participation in a forward defense, then the present size and structure of the U.S. Army, over half of which is stationed in or slated to reinforce Germany, can no longer be justified.

A modest reduction in the size of the U.S. Army would permit a significant expansion in sea power and seaborne force projection capabilities—the medium of military power best suited as the cutting edge for dealing with contingencies in the Persian Gulf and elsewhere in the Third World where the United States is denied politically secure military access ashore.

Adopting a maritime strategy in place of the present focus on NATO's central front would not eliminate the need for substantial ground forces; history has repeatedly demonstrated (the U.S. Pacific campaign in World War II is a good example) that naval and air power alone are rarely sufficient to defeat a determined and competent adversary. A strategy of the kind demanded by the political conditions governing U.S. military power in most places outside Europe, however, calls for ground forces different in character from the heavy, logistically ponderous armored and mechanized formations associated with a forward defense of Europe. It places a premium on comparatively light, strategically mobile units; on air-transportable forces; on forces deployed at or deployable by sea, and capable of being projected from sea to shore; and on forces able, if required, to take defended beachheads and other objectives. It places a premium, in short, on the kind of forces embodied today in the U.S. Marine Corps and the U.S. Army's 18th Airborne Corps and other specialized light infantry units.

The proposed alterations in the character and focus of U.S. general purpose forces would not necessarily require a significant increase in the present total active-duty military manpower of 2.1 million personnel, since a smaller army would in part offset a larger navy. A major expansion in existing U.S. force levels designed to cover adequately both the traditional U.S. commitment to Europe and the new strategic requirements outside the NATO area would in any event be politically difficult to sustain as long as key NATO allies refuse to pull their military weight, even for their own defense. It would also, as noted, be difficult to sustain economically. For U.S. force planners the real choices are thus likely to be made—and ought to be made—within the framework of modest increases in existing aggregate force levels. The issue is one of reallocation rather than major expansion.

The withdrawal of U.S. ground forces from Europe would be undertaken on the same premise that underlay the Guam Doctrine proclaimed by the Nixon administration in 1969, namely that our allies are more than capable of mustering the manpower and hardware for their own defense on the ground, although the United States will continue to provide air, naval, and (in Europe's case) nuclear forces for their defense. Thus, while U.S. ground forces would be withdrawn, U.S. tactical air forces would remain in place, along with a substantial naval presence. The inherent strategic mobility of naval and tactical air power, in contrast to heavy ground forces, makes European-based U.S. naval and air units available for rapid deployment to crisis areas outside Europe. U.S. theater nuclear forces would also remain in Europe, but only as long as their recurring modernization is not politically torpedoed by host governments. The United States should not be in the business of fielding palpably obsolete forces simply to accommodate allied hysteria on nuclear questions.

The retention in Europe of existing U.S. tactical air and theater nuclear forces, to which in Germany alone over sixty thousand personnel are assigned, would make it impossible for the Soviet Union to avoid early and heavy combat with Americans in the event of war, especially since the preemptive destruction of NATO air bases and nuclear storage sites is accorded the highest priority by Soviet force planners. Thus the argument, which may be anticipated in some European political circles, that a withdrawal of U.S. ground forces is tantamount to an abjuration of the U.S. commitment to Europe's defense would be valid only on acceptance of the preposterous assumption that an American president would simply walk away from a situation in which tens of thousands of U.S. military men and their dependents were being killed or wounded.

In sum, the United States would abandon neither its membership in NATO nor its commitment to Europe's defense; only the character of that commitment would be altered. Indeed, if attended by adequate compensatory allied measures, withdrawal of U.S. ground forces would stimulate a more effective division of labor within NATO. America's comparative military advantage has always resided in naval and air power, and the qualitative superiority of U.S. warships and combat aircraft remains unchallenged within the Alliance. In contrast, the Continental military traditions of Germany are still reflected in the *Bundeswehr*'s primary focus on the land battle. The quality of the German army and its weapons remains second to none in Western Europe.

A division of military labor along the lines suggested above, which ought to be welcomed by those allied political leaders who have expressed serious reservations about the quality of the U.S. All-Volunteer Army, could encompass U.S. procurement of European ground force weapons and equipment in exchange for European acquisition of U.S. tactical aircraft.

The withdrawal of ground troops would be unconditional (that is, carried out irrespective of future allied military behavior), although it would be conducted slowly and evenly, over a period of fifteen to twenty years, thus avoiding the kind of political shock and military disruption inherent in a precipitous Mansfield-style pull-out. An abrupt withdrawal forced by an aroused and ill-informed Congress must be circumvented at all costs. A declaratory program undertaken incrementally over fifteen to twenty years would serve as a strong hedge against politically destabilizing congressional intervention. It also would afford the allies sufficient time to undertake compensatory increases and improvements in their own forces, such as reequipping and upgrading the readiness of their reserve forces. Their failure to do so would simply reaffirm the wisdom of removing U.S. ground forces.

Second, sets of equipment prepositioned in Europe for U.S. reinforcing units based in the United States, along with war reserve stocks of ammunition and equipment maintained on the Continent for the U.S. Army Europe, would also be returned to the United States. The continued retention in the United States of costly ground forces dedicated to Europe's reinforcement would be unnecessary and incompatible with renunciation of U.S. participation in NATO's forward defense on the ground.

Some army units returning from Europe would be demobilized with the aim of achieving an overall reduction in the army's active force structure on the order of two to three divisions and 100,000 to 200,000 personnel. Candidates for elimination would be armored, mechanized infantry and other heavy, strategically immobile formations of the kind now stationed in Europe. Strategically mobile units like the 82nd Airborne Division would be retained in the force structure, and top priority would be accorded to development of light armored formations possessing a high level of tactical mobility and firepower at minimum expense to their strategic mobility. The need for such forces has already been recognized in the army's "AirLand Battle 2000" doctrine.

In partial compensation for smaller active army forces, selected National Guard and other reserve component units would be substantially upgraded in readiness and quality and integrated closely with active parent formations, whose deployability would be staggered according to anticipated need and the availability of strategic lift.

PROPOSED CHANGES
IN NAVY FORCE STRUCTURE

As noted, a reduction in the size of the NATO-oriented U.S. Army would yield budgetary resources for a major expansion in naval and seaborne force projection capabilities—the kind of military power best suited for most contingencies outside Europe. To be sure, sea power and sea-based intervention forces have limited utility in situations demanding sustained inland combat beyond the reach of amphibious assault forces and carrier-based air power. It is important to recognize, however, that the Arabian peninsula and most other economically critical spots in the Third World possess extensive and largely undefended coastlines, or are otherwise easily accessible from the sea by surface or heliborne amphibious forces. Moreover, implicit in the substitution of a maritime strategy for the present heavy investment in Continental warfare in central Europe is a deliberate avoidance of large-scale, sustained inland combat on the Eurasian land mass against first-line Soviet forces. The successful prosecution of sustained inland combat in the Third World would in any event be contingent on secure coastal military lodgments, which could be gained only by the ability to project military power from sea to shore. Finally, unlike forces withheld in the United States for rapid deployment overseas, a sea-based intervention force could be maintained on station in potential crisis areas, affording both quicker responsiveness and greater deterrence. In major contingencies requiring substantial transfer of forces from the United States, on-station sea power and force projection capabilities would serve as both the cutting edge of the U.S. military presence and the guarantor of secure access ashore for those reinforcements.

Meeting the new strategic requirements confronting the United States in the Persian Gulf, and elsewhere in the Third World where the United States does not enjoy the operational and logistical benefits of politically secure military access ashore in peacetime, demands significant alterations in present U.S. naval and seaborne force projection capabilities.

First and foremost is the need for a larger navy, of perhaps six hundred to eight hundred ships. The optimum size of the U.S. fleet has been a subject of controversy throughout American history; there is a virtual consensus among force planners today, however, that the existing fleet is inadequate to meet a three-ocean commitment, an inadequacy manifest in the endless difficulties the U.S. Navy has encountered in maintaining even one carrier battle group in the Indian Ocean without seriously degrading naval commitments in the Atlantic and Pacific oceans.

There is, moreover, a growing recognition that a substantial expansion in American sea power is incompatible with a continuing fixation on endowing most ships with the maximum combination of operational capabilities. The result of this fixation—evident in the present fleet—is reliance on evermore expensive and technologically fragile platforms that can be obtained only in steadily diminishing quantities and at the price of sustaining an adequate simultaneous force in critical areas. A significant increase in the size of the U.S. Navy can be gained only through acceptance of smaller, less expensive, more specialized ship designs, including light carriers, diesel-electric submarines, and merchant vessels modified for selected auxiliary and supporting combat missions. The aim of simply expanding the navy's present force structure, which is vested largely in a handful of multi-billion-dollar big-deck carrier task forces dedicated to surviving a war with the Soviet Union, is neither fiscally feasible nor warranted by likely operational requirements in the Third World. The issue is not big-deck nuclear carriers and $1.5 billion nuclear-propelled ballistic missile submarines versus our smaller, simpler, and cheaper surface and subsurface platforms; the issue is rather the desirability of supplementing the navy's present force structure with a larger number of smaller, less expensive ships suitable for comparatively less demanding maritime contingencies in the Third World. At some point numbers do count, and the U.S. Navy must be prepared to make an investment in numbers, even at the expense of individual ship capability.

An investment in numbers would seem especially imperative in light of the commitment to regaining a maritime superiority officially defined as an ability to "prevail" simultaneously over "the combined threat of our adversaries" in the Pacific, Indian, and Atlantic oceans, including the Norwegian Sea. To prevail in the Indian Ocean and Norwegian Sea alone would require the commitment of at least six carrier battle groups, severely denuding naval coverage of such other vital areas as the Caribbean, western Pacific, and the Atlantic. That such a definition of maritime superiority can be satisfied simply by the addition of three new big-deck carrier battle groups to the present twelve is difficult to fathom. Several more would seem to be required.

Increases in present levels of amphibious shipping and naval gunfire support, now at their lowest point since the late 1940s, are also necessary if the United States is to possess a comprehensive seaborne force projection capability that is truly independent of the political good will of unstable potential host countries in the Third World. The U.S. Navy's current sixty-seven active and reserve amphibious vessels are capable of lifting only one of the Marine's Corps's divisions, and since the ships are scattered throughout the navy's various fleets, a minimum of thirty days would be required to assemble in one place the shipping necessary to mount a division-sized assault. The Joint Chiefs of Staff force planning requirement for 1986 specified a minimum of two divisions' worth of amphibious shipping, which would permit the continuous deployment of a brigade-sized assault force in the critical Persian Gulf region.

To enhance naval gunfire capabilities, particularly all-weather fire support for amphibious forces during the assault, four *Iowa*-class battleships have been recalled to service. This solution is inadequate, however, since the enormous firepower of their 16-inch naval rifles is distributed among but four platforms, only one or two of which, given the navy's ship rotation policies, is likely to be available at any one time. Consideration should be given to the installation aboard the Navy's thirty-one *Spruance*-class destroyers of the new and fully tested Mark 71 lightweight 8-inch gun, and to recalling the two *Salem*-class heavy cruisers (each mounting nine automatic 8-inch guns) now in mothballs.

Expanded investment in maritime prepositioning also would seem imperative. Present plans to preposition a marine division's worth of equipment afloat in the Indian Ocean should be enlarged to include a second division set, which could easily be obtained from prepositioned U.S. Army stocks withdrawn from Europe. The second set should be for an armored or mechanized infantry division. It makes little sense to preposition light divisions afloat while attempting to fly or ship in heavy divisions. Maritime prepositioning, however, is unavoidable, given the refusal of potential host nations in the Persian Gulf and elsewhere in the Third World to permit the United States to preposition equipment and combat supplies on their territory. The inherent mobility and security of ships at sea also provide greater military flexibility in a crisis as well as substantial invulnerability to the kind of terrorist and guerrilla attacks that shore-based sites almost certainly would invite.

PROPOSED CHANGES IN THE RDF FORCE STRUCTURE

Finally, in concert with the above measures, the present Rapid Deployment Force should be replaced by a comparatively small, agile, tactically capable intervention force that is based at and supplied from the sea, governed by a single, unified command, and supported—as proposed—by expanded sea power, especially forcible entry capabilities. Such an intervention force would stress quality at the expense of size, immediate responsiveness at the expense of delayed augmentation from the United States, and logistical self-sufficiency at the expense of dependence on facilities ashore.

CONCLUSION

The proposed fundamental restructuring and reorientation of U.S. military power would be accompanied by delineation of a new U.S. strategy predicated on an explicit recognition of the strategic imperatives imposed on the United States by NATO's disintegration as an effective collective security organization and the rise of new and unique threats to American security outside Europe. The hallmark of the strategy would be avoidance of major sustained inland ground combat in Europe against Soviet forces, whose requirements can and should be met by U.S. allies directly threatened by Soviet and other hostile ground forces and by increased reliance on military power capable of operating effectively on and along the Eurasian periphery. It is a strategy not only dictated by the strategic realities now confronting the United States, but one also far more congruent with America's geographic position as an island continent possessing profound security interests across the seas. America's natural advantage has always resided in sea power, and the time has come to exploit that advantage to the utmost.

10

HEAVY VERSUS LIGHT FORCES:
A QUESTION OF BALANCE

John D. Mayer, Jr.

Mayer argues that the U.S. force structure has too few heavy (armor and mechanized infantry) divisions to effectively counter the Soviet-style heavy divisions present in Europe, southwest Asia, and northeast Asia. He maintains that three light army divisions are adequate to meet possible insurgencies and that the remaining eight light army divisions in the active and reserve force should be converted to heavy divisions. Mayer sees current initiatives in upgrading strategic sealift capabilities as resolving the problem of strategic deployability presently facing heavy divisions.

INTRODUCTION

In a 1980 White Paper detailing his vision of the army of the 1980s, General Edward C. Meyer emphasized the need for improving the Army's ability to project combat power worldwide.[1] His proposal for "lighter, more capable forces" contrasted sharply with the direction in which the army had been moving. An underlying assumption of his proposal was that the army could no longer focus solely on its NATO mission but must look more broadly at the world and be prepared to move a relatively large, capable force anywhere, in the least possible time.

Because the army was primarily oriented toward the defense of Europe, its plans had called for the conversion of light infantry divisions to heavy mechanized divisions over a period of time. The theory was that light infantry would be much less effective in the defense of Europe than heavy or mechanized infantry with their large number of tanks and armored vehicles. Meyer and other critics of this theory argued that the planned conversions would further orient the army toward the European theater, reduce the army's flexibility to respond rapidly elsewhere in the world, and cost a large amount of money to acquire the tanks, artillery, and armored vehicles necessary to convert a light infantry division into a heavy mechanized division. As a result, the army sought relief from further "heavying up" (as these conversions became known) by proposing to greatly improve light infantry without converting them to heavy mechanized divisions. A decision was made to defer the conversion of the 9th Infantry Division to a heavy division and designate it instead as the test bed for a High Technology Light Division (HTLD).

This action fueled the longstanding "heavy" versus "light" controversy in that it signaled a moratorium on "heavying up" the army. In some circles it was seen as an opportunity to reverse the heavying up process and perhaps even to convert some of the CONUS-based heavy divisions to lighter, more capable divisions.

Improvements that enhance the overall tactical mobility and firepower of light divisions are long overdue. But light forces alone cannot be relied on for successful execution of offensive actions against much of the expected threat. Only heavy forces currently possess sufficient tactical mobility and firepower to mount offensive operations. It is the thesis of this chapter that the current mix of heavy and light forces, far from being too heavy, may not even be consistent with future tactical doctrine, considering the nature of the threat they are likely to face.

The first section of this chapter looks at the mix of heavy and light forces currently available and the nature of the expected threat. The second section examines critical issues associated with the heavy-versus-light-division debate: rapid deployment, offensive power and battlefield mobility, and affordability. The concluding section presents alternatives for organizing future light and heavy army divisions in order to capture the benefits of both light and heavy units and to strengthen the total force capability.

CURRENT U.S. FORCES AND GLOBAL REQUIREMENTS

It would be a serious mistake to view the heavy-light mix from the perspective of the active army alone. U.S. ability to respond to national commitments is based on the total force capability. General Meyer recognized this when he stated that "capabilities of the other services will play an important role in determining the precise force for a specific operation."[2] The natural extension of this concept is that the capabilities of both the army and the marines must play an important role in structuring the total force capability.

Table 10.1. U.S. Divisions

Service	Heavy	Light
Army		
Active	10	6
Reserve	3	5
Marine Corps		
Active	0	3
Reserve	0	1
Total	13	15

Source: U.S. Department of Defense, *Annual Report to the Congress, Fiscal Year 1983*, p. III-5.

Heavy forces are generally structured alike, although the type of equipment in each may differ. This is not the case, however, for light forces. Army light forces range from the very light and deployable 82d Airborne Division to the fairly heavy 2d Infantry Division. A typical light division in the active and reserve forces consists primarily of light infantry battalions supported by one mechanized infantry and one armored battalion. This type of division has the least tactical mobility and antitank firepower of any of the army divisions (with the possible exception of the airborne division), yet eight of the twenty-four army divisions are configured roughly this way.

Marine divisions differ significantly from army light divisions in structure and capabilities. Consisting of approximately seventeen thousand people, these divisions normally have three infantry regiments, a tank battalion with seventy M60 tanks, an assault amphibious vehicle battalion with 208 amphibious landing vehicles, an artillery regiment with 105-mm, 155-mm, and 8-inch howitzers, and a reconnaissance battalion. A Marine Corps air wing with helicopters and fixed wing aircraft usually accompanies the division into combat. Although large in structure, these divisions are primarily light infantry divisions and should be considered as such in assessing total force capability. Table 10.1 shows the current U.S. division structure.

Indications are that this structure may change slightly over the next several years. Army plans call for consolidating three separate reserve component brigades to form an additional reserve component division, and for converting the 9th Infantry Division into the prototype High Technology Light Division by 1986. The exact structure and equipment for the division are still being tested and evaluated.

From the present structure of U.S. forces, one might conclude that much of the threat they potentially face is light and technologically unsophisticated. This is not the case. In fact, in the area of the world where we presently place our greatest military emphasis, the threat comes from armor-heavy forces with a high level of technological sophistication.

The threat to Europe is, and will continue to be, heavy armor, since that is basic to the composition of the Soviet and other Warsaw Pact armies. In the Far East, a review of the threat posed by the North Koreans contributed to the decision to retain the 2d Infantry Division in Korea. In southwest Asia and the Persian Gulf area, the composition of the threat has changed dramatically in the past six years with the proliferation of Soviet equipment in the forces of Libya, Iraq, and Syria. General Meyer has stated:

> Five years ago I would have put a different kind of force into the Middle East and into the Persian Gulf than I would today, because there was far less sophisticated equipment in that area than there is today. We must keep in mind that we do not decide what type of equipment we need. That decision is made for us by the Soviets and the equipment they are proliferating. In other words, the kind of equipment that we find around the world that has to be considered.[3]

These scenarios calling for armored units represent the most serious threat that ground forces should expect to face. Lighter forces are appropriate for countering insurgent activity in Africa, Central and South America, and Southeast Asia in order to assist friendly government forces. It is unlikely that counterinsurgent actions would require a large number of heavy forces. Rather, these would be lighter, mobile infantry forces well schooled in such operations.

Light forces are always useful to a degree. Their greatest utility is in areas where the threat is light and relatively unsophisticated. They can be employed to a limited extent against a heavy armor threat, but they cannot provide the offensive power needed to defeat such a force. Improvements in light forces have centered on upgrading their antitank defensive capability and their ground mobility. Recent testimony before the House Committee on Armed Services indicated that with these improvements "the light forces . . . will be well suited for defense and limited offensive actions, operations in urban areas and rear areas."[4] These steps to enhance light forces are long overdue. It would be a mistake, however, to see these improved light forces as a total substitute for armored forces.

MAJOR ISSUES IN THE LIGHT VERSUS HEAVY DEBATE

Deployability. Proponents of light forces often argue that the army must have more light divisions capable of being deployed rapidly by air. Clearly, as shown in table 10.2, a heavy division does not deploy as rapidly by air as does a light division. But there are several aspects to this. Even the lightest division, the 82d Airborne, with its necessary support would require two to three weeks to deploy to southwest Asia, assuming use of virtually all military transport.[5] Although some of the combat units could be there in a matter of days, their limited mobility and offensive striking power limit the environment in which they can be employed and the threat they could face. In contrast, a mechanized division placed aboard fast, roll-on/roll-off (RORO)

Table 10.2. Time to Deliver One Army Division to Southwest Asia, Using All Available Airlift or All Fast Sealift

Type of Division	Days Required by Air	To "Close" by Sea
Airborne	14	24
Airmobile	14	24
Mechanized	27	24

Source: U.S. Airlift Forces: Enhancement Alternatives for NATO and Non-NATO Contingencies, Congressional Budget Office (1979).

ships would arrive with much of its support in southwest Asia within three to four weeks.[6] Once there, moreover, it would have the offensive capability suitable for countering the expected threat.

In short, one heavy division with sufficient support to sustain itself can be deployed by sea in less time than two light infantry divisions can be deployed by air. Once deployment by sea begins, it can be sustained at a much higher tonnage rate than air deployment. Sealift is not a substitute for airlift in the opening days of mobilization. Rapid delivery of small numbers of light forces may have an enormous political effect or deterrent effect upon an aggressor, even though their combat utility might be limited in scope. But the deployment argument seems to justify only a limited requirement for light divisions, not necessarily the eleven currently in the army structure. The force projection capability of the United States may be better served by obtaining more fast sealift dedicated to deploying heavy divisions with their superior offensive tactical capability than by investing in more, albeit improved, light divisions to deploy by air.

Tactical Considerations. Recently, the army has begun to put forward a new tactical concept for the future. Entitled the "AirLand Battle," the new concept emphasizes maneuver and offensive operations. The concept has important implications for the future force structure in that it requires a force that is very mobile, yet possesses the necessary firepower to conduct offensive operations and defeat an armor threat. Currently, heavy divisions in the army have the equipment and structure to implement this doctrine; light divisions do not. Therefore, current light forces cannot execute the maneuver doctrine that the army proposes for the future. In the past, light division proponents have argued that they can fight an armor-heavy force by relying on their ability to dig in and provide reinforced overhead cover (using the traditional methods infantrymen have used for years) and engage armor with a multitude of antiarmor missiles. This "Maginot Line" type of approach is defensive in nature, however, and therefore not generally supportive of AirLand Battle requirements.

Table 10.3. Fiscal Year 1981 Direct Costs
(In millions of dollars)

Direct Costs	Infantry Division	Mechanized Division
Investment cost		
Nonrecurring	726	1,016
Recurring	47	67
Operating cost		
Nonrecurring	317	320
Recurring	400	409

Source: Army Force Planning Cost Handbook, U.S. Department of Defense Office of the Comptroller of the Army (May 1981), pp. IV–11, IV–14, 15, 20, 21.

The army recognition of this led to proposals to create a new "high technology division." The 9th Infantry Division at Fort Lewis, Washington, is currently testing the concept of a High Technology Light Division (HTLD). The object is to see whether high technology can provide a division with the deployability of an airborne division and the antitank combat power of a heavy division. The tests are designed to evaluate structure and equipment that will be consistent with the army's future tactical concepts. However, the testimony cited earlier before the House Committee on Armed Services indicates that the light divisions that evolve from the HTLD tests will be suited primarily for defensive and limited offensive operations. That testimony indicated further that the light divisions will not have the capability to defeat defenses fortified by armor forces. Such offensive operations would require tanks.[7] Even with projected improvements, these new light divisions may not have sufficient offensive firepower to replace heavy divisions in the AirLand battle roles.

Budget Implications. Resources will continue to be a constraint on force structure changes for the army. This is especially true now when the army is trying to modernize virtually all major combat systems across its current force. However, there is a myth about the relative costs of heavy and light divisions. As table 10.3 indicates, the initial investment for a heavy division is considerably higher than for a light division.[8] However, once the initial investment has been made, the cost of operating each is nearly equivalent. In the long run, a heavy division costs approximately 9 percent more than current light divisions. The table suggests that an argument for light forces based on operating costs may be overstated, especially when the relative effectiveness of both forces is considered. Generally, static and dynamic analyses indicate that the effectiveness of a heavy force exceeds that of a light force by a significant amount.[9] On a cost-effectiveness basis, therefore, the heavy force rates higher.

The cost differences between heavy and light divisions may narrow considerably, since planned improvements in light forces will not come cheaply. The projected average program cost in fiscal year 1983 dollars for light armored vehicles is over $786,000, a figure that is far higher than the slightly over $300,000 that the army had originally planned for. Development and acquisition costs for a Mobile Protected Gun (MPG) capable of providing rapid assault fire and antitank fire for the division will also be quite high. At least one army-sponsored study estimated that the cost of an MPG would be comparable to the cost of the Bradley fighting vehicle.[10]

Converting light divisions to heavy divisions is fiscally possible within a constrained budget if it is done over time. As the army continues to modernize with new tanks and fighting vehicles, older M60 tanks and M113 squad carriers will be available for issuing to newly converted light divisions. This would be an evolutionary process that effectively converted the current light infantry divisions at minimum expense. It would enhance the army's ability to execute its planned tactical doctrine with more divisions. It would provide an increased capability to the reserve forces where a large percentage of the army's light divisions are concentrated. When and if they are mobilized, reserves would most likely encounter an armor threat. This evolution of light divisions to heavy would demonstrate to the reserves that they are in fact an integral part of the national defense strategy and would signal a greater willingness on the part of the United States to meet the challenge of projected threats.

DIVISION STRUCTURE ALTERNATIVES

The army is currently revising the composition of both its heavy and light divisions. These plans, however, presume no change in the relative mix of heavy and light divisions in the army. Mix is an important issue that should be considered when decisions are being made on the future composition of heavy and light divisions. The army thus has an opportunity to implement its plans to modernize its forces while examining what should be the appropriate mix of heavy and light divisions in view of future missions, tactical doctrine, and threat force capabilities.

It may be time to consider some new alternatives to division compositions in light of changes in the threat forces, in the global mission, and in the tactical doctrine. An alternative composition for heavy and light divisions is examined below.

Current heavy divisions contain eleven maneuver battalions. Recently, the army announced that heavy divisions will convert to a "division 86" structure with ten maneuver battalions. Although major changes are to be made in the combat support units of the division, the remaining ten maneuver battalions will continue to reflect a mix between armor and mechanized infantry that closely parallels the current balanced structure.[11]

The German army has taken a fresh approach toward structuring its heavy divisions. Recognizing the fact that infantry units can play an important role in warfare and contribute to the effectiveness of heavy forces, the German army now contains two light infantry battalions in each division. These battalions come under the direct control of the division commander. He, in turn, is free to use them as he sees fit, depending on the terrain and enemy situation presented in his division sector. The German position on the role of light infantry is quite clear.

> The German Army is of the opinion that an "infantry concept" is no suitable substitute for the concept of tank-heavy mechanized formations which are capable of mobile employment, even in defense operations, and which are also able to counter the expected threat since such a concept will not enable us to give credibility to the concept of "flexible response." On the other hand, nonmechanized or light infantry is a means well suited to improve forward defense—especially under the environmental conditions prevailing in the Central Region—if employed as a supplementary capability.[12]

This approach is worth considering for heavy divisions in the U.S. Army. Future divisions could be designated as heavy divisions with a fixed mix of armor and mechanized battalions.[13] Two additional light infantry battalions could be assigned to a division under the direct control of the division commander. The light infantry battalions could be mobile in that their transportation would be light, wheeled vehicles. Vehicles would not have to be armored, since their purpose would be to transport light infantry quickly over roads. This concept is consistent with future tactical doctrine, since it would allow the division commander to use light infantry where their effectiveness is optimal[14] and to employ the armor and mechanized units for the main thrust of the maneuver. Conceptually, at least, the division commander would have the structural tools at his disposal to execute a successful mission regardless of the environment.

Alternative plans for light divisions might also be appropriate. The preceding discussion indicated that perhaps fewer, not more, light infantry divisions will be needed to counter expected threats. Maintaining separate configurations for airborne, airmobile, and light infantry divisions may not be appropriate or desirable. Although airborne and airmobile units do have a place in light forces, these could be incorporated within the total capabilities of a new light division.

Plans for the new High Technology Light Division do not provide sufficient airborne spaces or helicopters to allow the division to conduct airborne or air assault operations at the level of the battalion or higher. Although ground mobility improvements for the HTLD will be a major advance over current light divisions, bolder concepts may be appropriate. Hybrid divisions incorporating the best capabilities of airborne, airmobile, and high-technology divisions may be worthy of consideration. One brigade would be basically an infantry brigade, airborne qualified, capable of conducting airborne and airmobile operations. The divisions would need a battalion of Blackhawk helicopters to provide the necessary air assault lift. The remaining two brigades could be configured along the lines of the HTLD brigades. Each brigade would have three battalions, two mobile infantry battalions with tracked or wheeled squad carriers and one light tank battalion. The hybrid division could replace the airborne and airmobile divisions and the HTLD in the active army structure. By designing three divisions alike, oriented primarily toward worldwide rapid reinforcement missions, at least one division could be ready to deploy at all times.

These alternative force compositions reflect the belief that light infantry does have a place on the armor battlefield, as well as the importance of strategic deployability in developing a force mix and the possibility that initially, light infantry may be the only force capable of deploying rapidly. The proposed heavy forces could counter future threats and execute an offensive tactical doctrine. The light forces could fight and move on the battlefield regardless of the environment.

CONCLUSION

Recently, there has been much talk about the nation's ability to match national strategies with military capabilities. The secretary of defense has indicated that the interests of the United States are global in nature and not necessarily limited to a particular region of the world. This does not imply, however, that each service must structure its force so as to be able to respond to every contingency.

It is clear that the Soviet and Warsaw Pact emphasis on armor and motorized infantry units will continue far into the future. Likewise, Third World countries supported by the Soviets share the same emphasis on armor and motorized infantry. Soviet equipment and tactical doctrine are certain to be encountered when and if U.S. ground forces are committed in battle. Because of the current force structure, much of the U.S. response to this kind of threat will be made with light forces.

The Marine Corps, with a special amphibious mission, will continue to be a relatively light force with a global orientation. The U.S. Army should also maintain a global orientation, but its force need not be predominantly light. The army should continue to orient itself to the Soviet threat and to the Soviet-style threat of Third World countries, but this does not mean that it should emphasize light forces. The mix of light and heavy forces should be governed by the threat the army can expect to face, the strategy it will have to implement, and the unique capabilities of the other services that will complement the army's ground forces. While deployability should be a consideration, only a limited number of army divisions need be deployable by air; others can be moved by sea. The costs of operating light divisions are only slightly less than those of heavy divisions, but the effectiveness of a heavy division is much greater.

In view of the preceding discussion, it is very difficult to justify having eleven light divisions in the total army. Since reserve component divisions will certainly be late-deploying units charged primarily with a reinforcing mission, their composition should be based on combat effectiveness for the mission. Rapid deployment should not be a major factor for reserve component divisions. Since they will most likely face an armor threat on the European battlefield, they should be structured to counter that threat. Until it can be proven that light divisions, even new and improved ones, are more effective than heavy divisions on the European battlefield, reserve component divisions should be heavy.

Active component divisions, however, need to provide a balance of forces capable of fighting in Europe, southwest Asia, Korea, or any number of other places. Some emphasis, although not all, should be placed on developing light divisions that are rapidly deployable by air. As shown earlier, almost two complete light divisions could move to southwest Asia by air before the first heavy division arrives by sea. But once sealift arrives, the rapid deployment advantage of light divisions over heavy is very low. Unless it can be shown that the overall effectiveness of the light division is nearly equivalent to the effectiveness of a heavy division, the use of light divisions, beyond what is necessary for rapid mobility, may not be a cost-effective approach. Therefore, it is very difficult to justify six light divisions in the active army today. Certainly some light divisions are necessary, and at least two are needed for rapid mobility. But when you consider the potential conflict areas, the potential threat, and the combined capabilities of army and marine forces, the army's current mix of heavy and light divisions is certainly subject to question.

The structuring of heavy and light divisions is another area that needs close attention. This chapter has offered an alternative for each type of division, but other alternatives merit consideration. The army has an opportunity now to develop a total structure that will support future tactical doctrine and enhance the army's capability to fight effectively.

NOTES

1. Gen. Edward C. Meyer, Chief of Staff, U.S. Army, *A Framework for Molding the Army of the 1980s into a Disciplined, Well-Trained Fighting Force,* White Paper (1980), p. 1.

2. Ibid., p. 5.

3. "The Army of the Future," a conversation with General Edward C. Meyer, American Enterprise Institute for Public Policy Research (27 January 1981), p. 6.

4. House Committee on Armed Services, *Hearings on Military Posture and H.R. 2970,* 1982, pt. 2.

5. The fourteen days cited in table 2 assumes the use of virtually all military air transport. In actuality, much of the early-deploying aircraft in most contingencies would be used to deploy air force fighter squadrons. Therefore, the actual time for deploying the first army division by air would exceed fourteen days.

6. Eight SL7s have been purchased by the navy for deploying army heavy divisions. Although originally configured as container ships, four of these ships are being converted to the RORO configuration with funds provided in fiscal year 1982. Funds for converting the remaining four are requested for fiscal year 1984. Conversion should be completed by fiscal year 1986.

7. *Military Posture and H.R. 2970,* pt. 2.

8. Although these figures do not reflect any modernization costs, they provide a basis of comparison between heavy and light divisions.

9. Supporting analysis for the HTLD concept compared the relative combat power of the heavy divisions with that of infantry divisions. In that analysis, the army indicated that the heavy division has nearly twice the combat power of the standard infantry division.

10. In 1980, the army was concluding its work on a research and development program called High Survivability Test Vehicle-Lightweight (HSTV-L). This was the forerunner of the MPG program. To get a perspective on the cost of a future MPG system, a model was run that used the most likely design of an MPG at that time and projected a cost. That analysis indicated that in constant dollars, the MPG would be equivalent in cost to the fighting vehicle.

11. *Commanders Call,* DA Pamphlet 360–866 (1982), pp. 8–9.

12. "The German View of the Role of Infantry on the Battlefield," Report of a symposium jointly sponsored by the RUSI and the Commander, ACE Mobile Force (Land) (28 April 1980), p. 69.

13. The proper mix of armor and mechanized battalions could be decided in the future. Consideration should be given not only to the threat, but to the tactical doctrine that will have to be implemented.

14. The two light infantry battalions could be effective in prepared defensive positions using antiarmor systems to delay and disrupt an attacker's advance. Even under the maneuver concept, a forward defensive force will be necessary. Employment of the light infantry battalions in urban areas not suited for armor warfare or in heavily wooded areas not easily negotiated by tanks is also appropriate within a division sector.

V

MODERNIZATION AND
WEAPONS ACQUISITION ISSUES

Contentions concerning weapons design and defense procurement have headlined the public debate over the military reform agenda. The other portions of the discussion that address peacetime strategy, doctrine, force structure, and defense reorganization have proven to be of little interest to an American public disturbed about record budget deficits, unemployment, high interest rates, and the general condition of the economy. To the degree that the average citizen is concerned with defense, many have been attracted to modernization and weapons acquisition issues.

Why have other issues, which also hold potential for fiscal savings, not seized the public's attention? Congress, under public pressure to reduce record deficits, must consider the political liabilities that are part of any proposal to trim the defense budget. For example, reinstitution of the draft might well save more money and do more to improve the quality of the force than any other single action Congress could take. However, legislators consider support for the draft a political liability. Weapons acquisition issues, in contrast, offer politicians budget-cutting alternatives that have high political payoffs and relatively low political price tags—as long as the system is manufactured in someone else's district or state.

The taxpaying public is attracted to this portion of the reform agenda because the billions of dollars involved are attributable to specific weapons, which consequently serve as convenient targets for budget cutters. These issues and choices, unlike esoteric debates over strategic deterrence and arms control, can be presented in terms easily understood by the interested citizen.

Research, development, and acquisition cycles for modern weapons extend over many years. As a result, weapons systems development is plagued by uncertainties, sunk cost arguments, pork-barrel and follow-on incentives, technological imperatives, and large capital costs (which are difficult to justify or recover). In addition, deployed systems act to constrain most other aspects of military policy over the lifetime of the weapon. Finally, the extended production and procurement cycle forces budget outlays to be spread over many years. Reformers opposing overexpensive, undercapable weapons find political allies in OSD, OMB, and congressional budget cutters. Although motivated by various programmatic or fiscal concerns, these actors' political tactics converge on advocating the cancellation of whole weapons systems. In this way, it is argued, deletion of unnecessary programs will make possible long-run savings. This focus of the public debate is understandable in view of both the characteristics inherent in weapons systems design and procurement and the way the media have reported the debate.

Growing Soviet military strength has been cited by past and present administrations as justification for increases in the defense budget. In its efforts to increase overall U.S. defense capabilities, the Reagan administration—as did its predecessors—has run headlong into several built-in constraints. The first of these constraints is the ever present manpower and budgetary limits that flow largely from domestic political factors. The second is that the weapons that any administration attempts to field entered the development cycle more than a decade earlier.

In an effort to meet the Soviet threat, successive administrations, Congress, and the Pentagon have focused on weapons procurement as a partial answer to Soviet numerical superiority. Increased weapons acquisition is a highly visible, quantifiable, and, most importantly, politically inexpensive means of meeting the threat. However, the political and fiscal cost of matching Soviet military power weapon for weapon, man for man, is prohibitive. Therefore, increased procurement does not necessarily translate into more systems. Given these constraints, the trend in the weapons acquisition process is to exploit the sweetest and latest technological advantage, in an attempt to maximize battlefield effectiveness at the lowest possible force level. Furthermore, there has been a tendency to integrate this latest technology into these weapons *during* the procurement cycle. Such practices have been reinforced by the often-repeated argument that America's comparative advantage resides in its technological superiority.

The irony is, however, that since the procurement process tends to lag behind the pace of technological advances, there is an inevitable temptation to chase improvements in technology. The B-1B bomber, the M2 (Bradley) fighting vehicle, and the F/A-18 (Hornet) fighter are often-cited examples of this continual tendency toward integrating the latest technology. While critics have charged that these weapons fail to meet specified performance standards and have ballooned in cost, historically such arguments have received little support in the defense community. Today the debate has become even more polarized because the administration has invoked the ideological charge that the Kremlin is bent on "world domination" and is "the focus of evil in the modern world." Faced with meeting this immediate threat, supporters of the policies that produced the B-1B, M2, and F/A-18 have argued that given the constraints under which planners must operate, such weapons represent the optimal American response. These have proved powerful rejoinders to the reformers' critiques.

Many reformers argue that the high costs of today's weapons are caused by the Pentagon's fascination with technology. It is commonly argued that this fascination follows from America's cultural predisposition for technology-intensive over manpower-intensive means, or from a profit-oriented conspiracy within the military-industrial complex, or from repeated systems reengineering (to improve performance based on initial test and operational experience) during production. Accordingly, some reformers who stress the "quantity" approach propose substituting cheaper, simpler, better-tested weapons for those "quality" high-tech, gold-plated systems which, they claim, have inflated the defense budget and failed to meet performance expectations in the field. The persuasive public appeal of such arguments derives, obviously, from the alluring promise to deliver greater defense for less money.

To date, the protagonists concerned with this portion of the debate have argued that the use of the phrase "quantity versus quality" is unfair and has detracted from the true meaning of their individual messages. Perry states that for years the United States has relied on its nuclear forces to "paper over the deficiencies of our conventional forces." He argues that the selective use of high technology provides the best offset strategy to counter Soviet capabilities. Perry makes the case that the integration of microelectronics technology will improve performance, reliability, and maintainability, and will reduce the cost of future weapons systems.

Sprey points to a reduction in the procurement of major systems, brought about by increased costs, not decreased real expenditures, as causing a "quantity" problem. He, like Perry, insists that there is no dichotomy between quantity and quality. Sprey argues that those responsible for weapons acquisition have become enamoured with the high-tech solution. He concludes that this reliance on complexity prevents us from using advanced, simple technology to meet the Soviet threat.

11

DEFENSE REFORM AND THE QUANTITY-QUALITY QUANDARY

William J. Perry

Perry defines the ultimate test of U.S. military equipment as being able to prevail in combat over the Soviet Union. For the last two decades, the United States has failed to remedy conventional force deficiencies, relying instead on nuclear forces. Even worse, due to cheaper labor costs the Soviets are able to build two to three times more equipment on the dollar than is the United States. Given this cost asymmetry, Perry argues, the United States should selectively exploit advanced technology to overcome numerical inferiority. He offers "stealth" and microelectronics technologies as examples that the West can use to escape the quantity-quality quandary.

The so-called quantity-quality controversy centers on the issue of how to optimize the tradeoff between quantity and quality in the design of U.S. military equipment. To discuss this issue intelligently, we must first decide on a criterion of optimization; that is, we must decide what is the most critical and demanding task for this equipment. The effectiveness of U.S. forces must be measured relative to those of the Soviet Union. American forces may face less challenging tasks, but the United States must design them so that they could prevail in combat with the forces the Soviets actually have or are likely to have in the future.

If the principal test is the adequacy of U.S. defenses vis-à-vis the Soviet Union today, unfortunately, we flunk that test and have flunked it for a good many years. For the last few decades we have leaned, instead, on our nuclear forces to compensate for this failure; that is, our nuclear forces have been used to paper over the deficiencies of our conventional forces. This was the cheap and convenient way of meeting the Soviet threat. The time is fast approaching when that will no longer be an adequate solution. In fact, it is already a very dangerous solution to the problem, given the Soviets' present nuclear capability.

Therefore, the primary military problem of our day is how to improve our conventional military forces so that they are able to stand up to the conventional forces of the Soviet Union in a European conflict. What is the strategy? What are the tactics? What is the doctrine? and Which is the equipment that will allow us to do that? It is particularly unhelpful to frame these questions in terms of quality versus quantity arguments; neither choice would allow us to win a competition with the Soviet Union.

Just as one rejects the quantity-quality dichotomy as a useful framework for evaluating the opposing forces' weapons systems, one must also reject these extremes as reasonable approaches for designing weapons systems and force structures. That is, neither a small, high-tech, nor a large, low-tech, force approach can achieve optimum defense effectiveness. Rather, this chapter argues, selective use of high technology provides the best offset strategy to counter Soviet capabilities: enhanced combat capabilities plus long-run fiscal savings. Effective, selective integration of technology offers cheaper weapons than the two extremes rejected above because of improved benefit-cost ratios and reduced unit costs resulting from technologically-enhanced production techniques. Several weapons systems and technology sectors are discussed to illustrate the validity of America's best offset strategy to the Soviet threat: integration of selective technology to improve performance, reliability, and maintainability, and to reduce cost.

QUANTITY VERSUS QUALITY?

Selecting only quantity is not an option that is realistically open to the United States. The Soviet Union already has about a two- or three-to-one advantage in manpower and equipment, and they continue to build somewhere between two and three times as much equipment as the U.S. in almost every category. There is no simple solution to that problem; building three times as many tanks at a third the cost is not viable. It is not simply a question of whether those cheaper tanks would be adequate; there is still the problem of how to man them. Following that policy would double the size of our army. In fact, not coincidentally, the army would end up the same size as the Soviet army.

That may be a conceptual solution to the problem, but it is not politically feasible. The Soviets are able to build two to three times as much equipment, not because they build cheaper and simpler equipment, but because of their key advantage of cheaper manpower. For example, about one-fourth of their defense budget is allocated to manpower costs, whereas in the U.S. about half of the defense budget is allotted to manpower costs.[1] As a result, the Soviets can allocate about half of their defense budget for equipment, while the U.S. can assign a little over one-fourth. Even with equal defense budgets, therefore, the Soviets are able to spend about twice as much as the U.S. on equipment.

It would seem that there is no quantity-quality controversy in the Soviet Union. In fact, the Soviets do not have to select between quantity and quality; because of their cheap manpower, they are able to choose both. And that poses what Leonard Sullivan, Jr., has aptly called America's quantity-quality quandary. The United States has a quandary because we are not able to choose between quantity and quality. Quality cannot be lowered because the Soviets are competing qualitatively. In fact, they are already equal in some areas and are not far behind in others. Therefore, lowering quality would cause the U.S. to become inferior in performance in addition to being outnumbered. At the same time, the United States cannot increase its quantity significantly because of the high production costs and the prohibitive costs of manning larger quantities of equipment.

The quantity-quality quandary is a serious dilemma for which no simple or certain solution can be prescribed. The conditions that allow the Soviet Union to solve this problem—cheap labor, high priority for the military, and high priority for technology—are not feasible in the United States. What follows are some actions open to the United States that are not solutions. Cutting the cost of American equipment in half, as advocated by some, is not a solution, for the reasons described. At the same time, increasing the performance of American fighter aircraft, tanks, and ships also is not a solution. The United States is already designing these systems close to the "knee" in the cost-performance curve. Therefore, additional large increases in unit cost would yield only small improvements in performance, which would not measurably offset the two-to-one numerical disadvantage the United States faces.

ESCAPES FROM THE QUANDARY

The United States has only three generic ways of dealing with the quantity-quality quandary. The first is to take maximum advantage of the geopolitical factors in America's favor—geography, allies, economic strength, and political stability. For example, cooperation on armaments in NATO, although exceedingly difficult to implement, is necessary. If the United States is to offset the Soviets' advantage of cheap labor, the relative advantage of having allies who are economically strong and technically advanced must be exploited. It is too often forgotten that the United States has as military allies the most advanced industrial nations in the world: Japan, Germany, Britain, France, Italy, the Netherlands, Belgium, and Norway. In aggregate, the Soviets do not outnumber the West; if we could find some effective way of using our allies, we could deal with the numbers problem that way.

Second, the U.S. should take advantage of better-motivated and better-trained manpower. Because that is not done today, the United States is failing to exploit one of its greatest potential advantages. Turning that around is perhaps more important than anything else the United States can do to upgrade its defense capability.

Third, the most publicized and least understood solution to U.S. numerical inferiority vis-à-vis the Soviet Union is found in the selective exploitation of technology. An example is the integration of "stealth" and electronic countermeasure technologies in the stealth bomber and cruise missile, in order to enhance U.S. capabilities to penetrate massive Soviet air defenses.

Contrary to the public discussion of stealth, which has been focused entirely on the strategic bomber, "low observables" technology (stealth techniques) will be incorporated to some extent in all future U.S. military aircraft and missile systems. For example, reduction of a fighter bomber's radar cross-section from ten square meters to one square meter decreases the detection range by a factor of two. Consequently, the air defense system has only half the time to detect, identify, and engage a low-flying, fast-moving aircraft on a penetration mission. Ultimately, air defenses will be almost completely degraded by very low observability systems whose electronic signatures are virtually eliminated.

Air-launched cruise missiles (ALCM) began deploying in 1982. Because an ALCM has a radar cross-section only one-thousandth that of a B-52 bomber, it can be considered the first stealth weapon and can defeat existing Soviet air defenses. The next generation of stealth programs will apply this technology to tactical airplanes, strategic bombers, and the ALCM follow-on. Stealth technology will be pervasive, and when used in conjunction with electronic countermeasures and evasive maneuvers will nullify any advantage that the Soviets may derive from their enormous investment in air defense.

There is a special synergism created by combining stealth and electronic countermeasures (ECM). For example, if the cross-section of a military aircraft is reduced by a factor of 100, then the power required for any given level of ECM effectiveness may be reduced by the same factor. This means that an ECM system requiring large, complex, high-power tubes may be replaced with a system that is entirely solid state. Stealth, therefore, allows an airplane to achieve the same level of ECM effectiveness, while reducing the ECM component's complexity, cost, and weight, and increasing reliability as well.

That stealth makes the task of radar jamming less demanding does not mean that the United States should allow its state-of-the-art ECM capability to lag. Advancing ECM technology is imperative in order to cope with the rapidly expanding threat environment, which soon will include new Soviet fighters and a long-range interceptor equipped with a look-down/shoot-down capability, a modified IL-76 airborne warning and control system (AWACS), and SAMs using monopulse radars, which pose particularly difficult problems to an ECM system.

As illustrated by the prospects for stealth, the selective use of technology yields major performance increases in weapons systems. In addition, effective use of technology presents a more cost-effective solution to current Soviet advantages in both quantity and quality.

In aggregate terms, the Soviet Union currently fields more than forty thousand main battle tanks, compared to just ten thousand for the United States. Moreover, the balance in tank inventories will deteriorate further as the Soviet Union produces its newest tank, the T80, at a rate of two thousand units per year, or twice the number of tanks the U.S. hopes to produce during the same period. The best offset strategy does not call for the U.S. to procure thirty thousand additional tanks.

Nor does it suggest that we try to create a tank that is four times as effective as the Soviet tank. Lanchester's famous treatise on military combat derives a square-law relation between quality and quantity. Thus, American tanks would have to be sixteen times as effective as Soviet tanks in order to offset the four-to-one Soviet quantitative advantage. Considering that Soviet tanks are already quite impressive, this is not a realistic option.

The alternative is to deploy the most effective and cost-efficient mix of armor and antiarmor in numbers sufficient to meet the numerically superior threat. Critical to this approach is the U.S. ability to finesse the quantitative imbalance by deploying antitank guided missiles, which exploit the technology of precision-guided munitions (PGMs).

Whether the United States can or should rely on antitank weapons to compensate for its inferiority in tanks is a question that has plagued American defense analysts and military planners for the last fifteen years. It often seems as if each new development in target acquisition has sparked renewed debate on this issue. Yet the simple fact is that although they are not the only answer to the overwhelming superiority of Soviet tank forces, PGMs are crucial. Even as the United States proceeds with production of the M1 tank, America will still be outnumbered in tank forces by four to one.

The vast array of antiarmor weapons under advanced development today has come a long way from the crude and unreliable devices used in World War II. Major advances in smart weapons now permit accuracies that promise a "one shot, one kill" capability. Contemporary precision-guided munitions, moreover, may be deployed in a variety of ways. The multiple configurations include an antitank guided missile that can be fired from an airplane, a different model that can be fired from a helicopter, and still another model that can be fired from a portable weapon—the modern bazooka. The same technology can be incorporated in artillery projectiles, allowing a 155-mm artillery round that can make a direct hit on a moving tank at a range of ten miles. Coupling the large quantity of U.S. self-propelled 155-mm artillery with the so-called Cannon Launched Guided Projectile, the Copperhead, converts an antipersonnel barrage weapon into a very effective antitank weapon.

In order to ensure the viability of the best offset strategy, it is essential that the United States maintain a vigorous effort on all three generations of precision-guided munitions. First-generation PGMs, such as the TOW (tube-launched, optically-tracked, wire-guided) missile, were developed in the mid-1960s and have been in service for years. These accurate, relatively inexpensive weapons, however, have two major drawbacks. First, they are weather dependent; second, the wire guidance device makes the operator vulnerable to counterfire.

Second-generation laser-guided PGMs, such as the Copperhead and Hellfire, were developed during the 1970s and are beginning to enter NATO inventories. This generation of antitank weapons incorporates significant advances in lethality and operational flexibility, but still has problems of weather dependence and operator vulnerability. These first- and second-generation PGMs will be the mainstay of NATO forces through the 1980s. Considering that the Warsaw Pact, as of 1980, had twice the number of antitank missiles in central Europe as did NATO, the West should not curtail the production and deployment plans for these weapons until third-generation systems are well into production.

Third-generation PGMs will be "fire and forget" systems and will thus greatly reduce the problems of operator vulnerability and weather limitations. By overcoming the most serious operational deficiencies of current PGMs, they will give NATO a real competitive edge in ground combat. The technologies that are now under development for this generation include millimeter-wave radar and infrared sensors configured in focal plane arrays, which are clusters of approximately one thousand individual sensors, each on a tiny chip. The resolution of these sensors is sharp enough to distinguish a vehicle the size of a tank from one much smaller or larger, thus permitting selective targeting. The incorporation of such technologies will allow third-generation PGMs to operate effectively in conditions of poor visibility and with less susceptibility to suppressive fire and other countermeasures.

Significant advances in miniaturization in recent years have not only made weapons systems more efficient, they also have completely changed the nature of what is possible. Sophisticated sensors and computers, which a decade ago would have filled a large room, are now small enough to fit into an artillery shell. The Copperhead program, for example, depends on microelectronics technology to build sensors and computers small and rugged enough to fit inside a 155-mm howitzer shell, thereby converting it to an antitank guided missile. This could hardly have been imagined ten years ago.

The U.S. Tank Breaker, which is a missile under development that will use focal plane array, infrared guidance, and a shaped-charge warhead, will allow an infantryman to engage a main battle tank. Still more ambitious is the

Assault Breaker, which is a long-range system designed for interdicting rear-echelon enemy armor. This system entails a large warhead filled with thirty to forty submunitions. Using infrared or millimeter-wave sensors, the submunitions are independently guided to multiple targets. One Assault Breaker, therefore, could engage an entire company of tanks. These new technological developments, embodied in third-generation PGMs, will provide a true fire-and-forget capability and will make an enormous difference in managing the vast asymmetry in U.S.-Soviet tank forces.

It is important to qualify discussions of technologically-induced increases in weapons performances with a caution to avoid problems associated with the "knee" of the cost-performance curve. Simply put, this means avoiding attempts to achieve the last 10 percent of performance in a system. Diminishing marginal returns generally induce large cost increases as performance increments are pushed to the limits of a system's "performance envelope."

Particularly in complex systems, it is more feasible to analyze marginal cost-benefit returns of various components of the system. For example, analysis of how to enhance performance in fighter aircraft must evaluate a particular aircraft as a platform to be compared with alternative add-on packages of avionics, fire control systems, and weapons, versus alternative aircraft platforms featuring the same add-on packages.

Tactical aircraft illustrate technological contributions to performance that are often misunderstood and invite controversy. The question of how to offset the current two-to-one Soviet numerical superiority in tactical aircraft often invites advocacy of either extreme solution: a large, low-technology force or a small, high-technology force. Some proponents of the "simpler-but-more" school, for example, argue that the United States should abandon its costly pursuit of "technological perfectionism" and build, instead, large quantities of simpler and less expensive airplanes. The flaw in this approach, of course, is that the latest generation of Soviet tactical aircraft is more complex than its American counterparts.

The crux of the problem in tactical fighter development turns on a steady improvement in performance of Soviet tactical aircraft. Ten years ago, American airplanes were so superior to their Soviet counterparts that the United States could still compete successfully, despite a two-to-one disadvantage. But Soviet frontal aviation has progressed from a predominantly defensive force to one with improved offensive capabilities for theater warfare: improved maneuverability, extended range, and upgraded avionics and weapons. The most striking change in the Soviet approach to aircraft design is the fact that all but one of the latest generation of Soviet fighters have variable swept wings, adding both complexity and cost to the airplane, as well as rendering it more difficult to maintain.

Advocates of the "superior quality" approach, in contrast, emphasize that by capitalizing on American technological superiority, the United States can continue developing and deploying sophisticated, highly capable aircraft and avionics systems that are superior to those of the Soviet Union. But extreme proponents of this school generally underestimate the importance of numerical requirements. And by succumbing to a technological syndrome, they are often reluctant to procure systems that fall short of perfection. Framing the debate in quantity-versus-quality terms, therefore, is singularly unhelpful and often misleading.

To repeat the theme of this chapter, technology should be applied selectively, and only when it yields significantly superior war-fighting capabilities. For example, in clear contrast to the Soviets' increased use of variable wing technology in combat aircraft, the United States has abandoned variable geometry wings on the F-15, F-16, and F-18 in favor of less costly and more reliable designs. These important trends are too often overlooked by quantity and quality advocates.

In line with the quantity-quality controversy and debate over the most appropriate weapons design approach, important lessons can be derived from the AIMVAL/ACEVAL exercises held at Nellis Air Force Base in 1977. In dogfight situations, for example, numbers of available aircraft are crucial to successful engagements. Incremental increases in performance advantages simply do not offset four-to-one quantitive disparities. Therefore, weapons and operational strategies should be developed that minimize the risk of having to engage in dogfights when outnumbered. This can be effected by achieving superior tactical intelligence (so that we can avoid scenarios where we are outnumbered) and by developing the means to attack multiple targets at long ranges (so that we can reduce the numerical disadvantage before we reach dogfight ranges). Although some dog fights will always be unavoidable, improved intelligence and improved air-to-air missiles can act as powerful equalizers by reducing the probability that U.S. fighters will have to engage Soviet aircraft in dogfights at a significant numerical disadvantage. The key to this approach is the transfer of technological sophistication from the airplane to the weapons system. Thus, F-16s procured in large quantities may be preferable to fewer of the more formidable F-15s if the F-16s are equipped with improved air-to-air missiles.

Two technologies are critical to the ability of the United States to maintain a performance edge in air combat. First, the United States can achieve an advantage in the avionics equipment that leads to "situation awareness," allowing a pilot to know at all times the type and location of all aircraft in his battle space. This information can be displayed electronically to the pilot in simple form and updated frequently in a matter of a few seconds. Such situation awareness requires a combination of advanced systems including the Airborne Warning and Control System (AWACS), NAVSTAR navigational satellites, and digital data communication systems, which relay the data from collection centers to individual pilots.

A second advantage will flow from the next generation of air-to-air missiles, particularly the Advanced Medium Range Air-to-Air Missile

(AMRAAM), which marks a revolutionary advance from present technology. AMRAAM employs terminal guidance and advanced signal-processing techniques, which give it a high probability of making a direct hit on low-flying targets in a heavy ECM environment. Its longer range, moreover, enables pilots to operate in stand-off engagements instead of dogfights. As a result, each pilot may intercept, at visual ranges, three or four enemy airplanes simultaneously. Significantly more impressive than the Sidewinder missile, which functions more like an advanced machine gun and is primarily useful in one-on-one encounters, AMRAAM allows the pilot to engage multiple fighters before they engage him. Thus, even if U.S. tactical fighter forces were outnumbered in a particular theater, situation awareness would enable the American pilot to avoid being outnumbered in his locality or region. And AMRAAM allows him to face an engagement in which he suffers from numerical disadvantage by intercepting multiple targets before they can attack him.

SUPPORTING INFRASTRUCTURE TECHNOLOGIES

There is a final application of technology important to defense that is different from the others described. Technology can also be used to reduce the cost and complexity and to increase the reliability and durability of military equipment. Often in debates this issue is framed as a trade-off between advanced technology performance benefits and increased operational problems caused by decreased reliability. The microelectronics technology that has been developed in the last decade, and that has been applied to a wide variety of commercial and consumer products, can lead to significant improvements in reliability and operability. Arguments relating technology to low operational readiness or low reliability do not refute this contention, since the relevant microelectronics technology is only five to ten years old and is just beginning to be incorporated in equipment that is in the field today. As this new microelectronics technology proliferates in deployed equipment, we will see substantial improvements in reliability and operability. The question is, How hard should we push to get those benefits into equipment in the future? My belief is we should make a dedicated effort to employ microelectronics for the resulting reliability and operability benefits, almost independent of the performance benefits achieved.

Performance-reliability-cost trade-offs can best be avoided by integrating into weapons advanced technologies in which the United States is preeminent: microelectronics and computers. For example, U.S. integrated circuit technology portends increased system reliability, since greater component density will decrease the number of potentially unreliable interconnections between integrated circuit chips. The program will also result in major savings in cost, weight, size, and power.

Microelectronics technology also reduces equipment costs. The notion that technology increases equipment costs has no basis in reality. Complexity, not technology, is the culprit. It is electromechanical equipment, not microelectronics equipment, that is rising in cost, together with other commodities. For example, a car purchased in 1950 for $1,000 would cost $10,000 today; home prices have soared from $10,000 to $100,000; in fact, almost every category of consumer purchases has seen a tenfold increase in price in the last few decades, except electronics. In 1950, a black-and-white television set listed for about $500. The equivalent set today may be purchased for $100. Even the more sophisticated color set runs about $500. Similarly, the cost of a calculator has been reduced from $1,000 for the electromechanical model of the 1960s to $10 for today's solid-state model. And computers have gone from a few million dollars to a few tens of thousands for the equivalent capability. Considering that electronics is the only area of human endeavor where costs have been decreasing by factors of 10 to 100 in the last few decades, it is obvious that the selective application of electronics is the key to limiting defense costs.

Thus, while the United States has experienced a technology inflation as well as a cost inflation in military equipment since World War II, the added cost generally has been used to incorporate new technology that has substantially increased military effectiveness. Critics who argue that the United States should use technology to reduce equipment costs rather than to improve performance generally overlook the state of Soviet advances. Still, a very real problem occurs when multiple state-of-the-art innovations that rely on immature technology are incorporated into a single weapons system. As in the F-111A program, this leads to technical difficulties, increased operating costs, expensive modifications, and lower readiness rates. While the better is not always the enemy of the good, too many unproven innovations in a single system are bound to cause problems, not to mention cost overruns.

Microelectronics technology has generated an additional, corollary benefit beyond enhanced weapons performance characteristics and reduced production costs: training of weapons operators on simulators. This same technology makes possible various types of simulators, which can bring about revolutionary improvement in the training of equipment operators. Computer simulators have the ability to recreate, at a reasonable cost, the level of fast-paced decision making that is required for many combat environments. Such conditions are often too dangerous and too expensive to duplicate in reality. By reproducing all the equipment that a tank-gunner, for example, would operate, simulators can employ two-sided combat scenarios (similar to video games). Leading to vast improvements in operator proficiency, simulators will help reduce what Clausewitz called the "friction" of war.

CONCLUSION

Military reformers often confuse technology with complexity, but they are not synonymous. It is important to realize that one can have the benefits of technology without suffering the problems of complexity. Many critics of technology are thinking of the technology of an earlier era. Examples of what could or could not be done with technology in the Korean War or the Vietnam War are not as relevant to today's debates. In the field of electronics and computers, there have been three generations of technological developments since those days. Today's technology offers the potential for low-cost, reliable, and effective solutions to military problems. The reform movement's effectiveness is handicapped to the degree that it fails to appreciate the one great advantage that this country has in its competition with the Soviet Union; namely, its technological advantage.

In sum, the 1980s will be a dangerous period for the United States because of the serious challenges posed by the Soviet Union. The United States is capable of meeting these challenges, but a determining factor in its success will be an intelligent and energetic exploitation of American technology. Soviet leaders, however, also recognize the crucial importance of technology. Former Premier Brezhnev once said, "In the competition between the two world-opposed forces, science and technology will play a critical role, and this makes further advances in science and technology of decisive significance." But Brezhnev was only half-right: he had the right strategy, but the wrong country. The application of this strategy requires access to ongoing technological innovations, and, fortunately, this is an area in which the United States excels. Technological innovation flourishes in an environment of free enterprise and free expression such as enjoyed in America. Based on intelligent integration of selected technologies and thorough testing under realistic combat conditions, it is this approach that offers the best prospects for the future U.S. defense posture vis-à-vis the Soviet Union.

NOTE

1. Department of Defense, *Annual Report: FY 1982* (Washington, D.C.: Government Printing Office, 1981), table 13–3, shows defense manpower outlays for FY 1982 as $89.5 billion. Table 16–1 shows total defense outlays as $180 billion.

12

THE CASE FOR BETTER AND CHEAPER WEAPONS

Pierre Sprey

In this chapter, Sprey starts by demonstrating the "staggering decrease" in quantities of U.S. weapons produced each year—despite increases in procurement expenditure. Using both historical case examples and current combat criteria, he proceeds by testing the proposition that expensive, complex weapons are generally more effective than any cheaper, simpler alternatives. He then reapplies the same combat criteria to key Soviet weapons to test whether Soviet weapons "quality" forces us to favor the expensive, complex systems. His evidence shows that the "quality versus quantity" dichotomy has no basis in technical or tactical fact. Sprey concludes by proposing a different approach to building larger and more effective forces at reasonable cost.

Much of the defense debate, unfortunately, revolves around buzz words. "Second echelon," "power projection," and "smart weapons" come to mind as examples of particularly imprecise and misleading terms. One of the most fashionable buzz words used to defend the complexity and high cost of current weapons is "quality versus quantity." This slogan is intended to characterize the fundamental weapons procurement dilemma as a choice between a few superb but unfortunately expensive weapons or large numbers of cheap but ineffective weapons. The issues underlying this rather shallow characterization reach down to the roots of our deteriorating combat capabilities: it is these underlying issues that are worth pursuing.

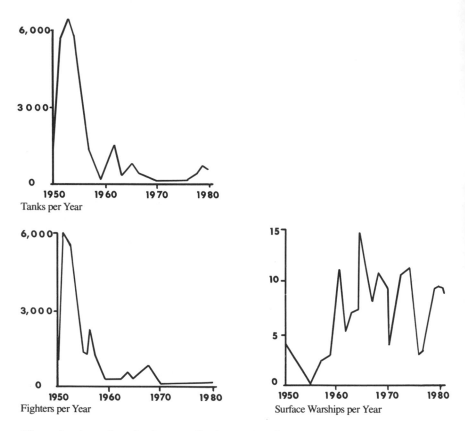

Figure 2. Annual production rates for three types of weapons.

Let us start by examining how much of a "quantity" problem we have. Figure 2 traces the annual production rates since 1950 of three of our most important weapons: tanks, fighters, and surface warships. In 1952, we produced over sixty-five hundred tanks; today we are producing about seven hundred per year. In 1951, we procured over six thousand fighters; today, we are buying fewer than three hundred. Surface combatant ship deliveries peaked in 1963 at fifteen per year; for 1984 we are down to eight, and by 1987 we'll be down to three per year. This amounts to a staggering decrease in quantity over the last twenty to thirty years.

To understand the causes of this decrease it is necessary to look at spending, then and now, for the tanks, fighters, and ships produced. The tanks we produced in 1952 cost us about $2 billion in FY 83 constant dollars. We are spending the same amount today to buy one-tenth as many tanks. The more than six thousand fighters we budgeted in 1951 cost about $7 billion (FY 83). In the FY 83 budget we are buying one-twentieth as many fighters for over $11 billion. Ships present a similar picture. One thing is clear: decreasing real expenditures are not the cause of the quantity problem.

THE ARGUMENT FOR "QUALITY"

In this discussion, I shall follow the steps of the typical argument for "quality" weapons and, wherever possible, test each step against the evidence. There are three steps to the typical argument:

Step 1. *We have always bought the best for our boys, and the best costs money.* This is easily tested by looking at a sample of weapons that worked notably well in past wars and seeing whether they typically cost more than the ones that did poorly in combat.

Step 2. *No matter what happened in the past, the only real world alternatives we face today are between expensive but very effective systems and cheaper, much less effective ones.* This proposition can be tested by looking at a sample of today's expensive systems and their cheap alternatives, across a spectrum of missions.

I shall then compare in some detail the effectiveness of the expensive system versus the cheap alternative in two of these missions, armor and air-to-air combat. I shall use explicit effectiveness criteria based on combat experience.

Step 3. *In any case, much as we would like to choose the simple, cheap alternative, the rapid increase in Soviet quality forces us to select the option of fewer, more complex, more costly weapons.* The validity of this final step can be directly tested by evaluating the latest Soviet quality tank and quality fighter against exactly the same set of effectiveness criteria used in step 2 to compare the simple to the complex U.S. tanks and fighters.

The evidence assembled in testing these three propositions should lead to some useful overall insights on the connection, or lack thereof, between complexity and effectiveness.

HISTORY: WERE THE BEST WEAPONS THE MOST EFFECTIVE?

Table 12.1 represents a sample of inexpensive weapons that were notably successful in World War II and Vietnam combat, together with their expensive counterparts or alternatives.

It is appropriate to start with the most basic and, in some ways, the most important weapon of war, the rifle. In the first infantry actions of the Vietnam conflict, American troops were usually equipped with the M-14, the heavy, handsomely fabricated 7.62-mm weapon strongly preferred by the Army hierarchy over the light and much cheaper 5.56-mm AR-15.[1] In the initial firefights against Viet Cong using the fully automatic AK-47, the slow-firing M-14 came off second best; the Viet Cong usually established fire superiority, and M-14 riflemen suffered unfavorable casualty exchange ratios. But during the same period, U.S. Special Forces units and some South Vietnamese infantry were using the AR-15 and achieving very favorable results in firefights against the AK-47.[2] In both operational tests and combat, the $75 AR-15 proved to be more accurate, more reliable, and remarkably more

Table 12.1. Historical Test: Were Expensive Weapons Better in Combat?

Problems

Type of Weapon	Cheap Winners	Expensive Losers	Why?
Infantryman's rifle (Vietnam)	AR-15 ($75)[a]	M-14 ($295)	AR-15 better in actual firefights: —Riflemen carried 3 times as many rounds —Each round more lethal, accurate —AR-15 (not M-16) more reliable in test and combat
Tank (WWII)	T34	Panzer IV	T34 won: —Far more reliable in mud and ice —Higher velocity, more lethal cannon —Wide tracks prevented bogging in deep mud
Artillery (Vietnam)	105-mm Towed ($170,000)	175-mm Self-Propelled ($560,000)	175-mm SP less useful: —Frequent chassis breakdowns and gun tube replacements —Much lower rate of fire
Surface warship (WWII)	Japanese destroyer (2,500 tons)	U.S. cruiser (12,000 tons)	Destroyer won in surface battles: —Had reliable, large, lethal torpedo; U.S. cruisers removed torpedoes before war —Torpedoes dominated guns in night surface battles
Air-to-Air missile	AIM-9D/G Sidewinder ($14,000)	AIM-7D/E Sparrow ($44,000)	AIM-9D/G more lethal: —In air combat over North Vietnam, AIM-7 D/E had 3% to 10% probability of kill, ⅓ that of AIM-9D/G
Air-to-Air fighter (WWII)	P-51 ($51,000)	P-38 ($125,000)	P-38 failed in Europe: —Too large and visible —Too sluggish in roll, turn —A hit on *either* engine frequently fatal

[a]Weapon costs are in current dollars.

lethal than the $295 M-14. Equally important, the light gun and light cartridges permitted the rifleman to carry three times as many rounds in his fighting load. The disparity in combat results between the two rifles was so marked that General Westmoreland, reluctantly and against the bitter opposition of the army staff, ordered that the AR-15 be issued to all U.S. troops in Vietnam.[3]

Moving back in time to World War II and the eastern front, scene of the largest tank battles in history, the two principal tanks facing each other were the primitive, crudely fabricated Soviet T34 and the beautifully engineered and machined German Panzerkampfwagen IV. The skilled and experienced German tankers were shocked by the superiority of the Russian tank. Crude and simple it was. Nevertheless, its wider tracks allowed it to move when German tanks were bogged down in the deep Russian mud. When the finely crafted running gear of the Panzers was frozen stuck, the sloppy tolerances of the T34s kept them rolling. The T34's low sloping armor and its less flammable diesel fuel made the Panzer IV's short, low-velocity, 75-mm cannon seem puny and inadequate; in contrast, the high-velocity, long-barreled 76.2-mm, and later 85-mm, cannon of the T34 could penetrate and destroy the Panzer IV from any direction. Tank for tank, the cheaper T34 was more effective than the more expensive Panzer IV. Even worse for the Germans, the Russians were able to produce more than three for every one the Germans produced, in part due to the relative simplicity of the T34. The superior effectiveness and much greater numbers of the T34 were a crucial factor in winning the war for the Russians.

Though all the examples in table 12.1 are worth discussing, one final example is selected here: the P-51 fighter versus the P-38 fighter in World War II European air-to-air combat. The Army Air Force's "school solution" fighters for defeating Messerschmitt 109s and Focke-Wolf 190s were the large and expensive P-38 and P-47, respectively $125,000 and $90,000. The P-51 was a much lower priority project that had to be ordered by the RAF as a close support aircraft in order to survive at all.[4] High losses in actual combat against German fighters showed that the complex, expensive P-38 was an unsatisfactory solution, and it was ordered removed from Europe by the AAF theater command during the spring of 1944. Why? Although the P-38 was fast, it was too large and too visible, too sluggish in transient maneuvering. It also suffered from twin engine vulnerability—that is, if *either* engine was hit, the aircraft was likely to burn or explode.[5]

By the time the P-38 was forced to withdraw from Europe, the P-51 was establishing itself as one of the finest fighters of the war. The superior effectiveness of the P-51 is common knowledge; that it was also one of the least expensive fighters of the war at $51,000 apiece is less widely known.

TODAY'S CHOICES: ARE THE EXPENSIVE ONES MORE EFFECTIVE?

Table 12.2 shows a sample of today's important military missions or functions and, for each, the expensive weapon that we have elected to buy. For each expensive choice, a much cheaper alternative is shown. Cost differences range from two to one to seventy-five to one, so clearly the cheaper choices permit building much larger forces. Can we be sure the differences in effectiveness go the other way?

Effectiveness comparisons in two of the table 12.2 mission areas, armor

Table 12.2. Today's Choices: Are the Expensive Ones More Effective?

Mission	Cheap	Expensive	Cost Ratio	FY 82 $
Armor	M60A1	M-1	1:3	.9M/2.7M
Air defense	Oerlikon 35-mm	DIVAD	1:30	.35M/10M
Antitank	106 recoilless rifle	TOW	1:30	.25K/7.5K
ASW escort	Kortenaer	Spruance	1:4	140M/600M
Submarine	210 (diesel)	SSN-688	1:8	70M/600M
Air-to-Air	F-16A	F-15 A/C	1:2	15M/30M
Tank hunting	A-10	F-15E	1:5	8M/40M
Close support	A-4M	AV-8B	1:3	8M/25M
Interdiction	A-7	F-18	1:3	11M/35M
Antitank ammo	30-mm	I^2 Maverick	1:75	1K/75K (per firing)

and air-to-air, will be examined in subsequent sections. Only brief comments can be offered here on some of the other choices.

In air defense, recent firing tests show that the army's new antiaircraft gun, the DIVAD (Division Air Defense), like all previous radar-directed guns, will do poorly against nap-of-the-earth helicopters and maneuvering attack fighters. In contrast, old optically-aimed guns (even though they had much slower ballistics than the high-velocity Oerlikon 35-mm of table 12.2) with well-trained or experienced gunners have done devastatingly well against Western fighters and helicopters in the Korean, Vietnam, and Israeli wars, as evidenced by the four thousand or more jets they shot down—almost all of the them during a maneuvering attack pass.[6]

In heavy antitank weapons, there are reasons to believe that the TOW (Tube-Launched, Optically-Tracked, Wire-Guided) missile may do nearly as poorly as the .013 probability of kill scored by the Soviet Sagger antitank missile in the Yom Kippur War. Although the TOW probably has somewhat more accurate guidance than the Sagger, it suffers from similar deficiencies in excessive exposure of the gunner during missile guidance and an unacceptably low rate of fire (.7 to 1.0 rounds/minute). The 106-mm recoilless rifle, though old and far from the best in today's recoilless rifle technology, can get 8 rounds per minute and can hit well out to eight hundred meters, which covers at least 75 percent of all firing opportunities experienced in actual World War II and modern Israeli tank combat. It also costs one-thirtieth as much per round as the TOW, ammunition being the dominant cost for both systems. It seems unlikely that a war reserve stockpile of one-thirtieth fewer TOW rounds than 106-mm rounds will defend us better against a sustained attack by twenty thousand or more tanks in central Europe.

In submarine warfare, the United States Navy has long since abandoned the diesel-electric attack submarine in favor of the faster and longer-range nuclear submarine. When operating on batteries, however, modern diesel-electric submarines are much quieter than nuclear submarines, need to snorkel only 5 percent of the time, and can go twelve thousand nautical miles or more. We could have eight twelve-hundred-ton diesel-electric submarines for every SSN-688 foregone. Given that ultra-quite diesel-electrics rarely fail to sink high-value surface warships in NATO exercises and usually win against nuclear boats in sub-to-sub exercises, is the diesel-electric the less effective choice for any and all submarine missions? The Soviet, French, and British navies clearly think otherwise.[7]

When effectiveness is examined, not by trusting mechanistic computer models of combat or by believing technological promises, but by understanding actual combat and field test evidence, then similar doubts can be raised about each of the remaining expensive choices in table 12.2. Not a single one of the ten expensive choices is *clearly* more effective; in at least seven cases, the available combat or test data support an opposite conclusion.

AIR-TO-AIR EFFECTIVENESS: F-15 VERSUS F-16

The first mission area in which I shall compare, in somewhat more detail, the effectiveness of an expensive alternative with a cheaper one is the air-to-air mission. I shall compare the $30 million F-15 (1982 dollars) and the $15 million F-16 in terms of the four principal effectiveness characteristics that contribute to victory in air-to-air combat: achieving surprise and avoiding being surprised; outnumbering the enemy in the air; outmaneuvering the enemy to reach firing position (when surprise fails); and achieving reliable kills within the brief firing opportunities presented by combat.[8]

Surprise is first because in every air war since World War I, somewhere between 65 and 85 percent of all fighters shot down were unaware of their attacker. The F-16 is superior in achieving surprise because it is about half the size of the large and highly visible F-15; even more important to visual detection, the F-16 smokes half as much as the F-15 (though good engines for fighters should not and do not smoke at all). Advances in radar signal detection are likely to force both fighters to turn off their radar most of the time to assure surprise against an enemy equipped with a competent radar warning receiver. When both have their radar on, current training engagements show that the F-16 detects the F-15 at about the same or longer distances, due to the F-15's much larger radar reflectivity.

Second, in outnumbering the enemy in the air, the F-16 has a sizable advantage. We can buy and operate two F-16s for the same cost as one F-15. In addition, each F-16 can fly about 50 percent more sorties per day than an F-15, due to its considerably lower failure rates and maintenance requirements. Thus, for every F-15 we forego, we can have three times as many F-16s actually facing the enemy in the air.

Third, in outmaneuvering the enemy, the F-16 has a moderate advantage over the F-15. The F-16 accelerates noticeably faster than the F-15, particularly in the all-important transonic region.[9] In maximum turning performance, the two fighters are closely matched. However, the F-16 can transition from one maneuver to another much more quickly than the F-15, due to its superior roll and pitch performance. As for range and combat endurance, despite its smaller size the F-16 is considerably better; for instance, its air-to-air mission radius is at least 50 percent better than the F-15A's.[10]

Finally, in achieving kills within a brief firing opportunity, both fighters are essentially equal. Both carry the same gun and the same Sidewinder infrared missiles. The F-15 has an apparent advantage in that it also carries the Sparrow radar missile. On closer examination, this proves to be of little or no advantage: in Vietnam, the Sparrow had a kill rate of .08 to .10, less than one third that of the AIM-9D/G—and new models of the Sparrow do not appear to have corrected the major reasons for this disappointing performance. Even worse, locking-on with the Sparrow destroys surprise because of the distinctive and powerful radar signature involved. The 1973 and 1982 Israeli combat experience seems to confirm the insignificance of Sparrow: in Lebanon, the radar missile contributed less than 15 percent of air-to-air kills, and none of these were outside visual range.

In summary, in three of the four effectiveness areas critical to winning air-to-air battles, the cheaper F-16 is clearly more effective than the twice-as-expensive F-15, while in the one remaining area the two fighters are equal.

TANK EFFECTIVENESS: M1 VERSUS M60A1

The second detailed effectiveness comparison, one considerably more complex to analyze than air-to-air combat, looks at the new $2.7 million M1 tank against its predecessor, the $0.9 million M60A1. The two will be compared in terms of six effectiveness characteristics critical to success in armor operations: operational mobility of tanks; numbers available at the point of engagement; machine gun effectiveness, particularly against close-in infantry threats; mobility in sudden tank-versus-tank or tank-versus-antitank firefights; time to kill multiple threats such as an enemy tank platoon; and crew survival in the face of enemy infantry weapons, mines, and tank weapons.[11]

Operational mobility—that is, the speed with which complete armor units (not individual tanks) can be moved over distances of, say, fifty to two hundred miles—is addressed first because surprise and arriving before the enemy has time to prepare defenses are the best guarantors of success and survival in tank operations. An M60 battalion will arrive at a distant objective considerably sooner than an M1 battalion, mostly because of one critical advantage: M60s break down between one quarter and one fifth as often as

M1s, based on the army's operational tests, and take about half as long to repair when they do break down.[12] A further impediment to fast unit moves is that the M1 needs to refuel 40 percent more often than the M60 (every 127 miles versus every 175 miles) and needs to carry along nearly twice as many fuel trucks. The fact that when it is running reliably the M1 can average 25 percent better sustained speed than the M60 (twenty-five versus twenty miles per hour over secondary roads in Operational Test II at Fort Bliss) is hardly enough to offset the crippling effects of excessive breakdowns and high fuel consumption.[13]

Next in importance is the number of tanks actually brought to bear on the enemy. Three M60A1s can be procured for the cost of one M1. But the M60 has an additional two-to-one advantage in daily availability for combat (85 versus 43 percent, based on the Army's analysis of the M1's Operational Tests II and III). This means that for a given budget we will bring to bear six times fewer tanks if we choose M1s over M60s. If we include the much larger number of M1s that will be down for combat damage repairs, the M1's effective force size may be less than one-tenth that of the M60.[14]

Third, in machine gun effectiveness, the M1 has some significant disadvantages. Due to the flat and very wide turret roof, fields of view (hatch open and closed) and machine gun fields of fire are poorer than for the M60 in the close-in zone where simple bazooka-type infantry antitank weapons are such a dangerous threat to tanks. Further, two of the three M1 machine guns are nearly unusable: the commander's machine gun is, to quote the crews, "impossible" to aim due to quick power traverse and slow manual elevation controls; the loader's hatch machine gun[15] has a mount that has been breaking in peacetime testing ever since 1977 and is too flimsy to last in combat.

Fourth, in firefight mobility, each tank has advantages and disadvantages. The M60 is slightly better in deep mud and sand due to lower ground pressure (eleven versus thirteen pounds per square inch); it is much faster and more controllable in slick mud and snow where the M1's slippery, nonremovable rubber track pads limit it to hills no steeper than a gentle percent grade. Over rough ground, the M1 has a softer ride but has to restrict speed more than the M60 in maneuvering around obstacles due to fear of track misguides, which can cause major damage to the final drives. The M1 is slower in short dash acceleration due to the several seconds of lag inherent in turbine engines; however, in longer accelerations (say, beyond one hundred feet) its higher horsepower gives it the advantage.

Fifth, in firepower—more precisely defined as time to kill multiple enemy tanks—the M1 and M60 should be about equal, since they have the same gun with the same ballistic and approximately the same time to aim.[16] However, in training range firings the M1 appears to be one or two seconds slower than the M60's seven seconds between aimed rounds due to the M1's very cramped loader's station. In ability to sustain a given rate of kill, the M60 has a slight advantage with sixty-three rounds on board as opposed to only fifty-five for the M1. When the M1 converts to the larger 120-mm gun, its sustainability will fall to a clearly inadequate forty rounds—half of the eighty to eighty-five rounds considered adequate by U.S. and German armor users, based on their combat experience in World War II.

The final effectiveness characteristic, crew survival, can be assessed only on the basis of live firings against tanks loaded with the three principal hazards that kill crew members: ammunition, hydraulic fluid, and fuel. For the M1 and M60, no clear comparison is possible due to the army's long-standing tradition of not using live firings against combat-loaded tanks to test them for their greatest vulnerabilities.[17] The M1 has significantly better crew protection than the M60 against Sagger-size shaped charge antitank weapons from the front 180 degrees, due to its Chobham armor, which was specifically designed to defeat shaped charges.[18] For the rear 180 degrees, the M1 has ordinary plate armor slightly thinner (though harder) than the M60's and both tanks are easily penetrated by standard bazooka-type antitank weapons such as the ubiquitous Soviet RPG 7. Which tank is more likely to burn or explode given an RPG-7 hit from the rear 180 degrees cannot be known without side-by-side live firings.[19] Moving from infantry to tank threats, the most important Soviet tank cannon rounds, the high-velocity solid projectiles used by the T62, T64, and T72, penetrate both the M1 and the M60 from almost any direction—a fact only recently admitted in open congressional testimony. Give that both tanks can be readily penetrated by standard tank cannon rounds, only live firings tests can show which one is less likely to burn its crew.

One last point, which weighs somewhat against the survival of M1 crews, is the much greater heat of the turbine compartment and its jet exhaust as compared to the diesel exhaust; the M1's heat can be seen with an infrared viewer at more than five times the typical visual detection distance—and, under many conditions, the rising heat gives away the tank's position, even when it is in complete defilade.

Summing up, in four of the six characteristics essential to tank effectiveness, the M60A1 is clearly superior to the three times more expensive M1; in the remaining two areas, testing to date is inadequate to tell whether a clear advantage accrues to either tank.

DOES SOVIET "QUALITY" FORCE US TO ADOPT COMPLEX, EXPENSIVE SOLUTIONS?

The T72. The most direct way of addressing the question of Soviet quality is to assess the latest Soviet weapons, using precisely the same effectiveness criteria we have used to compare alternative U.S. systems. As a first example, we can use the tank effectiveness criteria of the previous section to assess the T72, the current Soviet first-line tank.

In operational mobility, the T72 is slower than the M60A1 in three respects. It is likely to break down more often, since it is a heavier tank based on the same unreliable powertrain as the T62.[20] When running, its sustained speed on secondary roads is probably about fifteen miles per hour to the M60's 20, mostly because of the harshness of the Soviet short-travel suspension. And range will be a little less than the T62's, which has at least one-third less range on internal fuel than the M60. The only mobility advantage of the T72 over the M60 is its lighter weight, which allows it to cross a wider range of bridges, particularly the secondary road bridges important in achieving surprise.

In numbers available to engage the enemy, there is no reliable cost comparison of the M60 and T72 on which to base calculations. But we know that the Soviets produce at least 1500 to 2000 T72s per year (out of a total annual tank production of 2500 to 3000). Thus, they are producing two to three times as many T72s as the 720 per year production rate that we are trying to achieve with the M1—or nearly twice as many as the 800 to 1200 rate we maintained for some years with the M60.

In machine gun effectiveness, both tanks have two reasonably effective weapons, but the T72 can carry only one-third of the six thousand-round ammunition load of the M60. This will severely constrain the T72 in suppressing or eliminating infantry antitank threats.

In battlefield mobility, the T72 has about the same ability to move in mud or sand as the M60 but poorer rough ground mobility due to its harsher suspension and slower steering. Acceleration of the two tanks at low speeds is about equal, except for a T72 advantage in initial jump due to its more efficient, nonautomatic transmission.

Rate of kill is a glaring weakness of the T72. The T72 has the unreliable, crew-endangering autoloader first introduced in the now-failed T64.[21] The autoloader is claimed to have an eight- to nine-second reload cycle, but the practical time between aimed shots is probably double this; even worse, when the autoloader fails, which appears to be a frequent occurrence, the T72 is probably not capable of better than a nearly unusable forty-five seconds between aimed rounds (since the crew no longer includes a loader). In addition, the Soviet cannon projectile, which is steel or possibly tungsten, is much less incendiary than the depleted uranium of the M60 and M1 penetrator. Nor can the T72 sustain firing as well as the M60, since it has only forty rounds on board, compared with the M60's sixty-three rounds.

Finally, crew survival appears to be the major Achilles heel of the T72, probably even more so than in the T62. We have a fairly good idea of how poor the chances of a T62 crew are: air force live firing trials with the GAU-8 30-mm cannon of the A-10 showed the T62 to be almost exactly twice as likely to burn or explode as the U.S. M47, a tank slightly less well armored than the M60. These findings are confirmed by Israeli tank combat reports of how easy it was to "brew up" a T62 in 1973 and 1982. The T72's protection differs from the T62's in only two respects: the front of the turret and the glacis plate have an extra 50 mm of unknown armor material, and the auto-loader has forced a different internal arrangement of the T72's new, larger, two-piece ammunition.[22] Did the extra T72 armor help? The fate of the Syrian T72 crews in the Bekaa Valley underscores how irrelevant the predictions of paper vulnerability analyses are and how much we need live firing results: unlike the T62, essentially every T72 hit by an Israeli round exploded.

Thus, in five out of the six critical effectiveness criteria, the T72 is deficient relative to the M60. This is not strong support for the case that Soviet tank quality forces us to field a tank of unprecedented cost and complexity such as the M1, especially when the M1 shows effectiveness deficiencies relative to the M60.

The MiG-23.   The four air-to-air effectiveness criteria used in the F-15 versus F-16 comparison can be used equally well to assess the MiG-23, the current Soviet first-line fighter that is replacing the MiG-21.

The MiG-23 has considerably less ability to achieve surprise than the F-16 because it is at least 50 percent larger. It is, in fact, nearly as big as an F-105. Even better for us, the MiG-23 is the first Soviet fighter that smokes heavily. As a result, the MiG-23 is much easier to find and surprise than an F-16—or than its predecessor, the MiG-21.

In numbers in the air, the MiG-23 represents a lesser threat than the MiG-21 insofar as its complexity forces the Soviets toward lower production rates and poorer wartime sortie rates. Nevertheless, the Soviets still produce at least five times more MiG-23s than we produce F-16s.

In maneuvering to firing position, the MiG-23 suffers its most severe disadvantage: its acceleration and turn capabilities are quite close to those of the F-105, a late fifties tactical nuclear attack aircraft that makes no pretense of being an air-to-air fighter.[23] In fact, the MiG-23 would probably lose a dogfight to an F-105 because the MiG's roll rate and endurance are inferior to the F-105's.

In weapons lethality, the principal MiG-23 weapons are the same as the MiG-21's: the 23-mm cannon (a gun of considerably lower rate and velocity than the U.S. 20-mm) and the Atoll infrared missile (a copy of older U.S. Sidewinder missiles). In addition, the MiG-23 mounts a bulky radar, larger than the MiG-21's radar and perhaps most comparable to the non-lookdown pulse radar of the 1962 F-4B. The MiG-23 also carries radar missiles of unknown capability. The Soviet radar/radar missiles have never been tested in combat and, consequently, are unlikely to be any better than the disappointing F-4/Sparrow combination.

As in the case of the latest Soviet tank, the MiG-23's inferiority in three out of four categories again casts doubt on whether Soviet quality forces us to choose more complex, costly options. In fact, it appears that the MiG-23 is a substantially less dangerous opponent than the MiG-21 it is replacing.

One additional point is worth noting: for the T72 and MiG-23, the *one* effectiveness area in which each was superior to its U.S. counterpart was the numbers available in combat. In view of this, it is difficult to understand how reducing already-low U.S. tank and fighter production rates in order to buy expensive M1s and F-15s represents an appropriate response to the Soviet threat.

INSIGHTS

The foregoing analysis leads to some insights that, in retrospect, may seem obvious:

1. There was and is no inherent dichotomy between quantity and quality.
2. Instead, the issue has always been to distinguish what works in combat from what doesn't work.
3. In the past, the weapons that were relatively costly or complex have not usually worked well in combat.
4. Weapons that proved remarkably effective in combat have almost always been relatively simple for their day.
5. This does not imply that all simple weapons work—we have many examples of how easy it is to field simple weapons that are ineffective, ranging from the .30 caliber carbine to the LAW (Light Antitank Weapon).
6. We can't make progress in designing for superior effectiveness if we can't define it.
7. To understand and define effectiveness—that is, what works in war and what doesn't—we have to spend much more time studying combat as it actually occurs. And we need to give much less credence to the hypotheses of technologists concerning how future combat *might* look.

There is no inherent contradiction between quality and quantity in weapons. But our now-entrenched defense of high-cost, high-complexity programs blocks us from using advanced, brilliantly-simplifying technology to achieve the large increases in both quality and quantity of weapons that the nation needs more desperately every year.

NOTES

1. Besides the "pea shooter" caliber, the AR-15 had two more strikes against it: it was privately designed outside the ordnance bureaucracy and it had the flimsy, mass-produced look of a Mattel toy.

2. About 85,000 AR-15s had been bought by the Advanced Research Project Agency (ARPA) during the period 1962 to 1964 and sent to Vietnam for combat evaluation.

3. This resulted in the superb reliability of the AR-15 being destroyed when the army "militarized" it into the Vietnam standard issue M-16. That event and its tragic conse-

quences in combat are beyond the scope of this discussion. See J. Fallows, *National Defense* (New York: 1981), pp 76–95.

4. Even the critical step of fitting the more powerful Rolls-Royce Merlin engine to the underpowered early P-51s was so bitterly opposed by the Wright-Patterson aircraft development bureaucracy that it had to be forced on the Army Air Force by White House intervention.

5. The P-38 had a better combat record in the Pacific war for reasons that are worth understanding when designing new fighters today: in Europe, the P-38 had little or no sustained speed advantage over German fighters; in the Pacific, it had close to 100-mph combat cruise speed superiority over the slow-cruising Zero and thus achieved an advantage in surprise while avoiding maneuvering engagements with the tighter-turning Zero.

6. Although radar fire control was available for the Soviet 85-mm and 57-mm batteries in Korea and Vietnam, as well as for the later ZSU-23-4, their preferred mode in combat against maneuvering attacks was optical aiming with radar range only. The model of Oerlikon 35 mm used as a low-cost alternative in table 2 is a towed, twin barrel mount with only optical computing sights.

7. Over half the Soviet attack submarine force consists of diesel-electrics, and the Soviets, despite repeated intelligence projections to the contrary, have continued to produce diesel-electrics to this day. In the Falklands, the one operational Argentinian diesel-electric—a modern German design—easily penetrated the British ASW (Anti-Submarine Warfare) screen around the British carrier, executed a close-in firing attack in which four torpedoes hit but failed to explode, and then easily evaded seventy-two hours of intensive British ASW search.

8. The derivation of these four effectiveness characteristics from the air combat experience of the last forty years is provided in more detail in a study and briefing by the author, "Comparing the Effectiveness of Air-to-Air Fighters: F-100 to F-18" (first presented to the American Institute of Aeronautics and Astronautics' "75th Anniversary of Powered Flight" Symposium, December 1978).

9. This acceleration advantage has grown in the last few years with the thrust deterioration of the F-15 engine, a deterioration that has not been experienced in the F-16 version of the F-100 engine.

10. Calculations performed according to the air-to-air combat mission fuel rules of the F-16 RFP. The F-16's surprising superiority in range can be attributed to its larger fuel fraction (i.e., weight of fuel divided by total aircraft weight) and its considerably lower cruise drag (which stems, in part, from the cleaner aerodynamic shapes possible in single-engine designs).

11. As in the case of air-to-air, these six effectiveness characteristics are based on detailed examination of U.S., German, and Israeli tank combat experience from 1940 to 1973, with particular emphasis on the views of successful armor commanders such as Wood, Patton, Balck, Guderian, Rommel, and Tal. A discussion of this background is available in the author's briefing, "Comparing the Effectiveness of Current Tanks" (first presented to the Congressional Military Reform Caucus, Spring 1981).

12. M1s in Operational Test (OT) III required nondeferrable maintenance every fifty-three miles, and each such repair lasted 2.6 hours, on the average. Using the army's more artificial criterion of "chargeable" systems failures (as judged by the army's scoring conference), the M1 failed every 99 to 105 miles in OT III; in the only side-by-side M60/M1 test (OT II at Fort Bliss), the M60A1 was scored at 492 miles between chargeable systems failures.

13. Based on the M1's average mileage of 3.86 gallons per mile demonstrated in OT II and OT III; this includes idling time and a high percentage of travel on secondary roads.

14. Israeli field maintenance teams were able to repair essentially all combat-damaged M60s in one to two days. M1s are likely to take much longer because, according to army M1 logistics studies, almost any serious hit on a Chobham armor panel will require depot-level repair to restore full protection, and, further, projectile damage to the gas turbine engine will require engine overhaul in the U.S.

15. A loader's hatch machine gun that worked, such as the one on the M48A5, would be useful and an advantage over the M60, which has only two machine guns. The 1973 war taught the Israelis how critical machine guns are for defending tanks against RPG-7s and Sagger missiles; in response, they added a loader's hatch machine gun to the M60 and doubled the ammunition stowage from 6,000 to 12,000 rounds.

16. Under the extreme time pressure to kill before being killed, neither tank will use ballistic computers and rangefinders (laser or optical) in serious combat because they cost on the order of three to five seconds in time to fire. Instead, they will use the fixed battlesight, particularly since there is no need for ranging when engaging at less than 1,000 meters. Combat records for several hundred World War II tank engagements (confirmed by 1973 and 1982 Israeli reports and NATO terrain measurements) indicate that about 85 percent of engagements will be at less than 1,000 meters. Indeed, about 50 percent will be at less than 500 meters. In this dominant battlesight mode, the M1 is likely to be less accurate than the M60 because it is considerably more difficult to boresight and zero and is experiencing problems in retaining boresight and zero, due to its lack of a simple mechanical battlesight independent of the complex, drift-prone electronics of the M1 gunner's sight.

17. There were a small number of live firings against a combat-loaded M1, but they were designed to show success, not to probe for weaknesses. Instead, the army continues to rely on computerized tank vulnerability models that, based on test, have proven to be incapable of predicting probability of fire and explosion to within a factor of four.

18. It should be noted that the Sagger guided missile did not prove to be a major threat to Israeli tanks in the 1973 war after the initial surprise, requiring an average of eighty firings per kill according to published Israeli accounts.

19. Arguments can be made either way. The M1 might be more flammable because it has more ammunition high up in the tank, more fuel, much hotter engine surfaces, and more of the army's extremely (and unnecessarily) flammable hydraulic fluid. In contrast, the M1 may be less flammable because it has automatic fire-sensing extinguishers (which fail frequently) and an armored, hydraulically-operated door to separate the crew from most of the ammunition (which may be left open in combat due to jamming, unreliability, and loader fear of door-caused injuries).

20. The T72 is two or more tons heavier than the T62 and appears to have added a supercharger to the T62's diesel engine, changes that are not likely to increase reliability. Users complain that the T62 has significant breakdowns every 100 to 125 miles; for details of Soviet tank unreliability, see S. Zaloga, *Modern Soviet Armor,* (New York; Prentice-Hall, 1979).

21. In 1979, the Soviet T64s in eastern Europe were ordered to stop using the auto-loader due to its tendency to feed parts of the gunner into the breech.

22. This add-on armor lamination led to U.S. intelligence projections attributing "magic" special armor properties to the T72's hull. Despite this, the Israelis' ordinary 105-mm tank cannons (some using Israeli APFSDS rounds) had no trouble in penetrating

and exploding about a dozen Syrian T72s in a few minutes, when the T72s first showed up right at the end of its Bekaa campaign.

23. Acceleration and turn can be judged by calculating wing loading and thrust-to-weight from figures provided by *Interavia* or *Jane's Fighter Aircraft*. Acceleration right at Mach 1 should be relatively better for the MiG-23, since it can sweep its wings aft, though in this wing position its turn capability deteriorates so much that it becomes impossible to defend the MiG-23 against surprise bounces or SAMs.

VI

THE ORGANIZATION OF DEFENSE POLICY MAKING

Military reform proposals that focus on reshaping the defense establishment in terms of organization and process describe the current policy outputs as inappropriate or inadequate. Many then go on to describe various organizational changes that presumably would correct this problem. The implicit assumption, of course, is that the policy inadequacies are largely caused by organizational and procedural deficiencies. Reforms to correct these deficiencies, it is argued, would correct the policy inadequacies.

In this section the authors make such an assumption. To the degree that such an assumption is valid, what specifically do reformers hope to achieve in advocating such changes? Samuel Huntington points out that any such changes should address three basic goals: (1) to improve defense planning and preparation, (2) to improve the conduct of military operations, and (3) to make more efficient use of the resources available. Improvements in any or all of these would enhance overall defense posture and national security.

Reed approaches the defense policy process from the congressional perspective. The Senate and the House of Representatives, through the budget process, control the purse strings. Choices between defense and social programs are ultimately made on Capitol Hill. Since the Executive prepares and presents proposed budgets, it thereby determines to a great extent the final allocation of resources. Nonetheless, the Congress must approve it or modify it. As Reed points out, a problem arises in the balancing of the particular constituencies and interests that the Congress represents and the national interests that are often vaguely or poorly defined, and which Congress does not directly represent. Further, he argues, Congress is ill-equipped and poorly organized for dealing with military policy decisions. Despite Congress's apparent aspiration for greater assertiveness, as reflected by the Military Reform Caucus, the nature of military policy precludes congressional dominance. Therefore, the final allocation of resources for any budget year is often more a result of bargaining, compromise, and politics than it is an effort to meet national security needs.

Clark and Fagan argue the resource allocation question from a different perspective than Reed. They point out that the question is not merely one of overall allocation of resources to defense, but also, and perhaps more importantly, how those resources are allocated within the defense budget. In this regard they point out that the investment spending (for example, weapons procurement) portion of the budget is authorized in a current year but spent over a number of years (as the weapons are produced). This effect has at least three major implications. First, as the level of investment spending increases, the ability to adjust future defense budgets decreases. Second, increased investment spending also decreases the ability to reallocate resources in future defense budgets. Third, should political or economic reasons dictate a downward adjustment in future budgets, adjustments will be made in the manpower or operations and maintenance portions of the budget at the expense of defense readiness. Clark and Fagan also point out that in regard to manpower, it is cheaper in the long run to spend the extra money necessary to recruit quality soldiers, since they perform better and stay longer. Therefore, Clark and Fagan conclude, resource allocation analysis must address both the long-run and short-run, quantitative and qualitative, consequences.

Clark then goes on in a separate chapter to examine the impact of resource allocation among the armed forces upon the perceived validity of service roles and missions, and hence the services' receptivity to change. Since the defense pie is finite, Clark argues, a particular service's share of that pie is seen as confirming or threatening that service's role. This factor, when evaluated in conjunction with the degree of doctrinal autonomy a service has, can explain its willingness to innovate, accept, and adopt reform proposals. Clark maintains that as a service's share of the budget decreases and as its doctrinal autonomy decreases, greater receptiveness to reform will be demonstrated in an effort to increase budget share and autonomy. The converse holds as well. Clark concludes that the concern about interservice rivalry as a detractor from optimal defense effectiveness is not valid across all services, and that indeed this rivalry can be used to maximize innovativeness within the defense establishment.

General Jones, as a retired air force chief of staff and chairman of the Joint Chiefs, sees interservice rivalry in a different light. Jones agrees with Clark's evaluation of the services' focus on gaining large shares of the defense budget but does not see those efforts as being salutary. Rather, he argues, the very process prevents adequate integration of efforts, diffuses cross-service coherence, and results in an inefficient allocation of resources—a budget based on parochial service interests rather than a well-integrated plan. Jones argues that neither the civilian nor military leadership can gain control of the process under the current organization. He proposes, *inter alia,* strengthening the position of the chairman of the Joint Chiefs of Staff in order to provide timely and unified advice to the secretary of defense by overriding particular service interests. This would result, Jones maintains, in more efficient resource allocation, greater coherence in planning, and improved integration of effort in operations.

General Gorman points out that today's JCS reform proposals have, at their base, the same desires to improve military advice to their civilian leader as have been present for the last eighty years. He further points out that previous reforms and reorganizations have been diluted or abandoned, and that consequently the same problems have continued to plague the system. These problems arise from the "cultural" differences among the services as much as anything else and have been perpetuated because of fears of a dominant military. Gorman argues that these fears are unfounded and that the result of the Jones proposal, for one, would be a more effective military organization, better staffed and better prepared to meet the needs of its civilian superiors.

Odeen then provides a commentary on JCS reform. He identifies four areas where the current system is clearly deficient: (1) strategy development, (2) force structure and weapons requirements, (3) resource allocation advice, and (4) contingency and war planning. He then looks at some historical, political, and practical considerations that must be examined in analyzing any proposal for JCS reform. He performs some preliminary analysis by comparing the Jones proposal with a general staff proposal within the context of the considerations he proposed. Odeen concludes that more in-depth study of the various proposals is needed before a good decision can be reached, and he urges that both the study and the decision be made because of the importance of the issue.

13

TRENDS IN DEFENSE BUDGETING: MORTGAGING THE FUTURE

Asa A. Clark IV and Thomas W. Fagan

Clark and Fagan note that two characteristics are prominent in the defense budget increases of the early 1980s. First, they are concentrated in investment spending; second, future spending is constrained by previous procurement decisions. Clark and Fagan argue that these trends pinch out future policy discretion and "skew resource allocation priorities in favor of investment programs" at the cost of critical qualitative issues: for example, manpower and operational readiness.

Defense spending levels were dramatically increased in the first half of the 1980s in response to many factors, among which were continued high growth rates in Soviet military power, perceived nuclear parity between the superpowers, American reassertiveness, sufficient perceived distance from the haunting experience in Vietnam, and a groundswell of domestic conservatism. Driven primarily by greater investment spending (for research and development, procurement, and military construction), these expenditures reflected new priorities: in particular, a shift to a global, maritime-based strategy for general purpose forces, and modernization programs to renovate forces (especially strategic nuclear forces) neglected during the post-Vietnam era of impoverished defense spending.

Real defense spending was projected to rise by 1984 to the highest level since 1952 ($274.1 billion versus $283.4 billion in 1952, in constant 1983 dollars). Associated with these large spending increases are two characteristics that are central to this chapter's focus. First, these increases are concentrated in investment spending: 44.1 percent of the 1984 budget is allocated to research and development, procurement, and military construction, compared with 33.4 percent in 1980 and 31.0 percent in 1974. Given the long operational lives of weapons systems and investment spending, hardware deployments during the 1980s are sure to affect military policy through the year 2000. Other long-run effects of these hardware-intensive decisions, for example on manpower, will also shape future military policy.

Second, because appropriated investment dollars are expended over a time frame of more than five years, future spending is constrained by previous procurement decisions for major weapons systems. As a result, policy makers' discretion in forming future budgets is increasingly mortgaged. In addition, because procurement outlays are "back-loaded," austerity drives inevitably target more lucrative, vulnerable sectors (such as military pay, or operations and maintenance), which yield immediate budgetary savings.

What are the short- and long-run implications of these shifts? Is there an overarching, fundamental strategy that guides these choices? Can we be assured that U.S. security interests are best served by these policies?

In general, policy effectiveness and public accountability are served to the degree that short- and long-run consequences for the public's interest in the common defense are purposively considered. Conversely, however, the opposite effects obtain to the extent that short-term political factors unconnected to the public interest intrude. One solution to this critical concern, as suggested by classical pluralist theory, highlights the roles of competition, cooperation, and compromise in a system characterized by power diffused among political actors who hold diverse goals. What if, however, key aspects of defense policy have no political constituents who mobilize to effectively represent them? What if politically powerful constituents of defense policy subsectors operate as key decision-making actors and bias policy decisions? What if the structure of the policy process contains biases that operate quite independently of purposive choice?

Given the large degree to which the defense policy-making infrastructure is riddled with parochial, interest-serving individuals and organizations, the potential dangers raised by these questions are real. For example, the MX-basing controversy was driven as much by the relative sensitivity of state and local political constituents as by regard for particular geological or strategic considerations.

Given the powerful employment function of prime weapons production contracts, it is not surprising that congressmen, bureaucrats, and interest groups engage in free-wheeling politics to capture the plums represented by these contracts. These incentives and motives are understandable in view of the clearly discernible distributive consequences presented by such policy issues. However, these motives create political inertia for weapons procurement decisions quite apart from explicit assessment of larger questions. For example, what is the marginal net contribution of the weapon system to a broad mission legitimated by U.S. military strategy? How does this overall assessment of cost-effectiveness compare with those of alternative weapons systems? How does this overall assessment compare with other (non-weapons) expenditure proposals?

The public interest may be even less well served on issues in which there is no natural political constituent. For example, qualitative aspects of military policy such as operational readiness or leadership experience offer few identifiable and politically visible payoffs that would elicit a political constituency outside the military. Consequently, such critical qualitative elements are often ill served by policy processes fixated on balancing short-run, more easily identifiable political and economic tradeoffs.

This chapter, then, addresses these dilemmas by first discussing the political and fiscal parameters that substantially shape defense policy making, and the structural asymmetries that operate to skew resource allocation priorities in favor of investment programs without adequate qualitative appreciation for manpower and long-run readiness. This discussion is followed by an examination of the qualitative effects of ongoing quantitative decisions and an assessment of the implications of these trends for the future efficacy of U.S. armed forces. These aspects are presented to serve the chapter's primary purpose: informing the defense debate in order that public constituents of key qualitative components of military policy are created. In this way, sharpened analysis and broadened accountability will operate to help improve both short- and long-run defense policy effectiveness.

THE PROBLEM

The context of the problem can be explained in terms of five postulates. First, despite some erosion of the pro-defense consensus, Americans continue to believe in the necessity to commit substantially greater levels of resources in the 1980s to upgrade the armed services and the overall U.S. military posture. Acceptance of this necessity reflects public concern for renovating the military after the post-Vietnam period of relative fiscal poverty and, more fundamentally, one primary (although not dominant) world view, enunciated by President Ronald Reagan on 16 July 1980:

> We know only too well that war comes not when the forces of freedom are strong, but when they are weak. It is then that tyrants are tempted.

The second postulate, ironically both intuitively obvious and widely ignored, holds that a country's defense posture should be evaluated in terms of its capabilities and how they serve strategic purposes. Unfortunately, assessments of U.S. defense posture too often look only at aggregate (or, in the case of more thorough analyses, at interservice or interprogram) spending levels. This postulate is captured by James Fallows:

> The truly urgent military questions have little to do with how much money we spend. Indeed, more money for defense, without a change in the underlying patterns of spending, will not make us more secure, and may even leave the United States in a more vulnerable position than before.[1]

This tendency and its dangers are more fully discussed below.

The third postulate also renounces the tendency to view defense issues and policy choices in aggregate, quantitative terms. To quote an Israeli proverb, "Quality is more important than quantity—but is best in large numbers." This ethic is so pervasive in the politics of American defense policy that qualitative factors receive only secondary consideration. Perspectives that view defense in terms of "How much is enough?" are prone to give too little credence to qualitative and perhaps less tangible aspects of military affairs. Defense assessment should employ more disaggregate and qualitative analysis of resource allocations within the overall budgetary limit.

Fourth, although defense issues are "high politics" in which policy ought to derive rationally from a coherent set of strategic objectives, rationality is often overwhelmed by the pragmatism of politics. Because strategic objectives are difficult to identify, policy makers choose more tangible organizational and institutional goals as policy referents. Consequently, policy analysis of ends and means becomes confounded by goal bifurcation, and national security justifications are often invoked to serve parochial interests.

Fundamental to this theme is the contention that public officials' sincere commitments to the public interest are distorted, not by a corrupt desire to line their own pockets, but by creation of parochial but empirically useful goal and policy referents. As a result, in the name of national security considerations, officials may act to serve more parochial interests: organizational, institutional, constituent, even personal. As a consequence, factors not related directly to these parochial interests may receive only secondary consideration, if any. As Richard Garwin remarked:

> Sometimes I think none of it is real to them—the Congressmen. Getting elected is real. Making nice speeches is real. But not the idea that these forces might ever have to be used.[2]

Within defense budgeting, parochial interest serving ensures that great attention is paid to investment funding: research and development, procurement, and military construction. Representing almost half of the total defense budget, these appropriations categories are the game board on which pork-barrel politics are played.[3] More important, perhaps, than the magnitude of these three accounts is the fact that these allocation decisions commit a large quantity of funds, in zero-sum game fashion over the long term, and result in

Table 13.1. Trends in Federal Budget Deficits (Billions of Constant 1983 Dollars)

	1981 (actual)	1982 (actual)	1983 (est.)	1984	1985	1986	1987
				(baseline projections)			
Revenues	599	618	606	653	715	768	822
Outlays	657	728	800	850	929	999	1,072
Deficit	58	111	194	197	214	231	250
GNP	2,922	3,140	3,266	3,580	3,903	4,221	4,540
Deficit as percentage of GNP	2%	3.6%	6.1%	5.6%	5.6%	5.6%	5.6%
					(assumed gradual decline to 3.8% until 1988)		
(Assumed GNP deflator)			4.7%	4.6%			

Source: Congressional Budget Office: (1). *Reducing: Spending and Revenue Options,* February 1983, p. 1; (2). *The Outlook for Economic Recovery,* 1982, p. 52.

expenditures primarily to the civilian sector. As a result, investment decisions are carefully guided by interested and interest-serving congressmen.

In contrast, military pay and operations and maintenance dollars are allocated for short-term expenditures, usually in that budget year. Moreover, because these dollars are expended primarily to the armed services, few constituents external to the military are attracted. As a result, these "consumption" budget decisions are made fiscally more vulnerable by the absence of powerful political constituents.

The final postulate concerns the fiscal structure of and within defense budgeting. First, as everyone is painfully aware, federal budget deficits have become the rule. The last year in which the federal budget ran a surplus was 1969. As shown in table 13.1, this trend of budget deficits has accelerated in the 1980s: Congressional Budget Office analyses show that total real federal deficits rose from $58 billion in 1981 to $197 billion in 1984. As a percentage of the gross national product (GNP), real deficits climbed from 2.0 percent in 1981 to 5.6 percent in 1984. High deficit to GNP ratios will probably be sustained through the 1980s.

These large and growing deficits have serious implications for the economy. Assuming continued tight monetary policy, financing of the 2 percent real growth in budget deficits as a percentage of the GNP requires federal borrowing, primarily from the public. In addition to diverting funds from the private investment sector, federal borrowing exerts upward pressure in the financial markets on real interest rates (nominal rates less inflation). This is one of the primary reasons that real interest rates are maintaining their historic highs. As Senator Daniel P. Moynihan laments: "Taxes are a burden. Inflation is disorienting, but interest rates kill." Accordingly, federal deficits trigger political pressure to cut spending across the board. Arguments for spending cuts, it should be noted, focus on cutting rates of increasing defense spending, not on cutting absolute spending levels.

Although it is clear that federal deficits are not driven primarily by defense spending, the defense budget in particular is targeted for a variety of reasons: the traditional debate over "how much is enough?," the visibility of the defense budget (it is easy to single out specific measures to cut, for example, major weapons systems), and the comparative ease of controlling the defense budget relative to social programs.

Fully two-thirds of the federal budget is uncontrollable. In addition to their legal basis, the moral, social, and political implications of entitlement programs make them difficult to reduce (for example, Social Security benefits, farm price supports, medicare, medicaid, unemployment benefits). Because defense spending constitutes 70 percent of the controllable portion of the federal budget, budget cutters will inevitably want DOD to share the burden of measures necessary for economic recovery.[4]

To the degree that defense cutbacks are implemented, the consequences for specific programs and overall savings also reflect the fiscal structure *within* the defense budget. Total Obligational Authority (TOA) is the legal limit approved by Congress for buying and operating defense programs. Outlays represent, in contrast, actual expenditures during the current budget year. Total Obligational Authority is important because it is used by DOD, Congress, and the president to review details of the defense budget and to set actual defense dollar commitments. Because outlays lag Total Obligational Authority, however, when the President cuts TOA for a defense program, he may stop treasury checks tomorrow or he may stop checks ten years from now, depending upon the program. Therefore, depending on the appropriations category, cuts in TOA have differential effects on outlays.

As reflected in table 13.2, the rates at which budget dollars are actually spent differ substantially for each appropriations category. This means that these categories (for example, manpower, procurement, military construction) present different outlay savings returns on budget TOA cutbacks. For example, $.98 of $1.00 cut in military personnel will be saved in the first year. In contrast, only $.03 per $1.00 cut for ship building is saved in the first year. Even when these lags are known, few realize how little in front-end savings is achieved by what appear to be major cuts in defense programs TOA.[5]

Three important consequences follow from these inherent differential outlay rates. First, the incentives facing policy decisions to generate short-run fiscal savings are structurally biased to protect investment sectors (procurement, research and development, military construction) and, conversely, to expose short-run consumption sectors (military personnel, operations and maintenance). Second, to the degree that defense budgets reflect decisions to grant funding priority to long-run investment sectors, future budget authority

Table 13.2. Outlay Rates per Dollar of Total Obligational Authority, by Defense Appropriation Category

Appropriations Category	Budget Year				
	1	2	3	4	5
Military personnel	.98	.02	—	—	—
Operations & maintenance	.80	.17	.02	—	—
Procurement:					
Aircraft	.10	.40	.30	.10	.10
Missiles	.30	.55	.14	.01	—
Ships	.03	.13	.14	.14	.55
Research & development	.59	.34	.05	.01	.01
Military construction	.10	.47	.13	.10	.10

Source: Congressional Budget Office, 1983.

discretion is mortgaged to the stream of future outlays generated by past investment-intensive decisions. As reflected in figure 3, subsequent budget regimes are increasingly constrained by the combination of fiscal ceilings and TOA budgeted in prior years. Policy discretion becomes increasingly circumscribed. As discussed earlier, this circumstance is made operative by the force modernization decisions of the early 1980s.

Finally, this structure of differential outlay rates operates to drive a wedge between short- and long-run evaluations of trade-offs: for example, readiness versus modernization. A decision to generate fiscal savings is a decision to decrease short-run readiness and to mortgage future budget authority to outlays for procurement that was spared in the economy drive, perhaps independently of programmatic policy. A decision to expand defense spending is a decision to mitigate short- and long-run tradeoffs, but one which also mortgages future budget discretion, again perhaps independently of policy.

What is more insidious, in terms of severity of consequences, are the long-run effects of short-term economy decisions. That is not to say that these pernicious effects are either understood or intended by policy makers when choices are made. For example, the long-term consequences of cutbacks in military personnel funding are severe and generally unintended.

ASSESSMENT OF EFFECTS

Defense spending through the 1980s will be shaped primarily by the intersection of several forces: the modernization and build-up programs launched in the early 1980s, increasing congressional and public disenchantment with sustaining the defense build-up, fundamental concern for the economy and equitable sharing of increasing fiscal constraints as part of economic adjustment burdens, increasing public suspicion of responsible defense man-

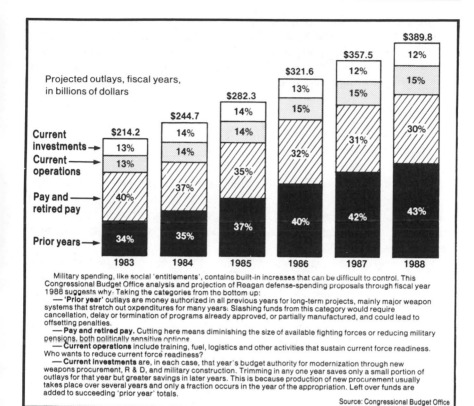

Figure 3. Cut defense spending? Here's the catch. (© 1983 by The New York Times Company. Reprinted by permission.)

agement sparked by a rash of reports of long-term undercosting of major weapons systems, and the political and structural forces described earlier.

To the extent that the defense sector is required to curtail projected TOA rates of increase in order to reduce defense outlays and help relieve the federal deficits problem, a variety of targets suggest themselves:

1. Cut military personnel outlays by reducing or capping pay, allowances, and bonus compensations

2. Cut funding for operations and maintenance by reducing outlays for training and maintenance

3. Terminate contracts for procurement of major weapons systems

4. Cut force structure by reducing personnel strengths of the services and defense civilians

5. A combination of these and other measures

It is outside this chapter's scope to present and analyze specific proposals for defense cutbacks. Many alternative defense posture statements and budgets are available in the ongoing debate.[6] Rather, analysis of spending implications will focus on the first two targets, both of which have qualitative considerations that are poorly understood and without political constituencies outside the military: military personnel and operation and maintenance. A number of studies have examined the fiscal and policy consequences of the other targets.

QUALITATIVE CONSIDERATIONS: MILITARY MANPOWER

For reasons developed above, there will always be pressure to cut defense spending, pressure that will always be focused on military personnel funding levels. Therefore, it is imperative that both public levels of understanding and quality of policy analysis be raised and attuned to long-run, qualitative consequences.

This section argues against cutting planned pay increases and bonuses for the current force. Specifically, it is argued (1) that evaluation of the success of the All Volunteer Force (AVF) should focus upon the army; (2) that high-quality recruits are cheaper in the intermediate and long run; (3) that changes in pay and benefits attract high-quality recruits and soldiers much more than less qualified recruits and soldiers; (4) that the GI Bill is more important and could cost less than many studies suggest; and (5) that lack of financial support for the All Volunteer Force may unwittingly cause it to unravel.

Continuation of the AVF, with appropriate pay and benefits schedules, however, yields soldiers who perform better and stay in the service at a higher rate (thus enhancing the quality, experience, and cohesiveness of the NCO corps) and is cheaper overall. Although contradicting all conventional wisdom, this course of action enhances short- and long-run readiness more than alternative manpower policies: a return to the draft (politically infeasible) or continuation of the AVF, but with pay and benefit cuts.

The debate about the draft versus the All Volunteer Force has obscured important issues over the years. One such key issue concerns the use of aggregate DOD data to compare the draft and the AVF. The air force and navy have always had volunteers (many of whom enlisted, however, to avoid the draft). Between 1953 and 1973, 32.4 percent of all males entering the armed forces were drafted. Of those, 98.0 percent were drafted into the army. During this period the army's strength was composed of 59 percent draftees (compared to 1 percent for the navy, zero percent for the air force, and 4 percent for the marines). Clearly, therefore, assessments of the AVF must examine manpower data for the most draft-dependent service: the army.

A second issue that has obfuscated manpower debates has been the focus on quantitative strength and authorization levels, based on the presumption that soldiers are homogeneous. This presumption is false: smart, educated soldiers are better soldiers. This does not mean that all soldiers must be smart, but some must be.[7]

Table 13.3. High-Quality Male Recruits Displayed by Recruiting Year and by Their Current Year of Service within the Army

Recruiting Year	Year of Service	I-IIIa Recruits	High School Graduate I-IIIa Recruits	Percentage of this year group who are High School Grad I-IIIa in the current Army Inventory
1968	15	214,100		43.4
1969	14	191,500		42.5
1970	13	131,200		43.7
1971	12	102,600		45.2
1972	11	94,900		47.5
Shift to All Volunteer Army				
1973	10	50,100		46.2
1974	9	80,200	43,544	47.4
1975	8	87,300	53,387	46.8
1976	7	82,900	52,015	40.0
Loss of the GI Bill				
1977	6	47,900	33,000	30.0
1978	5	36,500	26,000	30.2
1979	4	33,000	22,300	27.0
1980	3	35,300	25,500	19.7
1981	2	41,800	31,900	28.3
1982	1		43,300	41.4

Sources: Bernard D. Karpinos, *Male Chargeable Accessions: Evaluation by Mental Categories (1953–1973)* (Alexandria, Va.: Human Resources Research Organization, 1977); Thomas W. Fagan, Office of Economic and Manpower and Analysis, United States Military Academy.

Note: I-IIIa refers to the top 50% of recruits by entrance mental aptitude scores.

The soldiers currently in the army reflect the quality of the recruits each year for the past twenty years. If there was a large number of high-quality recruits in fiscal year 1966, they will be reflected in a high percentage of high-quality soldiers in their eighteenth year of service in 1984. When a large number of high-quality recruits enter the army, they stay in the army and sustain high levels of quality soldiers in each year group's inventory (see table 13.3). The shift to the All Volunteer Force (1973–1976) did not dramatically affect quality recruits and, subsequently, has not affected the inventory of high-quality sergeants. Caps on military pay and the loss of the GI Bill in 1976, however, dramatically affected the army's ability to attract quality recruits and the subsequent inventories of quality young soldiers. This quality "bubble" is why the army leadership supports a GI Bill.

The upturn in army recruiting in fiscal year 1981 is a positive sign and reflects the management efforts by managers and recruiters within the United States Army Recruiting Command. Nonetheless, this upturn still falls far short of the quality levels of the 1973–1976 period. What measures are required to continue and accelerate this trend? Before policy makers can intelligently address this central question, a number of other fallacies obfuscating manpower analyses must be exploded. These fallacies are termed myths because although almost everyone accepts these contentions as valid, they are patently false.

Myth 1:   Less qualified soldiers reenlist at higher rates. Therefore, if the army reorients recruiting to attract more qualified soldiers, it will not help itself in the long run because high-quality soldiers fail to reenlist.

In 1976, 20 percent of high school recruits stayed in the army, compared to only 13 percent of the non-high school recruits. High school recruits reenlisted at almost twice the rate as non-high school recruits.

The confusion about this phenomenon results from continued focus upon reenlistment rates. Figure 4 shows that high school graduates (HSG) stayed at a 20 percent rate, while non-high school graduates (NHSG) stayed at only a 13 percent rate. However, 41 percent of the NHSG reenlisted, compared to only 36 percent for the HSG. The strange inversion is caused by the proportions of those who quit: 68 percent of the NHSG quit, or were ineligible to reenlist, compared to only 44 percent of the HSG. More quality recruits reenlisted, but substantially more were eligible. Consequently, the quality recruit reenlistment rate *appears* to be lower. The reenlistment, or stay, rate is the important measure and should be the focus of manpower research, inquiry, and policy. It is this rate that reflects the NCO experience, stability, quality, and cohesiveness so critical for the leadership of the modern army, particularly in light of the requirements for maneuver warfare.

Myth 2:   High-quality recruits are more expensive than low-quality recruits.

This myth is the result of a unidimensional focus upon recruiting costs. Although the higher-quality recruits cost more to recruit, they are much cheaper to train and maintain. As suggested by figure 4, they also stay in the army much longer (they do not quit), and they are more productive (they are promoted faster). For example, consider the current recruiting requirements necessary to yield one thousand sergeants in 1990 to help man the Bradley infantry fighting vehicle. Applying the reenlistment percentages found in figure 2, 5,297 high school graduate I-IIIa soldiers would need to be recruited today. Similarly, 6,671 non-high school graduate I-IIIa soldiers would need to be recruited today. The 1,374 soldiers not accounted for would have to be trained and paid over the intervening eight years. These costs overwhelm the initial recruiting costs. This phenomenon consistently emerges regardless of the job or career management field under consideration: there simply is not a one-to-one comparison of high-quality and lower-quality recruits. In short, the army could recruit fewer and fewer people if given the resources to focus on those of higher quality.

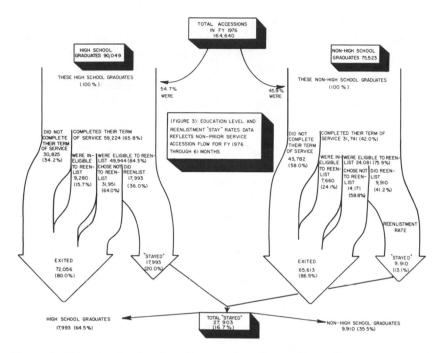

Figure 4. Education level and reenlistment "stay" rates (data reflect non-prior service accession flow for FY 1976 through 61 months).

Myth 3:   Relative to high-quality recruits, pay increases do more to motivate lower-quality (high school dropouts) recruits to enlist, and, subsequently, to reenlist.

Of all of the myths, this is the most insidious. It suggests that the army cannot solve its quality "bubble" problem with pay or bonuses. Moreover, it suggests that increases in pay and reenlistment bonuses will decrease the proportional quality of the force. Although many econometric studies have supported this contention, virtually all these studies are fatally flawed because the data on which the analyses are tested fail to satisfy a variety of technical, statistical assumptions of these analytical techniques.[8] When estimation techniques are corrected for this problem, however, studies show that in fact pay and bonuses attract and affect high-quality soldiers substantially more than low-quality soldiers with respect to both reenlistment and enlistment. Consequently, erosion of pay or bonuses will adversely affect the long-run quality of armed forces personnel.

Myth 4:   Educational benefits are less important than bonuses. Educational benefits do not attract and retain soldiers as much as the military believes they do.

The young people who enter the military are recruited from a segmented labor market. College students or college aspirants are motivated to join by programs like the Army College Fund or the GI Bill. Talented apprentices or members of the labor force are motivated by pay and bonuses. As is obvious from inspection of figure 4, the GI Bill's education benefits substantially increase both the pool of potential recruits and the proportion of high-quality recruits. Studies drawing contradictory conclusions are statistically flawed (for the same reasons discussed earlier) and fly in the face of intuition. Moreover, education benefits are not as costly as many suggest.

The AVF is a viable concept if provided financial support, as suggested by the analyses used to reject these myths. By focusing on important qualitative manpower parameters such as aptitude scores, schooling, and stay rates, policy tools like military pay, reenlistment bonuses, and education benefits can be manipulated to attract and retain higher-quality soldiers who are cheaper, perform better, and provide more experienced leadership in a more cohesive NCO corps in the long run.

Conversely, if military personnel funding is cut to redress short-run cash flow problems, the success of the AVF may be jeopardized. Therefore, it is imperative that these short-run decisions be reached following rigorous analysis of the long-run consequences for the integral support of effective manpower and defense policy. A decision this year to save outlays and reduce deficits by capping military pay is a decision to reduce the overall quality of the NCO corps over the next twenty years.

QUALITATIVE CONSIDERATIONS: OPERATIONS AND MAINTENANCE

Budget dollars appropriated for operations and maintenance are spent on a variety of consumption components that primarily affect short- and near-term combat readiness: training and exercises (ammunition, fuel, transportation, training areas and facilities), maintenance (parts, facilities, training of maintenance personnel), and war stocks (ammunition, fuel, spare parts).

The yield of O&M funding derives from enhanced operational readiness resulting from intensive, realistic training and maneuvers—payoffs that are somewhat subjective, difficult to assess, and politically invisible to the public. Because these payoffs are difficult to explicitly measure, compare, and evaluate, it is hard to assess the net return on O&M dollars. For example, to what extent is the operational readiness of army forces in Europe enhanced by annual Reforger exercise? Are the dollars spent on Red Flag exercises justified by higher air force tactical fighter readiness? Is the increment in U.S. Sixth Fleet combat readiness worth the high cost of supporting O&M funds? How can the relative returns on O&M dollars be compared across service exercises? How can the marginal cost-effectiveness of readiness be evaluated and compared with spending returns for procurement, research and development, or manpower?

Given the diversity, invisibility, and nonquantifiability of returns on O&M spending, arguments for expanding, sustaining, or defending O&M dollars are severely handicapped. This problem is compounded when budgetary trade-offs are assessed between O&M and, for example, procurement spending.

There is a second reason why there will always be pressure to focus defense spending cutbacks on O&M budget authorizations. As in the case of military personnel funding, O&M budget authorizations are front-loaded (a high outlay rate in the budgeted year) and are consumed in the short run by the military services (for example, fuel for steaming and flying time, ammunition, spare parts, maintenance services). Therefore, O&M funds are vulnerable to economy drives because cutbacks yield immediate savings in defense outlays. Moreover, because these outlays primarily represent internal consumption spending, few constituents external to the armed services are attracted to act as political allies in budget battles.

The consequence of these structural (political and fiscal) characteristics is a continuous downward bias against O&M funding. As a result, irrespective of any policy decision to give priority to long-run modernization over short-run readiness, and reinforced by the absence of public understanding of the qualitative implications for force readiness, the U.S. defense posture is continually eroded by qualitative shortcomings. Forces that are severely constrained in realistic, joint, battle-oriented training cannot be ready for combat.

Again, this result may be judged on one set of terms if it follows from a purposive policy decision. If, however, this result follows from a structurally-induced stream of nondecisions, the public interest of national defense is being unintentionally violated. The conclusion is the same: short-run decisions should reflect explicit analysis of long-run consequences for defense tradeoffs among readiness, modernization, and fiscal constraints.

CONCLUSION

It is clear that defense spending projected for the 1980s will be increasingly scrutinized for soft areas from which outlay savings can be squeezed. To the extent that reports of chronic undercosting of weapons purchases remain true in the 1980s, the projected $1.6 trillion in outlays will prove inadequate to finance the defense buildup. Administration attempts to further increase defense budget rates will likely trigger fierce public backlash against defense spending in general.

This chapter has discussed short-run structural factors impinging on defense policy making. Because defense spending is the largest controllable sector in the federal budget, and because outlay rates vary widely across defense appropriations categories, structural incentives operate to protect or to sacrifice different components of defense spending *without regard to policy*. Furthermore, because these defense appropriations categories are coveted to varying degrees by constituent-serving congressmen and force modernization advocates within the DOD, for example, rational and coherent policy making falls prey, to a large degree, to short-term concern for distributive consequences of resource allocations.

It is imperative that long-run aspects of defense be protected by active and effective political constituents, or by a policy process that forces decision makers to confront long-run trade-offs. It is not difficult to construct a rational analytic methodology. One approach explicitly identifies long-run objectives, then "grows policy requirements back" to the present. Another approach "grows" current policy parameters forward to derive shortfalls relative to the long-run objectives. These shortfalls provide the basis for adjustments to growth rates and/or long-run objectives. In either case, a methodological framework is established that forces explicit assessment of short- and long-run tradeoffs in policy goals and resource allocations.

Although difficult to operationalize, such planning schemes are conceptually not difficult and have been operative, in various forms, for years. The best planning methodology, however, is compromised by the structural factors discussed here, unless active and effective political constituents of the qualitative and fiscally vulnerable defense sectors are created and sustained. Only then is a political climate generated in which these equally vital, but politically more vulnerable, sectors are protected.

NOTES

1. James Fallows, *National Defense* (New York: Random House, 1981), p. xv.

2. Ibid., p. 184.

3. Incisive studies of budget controllability and defense pork-barrel politics include John A. Ferejohn, *Pork Barrel Politics: Rivers and Harbors Legislation, 1947–1968* (Stanford, Calif.: Stanford University Press, 1974); and Steven Rosen, *Testing the Theory of the Military-Industrial Complex* (Lexington, Mass.: Lexington Books, 1973).

4. This argument is complex: Defense spending stimulates the economy through DOD employees' spending on consumer goods, infrastructure programs (military bases and installation), and procurement contracting. These must be weighed against the effects of overseas spending, deficit spending, and the multiplier effects of alternative uses of defense dollars. DOD estimates indicate that the net effects of these factors result in $.50 saved in that year for each dollar cut from the defense budget.

5. The Department of Defense, *Annual Report: FY 1984* (Washington, D.C.: Government Printing Office, 1983) reports that outlays represent 88 percent of TOA for each budget year in the 1980s. Because these outlays reflect both old (carryover) and new budget authority expenditures, this figure understates the outlay-lag effect, particularly for procurement-heavy budgets. See figure 1.

6. One such study, conducted by the Congressional Budget Office, (1) canceled the B-1 bomber; (2) substituted an engine that was cheaper by twelve million dollars per copy for 7,615 tanker aircraft, (3) canceled two of the navy's carriers, (4) canceled seven one-billion-dollar Aegis cruisers, (5) canceled ten nuclear submarines, (6) canceled 1,440 M1 tanks, (7) canceled 6,480 M2 infantry fighting vehicles, (8) canceled F/A-18s for the navy's thirty light attack squadrons, (9) modified retiree benefits, and (10) reduced or realigned 157 bases. These cutbacks saved less than one billion dollars in outlays in fiscal year 1983, or one-half of one percent of the deficit. Although those projected savings will increase through 1987, they yield little political capital to a current administration.

7. For purposes of this discussion, the "high- versus low-quality soldier" distinction is delimited by high school graduation. The analysis also holds if Category I-IIIa recruits are compared with Category IV recruits. Category levels refer to quartile scores of recruits on the Armed Services Vocational Aptitude Battery. Category I-IIIa recruits include the soldiers scoring in the top 50 percent of all entering soldiers. Use of terms such as high- or low-quality soldiers, it is recognized, is value-laden, and perhaps even pejorative. It is also, however, a crucial distinction for the effectiveness of the armed services.

8. These studies are flawed because they apply regression or ordinary least squares upon data for which the technique is inappropriate. Essentially, an assumption of regression analysis is violated, and conclusions or coefficients that result from that analysis are not near the true coefficients (they are biased) and will never be near the true coefficients (they are inconsistent). This error is called sample selection bias. In order to judge the effects of pay fluctuations on various categories of prospective recruits, income elasticities must be estimated. Difficult in and of itself, this estimation also requires data that are prohibitively difficult to get, such as income levels of alternative employment for prospective recruits.

14

CONGRESS AND THE POLITICS OF DEFENSE REFORM

James W. Reed

Reed examines the reasons why Congress has become a more assertive defense policy innovator. Chief among these is congressional frustration over a historical inability to influence the strategic components of U.S. military policy. He identifies and discusses changes that have taken place over the last twenty years which may explain this activist trend. Reed concludes by evaluating the impact of the Military Reform Caucus to date and in the future.

While not an unprecedented phenomenon, the current movement to effect change in our defense establishment displays certain features that distinguish it in some measure from earlier reform efforts. Military reform in the 1980s has come to embrace a spectrum of issues that is at once more pervasive and all-encompassing than many, if not all, of the earlier reform campaigns. The current reform agenda casts a wide net, one that captures issues on a macroscale (Should the United States pursue a maritime or coalition strategy?) as well as micro- (Should the military services retain their "up and out" promotion policies?).

Although the contemporary military reform effort traces its origins largely to sources outside Congress, one of the more interesting developments is the degree to which it has lately taken root in Congress. This is not to say that the military reform movement is exclusively or even primarily a congressional enterprise—indeed, much of the impetus for change has emanated from within the services themselves. Nonetheless, one of the more highly visible dimensions of the reform movement has been a significant segment of Congress that has endeavored to enhance considerably its influence over the formulation of defense policy.

That some in Congress should see themselves as a wellspring for defense reform may strike many as an oddity. Indeed, in commenting recently on the tendency for policy makers to choose the "politically palatable" alternative over the "proper" course of action, former chairman of the Joint Chiefs of Staff General David Jones said, "Congress is as responsible . . . for the defense problems we have today as the Pentagon."[1]

Why, then, has the current effort to reform the military, unlike many of its predecessors, evolved in some measure as a congressional initiative? The argument to be made here is that the defense reform movement in Congress, particularly as represented by the Military Reform Caucus, can be understood as an effort to redress Congress's longstanding incapacity to affect significantly the defense policy formulation process in the executive branch. Both the agenda and the *modus operandi* of the reform caucus are indicative of Congress's desire to move beyond its more traditional role in the defense policy sector toward a more assertive role as a policy innovator. In making this argument, we begin by describing the defense policy-making environment; we contrast the executive and congressional roles in the defense arena and their respective budget-making processes; and we examine the military reform movement in Congress as a vehicle by which to mitigate congressional handicaps in the policy process. We conclude with an appraisal of the military reform movement's prospects as a source of policy innovation in Congress.

THE POLITICS OF MILITARY POLICY

Political choices, by definition, pose difficult dilemmas for those who must make them. It is the nature of choices concerning military policy, however, that the dilemmas they pose are doubly acute. In a study that has perhaps not been improved upon in the nearly two decades since it was published, Samuel Huntington observed that military policy "exists in two worlds."

> One is international politics, the world of the balance of power, wars and alliances, the subtle and the brutal uses of force and diplomacy to influence the behavior of other states. . . . The other world is domestic politics, the world of interest groups, political parties, social classes, with their conflicting interests and goals.[2]

Huntington argues that "military policy can only be understood as the responses of government to conflicting pressures from its foreign and domes-

Table 14.1. Public Views on Defense Spending

Pollster	Date	Increase (%)	Decrease (%)	Maintain Current Level (%)
NBC/AP	Nov 1981	34	14	47
CBS/NYT	Apr 1981	54	9	34
CBS/NYT	Jan 1981	61	7	28
CBS/NYT	Feb 1980	64	6	23
NBC/AP	Dec 1979	51	9	31
NBC/AP	Sep 1979	38	16	36
Gallup	Jul 1977	27	23	40
Gallup	Jul 1969	8	52	31
Gallup	Feb 1960	21	18	45
Gallup	Mar 1950	64	7	24

Source: Public Opinion (December/January 1982).

Note: "Don't know" responses not shown.

tic environments."[3] Further, military policy can be viewed over time as displaying phases of equilibrium and disequilibrium. Equilibrium occurs when "no sharp conflicts exist among the dominant goals of domestic policy, military policy, and foreign policy; and no major changes in policy are taking place."[4] That is, the dilemmas inherent in military policy will be amplified during periods in which policy makers find the imperatives of the domestic and international environments to be pulling them in clearly contradictory directions. To the degree that Congress is both a reflection of and sensitive to mass attitudes, it is particularly vulnerable not merely to the dichotomy posed by the nature of military policy but also to a range of other dilemmas that surface with special intensity in Congress.

At least in theory Congress serves to represent the views of the body politic, but on issues of defense the views of the body politic have generally been ambiguous and unstable. As the 1980s unfold, opinion surveys indicate that more than 60 percent of all Americans sense that the United States currently possesses military forces inadequate to the challenge posed by increased Soviet military power.[5] This growing unease with the adequacy of U.S. military strength was translated in the mid-1970s into heightened public support for increased defense expenditures (table 14.1).

Contrary to popular belief, however, it is not clear that the consequent increases in defense spending, evident since 1979, have necessarily been at the expense of spending on domestic programs. In fact, since 1970 spending in non-defense related areas has increased at a rate sharply higher than that of spending on defense (fig. 5). Moreover, the greater part of federal spending in non-defense areas currently goes for interest on the mounting federal debt, entitlement programs, and other so-called "uncontrollable" expenditures.

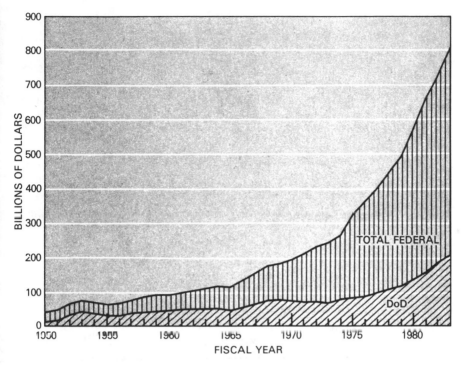

Figure 5. Aggregate federal spending (current $). (*Source:* Report of the Secretary of Defense to Congress, 1 February 1983, 63.)

Nonetheless, in an era of a burgeoning federal budget, a budget deficit perilously close to the $200 billion mark, record high interest rates, and double-digit unemployment, there is a perception that the domestic policy goals of Americans have been jeopardized. Public support for further increases in defense spending has thus waned (even while Soviet military forces continue to grow),[6] and the result has been the germination of a military reform movement in Congress that offers the beguiling promise of greater U.S. military strength at lower cost.

Faced with such conflicting cues from its domestic and foreign environments, it is hardly surprising that congress should find it difficult to achieve a stable internal consensus concerning the appropriate level of defense expenditures. But congressional efforts to promote consensus on matters of military policy are hampered still further by other salient dimensions of the policy-making environment. First among these is the often-noted erosion of a "spirit of bipartisanship" in foreign policy. Stemming primarily from our failure in Vietnam, Americans lost, as George Quester put it, a "common agreement . . . about what positive goals the United States could accomplish through its foreign policy."[7] With respect to military policy, evidence of this frayed consensus is to be found in the greater propensity of Congress to challenge defense programs. The debate in the late 1960s over an antiballistic missile (ABM) and the continuing debate over the fate of the MX missile are only two of the more noteworthy illustrations.

A second factor, one related to the first, is that while Americans may evince general agreement on the need for greater defense spending, that agreement is both fragile and ambiguous and, therefore, may lack usefulness as a guide to policy choices. Left unanswered are the critical questions: How much is enough? To what ends should American military power be directed? What tools should constitute the American power posture? Accompanying the growth in support for military spending has been a greater selectivity on the part of Americans concerning the end to which our military resources should be directed.[8] Even were such areas of ambiguity to be resolved, a general willingness on the part of the public to support higher defense spending may be of little practical use to a congressman forced to choose between added appropriations for an F-16 or an F-15 fighter aircraft.

Thirdly, beyond the dichotomy between our domestic and foreign environments, congressmen are faced with the added dilemma of choosing between the national interest broadly defined or the more parochial interests of their constituents. In responding to a new congressman's query as to how he should resolve that dilemma, the late chairman of the House Armed Services Committee, Representative Carl Vinson (D. Ga.), replied, "If you don't represent the nation as a whole and have your horizons beyond the limits of your congressional district, we don't need you in Congress." But then he added, "By the same token, if you're not representing your district, you won't be in Congress long enough to make a difference."[9]

Especially within the relevant committees, a minimal degree of consensus within Congress, sustainable over a period of time, is the precondition to effective congressional action in any policy area. In a context of resource scarcity, magnified threats, and uncertainty, policy choices on military matters pose special difficulties for Congress. Many of the factors described here pose relatively constant and enduring challenges to congressional policy making. Certain other aspects of the defense policy making environment, however, become particularly problematic during periods of disequilibrium. It seems reasonable to argue that Americans find themselves in the early 1980s in a period of defense policy disequilibrium; the military reform movement itself is testament to that. As a result, Congress is likely to find its efforts to craft an enduring consensus on military matters a particularly troublesome task in the period that lies ahead.

THE ASYMMETRY OF THE CONSTITUTIONAL BALANCE

The complexity that characterizes the environment of military policy making is magnified still further by the constitutional division of powers between the executive and legislative branches of government. Mindful of the need to serve the twin aims of centralizing authority for national security policy while establishing a counterweight to check the growth of presidential power, the Founding Fathers seemingly gave preference to the latter.

The only constitutional power over military policy explicitly granted to the president is the authority vested in him as commander in chief under Article I, Section 2. Congressional powers, however, as specified in Article I, Sections 8 and 9, extend more broadly to include the authority to declare war, to raise and support armies, to provide and maintain a navy, to make rules for the government and regulation of land and naval forces, and to provide monies for such forces.

As Richard Neustadt has emphasized, rather than create a government of separated powers, the Constitution set up a government of separate institutions with shared powers.[10] Thus was served the framers' intent that each branch should function to check the power of the other branches. While the balance of enumerated powers would appear to give Congress the upper hand, the realities of military policy making have produced a different outcome. The mandated sharing of powers between the executive and legislative branches has, on issues of military policy, resulted in greater presidential control over policy. Several reasons are apparent for this presidential preeminence.

The first is the difference in the types of decisions that tend to be focused in each branch. Huntington argues that issues of military policy can be divided into two categories: strategic and structural.[11] Strategy pertains to the "units and uses of force." That is, strategic decisions govern the size and composition of forces, the deployment of those forces, and their doctrinal employment. In contrast, structural decisions deal with the procurement and allocation of military resources, "the men, money, and material."

This distinction is key, first, because the nature of the military policy-making process is such that procurement decisions ideally flow from previous strategic decisions. A decision to procure a certain number of F-16 fighters, for example, should be the end product of a series of strategic decisions that include analysis of the threats; assessments of the adversary's capabilities; choices on doctrine; decisions on aggregate force structures; and, finally, choices among alternative types and numbers of weapons systems. Clearly, narrow-minded considerations often intrude in a fashion that attenuates the intended link between procurement and strategy; nevertheless, procurement decisions are generally judged to be intelligent to the extent that they reflect longer-range strategic imperatives.

Further, the distinction is important because structural decisions tend to be based more upon cues from the domestic environment, while strategic decisions stem from the international environment. For example, choices concerning resource allocation, such as military manpower issues, tend to be more sensitive to the constraints inherent in the domestic policy arena. Decisions concerning how that manpower is to be organized and employed, however, stem more clearly from planning assumptions concerning likely theaters and adversaries.

The balance of constitutionally enumerated powers aside, Huntington observes that "in the American system of government, decisions on strategy are largely executive decisions, decisions on structure normally require both executive and legislative action."[12] Thus, in a very real sense Congress finds itself dealing only on the margins of military policy with those issues most susceptible to domestic pressures.

Executive dominance in military policy has been reinforced by a second factor: the bureaucratic advantages inherent in the presidency. In a pattern strengthened by history and tradition, especially during wartime, the president has wide latitude to seize the initiative, to gather and control access to information, and, subject to some limitations, to act unilaterally. Clearly a more cumbersome institution, Congress finds itself reacting to the bureaucratic initiatives emanating from the executive branch.

A third factor has been a congressional predisposition to defer to the supposed expertise of officials in the executive branch. Such acquiescence has generally taken the form of granting the president his major defense programs, if not more. As Congressman Les Aspin noted, "Uniforms are identified with expertise; the higher the rank, the greater the expertise. . . . When it comes to national security matters, there is a tendency to 'play it safe.' Playing it safe usually means buying more.[13] While the advent of a military reform movement in Congress testifies to a greater congressional willingness to challenge such expertise, Congress as a whole still seems reluctant to cancel outright the major defense initiatives of the president.

None of these three factors presents a totally insurmountable barrier to greater congressional participation in military policy formulation. A fourth factor, though, serves both to reinforce and to perpetuate the impact of the others. The executive-legislative asymmetry in control over military policy is due perhaps more than anything to the wholly distinctive budgetary processes in each branch.[14] While the budget-making process in the Pentagon strives to approximate patterns of rational decision making through the application of systems analysis techniques, defense budgeting in Congress is politics writ large. The distinctive patterns are critical, since they pose significant obstacles to greater congressional participation in defense budget making. And as Arnold Kanter observes, "Budget outcomes are the quantitative statements of defense policy."[15]

These important points merit explication in some detail.

BUDGET MAKING IN THE PENTAGON

Secretaries of defense have long recognized that their ability to shape military policy hinges upon their ability to control the budgets of the military services. Since the Defense Reorganization Act of 1947, which unified the budgets of the services under the control of the secretary of defense, the history of defense budgeting through at least 1968 is a history of increasingly centralized control within the office of the secretary of defense (OSD). The "McNamara Revolution" of the early 1960s brought the trend toward increasing centralization to its apogee with the introduction of the Planning-Programming-Budgeting System (PPBS) to the defense budgeting process.

When viewed through the lenses of different models of the decision process, PPBS displays elements both of rationality and of the bargaining associated with bureaucratic politics.[16] The former is evident to the degree that PPBS is a management system "designed to translate national security goals into objectives, to define programs to meet those objectives, and to evaluate which weapons systems and force structures accomplish the objectives at least cost in budgetary and political terms."[17] In essence, PPBS uses systems analysis to solidify what had been a rather tenuous link between the planning and budgeting processes within the Pentagon.

Two features in particular made that link explicit. First, rather than making decisions based upon the traditional budget categories of personnel, procurement, R&D, operations and maintenance, and so on (as Congress continues to do), internal defense planning grouped budget decisions according to principal missions or programs, even though such categories cut across service lines. Examples of such programs were strategic forces, general purpose forces, airlift and sealift, and supply and maintenance. Second, although previous budget projections had been made on an annual basis, under PPBS a Five-Year Defense Program (FYDP) was published containing detailed tabulations of force levels, manpower, weapons systems, and costs for all of the services. The FYDP is updated annually and extended for an additional year.

The process by which the Pentagon prepares the FYDP involves a formalized sequence of events extending over twenty months.[18] Initially, the Joint Chiefs of Staff update the FYDP by preparing a strategic assessment and recommendation of force structure requirements that is unconstrained by fiscal limitations. Next, in consultation with the Office of Management and Budget, the secretary of defense issues detailed guidance on strategy and fiscal ceilings, which provides the basis for a revised JCS memorandum on force structure levels. Concurrently, each service prepares its own memorandum detailing how the decisions on force structure should be translated into specific program objectives. Where discrepancies arise, as they inevitably do, either between the various service proposals, or between a service's position and that of the JCS, they are resolved by consultations between the services and the secretary of defense. Once a decision is reached, the FYDP is updated and the budget proposals presented to Congress.[19]

Defense budget making in the Pentagon remains a highly politicized exercise in that the outcome reflects both externally imposed fiscal constraints and a substantial degree of bargaining and compromise among the services and between the services and the secretary of defense.[20] Nonetheless, PPBS as a process has an inherent range of advantages for the Pentagon. It allows decision makers to make budgetary decisions rooted more clearly in the criteria of the national interest; considers budget choices on an integrated, cross-service basis; provides for the explicit evaluation of alternatives at the highest levels; permits policy makers to judge more readily the future implications of present decisions; and makes use of open, quantitative techniques of analysis.[21]

While in practice the defense budgeting process is a complex and politicized one, it is—especially in contrast to the congressional analogue—a relatively disciplined, orderly, and coherent process. By rigorously applying techniques of systems analysis, officials are better able to assess the degree to which various budget alternatives provide cost-effective means to achieve defense-wide objectives as negotiated among the services, the JCS, and the secretary of defense. By explicitly identifying the costs and benefits associated with various budget options, the decision process is better able to approximate patterns of rationality.

Several points that are important to the analysis here emerge from this discussion. First, with the advent of program budgeting and multiyear defense planning under PPBS, the services are pressed toward some higher level of integration in terms of strategic assumptions and service objectives. That is, the budget process forces the strategic decisions—decisions concerning "the units and uses of force"—to be considered on an interservice basis. Disagreements that persist among the services are ultimately reconciled by decisions imposed upon them by the secretary of defense. As a result, through negotiation or fiat, choices are made that reflect priorities among theaters, missions, and weapons systems. Although the PPBS process itself does not produce joint or shared doctrine, the choices and trade-offs that it requires are often prerequisites to rationalized doctrines; thus, the defense budgeting process perhaps enhances the opportunities for the services to integrate their respective doctrines.

Second, whatever integration of assumptions, objectives, and doctrines is achieved occurs largely through a process of intra-DOD bargaining and compromise that is circumscribed by fiscal ceilings and budget deadlines. In this fashion, PPBS acts as an internal consensus-building mechanism that allows for organizational due process at every step. As the process is played out, each service is afforded channels through which to influence decisions made on a programmatic or defense-wide basis. Rational assessments of program alternatives require some minimal degree of consensus on the underlying strategic issues; as an inherently political process, PPBS provides a mechanism through which that consensual prerequisite may be obtained.

Lastly, and for our purposes most importantly, the budget-making process in the Pentagon generally excludes congressional participation in decisions on the important strategic issues that influence, if not determine, procurement. To be sure, particular congressmen or committees may become the bureaucratic allies of services attempting to defend their programs or chosen weapons systems;[22] but such marriages of convenience usually occur at the initiative of the services, not Congress. Since the relevant PPBS documents are tightly controlled, avenues for congressional influence in the Pentagon's budget-making process are opened largely at the discretion of the military services. And even where selected legislators may be granted access, such limited participation by individual congressmen does not necessarily translate into effective participation in the defense budgeting process by Congress as a whole.

A CHANGING CONGRESSIONAL ROLE?

The conventional wisdom of recent years has ascribed to Congress a more assertive role in the arena of foreign and national security policy making.[23] Evidence of this congressional resurgence, principally a reaction to the excesses of an "imperial presidency" during Vietnam and Watergate, are plentiful: the War Powers Act of 1973; the Case Act in 1972 requiring disclosure of executive agreements; congressional intervention in intelligence policy; and more. But while the net effect of these congressional initiatives has been profound, it is far from clear that Congress's ability to influence military policy has been enhanced. As one perceptive study noted:

> The result of these changes has been increasingly effective congressional oversight in virtually every aspect of defense policy save one: force design decisions— decisions that relate broad foreign policy and national security objectives to the size, character, and equipment of the armed forces. . . . These are the most critical decisions, because they drive the defense budget, dominate the design of weapon systems, and define the kinds of wars the armed forces will be able to fight. Congress at present simply does not have the institutional mechanisms to examine force design questions, with the result that oversight of overall defense policy is limited.[24]

The reasons for this emerge as one contrasts the budget-making process in Congress with that of the Pentagon.

It is a truism to state that Congress's most effective lever over defense policy is its control over the Pentagon's purse strings. But the congressional budget process is a bifurcated process that, despite recent reforms, tends to fragment control over the military budget, thus compounding the difficulties inherent in congressional efforts to influence military policy. Traditionally, congressional control over the federal budget was divided in each chamber between authorizing committees, which examined specific functions or programs, and the Appropriations Committees, which approved the actual expenditures of funds according to earlier authorizations. After World War II the defense budget was scrutinized not merely by the Appropriations Committee but also the Armed Services Committees whose function it was to authorize expenditures.

The Armed Services Committees, however, do not deal with the defense budget in its entirety. Beginning from a relatively narrow focus prior to 1960 that included authority only over military construction, the two Armed Services Committees have steadily expanded their purview over defense expenditures to a point that currently encompasses roughly one-third of the total defense budget. Included within that portion, though, is authority over the procurement of virtually all weapons systems, military construction, and R&D. Until 1974 effective control over the defense budget as a whole rested with the two Appropriations Committees, especially the defense subcommittees therein.

In 1974 Congress enacted the Budget and Impoundment Control Act in an effort to, among other things, bring greater discipline and coherence to the decentralized process by which Congress dealt with federal revenues and expenditures.[25] Under this law newly created Senate and House Budget Committees were empowered to report to their respective houses resolutions that established aggregate budget ceilings and, importantly, allocated budget authority among sixteen broad functional categories, one of which was defense. The Armed Services and Appropriations Committees, however, continued to guard jealously their sole prerogatives to make line-item amendments to the authorization and appropriations bills, respectively.

In addition, the new budget act considerably expanded congressional staff resources. The Budget Committees were authorized staffs numbering sixty-five in the House and eighty in the Senate. Perhaps more significantly, the act also created the Congressional Budget Office (CBO), numbering about two hundred people, which provided Congress an in-house policy analysis and economic forecasting capability. Increasingly, Congress found itself less reliant upon the Pentagon for analysis of policy and budget alternatives.

The changes brought about by the 1974 budget act converged with a trend toward increasing congressional willingness to challenge the executive branch on foreign and defense policy. Frustration with the conflict in Vietnam and a greater appreciation in Congress for the potential leverage inherent in the budget combined to mitigate the traditional predisposition in Congress to "play it safe" with the defense budget. In many cases the members of the new budget committees were either fiscal conservatives bent on reducing federal spending or liberals who yearned to rein in the administration's foreign and defense policies by cutting the budget. The net result throughout the early 1970s was a pattern of defense budget cutting by Congress that, while the amounts were not large (generally under 5 percent), did reverse the earlier tendency to rubber stamp, or even increase, the Pentagon's budget requests.[26] Perhaps more significantly, Congress displayed a newfound willingness to eliminate or reduce certain line-item programs in the defense budget. Reductions in the C-5A and F-111 procurement programs and outright cancellation of the Cheyenne attack helicopter and MBT-70 main battle tank illustrate this greater congressional assertiveness in the defense budget process.

But it is far from clear that this congressional assertiveness necessarily translates into a more constructive congressional role in shaping military policy. The weapons systems that become targets of congressional budget cutters tend to be those that attract adverse publicity due to poor performance or cost overruns. Congressional intervention in the defense budget process displays no underlying strategic rationale. Congress continues to deal with the marginal structural issues, while the more important strategic decisions remain relatively immune from legislative scrutiny. One study of the reformed budget process in Congress noted that:

> Unfortunately, nothing in the new process provides Congress with a means of examining force design—the central linkage between weapon systems, manpower levels, budget components, military strategy, and broad national security objectives.[27]

The sources of this congressional incapacity to affect the important strategic decisions that shape military policy are manifold. Fundamental to all of them, however, is what some in Congress perceive to be a lack of congressional access to the budget-making process in the Pentagon; but in a sense that is the least important reason, since Congress could, were it so inclined, mandate procedures that would give it access to the PPBS documents.

A second reason pertains to the imprecision of the tools available to Congress to deal with the budget. Reductions in the overall defense budget or cancellation of particular programs are notably blunt instruments by which to shape defense policy.[28]

Third, despite the budget reforms, control over the defense budget remains fractionated among the Armed Services, Appropriations, and Budget Committees, each of which has its own priorities and objectives. No institutional mechanism exists by which to make decisions on a fully integrated, rational basis. In establishing overall budget ceilings, the Budget Committees must make assumptions about what programs are to be included or eliminated, thus, "the Budget Committees have de facto access to and a measure of control over the same defense issues heretofore the exclusive preserve of the traditional defense committees."[29] Moreover, the proliferation of committees dealing with the defense budget merely provides additional access points for special interest groups seeking to shape budget decisions according to their parochial concerns.

Fourth, Congress continues to make budget decisions on an annual cycle in contrast to the multiyear planning and programming of PPBS. Strategic decisions by their nature extend over a period of years, thus, Congress is handicapped in trying to compete with a budget-making system that, while it can be updated, forces Pentagon planners to make strategic assumptions and prioritize objectives as prerequisites to an assessment of budget alternatives.

In allowing decisions to be made incrementally, the annual budget cycle in Congress does not require similar strategic choices or any ordering of defense objectives.

Lastly, but clearly most importantly, the very dynamics of the budget process in Congress distinguish it from that of the Pentagon. Institutionally, Congress functions to aggregate the particular and competing interests of an expansive constituency. Consequently, budget making in Congress is a wholly political process characterized as much by conflict as compromise. It is Congress where the dilemmas inherent in military policy—the trade-offs between the domestic and foreign environments, between the parochial interests of constituents and the broader national interest—surface with such regularity. As Les Aspin observed:

> What many advocates of congressional reform really seem to want is . . . to turn Congress into a kind of Brookings Institution or Systems Analysis Office, studying alternative budgets and making decisions about "how much is enough." They would like to see a Congress gathering and weighing information and making rational decisions on that basis, but they fail to take into account that Congress is based on politics. Legislative conflicts in Congress are resolved more often than not by political pressure, not by any rational presentation of the issues.[30]

Rational decision making, by definition, requires consensus on goals and objectives. Clearly, defense budgeting in both the Pentagon and Congress are fundamentally political processes; the budget process in the Pentagon, however, displays a modicum of coherence unmatched by its congressional counterpart. What Congress so critically lacks, and what the Pentagon derives through PPBS, is an institutional mechanism by which to promote consensus on strategic objectives and priorities. Absent from Congress is a device capable of reconciling the diverse priorities of the many committees and congressmen who shepherd the defense budget through Congress. In reaching decisions on the defense budget, Congress is able to attain a transient consensus on structural issues; the critical strategic decisions, however, remain the special preserve of the Pentagon.

MILITARY REFORM IN CONGRESS

If the analysis to this point is sound, we are provided an important conceptual basis by which to understand the evolution of the military reform movement in Congress.

The congressional reflection of the military reform movement is the Military Reform Caucus, a bipartisan, highly diverse group cofounded in 1981 by Senator Gary Hart (D., Colo.) and Representative G. William Whitehurst (R., Va.) "in hopes of surmounting the institutional barriers to deliberating strategy."[31] Simply put, the Military Reform Caucus, which numbers over fifty members, is "an ideologically varied group that is trying to persuade

Congress to debate not just dollars and hardware when considering Defense Department spending, but also military concepts."[32] The agenda for the reform movement in Congress has been broad in scope, including issues of doctrine and strategy, personnel policies, education and training, and weapons design and acquisition.

In our effort to account for the evolution of the Military Reform Caucus, academic rigor requires that we be skeptical of single-factor explanations. And, to be sure, one can attribute some aspects of the Military Reform Caucus to the overriding desire of some congressmen and senators to cut the defense budget, irrespective of the underlying rationale; to the personal motives of some members of the caucus; or to the growth of congressional staffs and the consequent ability of Congress to dabble in issues heretofore untouched. By looking beyond the more prosaic possibilities, however, one can see a more profound explanation, one relating to congressional frustration over its historic inability to influence significantly the strategic components of our military policy. From this perspective, the Military Reform Caucus can be viewed as an institutional mechanism that functions at least implicitly to affect strategic, not mere structural, decisions on military policy by shaping a consensus in the caucus, and more broadly in Congress, on the strategic and doctrinal assumptions that undergird military policy.

Such informal caucuses are not uncommon in Congress. The Military Reform Caucus, while relatively unique in its bipartisan, bicameral composition, in fact has its own pedigree. The Members of Congress for Peace through Law (MPLC) was a similarly bipartisan, bicameral caucus established in 1966 "to coordinate Congressional concern for world peace into specific actions."[33] Numbering as many as ninety-eight congressmen and senators, the MPLC was a relatively liberal group whose focus included such diverse areas as military spending and U.S. policy toward the Middle East, China, the United Nations, and, of course, Vietnam. Though congressional caucuses are a commonplace, such bicameral groupings, designed to promote consensus building on a bipartisan basis, remain a relatively unique occurrence.

In terms of its composition, goals, and practices, the Military Reform Caucus arguably serves an institutional role within Congress as potential integrator and reconciler of competing views on the critical strategic decisions. In this sense, the reform caucus conceivably performs the political functions in Congress that PPBS serves in the Pentagon. The diversity of the caucus's membership is suggested by table 14.2; hidden within the aggregate numbers is a political spectrum that includes at once some of the most conservative as well as the most liberal members of Congress. One cannot casually dismiss the caucus as a collection of amateur strategists disgruntled by a failure to secure assignment to a committee with standing on the defense budget. The committee assignments reflect that roughly half of the caucus's membership hold positions on at least one of the three congressional commit-

Table 14.2. Composition of Military Reform Caucus

	By Chamber	
	House	Senate
Republicans	28	5
Democrats	15	8
Total	43	13

	By Committee Assignment[a]		
	Armed Services	Appropriations	Budget
Republicans	H = 8 S = 2	H = 1 S = 2	H = 1 S = 1
Democrats	H = 8 S = 3	H = 1 S = 3	H = 2 S = 3

Source: Membership listing for Military Reform Caucus in *Naval War College Review* (July–August 1982).

Note: Two senators and twenty-six representatives associated with the Military Reform Caucus were not assigned to any of the above three committees.

[a] Some members are assigned to more than one of these committees.

tees dealing directly with the defense budget. But perhaps more importantly, the caucus generally defines itself as part of a broader military reform coalition including "(mostly younger) military officers, civilian defense analysts, and members of Congress."[34]

While the reform agenda has included proposed changes in the personnel and weapons acquisition processes within the services, it seems clear that for most members of the military reform movement a fundamental revision of our military doctrine has been the conceptual centerpiece.[35] Recognizing the degree to which doctrinal choices determine procurement patterns and define personnel requirements, which together constitute the structural aspects of military policy, a significant element within the reform caucus has focused on forming a consensus within Congress, and more importantly within the military services, around the precepts of maneuver warfare, its preferred doctrine.

That the overriding objective of the Military Reform Caucus is to foster consensus on defense issues is reflected in large measure by the reluctance of the caucus to define more explicitly its other goals. Agreement more readily results from ambiguity than specificity. For this reason, clearly defined statements of the reform caucus's goals are relatively rare, but one such statement illustrates this tendency toward ambiguity:

> Our goals are two: first, we want to create a broad, enduring national consensus in favor of a stronger defense. Second, we want to build a military which cannot only deter war, but, if conflict does occur, can win at the conventional level.[36]

Preferring to agree on generalities rather than to disagree on specifics, members of the reform caucus have for the most part avoided internal practices that would impose hierarchy and discipline on the caucus or force it to make collective decisions on issues. To do so would run counter to the overarching purpose of the Military Reform Caucus. Thus far the caucus has declined to appoint a formal head and has been reluctant to establish its own separate staff. No effort has been made to draft an agreed-upon reform defense budget, nor is one likely. Such initiatives would tend to disrupt the consensus-building process and would detract from the caucus's primary concerns: "issues such as style of war, doctrine, unit cohesion, the direction of military education, and the way the armed services make decisions."[37]

Beyond efforts to promote a general consensus within the councils of the Military Reform Caucus, members of the broader reform movement have undertaken an ambitious campaign to influence directly thinking within the military services since, as one reformer notes, "The foundation of any genuine military reform in the United States is a receptive Pentagon."[38] Targeted at the important service schools and key military units, especially in the army and marines, the objective of such efforts has been to promote in each service groups of officers sympathetic to the reformers' doctrinal precepts. To the extent the reform caucus reaches beyond its own circle to influence the Pentagon or the public at large, it exercises what Huntington described as the "lobbying functions of Congress."[39]

In sum, if, as has been the argument here, Congress's inability to affect military policy is essentially political—that is, stems from an inability to obtain an enduring consensus on the strategic components of military policy—then the Military Reform Caucus can be viewed on one level as an informal institutional mechanism that functions to achieve that end by integrating and reconciling the parochial and partisan interests of Congress. In its efforts to influence the key strategic components of military policy, the Military Reform Caucus attempts to move Congress beyond its traditional role of budgetary oversight of military policy toward a more assertive role as a policy innovator.

The irony may be, though, that so much as the Military Reform Caucus represents an effort to change the way the military does business, so too does it reflect an effort to affect the way Congress does business. The reform caucus urges Congress to transcend parochial interests and make decisions on military policy based on higher-order values.

CAN CONGRESS INNOVATE?

What successes has the Military Reform Caucus achieved to date? Most observers would agree that any tangible accomplishments of the caucus have thus far not been evident. As one member of the reform movement notes:

Despite a promising start heralded by much publicity and even official interest, the military reform movement on Capitol Hill has made little headway in reforming the military . . . the caucus cannot take credit for a single piece of significant reform legislation.[40]

Many observers of Congress would argue that, the early disappointments notwithstanding, Congress is institutionally capable of playing a positive role as a policy innovator and serving "as a seedbed and greenhouse for long-range policy development."[41] Some have argued that the congressional role in military policy making would be enhanced were Congress to effect budgetary reforms requiring Congress to deal on a multiyear basis with the budget as does the Pentagon.[42] Arguing more from a political than a procedural standpoint, others have suggested that the congressional Military Reform Caucus would be made more effective were it to restrict its membership only to those seated on committees empowered to deal with the defense budget.[43] But our discussion here cautions against easy acceptance of such sanguine assessments.

Congressional difficulty in promoting an enduring consensus on defense issues stems fundamentally from the character of Congress as a political institution. For Congress to assert itself as a policy innovator in the defense arena would require a more pervasive and persistent consensus on military issues than has thus far been evident. The handicaps that inhere in Congress as an institution, however, are greatly exacerbated by the very nature of military policy. Given the duality of military policy, the sense in which it exists both in the arena of domestic and international policy, it is difficult to imagine any set of issues—perhaps with the exception of foreign trade—on which agreement is likely to prove more elusive.

That Congress possesses the requisite resources to influence in some measure the process of defense policy formulation is beyond doubt. The expansion of committee staffs and the creation of the Congressional Budget Office have provided Congress with analytical capabilities that are in many respects the equal to those within the Pentagon. But such resources, while necessary, may not be sufficient for Congress to play a more creative role in the defense policy process.

Our earlier discussion suggested that the impulse to alter military policy is likely to be greatest at times of policy disequilibrium, that is, during periods wherein the imperatives of domestic and foreign policy are most clearly discordant. It is, however, at those times when the domestic and international goals of policy makers are so acutely disjoined that congressmen are likely to find defense policy innovation most problematic. Changes in policy direction generally require that someone's vested interest be tread upon. But what congressman would be eager to make the concessions necessary to achieve a consensus on military policy if to do so would imperil the domestic goals of his constituents? During a period of economic uncertainty and high unemployment, who shall be first to offer up the defense contracts in one's district in order to achieve a more rational defense posture? If, indeed, the 1980s hold out the continued promise of increasingly strained fiscal resources in the face of expanding threats to our national interest, there seems little promise that the Military Reform Caucus or the Congress as a whole will find it possible to seize the initiative in crafting military policy.

In all of this one unavoidably confronts the normative question of whether Congress *should* innovate in the area of military policy. Should congressional participation in the process of defense policy formulation properly extend beyond its traditional oversight function? One former senator offered this admonishment: "God help the American people if Congress starts legislating military strategy."[44] Indeed, there would appear to be some considerable validity in the argument that Congress, as the principal focal point of diverse special interests, is institutionally ill-suited to the task of influencing defense policy making beyond the next fiscal year.

This pessimism, however, is not to deny the usefulness of the military reform movement in Congress. While military policy innovation may go beyond what is possible, or even desirable, in Congress, such challenges serve constructive ends in prodding the armed services to deal openly with contentious issues and to justify or amend their current practices.

NOTES

1. Interview with General David C. Jones, *MacNeil-Lehrer Report,* PBS, 7 February 1983.

2. Samuel P. Huntington, *The Common Defense: Strategic Programs in National Politics* (New York: Columbia University Press, 1961), p. 1.

3. Ibid., p. x.

4. Ibid., p. 7.

5. Alvin Richman, "Public Attitudes on Military Power, 1981," *Public Opinion* (December/January 1982): 44.

6. See "Defense is Tempting Target for Members of Congress Faced with Budget Deficits," *Congressional Quarterly Weekly Report,* 20 February 1982, pp. 309–14.

7. George Quester, "Consensus Lost," *Foreign Policy* 40 (Fall 1980): 18.

8. Richman, "Public Attitudes on Military Power, 1981," pp. 45–46.

9. Cited in Capt. Brent Baker, "National Defense and the Congressional Role," *Naval War College Review* 35 (July–August 1982): 11. Congressman Les Aspin (D., Wis.) makes the point more pungently: "Congressmen vote the way they do primarily because of their constituents, and this is particularly true when it comes to votes pertaining to defense." See Congressman Les Aspin, "The Defense Budget and Foreign Policy: The Role of Congress," *Daedalus* 104 (Summer 1975): 155.

10. Richard E. Neustadt, *Presidential Power* (New York: John Wiley & Sons, 1969), p. 33.

11. Huntington, *The Common Defense,* pp. 3–7.

12. Ibid., p. 5.

13. Aspin, "The Defense Budget and Foreign Policy," p. 157.

14. Nancy J. Bearg and Edwin A. Deagle, Jr., "Congress and the Defense Budget" in *American Defense Policy,* 4th ed., ed. John E. Endicott and Roy W. Stafford, Jr. (Baltimore: Johns Hopkins University Press, 1977), pp. 335-54.

15. Arnold Kanter, *Defense Politics: A Budgetary Perspective* (Chicago: University of Chicago Press, 1979), p. 6.

16. For a fuller treatment of the PPBS approach to defense budgeting, see Amos A. Jordan and William J. Taylor, Jr., *American National Security: Policy and Process* (Baltimore: Johns Hopkins University Press, 1981), pp. 178-200. Also see Lawrence J. Korb, "The Budget Process in the Department of Defense, 1947-77: The Strengths and Weaknesses of Three Systems," *Public Administration Review* (July/August 1977): 334-46.

17. Jordan and Taylor, *American National Security,* p. 199.

18. Korb, "The Budget Process in the Department of Defense, 1947-77."

19. The unconstrained JCS estimate of force requirements is found in volume 2 of the Joint Strategic Objectives Plan (JSOP). Fiscal ceilings are set out in the secretary's Planning and Programming Guidance Memorandum (PPGM) from which the JCS produces the fiscally constrained Joint Forces Memorandum (JFM), while each service prepares its own Program Objectives Memorandum (POM). As the discrepancies between the POMs and the JFM are resolved, the secretary's final decisions are reflected in the Program Decision Memoranda (PDM).

20. Kanter, in *Defense Politics,* analyzes the budget process from the standpoint of bureaucratic politics.

21. Korb, "The Budget Process in the Department of Defense, 1947-77," p. 340.

22. Kanter, *Defense Politics,* pp. 37-44.

23. See Richard Haass, *Congressional Power: Implications for American Security Policy,* Adelphi Paper no. 153 (London: International Institute for Strategic Studies, 1979) for an analysis of congressional resurgence in foreign and national security policy making.

24. Bearg and Deagle, "Congress and the Defense Budget," p. 337.

25. See Bearg and Deagle, "Congress and the Defense Budget," for a detailed treatment of the circumstances leading to, and the impact of, the 1974 Congressional Budget and Impoundment Control Act.

26. Ibid., pp. 344-45.

27. Ibid., p. 349.

28. One prominent member of the Military Reform Caucus recently released a comprehensive defense budget proposal, which included criticism of the navy's funding request for the DDG-51 Aegis cruiser. The DDG-51 was alleged to be ill suited for antisubmarine warfare, since it lacked an on-board hanger for helicopters. The solution: cancel the program. Sen. Gary Hart, "A Military Reform Defense Budget for FY 1984," mimeographed copy.

29. Bearg and Deagle, "Congress and the Defense Budget," p. 347.

30. Aspin, "The Defense Budget and Foreign Policy," pp. 163-64.

31. "'Reform' Caucus Challenges Pentagon Judgments," *Congressional Quarterly Weekly Report,* 17 April 1982, p. 867. For fuller treatment of the history, composition, and goals of the Military Reform Caucus, see Jeffrey Record, "The Military Reform Caucus," *Washington Quarterly* 6 (Spring 1983): 125-29.

32. "Caucus Challenges Defense Concepts," *New York Times*, 12 January 1982, p. B8.

33. See "Bipartisan Congress Group Seeks to Influence Congress," *Congressional Quarterly Weekly Report*, 31 July 1970, pp. 1952–56. One of the originators of the MPLC was Sen. George McGovern (D., S.Dak.) for whom Gary Hart later became presidential campaign manager.

34. Gary Hart, "What's Wrong with the Military?" *New York Times Magazine*, 14 February 1982, p. 16.

35. See Sen. Gary Hart, "The Case for Military Reform," *Wall Street Journal*, 23 January 1981. Hart asserts that "unless we re-examine our entire concept of land warfare, it won't do much good merely to spend more money to buy more hardware."

36. Sen. Gary Hart, mimeographed letter accompanying "A Military Reform Budget for FY 1984," dated 14 March 1983.

37. Ibid. In offering his own budget proposals for FY 84, Sen. Hart was careful to dissociate them from the Military Reform Caucus as a whole.

38. Record, "The Military Reform Caucus," p. 126.

39. Huntington, *The Common Defense*, pp. 135–46.

40. Record, "The Military Reform Caucus," p. 126.

41. John R. Johannes, "The President Proposes and Congress Disposes—But Not Always: Legislative Initiation on Capitol Hill," *Review of Politics* 36 (July 1974): 369. For an in-depth analysis of Congress's ability to serve as a source of policy innovation, especially in domestic policy, see Gary Orfield, *Congressional Power: Congress and Social Change* (New York: Harcourt Brace Jovanovich, 1975).

42. Bearg and Deagle, "Congress and the Defense Budget," pp. 351–53.

43. Record, "The Military Reform Caucus," p. 128.

44. Cited in Huntington, *The Common Defense*, p. 135.

15

INTERSERVICE RIVALRY AND MILITARY REFORM

Asa A. Clark IV

How do the services view reform? Clark contends that there is no one answer to this question because "differential propensities for reform are observable among the services." These are explained by relative shifts in each service's doctrinal roles, missions autonomy, and budget share. For example, such shifts explain, in large part, reform activism in the army and marines, and air force and navy disinterest in military reform issues.

Some reformers focus their charges on the lack of coherent national and military strategies or on the "technological fascination" component of American strategic culture. Most reform issues derive, however, from charges of fundamental systemic flaws within the military.

Analyses of charges made by reformers and of recommended corrections of these "flaws" have been presented in earlier chapters of this book. As we have seen, most of these discussions collapse systemic indictments to charges and reform proposals about specific functions, weapons systems, or services. In this sense, the primary thrust of the reform movement operates at the micro-level of the individual military services. Clearly, some reform issues are more macro-oriented: for example, reorganization of the Joint Chiefs of Staff, aggregate defense budget priorities, and alternative military strategies. However, concrete charges and proposed reforms generally target the particular military services.

If the focus of military reform charge and response is in and about the services, then the services are critical players—in terms of their relative receptivity to external reform dialogue and internal reform initiatives—in determining to what degree the military reform movement achieves, in Lupfer's words, criticism or constructive reform.

How, then, do the services view reform? For simplicity's sake, reform and innovativeness are assumed to be conceptually identical. Although there clearly are differences worth distinguishing, these are foresaken in order to simplify examination of a service's general propensity for reform and innovation, whether internally generated or externally stimulated.

Two perspectives can be quickly dismissed. One view holds that the military is fatally bureaucratized and, therefore, resists reform as a threat to existing operating norms and resource levels. For example, Luttwak charges that the military's failure in Vietnam derived from the total absence of strategically relevant innovativeness in understanding ends and matching appropriate means to these ends. Specifically, Luttwak indicts the services for developing roles and missions in Vietnam "which allowed funds to be claimed for expansion, without changes of structure or function disturbing to the hierarchical or organizational orders of things."[1]

A second view holds that one intrinsic aspect of military professionalism involves dedication to continuous concern for innovativeness aimed at matching commitments and capabilities. The military professionalism view is exemplified by General Maxwell Taylor's personal campaign to shift U.S. strategy from massive retaliation to flexible response.[2]

As stated earlier, however, neither of these ideals obtains in practice. On the one hand, the military falls short of the professional innovativeness model; on the other hand, widespread internal reform and innovation belie the status quo bureaucratic model. In fact, differential propensities for reform are observable among the services: ranging from the activism of the marine corps and the army, to the interest of the air force, and finally, to the disinterest of the navy.

If the services' respective reform tendencies fall varyingly along a continuum between the bureaucratic and professional poles, how can these variances in receptivity to reform be explained? This is an important question— understanding of "service reformism" can provide the basis for measures explicitly aimed at catalyzing and sustaining constructive defense reform within and among the services.

Accordingly, this chapter examines the forces affecting the relative innovativeness of the individual services in order to explain their differential reform tendencies. Beginning with the presumption that organizational motives, incentives, and constraints count heavily, this chapter examines the services' organizational terrain in order to assess whether each service's organizational milieu operates as an opportunity for, or an obstacle to, reform and innovativeness. Specifically, it is hypothesized that services innovate doctrinally and technologically as a function of perceived autonomy in roles and missions and trends in budgeting for these roles and missions. Assessment of a service's relative doctrinal autonomy and budgetary prosperity will aid in understanding how and why that service views and reacts to the reform impetus.

Before this assertion can be examined in detail, the military services' organizational environment must be conceptualized. A framework for understanding these bureaucratic impulses, the organizational rivalry model, is briefly described and justified. Following examination of the phenomenon of innovation, specific hypotheses are presented and discussed in terms of a number of cases. Finally, these propositions are used to account for the differences in propensity to innovate across the services. In addition, these propositions are useful for forecasting the implications of announced Five Year Defense Programs (through the 1980s) for service innovativeness and reformism.

ORGANIZATIONAL RIVALRY: A FRAMEWORK FOR EXAMINING INNOVATIVENESS

The organizational perspective generally reflects the methodology suggested by Axelrod's version of the inference pattern of the bureaucratic paradigm: "Which agencies use what tactics to pull with how much effort in what policy space on what issues in what direction?"[3]

Organization theorists maintain that specific answers to this question are largely derived from organizational characteristics such as organizational self-interest and rational behavior, information costs, limited analytic capabilities, and uncertainty. Although the organizational model presumes that agency behavior is profoundly influenced by self-interested concern for agency autonomy and survival, these motives are viewed as derivatives of deeply held perceptions that the agency is, in fact, committed to effectively serving the public interest.

Organizations act rationally to attain their goals: typically, "power, income, prestige, security, convenience, pride in excellent work, and desire to serve the public interest." More generally, organizations seek influence, missions, capabilities, morale, "organizational essence," effective performance of social functions, survival, and budget maximization. Chief among these goals are organizational survival and autonomy.[4]

Defined by Katz as the degree of relative freedom from external constraint, autonomy facilitates survival.[5] In addition, organizational autonomy stabilizes the agency's environment, neutralizes intrusive threats to its functional domain, and legitimates stable claims to budget dollars, time, issues, information, and personnel.

One behavioral manifestation of organizational autonomy and survival motives is bureaucratic expansionism. Organization theorists speak of organizational expansionism as a technique for stabilizing a bureau's environment by reducing uncertainties, coordination costs, and external interdependencies.[6] Betts argues, for example, that "military leaders prefer poverty with autonomy to wealth with dependency."[7]

Organizations expand because dynamic growth (1) attracts capable personnel; (2) generates power, income, and prestige; (3) assuages internal conflict; (4) helps improve output quality and chances for survival; (5) generates economies of scale; (6) boosts research and development; (7) helps to stabilize the bureau's external environment; and (8) enables bureau leaders to avoid confronting marginal cost and marginal value considerations.

How do organizations expand and in what direction? A first answer is provided by Thompson's study of an organization's interactions with its environment.[8] In order to maintain autonomy over its functional domain, a bureau will expand its activities in order (1) to protect core operations from environmental influences, (2) to place its control boundaries around important contingency activities and (3) to integrate its activities vertically.

Thompson's implicit assumption of an internal hierarchical ordering of bureau activities acting to guide expansion is refined by Kanter.[9] Rejecting claims that organizations are mindlessly aggressive and imperialistic, Kanter argues that organizations expand as necessary to monopolize capabilities and resources perceived as essential to fulfill organizational goals. Moreover, this expansionist drive for autonomy reflects a hierarchical ordering of goals. Activities that are tangential to what Halperin calls "the organizational essence" are sacrificed to protect core activities. "Organizational essence" refers to the view of the dominant group in the organization of what the primary missions and capabilities should be. Also reflecting influences such as organizational socialization, promotion, activities of competitive agencies, tradition, and client interests, this essence defines core activities and rationalizes their top priority over other, so-called peripheral activities.

Several propositions follow from the impact of organizational essence on an organization's conception of its interests. Obviously, a bureau advocates policies that sanction activities as defined by its organizational essence. Similarly, a bureau struggles more intensely for capabilities that support its essence than for capabilities relating to peripheral activities. Conversely, a bureau resists most intensely those efforts aimed at reducing activities supporting its essence. Not only are bureaus relatively indifferent to peripheral activities, but they may eliminate them in order to retain resource claims in support of essence-sanctioned activities.

Just as autonomy-based efforts to strengthen internal control elicit intraorganizational conflict, it is to be expected that autonomy-serving bureau expansionism generates interorganizational conflict. Whether organizational expansionism is functional or allocational, it is perceived as a policy intrusion and a threat to other bureaus' autonomy. Such territorial sensitivity causes bureaus to expend great time and energy in territorial struggles that create no socially useful product. These competitive organizational struggles are the lifeblood of the autonomy and survival for public service bureaus.

To the degree that bureau expansionism reflects qualitative versus quantitative change, expansionism represents innovation. Huntington conceptualizes innovativeness in the armed forces in terms of change in major functional programs or (as components of such programs) weapons systems, doctrine, force structure, organization, personnel, and deployments.

Organization theory identifies a variety of factors which reinforce organizational inertia and resistance to change. For example, Kaufman speaks of the natural inertia of the status quo, resistance caused by desires to avoid the disequilibrating trauma of change, inability to change caused by tunnel vision and rigid routines, and obstacles such as limited resources, rules and norms, and sunk costs.[10]

Nevertheless, organization theory also extensively develops the concept and relationships of change. First, organizations innovate to improve performance. In particular, organizations facing fast-changing environments are forced to innovate in order to maintain high performance levels. Other internal sources of innovativeness are personnel turnover, internal reorganizations, and changing technology.

In addition to internal inducements, innovativeness can be prompted by environmental forces. Change may be induced by an injection of resources or, alternatively, by budget and resource cuts that are perceived to threaten the organization's ability to perform its functions. Bureaus may innovate by staking out a new domain in order to diversify product lines or to increase the degree of monopoly supply of core products (those reflecting organizational essence). In this sense, innovation serves as one organizational strategy to preserve or protect organizational autonomy and resource claims. Finally, a bureau may innovate in organizational self-defense against the intrusion of another bureau into its policy domain.

This organizational behavior framework is applicable to any large organization; more so, clearly, to bureaucratic agencies facing resource, but not product or service, markets. The assumptions and dynamics of this framework are especially applicable in the defense sector because of the inherent policy nature of the provision of defense. Security, defense, and deterrence are difficult "products" to evaluate because these concepts are characterized by low levels of operationality. It is difficult to assess, for example, the relative security afforded the United States and its allies by a particular strategy or defense program. Short of the outbreak of war, it is similarly difficult to judge deterrence—of whom? from what? how? under what other circumstances? These questions are not methodological recreation: they illustrate the difficulty of attaching causality to the behavior of country B as a function of country A's defense policies.

One consequence of this operationality problem is that "national security" considerations are invoked to justify a cornucopia of programs and strategies. The problem is that national security considerations provide insufficient conceptual, operational, and empirical resolution to answer questions about these programs and strategies. Are they designed to redress "performance gaps" and, therefore, to augment U.S. defense posture at the margin, or do they reflect suboptimal resource diversions generated by the "follow-on imperative" of organizational inertia and parochialism? Do they represent equivalently effective marginal contributions to U.S. defense posture?

Second, because of the size and organizational complexity of the Department of Defense (DOD), defense policy is substantially constrained by bureaucratic behavior. The extensive economic impacts of defense policy and widespread defense sector clientele generate the often-intense politicization of defense policy making. This politicization is compounded by direct international-domestic linkages of defense issues; for example, overseas defense spending and dollar exchange rates, DOD hardware procurement and arms transfers. Politicization of the policy processes serves to create a milieu in which purely organizational impulses are freer to play.

Roles of organizational motives in a politicized policy process are reinforced by characteristics of the so-called military-industrial complex: huge capital requirements, high entry and exit barriers to the weapons production sector, the monopsonistic role of the DOD, and uncertainties (about threat capabilities, end-item performance requirements, development lead time).

To an extent found in no other bureaucracy, the DOD and defense policy making are beset with constant and intensive intraorganizational political infighting. Given the sheer scale and complexity of the defense sector, the politics of defense is made all the more unique by interservice competition and the paramount issue of civil-military relations. Not only do the military services possess

> bargaining advantages available to subordinates in any large organization performing complex tasks, but they also have been able to exploit the constitutional separation of powers and to draw upon the support of their domestic constituents and allies. As a consequence, the services can (within limits) resist, ignore, and contravene the directives of their superiors.[11]

Defense policy making is unique in that policy outputs are resource-intensive and highly controllable. Unlike many other federal bureaucracies, DOD outputs are predominantly resource-intensive (manpower, hardware, force structures, support operations, retirement benefits, contracts for research, development, and production, and so forth). Moreover, the defense budget continues to exhibit the increasingly rare characteristic of controllability. While that portion of the federal budget which is uncontrollable has increased from 60 to 75 percent over the last fifteen years, defense spending continues to account for roughly 60 percent of the controllable federal budget.

This substantial degree of allocative discretion in the defense sector further underwrites the extensive politicization of allocative decision making and acts to magnify the degree to which budgetary parameters are perceived to be the locus of the policy process.

ORGANIZATIONAL RIVALRY AND INNOVATIVENESS IN U.S. MILITARY POLICY MAKING

Having described the organizational behavior framework and justified its applicability to the defense sector, it remains to relate these notions to the armed services themselves.

The motives and incentives highlighted by the organizational rivalry model are manifested in the military services in terms of service parochialism and both inter- and intraservice competition. These and other behavior manifestations are best understood from the perspective of service roles and missions.

Service conceptions of their core roles and missions—those reflecting a service's organizational essence—are predictable and have continued generally to reflect the maxim that "armies walk, navies sail, and air forces fly." Based on combat medium rather than combat mission, these role conceptions have remained service-oriented. The essence of the air force is strategic nuclear deterrence through the capability to deliver nuclear weapons globally. Navy role conceptions are more diffuse. Although the essence of naval operations is sea control with combat ships, there is substantial disagreement over the best means: surface ships, naval aviation, or submarines. In addition, the strategic nuclear submarine fleet has emerged as serving a core mission. Missions of the marines hinge on the primacy of their force projection role. The essence of army operations revolves around capabilities for sustained land combat anywhere in the world. With some exceptions, these core role conceptions have remained fairly stable and have not been subject to challenge among the services. (The exceptions are important and are discussed below.)

The high degree of acceptance of the core missions contrasts sharply with the historical ferocity of interservice competition over secondary or peripheral missions. The intent of the National Security Act of 1947 was to formalize a system of interdependent service missions. Although core missions were legitimized with some success, this attempt to delimit secondary rules failed. The intention was admirable: each service would undertake secondary roles as necessary to support its primary mission (for example, land combat) within the constraint that no such undertaking would encroach on another service's core mission.

However, asymmetrical role interdependencies insured an asymmetrical distribution of dissatisfaction. For example, because the army was more dependent on the air force for air support (mobility, close air support, logistical support, medical evacuation) than the air force was dependent on the army (security of forward air bases), the army was certain to remain dissatisfied with what it perceived to be air force indifference to its needs.

In addition, interservice competition focusing on overlapping organizational and doctrinal support for peripheral missions resulted from the service expansionism and protectionism highlighted by the organizational rivalry model. One response to these constant squabbles was a continuous sequence of DOD efforts to define and mandate boundaries for roles and missions.[12]

For example, in 1947 the Key West and Newport agreements (entitled "Clarification of Roles and Missions to Improve the Effectiveness of the Operation of the Department of Defense") initiated a stream of role definition agreements revolving around guided missiles and ancillary air operations such as close air support and airlift. Because the functional capabilities of air operations span traditional service domains, the question of the degree to which each service would engage in air operations continues to generate controversy. DOD edicts to delimit air operations roles have dealt with parameters such as responsibility for research and development versus operations, range, weight, payload, and point versus area capability. Squabbles among the services over proprietorship or joint responsibility for overlapping roles and missions continue today and are inherent in the defense sector for reasons discussed earlier.

HYPOTHESES

If role conceptions and organizational essence serve as the means by which the services operationalize doctrine into their respective programs, by what specific dynamics do services respond to shifts in technology, doctrine, budget allocations, and threat definitions in order to preserve autonomy and effectiveness? The answer suggested by the organizational rivalry model, of course, hinges on the self-serving and competitive behaviors by and among the services. Although competitive policy making is not unknown in other federal departments, nowhere is intradepartmental conflict as extensive as in DOD.

In general, two dynamics are operative. First, the twin forces of organizational rationality and expansionism operate to induce services to attempt to expand all their roles and missions (particularly those supporting a service's organizational essence).

Second, a service that perceives itself to be losing in terms of mission autonomy or budget priorities can choose one of two strategies. The service can expand the arena of decision outside the DOD. To paraphrase Huntington, the greater the degree to which a service perceives itself "losing" because of a given doctrine, the more prolonged is the decision-making process within the executive, and the more extensive is the public debate of the doctrinal issue before the administration makes a final decision.

Alternatively, the dissatisfied service can choose to compete for a piece of the doctrinally-favored mission (accorded to another service). Conversely, of course, a service whose domain of legitimized roles and missions benefits from a particular defense doctrine is certain to advocate the status quo and resist efforts by other services to challenge its favored status.

These behavioral dynamics can be stated simply as follows:

1. A service attempts to maintain and expand core roles and missions
2. A service enjoying increasing doctrinal and resource support also attempts to expand peripheral roles and missions
3. A service confronted by decreasing doctrinal and resource support attempts to (a) maintain and expand core roles by reducing priorities for peripheral roles; (b) change (through public debate) defense doctrine to legitimize roles derived from its own organizational essence; and (c) adapt its role conceptions (innovate) in order to compete for a share of doctrinally and resource-sanctioned missions.

Whether the politics of service policy advocacy remain within the DOD arena or are expanded into public debate, and whether the political struggles occur primarily between a service and the DOD or primarily among the services, the driving force is likely to be service concern for translating the interplay of defense doctrine, roles and missions, and budget priorities into support for the service's role and missions through the dynamic strategies specified above. Because our concern here is with innovativeness and propensity to reform, we restrict our examination to the last strategy above.

A service's propensity for doctrinal reform (redefinition of roles, missions, and forces) is viewed as a function of a trend of eroding doctrinal justification and corresponding reductions in resource levels.

Technological innovativeness is more complicated because at least two distinctive aspects are subsumed: qualitative innovativeness, based on advanced technology research and development efforts, and quantitative production, in which force modernization is achieved through procurement of technology-intensive equipment. These aspects differ in terms of relative sequence in the acquisition process, time-lag, costs of purchase, and organizational incentives.

Qualitative innovativeness in the form of aggressive R&D efforts is likely to be pursued by a service perceiving itself to be losing doctrinal and resource support. Just as is the case for doctrinal reform, a "losing" service is prone to push state-of-the-art technology in order to expand or create new capabilities so that it can gain leverage for support of its roles and missions.

Quantitative innovativeness in terms of production and procurement of high-technology systems (step-level shifts in hardware density and sophistication), however, is a function of affordability. Davis observes that services have historically shown keen interest in extensive procurement of high-technology equipment in proportion to their overall budget prosperity.[13] The powerful appeal of high-technology procurement is somewhat offset by high investment costs, attendant pressures for cuts in existing programs, high uncertainties, and organizational resistance to the often extensive (and disequilibrating) perturbations of new technology. (Consider, for example, the implications of the new guidance, propellant, and engine technologies—packaged in cruise missiles—for deterrence, air defense, strategic force structure, and arms control.)

Examination of a few historical examples illustrates the plausibility of these hypotheses. Huntington relates how the new U.S. strategy of deterrence in the 1950s meant that defense programs now cut *across* traditional service roles and missions.[14] Funding priorities, based on those functions, were significantly redistributed among the services.

In this environment of opportunity for innovation, the air force, newly blessed with service autonomy and top funding priority, proved to be the most innovative service in terms of force modernization and expansion (that is, the most procurement-intensive), yet the least innovative in exploiting major new technology and devising new doctrine.[15] This is understandable, given the allocative priorities of Eisenhower's New Look.

The air force's modernization program directed almost the entire avalanche of new funds at strategic bomber development and procurement, and neglected guided missile development programs.[16] The inattention paid to all missile R&D programs (especially ICBM programs) clearly reflected the powerful influence of the air force's organizational essence.

This case illustrates that service funding for procurement is increased only with increased service budgets in order to avoid redistributive cuts in current programs (which provide immediate payoffs). This tendency is reinforced by the short time horizon of organizations in viewing returns on investments, particularly in light of the uncertainties of research and development.

Other cases illustrating similar air force "winner" motives include the Thor-Jupiter controversy, ballistic missile defense, and a long series of close air support disputes—all battles with the army in which innovativeness was profoundly stimulated or repressed by considerations of the budget and "doctrinal turf."

In contrast, "loser" motives were instrumental in army innovations. Stating that "the smaller the stake which a group has in existing programs, the more likely it is to push new programs," Huntington argues that the army's relative funding poverty induced keen interest in doctrinal innovation in order to carve out doctrinally-sanctioned domains within which autonomous roles and missions (and supporting funding) could be assured. These motives were manifest in army-led initiatives for continental defense, European defense, and limited war during the early 1950s.[17] Similar cases have been examined: army efforts to secure its own innovation of airmobile forces and operations in Vietnam and, subsequently, in Europe.[18]

The effects of "winner and loser" motives are not confined to air force-army disputes. Similar clashes have erupted between other services in their concern for unilateral and joint operational effectiveness: air force-navy (roles for nuclear-delivery aircraft launched from aircraft carriers; the submarine-launched ballistic missile program); army-marines (force projection roles); and among all the services concerning strategic mobility and close air support. In each of these cases, service innovativeness, based on concern for doctrinal roles and supporting resources, has keyed "turf battles"—some of which served to enhance joint defense (or more effective service programs),

Table 15.1. Innovativeness and Organizational Motives

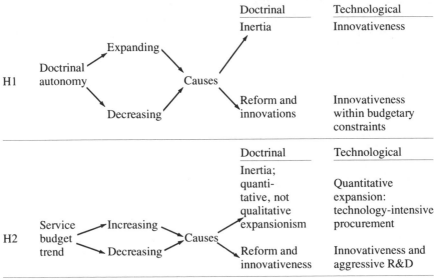

and some of which continue to reflect parochialism and relative neglect of necessary joint capabilities.

EMPIRICAL ANALYSIS: WHY THE SERVICES TAKE WHAT STAND ON REFORM

Two empirical propositions are postulated to link service innovativeness with "organizational milieu" variables: autonomy in doctrinal roles and missions, and trends in service budgets.

> H1: Imposed changes in doctrinally-based roles and missions inversely affect both technological and doctrinal innovativeness.
>
> H2: Imposed changes in budgeting levels inversely affect both technological and doctrinal innovativeness.

The predicted consequences of such externally-imposed shifts in a service's doctrinal autonomy and resource environment are explicitly specified in table 15.1.

How well are these predictions fulfilled in the respective organizational milieu trends and reform propensities exhibited by the services? Examination of doctrinal priorities is difficult and ambiguous. For instance, Secretary of Defense Weinberger's *Fiscal Year 1983 Annual Report* to Congress discusses, among other matters, the strategic importance of peacetime defensive

Table 15.2. Service Appropriations: Annual Percentage Change in TOA (Constant 1983 Dollars)

Year	Army	Marine Corps	Navy	Air Force	OSD	DOD
1981	11.3	8.0	9.6	12.2	17.3	10.9
1982	12.8	24.2	12.4	16.2	9.5	12.7
1983	10.4	9.6	20.6	13.8	15.6	13.2
Percentage change for period	19.4	11.0	26.2	24.4	21.4	21.6

Source: U.S. Department of Defense, *National Defense Budget Estimates for FY 1983* (March 1982).

measures (improved warning means, increased force readiness, enhanced military mobilization, and improved defense production surge capability), conventional forces that are more flexible and sustainable (particularly vis-à-vis non-European theaters), major modernization efforts across all nuclear forces programs and command/control systems, and vigorous arms control efforts.

The difficulties of discerning doctrinal roles and missions priorities from such a document suggest examination of recent budgetary trends instead. Although budget trends clearly are useful for examining the second hypothesis, fluctuations in these trends are also valid indicators of decisions about roles and missions. Because the outputs of defense policy are resource-intensive, and because the defense budget is highly controllable, budgetary trends directly signal policy decisions regarding roles, missions, force structures, and procurement. As a result, this analysis treats budgetary trends as the surrogate independent variable for larger policy decisions regarding doctrine: the autonomy and jointness of service roles and missions.

Table 15.2 shows the trends in spending—actually total obligational authority (TOA)—across the services during the Reagan administration's tenure. (Although the Fiscal 1981 budget was a product of the Carter administration, it is included because of the extensive supplemental appropriations added by President Reagan.)

Note the differential allocative patterns across the services within the increased spending envelope of the Reagan administration. Although overall TOA increases 21.6 percent in real terms during this brief period, both the army and the marines received proportionately less than the other services and OSD. Given the small absolute level of the marine budget, a rate of increase half that of even the army's is striking. These asymmetrical funding patterns are clearly illustrated in figure 6.

Although perhaps mitigated somewhat by the overall increasing defense budget, this erosion of army and marine relative "shares of the pie" predicts, according to the hypotheses, innovativeness and reform activism by these

DEPARTMENT OF DEFENSE
REAL GROWTH BY COMPONENT

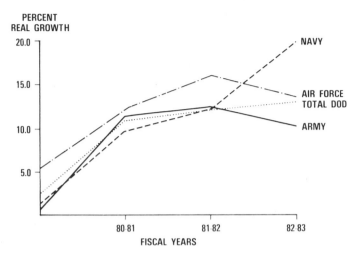

Figure 6. Department of Defense real growth by component. (*Source:* Department of the Army, *The Army Budget FY 1983*, 10.)

two services and, conversely, status quo-oriented disinterest in the reform movement by the air force and navy.

Before examining these relative service reform positions, however, it is useful to compare budget allocations at more disaggregate levels, in which budget priorities among roles and missions are more clearly discernible, and over a longer period of time. To the degree that budget allocation asymmetries across these measures (of service roles and missions relative to prosperity levels) are congruent with those suggested by table 15.2, the plausibility of the hypothesized predictions of service innovativeness and reformism is reinforced.

The data in table 15.3 suggest that the army's budget rebounded from the post-Vietnam war period of funding cutbacks to a greater extent than for the other services. This is misleading, however, because the major burden of these cutbacks during the first Nixon administration fell on the army. In fact, the army's share of the defense budget fell from 32.1 percent in 1970 to 24.6 percent in 1975. This trend reflects the reallocation of funding priority to the navy and OSD programs during the 1970s.

Table 15.3 confirms two points. Although the army budget recovered from severe cutbacks in the early 1970s, this recovery failed to keep pace with increased resource allocations to the other services. As a result, the army remained dissatisfied with both its absolute funding level and its share of the budget increases forthcoming in the Carter and Reagan administrations. Sec-

Table 15.3. Service Appropriations: Percentage Change in TOA within Administration (Based on Constant 1983 Dollars)

Administration	Army	Navy[a]	Air Force	DOD Total
Nixon	−41.4	−20.8	−13.4	−20.6
Nixon-Ford	+ 0.1	+ 1.9	+ 7.7	+ 5.5
Carter	+11.6	+ 1.9	+ 7.9	+11.4
Reagan[b]	+19.4	+24.4	+26.2	+21.6

Source: Computed from U.S. Department of Defense, *National Defense Budget Estimates for FY 1983* (March 1982).

[a] Separate budget data for the marines are unavailable. The navy figures, therefore, include the Marine Corps budget changes.
[b] Reflects changes for the FY 81–FY 82 budgets.

Table 15.4. Functional Allocation of Defense Spending: Percentage Change in Functional Share of Overall DOD TOA within Administration (Based on Constant 1983 Dollars)

Administration	Investment (Procurement, plus Research and Development)	Consumption (Operations and Maintenance)
Nixon	− 0.3	+ 3.1
Nixon-Ford	+11.0	− 0.1
Carter	+ 4.6	+ 0.1
Reagan (FY 81–FY 83)	+17.5	−10.2

Source: Computed from U.S. Department of Defense, *National Defense Budget Estimates for FY 1983* (March 1982).

ond, the last decade has witnessed a reallocation of funding priorities to favor air force, navy, and OSD-level programs at the expense of the army and the marines.

Are these trends confirmed in more disaggregate measures of resource allocation? One reform issue concerns evaluation of marginal combat effectiveness returns on investment for quality versus quantity weapons systems and force structures. This controversy pits the advantages of high-technology systems against the notion of shifting to low-technology, higher-density force structures, which would allow greater investment of resources. Although an extremely complex trade-off to evaluate, one crude measure of this priority is reflected in the relative budget share accorded to equipment investment (procurement, research and development) versus consumption (training, operations, and maintenance). As is evident in table 15.4, equipment investment exhibits an increasing trend since the mid-1970s (and an increase of 17.5 percent during the Reagan administration). This trend reflects decisions to modernize and expand U.S. force structures across the board. Also apparent in table 15.4, however, is long-term neglect and a recent decline in consumption spending (-10.2 percent for FY 81–FY 83).

These trends suggest a few implications. First, because the share of total DOD investment spending for the army and marines amounts to only 22 percent, this increased investment spending trend represents a net shift of budget dollars to the air force and navy (and to DOD "joint" programs). Juxtaposition of these investment-consumption trends, furthermore, suggests a zero-sum game redistribution of priorities from consumption-intensive activities (relatively more important to the army and marines) to investment-intensive activities (relatively more important to the air force and navy). To the degree that such an inference is valid, reform movement charges of the primacy of procurement over manpower and training orientations within DOD are substantiated.

Disaggregating spending priorities to the program level permits even better discrimination of changes in treatment of roles and missions. Again, trends are apparent in table 15.5 which are congruent with this emerging pattern of priority reallocation in favor of the air force and navy: spending for strategic forces for FY 81–FY 83 is up 21.0 percent compared to a 6.0 percent increase for general purpose forces and a 17.6 percent increase for mobility forces. It must be noted, however, that as the consumers for strategic mobility forces, the army and marines view higher funding of these assets as vital and as redress for long-overdue upgrading.

It is increasingly clear from this analysis of recent budgeting priorities that within the policy guidelines (of both the Carter and Reagan administrations) of substantial defense upgrading, priorities are shifting. The consequences of these shifting priorities for the funding, autonomy of roles and missions, and organizational morale of the different services are profound and asymmetrical. Clearly, we would expect the army and marines to adopt "loser" strategies as hypothesized: these include becoming more favorably inclined to innovativeness and to many of the thrusts of the reform movement. Concerned that these redistributive trends may begin to jeopardize their autonomy and their ability to conduct assigned tasks, it is to be expected that army and marine leaders, in their professional judgment, would be extremely interested both in organizationally-motivated innovative aspects of reform and in substantive reform charges congruent with their preeminent concern for the effective contribution of their respective services to U.S. national security. Conversely, the hypotheses suggest that the air force and navy would view these doctrinal and budget trends with equanimity and would espouse generally status quo orientations.

How can the services be categorized in terms of the pro- or antireform cells in table 15.1? Although the current reform movement is relatively young (tracing its roots to the mid-1970s), differential reactions to and participation in the movement are clearly evident across the services. Even the most critical nonmilitary reformers are quick to recognize and applaud the

Table 15.5 Program Allocation of Defense Spending: Percentage Change in Program Share of Overall DOD TOA within Administration (Based on Constant 1983 Dollars)

Administration	Strategic Forces	General Purpose Forces	Airlift and Sealift Forces
Nixon	−19.6	−38.5	−136.0
Nixon-Ford	+10.9	+15.0	+ 32.6
Carter	+ 2.1	+17.5	+ 22.5
Reagan (FY 81–FY 83)	+37.6	+26.3	+ 22.7

Source: Computed from U.S. Department of Defense, *National Defense Budget Estimated for FY 1983* (March 1982).

innovativeness of the marines and the army (and, in some cases, the air force). The navy, however, is generally viewed by reformers as paying little attention to reform charges. Innovativeness and reform, to be sure, are in the eye of the beholder; nevertheless, how well does the evidence support these contentions? Are the hypotheses substantiated?

In the early 1980s the navy finds itself in an ideal position: receiving substantial budget increases to modernize and build new forces (toward a six-hundred-ship navy) in support of roles and missions that are at the center of an evolving global maritime strategy. Based on the peacetime defensive and deterrent value of the "risk of our counteroffensive against . . . vulnerable points . . . at places where we can affect the outcome of the war . . . and are of an importance to him comparable to the ones he is attacking,"[19] the Reagan administration's forward strategy places a premium on a highly mobile, offensively-oriented U.S. Navy: "The most significant force expansion proposed by the Administration centers on the Navy, particularly these components of it having offensive missions."[20] In fact, navy procurement TOA has grown between FY 80 and FY 83 by 230 percent to account for 43 percent of the total DOD procurement.[21] Included in this huge force expansion are two new nuclear-powered aircraft carriers (and two associated battle groups), reactivation of four battleships, and major new construction programs in attack submarines, Trident SSBNs, and amphibious ships.

Two points are evident. To the substantial degree that navy roles and missions are doctrinally sanctioned by the new global maritime strategy, there are few incentives for navy interest in reform. Why advocate change of a policy structure that legitimates and supports navy missions almost across the board?

Second, the navy's build-up can be characterized more as a quantitative expansion of existing missions and forces than as a qualitative innovation in terms of new missions.[22] The bulk of the expansion constitutes modernization and new force structure increments to existing navy doctrine and structure. As such, this expansion represents follow-on programs more than program innovation. As a result of both these factors, it is not surprising that defense reformers and critics have met with a cool reception at the hands of the navy leadership.

Generally the same arguments apply for the air force. Although not as clearly favored as the navy by the doctrine and budgets of the early 1980s, the air force has been given a massive injection of modernization funds to upgrade and expand programs for the MX, the B-1 bomber, the Stealth bomber, F-15 and F-16 production, and airlift assets. In the FY 83 budget, the air force received 34 percent of DOD procurement funds.[23] As with the navy, because these funding levels are substantial and directed primarily at follow-on programs for existing missions, the air force has been an interested, but not overly active, reformer and innovator.

The army and marines have traditionally received the smaller shares of the defense budget pie. As shown in tables 15.2 through 15.5, moreover, their relative shares of the budget are declining as a result of the priorities shaped by the global strategy of the Reagan administration. How is the hypothesized prediction of consequent doctrinal innovativeness borne out for these "loser" services?

The Marine Corps has led the reform movement among the services. Demonstrating that "the smaller the stake which a group has in existing programs, the more likely it is to push new programs,"[24] marine company grade and general officers alike have advocated new priorities and new approaches. Representative of the professional ferment over doctrinal innovations such as maneuver warfare and its emphasis on leadership, flexibility, and esprit is the following question:

> Does the Corps lend itself to the maneuver warfare concept? Yes, it does, given its fairly small size, flexibility (land, air, and sea capabilities), and present technology favoring lightweight, highly mobile weapons.[25]

William S. Lind, defense analyst and military reformer, extends this doctrinal legitimation for the marines to future combat scenarios:

> There is no question Marines can meet the challenge. By adopting a maneuver concept of war, they can give the United States the capability it needs to defend its vital interests outside Europe. And by performing that task, the Marine Corps can assure itself a solid mission of unquestionable value.[26]

Similarly, the army continues to forcefully consider, adopt, and advocate doctrinal reform. As Wass de Czege pointed out in chapter 7, "Answering the Army's Critics: Doctrinal Reforms," the army's primary doctrine manual, FM 100–5, Operations articulates principles reflecting substantial integration of maneuver warfare precepts: for example, initiative, depth, agility. Moreover, the army has instituted many other systemic reforms: for example, recruitment, personnel, and training measures designed to reinforce unit cohesiveness; a concepts-based requirements system intended to link research and development to doctrinal parameters; and extensive field-testing procedures to develop high- and low-technology equipment that is reliable and compatible. In addition, the new combined arms doctrine, AirLand Battle, represents an extremely innovative approach to tactical doctrine in which many reform points have been adopted.

Although investment funding to modernize and upgrade capabilities of existing forces for flexible warfare has increased markedly in the early 1980s, the thrust of innovativeness for both the army and marines continues to focus on human capital aspects: recruitment, training, education, leadership, tactics, and so forth. As such, these innovations demonstrate parallel internal reform activism by these two services.

Doctrinal innovation has, however, created conflicts and sparked interservice squabbles. For example, both the army and marines (among others) vied for command jurisdiction over the Rapid Deployment Joint Task Force, a prize structural plum representing a new and major mission and sure to receive resources support under the defense strategy of the 1980s. This controversy was resolved, however, in 1981 by the decision to establish the RDF as a unified command. Another case of innovation-based, dissynchronous interservice coordination involves AirLand Battle, the new doctrine for fighting in Europe. Although touted as an innovative doctrine that truly achieves integrated joint operations, AirLand Battle advocates were chagrined when, in large-scale maneuvers in Europe in 1982, the air force was unable to provide any air support—a vital component integral to the new doctrine. These examples illustrate the discontinuities and politicization arising from the intersection of individual services' efforts to maintain, protect, and improve the roles, missions, and resources.

CONCLUSION

The central argument of this chapter is that these interservice differentials vis-à-vis reform and innovativeness are substantially explained in terms of organizational tactics to preserve service autonomy and effectiveness of operational domains and resources, in order that service readiness to provide for the common defense is assured. That is, services innovate and, alternatively, resist innovation. This chapter argues that these variant trends are largely accounted for by organizational incentives, constraints, and motives.

Critics of this viewpoint charge that the organizational perspective is both narrowly based and cynical in collapsing complex behaviors and professional motivations into a single-factor analysis hinging on competitive concern for organizational autonomy and effectiveness. While this approach does employ single-factor analysis, the high degree of non-operationality of national security policy making justifies the validity and legitimacy of such an approach. High-minded goals for enhancing operational readiness and managerial efficiency are the norm throughout the military leadership. However, the non-operationality of these motives creates a number of consequences: an absence of definitive parameters for guiding optimal decision making, honest and intense disagreement over various courses to effective defense, the sometimes indiscriminate use of "national security" justifications for marginal programs, and others. As a result, the defense policy making milieu is saturated with conceptual ambiguity. In this context, the rationalistic and optimistic professional military ethic reinforces natural proclivities to focus objectives, programs, and resources on easily identifiable organizational referents.

Other critics charge that although explanations of collective behavior (differential service interest in reform innovations, in this case) are important in an academic sense, understanding these motives is of no practical use. This argument is best articulated by Lindblom in his discussions of disjointed incrementalism and partisan mutual adjustment.[27] Briefly, these concepts explain how coordinated activities occur among self-serving actors in the absence of central authority, norms of cooperative adjustment, or even knowledge of actor motives. This reasoning suggests that there is some mean level of coordinated, joint interaction among the services which derives naturally from Lindblom's concepts and operates as an antidote to the organizational competitiveness dynamics highlighted in this chapter.

Two implications follow from this charge. First, whatever the explanations and motives of the services, they are constrained by cybernetic parameters to steady-state levels of organizational behavior (independent of service motives): parochialism, innovativeness, or joint cooperation. Second, whatever the service motives, these nondirected levels of coordinated activities ameliorate interservice competition and, consequently, rivalry-induced innovativeness. The result is, ironically, unintended levels of cooperation, coordination, performance "in the public interest," and perhaps, reduced innovativeness.

That such a benign assessment of service behavior is both desirable and interesting is undeniable. These implications do not accord, however, with the observable variability in service innovativeness and joint cooperation over the postwar period. The evidence clearly demonstrates that the services' efforts to provide for the common defense vary among one another and individually over time. It is also clear that the operationalizable referents against which the services evaluate these efforts hinge on doctrinally legitimized roles, missions, forces, and resource levels.

If the arguments of the organizational perspective discussed here are valid, what implications are suggested for service receptivity to reform issues? First, an understanding of these organizational imperatives must inform administration and senior defense policy makers. Given understanding of the critical role of service perceptions of the distributive consequences of strategic, doctrinal, and resource allocation policy decisions, senior level policy makers can adjust major policy decisions to influence service innovativeness and receptivity to reform recommendations. By manipulating the organizational milieu through budget changes to trigger "winner-loser" perceptions and the competitive dynamics discussed earlier, policy makers can exploit these motives to influence optimal service-level innovativeness, and performance in general. Through conscious manipulation of the factors impinging on the bureaucratic dynamics so universally disdained, it is possible to exploit these ineradicable dynamics as opportunities, not obstacles, for reform and innovativeness.

Specifically, the extent and quality of innovativeness (and overall defense performance) are served by balanced military strategies and doctrines in which each service is allotted diverse roles and missions. Strategic pluralism legitimates roles perceived as key to each service. By depriving no service of its doctrinal integrity, diversification of roles and missions tends to preempt bureaucratically inspired politicization of service positions.

So long as the existence of no service depends upon any single strategic purpose, no service has reason to oppose intransigently changes in strategic purposes. Organizational purpose is the partner of strategic flexibility.[28]

In addition to legitimating service autonomy, structuring roles for each service into most defense missions promises yields of improved joint defense performance, coordination, and innovativeness based on substantive, not bureaucratic, competition.

Major strategic decisions to redirect priorities among the services, however, disrupt these balances and the creative tensions of joint efforts on defense missions. Asymmetrical strategies, doctrines, and resource allocations trigger the "loser" service tactics discussed earlier: reduced priorities for roles peripheral to a service's organizational essence, further politicization of policy making by services scrambling for turf, and redirection of innovative efforts to politically expedient sectors promising shorter-term payoffs in missions and resources. Under such circumstances, organizational dynamics operate as obstacles to substantive innovativeness (the professionalism model), reform, and overall defense coordination.

The net, longterm value of major, imbalancing changes in military strategy must be assessed, consequently, by comparing the value of the new policy, discounted by the costs generated by the dysfunctional effects of major change, with the value of current strategy, to include whatever organizationally-induced payoffs accrue (as discussed above, for example, joint coordination, substantive innovativeness). Always difficult, net assessment must nonetheless consider these organizational effects.

What does this mean for the Reagan administration? As discussed earlier, it is difficult to judge the relative symmetry of the administration's strategy across the services: all services and many purposes are accorded top priority. However, the simple analysis of budgetary trends for the 1980s indicates major priority reallocations to strategic and naval forces. When aggregate fiscal pressures and public demands for a higher proportion of butter to guns intrude to lower projected rates of increase in defense spending, the politics of a decreasing-sum game will be triggered by the asymmetrical and disequilibrating effects of the Reagan administrations global strategy. Marine Corps and army reform campaigns reflect, in part, organizational motives in reaction to the hard times ahead in the late 1980s. While these efforts are to be applauded as benefiting the effectiveness of those services and U.S. security, it is less certain that the strategic shift represents an increment in U.S. security when the disruptive and dysfunctional effects of the resultant organizational dynamics are considered.

NOTES

1. Edward N. Luttwak, "Refocusing the Military Profession," *Marine Corps Gazette* (June 1981), pp. 60–65.
2. See Gen. Maxwell D. Taylor, *The Uncertain Trumpet* (New York: Harper & Brothers, 1959).
3. Robert Axelrod, "Bureaucratic Decision-making in the Military Assistance Program: Some Empirical Findings," in *Readings in American Foreign Policy, A Bureaucratic Perspective,* ed. Morton H. Halperin and Arnold Kanter (Boston: Little, Brown & Co., 1973), p. 170.
4. An extensive literature treats organizational rationality and behavior. Representative conceptual treatments: Anthony Downs, *Inside Bureaucracy* (Boston: Little, Brown & Co., 1967), p. 2; Morton H. Halperin, *Bureaucratic Politics and Foreign Policy* (Washington, D.C.: Brookings Institution, 1974), pp. 26–62; Richard M. Cyert and James G. March, *A Behavioral Theory of the Firm* (Englewood Cliffs, N.J.: Prentice-Hall, 1961), pp. 118–25; William A. Niskanen, *Bureaucracy and Representative Government* (Chicago: Aldine-Atherton, 1971).
5. Fred E. Katz, *Autonomy and Organization: The Limits of Social Control* (New York: Random House, 1968), pp. 18–21.
6. James D. Thompson, *Organizations in Action* (New York: McGraw-Hill, 1967), pp. 19–44.
7. Richard K. Betts, *Soldiers, Statesmen, and Cold War Crises* (Cambridge: Harvard University Press, 1977), p. 8.
8. Thompson, *Organizations in Action.*
9. Arnold Kanter, "The Organizational Politics of National Security Policy: A Budgeting Perspective," Ph.D. diss., Yale University, 1975.
10. Herbert Kaufman, *The Limits of Organizational Change* (Tuscaloosa: University of Alabama Press, 1971), pp. 5–40.
11. Kanter, "Organizational Politics," ibid., p. 7.
12. Such division of labor edicts are not unique, of course. Following in the shadow of the aircraft versus ship controversy ignited by Col. Billy Mitchell, navy sensitivity to charges that land-based aircraft threatened naval vessels on the high seas sometimes led to

absurd measures. For example, in 1937 when an Army Air Corps B-17 intercepted an Italian liner 600 miles at sea, the navy's violent protests forced the War Department to issue an edict prohibiting flights more than 100 miles from the coastline. See Edmund Beard, *Developing the ICBM* (New York: Columbia University Press, 1976), p. 232.

13. Vincent Davis, *The Politics of Innovation: Patterns in Navy Cases* (Denver: University of Denver Monograph Series in World Affairs, 1967), p. 60.

14. Samuel P. Huntington, *The Common Defense* (New York: Columbia University Press, 1961).

15. Ibid., pp. 284–89.

16. See Beard, *Developing the ICBM,* chap. 4, in which he describes fierce air force maneuvering to capture the guided missile development program and the subsequent air force neglect of that program in favor of manned bombers. Beard contends that the air force, occupying the high ground of deterrence doctrine and its supporting funding, sought responsibility for guided missile development in order to suppress efforts by the other services (particularly the navy) to gain a piece of the action. With top funding priority for the strategic deterrent mission that emphasized manned aircraft—the organizational essence of the air force—the newly created service had little incentive to promote technological innovation in the guided missile field.

17. Huntington, *The Common Defense,* pp. 312–53.

18. Michael H. Armacost, *The Politics of Weapons Innovation: The Thor-Jupiter Controversy* (New York: Columbia University Press, 1969), p. 3; Ernest J. Yanarella, *The Missile Defense Controversy* (Lexington: University of Kentucky Press, 1977), Frederic A. Bergerson, *The Army Gets an Air Force* (Baltimore: The Johns Hopkins University Press, 1980).

19. Caspar W. Weinberger, *Annual Report to the Congress, Fiscal Year 1983,* p. I-16.

20. Ibid., p. I-30.

21. Department of Defense, *National Defense Budget Estimates for FY 1983,* March 1982. By comparison, procurement for the air force has grown by 175%, for the army by 215%, and for the marines by 670%.

22. There may be possible exceptions: SLCMs (Sea-Launched Cruise Missiles), Trident II.

23. *Budget Estimates for FY 1983.*

24. Huntington, *The Common Defense,* p. 288.

25. Capt. G. I. Wilson, "The 'Maneuver Warfare' Concept," *Marine Corps Gazette* (April 1981): 50.

26. William S. Lind, "Defining Maneuver Warfare for the Marine Corps," *Marine Corps Gazette* (March 1980): 58.

27. Charles E. Lindblom, *The Intelligence of Democracy* (New York: Free Press, 1965).

28. Huntington, *The Common Defense,* p. 288.

16

WHAT'S WRONG WITH THE DEFENSE ESTABLISHMENT?

David C. Jones

General Jones outlines the recommendations for reorganization of the
JCS he made while chairman. Furthermore, he goes beyond his original
proposals and addresses those who misinterpreted him as calling for
an all-powerful chairman. Jones contends that his reform package would
strengthen civilian control by providing more balanced, timely, and
useful military advice to the secretary of defense. In addition, he proposes
changes in military personnel policies that would benefit the armed
forces in general.

At a late-afternoon meeting at the White House, President Reagan, who
had just returned from horseback riding at Quantico, turned to me in jest, but
with a touch of nostalgia, and asked, "Isn't there some way we can bring
back the horse cavalry?" My reply was: "Just wait, Mr. President. We are
starting by resurrecting battleships."

Below the surface of this lighthearted exchange lie two pervasive problems
within defense: (1) we are too comfortable with the past, and (2) we do
not make a sufficiently rigorous examination of defense requirements and
alternatives.

By their very nature, large organizations have a built-in resistance to
change. As the largest organization in the free world, our defense establishment—the Department of Defense—has most of the problems of a large

corporation but lacks an easily calculated "bottom line" to force needed change. At the core are the army, navy, air force, and Marine Corps: institutions that find it difficult to adapt to changing conditions because of understandable attachments to the past. The very foundation of each service rests on imbuing its members with pride in its missions, its doctrine, and its customs and discipline—all of which are steeped in traditions. While these deep-seated service distinctions are important in fostering a fighting spirit, cultivating them engenders tendencies to look inward to insulate the institutions against outside challenges.

The history of our services includes striking examples of ideas and inventions whose time had come, but which were resisted because they did not fit into existing service concepts. The navy kept building sailing ships long after the advent of steam power. Machine guns and tanks were developed in the United States, but our army rejected them until long after they were accepted in Europe. The horse cavalry survived essentially unchanged right up until World War II, despite evidence that its utility was greatly diminished decades earlier. Even Army Air Corps officers were required to wear spurs until the late 1930s.

But the armed services are only part of the problem. The Defense Department has evolved into a grouping of large, rigid bureaucracies—services, agencies, staffs, boards, and committees—which embrace the past and adapt new technology to fit traditional missions and methods. There is no doubt that the cavalry leaders would quickly have adopted a horse that went farther and faster—a high-technology stallion. The result of this rigidity has been an ever-widening gap between the need to adapt to changing conditions and our ability to do so. Over the last two to three years the American public has become increasingly concerned over our deteriorating position in military power and convinced that we must devote more to our defenses than we did in the 1960s and 1970s. But after serving on the Joint Chiefs of Staff longer than anyone else in history and under more presidents and secretaries of defense (four of each), and being a student of military history and organizations, I am convinced that fundamental defense deficiencies cannot be solved with dollars alone—no matter how much they are needed.

We do not think through our defense problems adequately, and we are getting less capability than we should from our increased defense budgets. There is reason to believe that faced with a contingency requiring a major joint operation, our performance would be below the level we should expect or would need.

No one element of our defense establishment is singularly responsible for our defense problems. The problems I shall identify, and for which I shall propose solutions, have existed too long to be the fault of any particular administration or of particular personalities in or out of uniform.

History books for the most part glorify our military accomplishments, but a closer examination reveals a disconcerting pattern:

1. unpreparedness at the onset of each new crisis or war
2. initial failures
3. reorganizing while fighting
4. building our defenses as we cranked up our industrial base
5. prevailing by wearing down the enemy—by being bigger, not smarter

We could do things poorly at the start of past wars and still recover because time was on our side.

The North was a striking example of a bureaucratized military establishment during the Civil War. Initially, the South had better leadership, was far more flexible, and was able to do a great deal more with its limited resources and forces. The North suffered early defeats and encountered many leadership problems, but finally won by virtue of overwhelming industrial output and military manpower.

We also had serious organizational problems during the Cuban campaign of the Spanish-American War. The interservice wrangling had been so great that the army commander refused to let the navy be represented at the formal surrender. Unfortunately, this was not the last case of split responsibilities and interservice conflicts obstructing our conduct of a war.

In the aftermath of the 1898 war, the services, particularly the army, instituted some organizational reforms. Despite a great deal of opposition, a Chief of Staff of the Army was created in 1903 and a Chief of Naval Operations was established in 1916. But the War Department (the precursor of the Department of the Army and the Department of the Air Force) and the Navy Department continued to be riddled with semiautonomous, often intractable fiefdoms, branches, corps, departments, bureaus, and so forth.

World War I was the most tragic example of trying to win a war through mass and attrition. Thousands of young men gave their lives to advance a few yards over the enemy trenches, only to be thrown back the next day at an equal cost to the enemy.

The emergence of the airplane as a major military asset during World War I should have alerted us to the need to adjust our doctrines and our organizations to changing realities. The continued development of air power could not help but blur the traditional distinction between land and naval warfare, but the nation reacted to this phenomenon in a traditionally bureaucratic manner: Each service developed in its own air power (today there are *four* air-power entities) and protected it with artificial barriers to obscure the costly duplications. One barrier, established in 1938 (later rescinded), prohibited any Army Air Corps airplane from flying more than one hundred miles out to sea.

The army and navy began World War II with authority and responsibility diffused. Each still had many semiautonomous agencies with little coordination below the chief-of-service level. Soon after Pearl Harbor, General George C. Marshall, the army chief of staff, streamlined the army by reducing the number of officers with direct access to him from sixty-one to six.

The navy also made some adjustments. (The services have since slipped back into the old patterns. The number of officers having direct access to most chiefs—especially when the joint system service is considered—is again very high.)

The Joint Chiefs of Staff were established early in 1942 as a counterpart to the British Chiefs of Staff Committee. Although the wartime chiefs addressed certain priority issues, to a great extent World War II was fought along service lines. General Dwight D. Eisenhower, in his United States (as distinct from his Allied) role, reported to General Marshall. In the Pacific, the difficulties of integrating the operations of the services resulted in the establishment of two separate theaters: the Southwest Pacific area, with General Douglas MacArthur reporting to General Marshall, and the Pacific Ocean area, with Admiral Chester W. Nimitz reporting to Admiral Ernest J. King, the chief of naval operations. Split authority and responsibility in the Pacific was a continuing problem and nearly caused a disaster during the battle of Leyte Gulf. Today the Pacific has been joined into one command, and our combat commanders now report directly to the secretary of defense rather than to their service chiefs. But the army, air force, navy and marine components of our combat commands report both to their service chiefs and to the combat commanders, and the service chiefs still have the greatest influence over their actions. Furthermore, many of the fundamental problems of the World War II joint systems still exist below the surface.

We won World War II despite our organizational handicaps, not because we were smarter, but once again because we and our allies were bigger. We had the time and geographic isolation to mobilize American industry and a superb code-breaking effort to aid our intelligence gathering.

As the war drew to a close, an exhaustive debate ensued on how to organize the postwar military. The army favored a highly integrated system, but the navy and others were strongly opposed, some fearing that the army would dominate any integrated system. The air force, then still a part of the army, supported integration, but was primarily interested in becoming a separate service.

Those opposed to integration were backed by stronger constituencies, including powerful forces in Congress, than were the advocates of unification. Arguments that unification threatened civilian control over the military soon dominated the debate. As it became quite clear to the advocates that major change was unlikely, a little-known and surprising effort was made to salvage true integration: Karl Bendetsen, then a colonel on the War Department general staff, but later the under secretary of the army, and then chairman of the board of the Champion International Corporation, was the prime mover. He had been designated by General Marshall as the War Department liaison officer for the unification project, dealing with the White House, the navy, and Congress. After several months of analysis, he concluded that in the absence of a new and bold initiative, unification as conceived by President Harry S Truman, Secretary of War Henry L. Stimson, and General Marshall had no chance of success.

In response to General Marshall's inquiry as to what such an initiative might be, Colonel Bendetsen responded that the only way to overcome the navy's resistance would be to do away with the War Department, transfer all of its elements to the navy, and redesignate that organization as the Department of Defense.

Instead of throwing the officer out of his office, General Marshall, one of the most consummate soldier-statesmen in our history, marched him straight to Secretary Stimson to outline the proposal. After an extended discussion among the three, Stimson called President Truman and asked for a meeting on this subject.

President Truman was intrigued by the idea and decided that the liaison officer should try it out on Secretary of the Navy James V. Forrestal. Though his first reaction appeared to be positive, Secretary Forrestal rejected the proposal, on the supposition that a single armed forces chief of staff could become too powerful and threaten civilian control. So after nearly two years of studies, debate, and political maneuverings, the National Security Act of 1947 emerged with a compromise military establishment: a loose confederation of large, rigid service bureaucracies—now four rather than three—with a secretary of defense powerless against them.

Ironically, Mr. Forrestal became the first secretary of defense and, after learning at first hand his impotence in dealing with service autonomy, told Karl Bendetsen, by then a civilian, that he, the secretary, had been wrong in rejecting Mr. Bendetsen's advice.

One of Mr. Forrestal's last acts as secretary of defense was to recommend a much more integrated Department of Defense, but changes came slowly. Amendments to the National Security Act in 1949, 1953, and 1958 strengthened the secretary's authority and expanded the size and purview of his staff, but did little to alter the relative influence of the joint military system and the services.

President Eisenhower had recommended a much stronger joint system in 1953 and 1958, and his wisdom was borne out by our conduct of the Vietnam War—perhaps our worst example of confused objectives and unclear responsibilities, both in Washington and in the field. Each service, instead of integrating efforts with the others, considered Vietnam its own war and sought to carve out a large mission for itself. For example, each fought its own air war, agreeing only to limited measures for a coordinated effort. "Body count" and "tons dropped" became the measures of merit. Lack of integration persisted right through the 1975 evacuation of Saigon, when responsibility was split between two separate commands, one on land and one at sea; each of these set a different "H-hour," which caused confusion and delays.

Our soldiers, sailors, airmen, and marines have acted bravely throughout our history. With few exceptions, our forces have performed well at the united level. And there have been bright moments at the higher levels also. The landing at Normandy, Patton's charge across France, the battle of Midway, and the landing at Inchon were brilliant strategic conceptions, valiantly executed. But these peaks in martial performance followed valleys in which the nation found itself poorly prepared, poorly organized, and imperiled by inadequacies in Washington. In the past, we had time to overcome our mistakes. Our allies often bore the initial brunt, and we had the industrial capacity for a quick buildup in the military capacity needed to turn the tide. Today we can expect no such respite. Our allies could not delay the Soviet Union while we prepared, and our industrial base has fallen into a state of disrepair. Nuclear weapons have added new dimensions that make constant readiness even more critical. If we are to deter another conflict, or to succeed if one be thrust upon us, we must be prepared to do things right on the battlefield the first time.

A sound defense posture should begin with sound long-term planning, a means to measure progress, and authoritative direction and control to ensure that all elements contribute to a well-defined objective. On the surface, our system appears to provide such an orderly approach. The process starts with a defense guidance document prepared by the office of the Under Secretary of Defense for Policy, based on administration policy and fiscal guidance and on inputs from field commanders, the services, the Joint Chiefs, the secretary of defense's staff, and other relevant sources. The services build their annual programs on the basis of the defense guidance's objectives and budget targets and then submit them to the secretary of defense. The secretary convenes a committee to review the documents and recommend changes to bring the service programs into conformance with the nation's priorities. After being submitted to the president and Congress for approval, the budgets are administered by the services and agencies assigned to the Department of Defense.

But this process begins to break down at the very beginning because the military strategy contained in the defense guidance always demands greater force capabilities than the budget constraints will allow. Some administrations have attempted to limit the requirements by calling for the capability to fight "one-and-a-half" or "two-and-a-half" wars, while others have proposed preparing for global war almost without limits. In any case, the guidance almost invariably leads to what the Joint Chiefs have long called the "strategy-force mismatch" as requirements outpace capabilities.

Current guidance is so demanding that developing truly coherent programs to carry it out is impossible even under the most optimistic budget assumptions. The guidance places high priority on the long-term survivability of our strategic forces if a nuclear war should occur. Spending programs now include improvements in strategic command and control, a new bomber force with the B-1 and cruise missiles (and eventually the Stealth bomber), new nuclear submarines with improved missiles, and the MX intercontinental ballistic missile. The guidance also requires a revitalized air defense, an expanded civil defense program, and possibly an antiballistic missile to protect the MX. Military developments in space will receive additional priority. At the other end of the nuclear spectrum, ground-launched cruise missiles and Pershing 2 intermediate-range ballistic missiles are planned for Europe to reinforce our position in arms control negotiations, or to restore theater nuclear balance if those negotiations break down.

These nuclear requirements are large indeed, but they pale in comparison with conventional force requirements—expenditures for conventional forces are about three times those for nuclear forces. Substantial improvements in European and Pacific operations are planned, and the ability to project power, especially in southwest Asia, is to be expanded. The DOD document *Defense Guidance* tells the services to improve the readiness of conventional forces, greatly increase strategic mobility capabilities, and build up the navy to provide maritime superiority. At the same time, they are to replace many weapons systems that are nearing obsolescence. And they are to provide greater sustainability so as to be able to fight a longer war. Improved industrial preparedness is also a goal.

There is simply not enough money in the projected defense budgets to do all this, but *Defense Guidance* does little to set meaningful priorities or mandate a search for new directions to maintain our security. This is not a problem unique to this administration.

Since requirements exceed resources, the military services invariably allocate resources among their traditional missions and seek ways to justify a greater share of the budget. But additional funds are likely to come from another service's share, so each attempts to outgame the others without sufficient regard for cross-service programs.

The vast array of service programs is then submitted to the defense committee. The name and composition of the committee may vary from administration to administration, but its function remains the same. Currently it is called the Defense Resources Board; its chairman is the secretary or the deputy secretary of defense, and it includes the service secretaries, assistant secretaries of defense, and the chairman of the Joint Chiefs of Staff. The service chiefs attend as observers.

Week after week, the board meets in an attempt to examine major issues, but the focus is primarily on the service programs, which include many hundreds of items deemed essential by their advocates. The board fusses over marginal changes in the service programs, but it is literally impossible for it to address them in sufficient depth or to focus on the most critical cross-service issues.

The Joint Chiefs of Staff and the Joint Staff are assigned a role in this process, but each service usually wants the Joint Staff merely to echo its views. Since four of the five members of the Joint Chiefs of Staff are also service chiefs, a negotiated amalgam of service views almost invariably prevails when inputs are finally proposed by the Joint Staff. The chairman of the Joint Chiefs of Staff is the only military member of the Defense Resources Board and can offer independent opinions, but the chairman has only five people working directly for him to sift through the various issues. (The Joint Staff belongs to the Joint Chiefs' corporate body, not to the chairman.) Consequently, chairmen traditionally focus on a few critical items. In my case, they were readiness, command and control, and mobility.

The result of this tedious process is a defense budget that is derived primarily from the disparate desires of the individual services rather than from a well-integrated plan based on a serious examination of alternatives by the civilian and military leadership working together. Inevitably, a secretary of defense either supports a total program that is roughly the sum of the service inputs (limited by fiscal guidance) or resorts to forcing changes, knowing that advocates of disapproved programs will continue their opposition into the congressional hearings.

But resource allocation by the board is only the beginning of the problem. The optimism expressed in program proposals seldom comes true. The chairman of the Defense Science Board, Norman Augustine, has written that over the last thirty years our major weapons systems have met performance goals 70 percent of the time (not bad), but have met schedules only 15 percent of the time and cost estimates only 10 percent of the time, even after accounting for inflation.

As costs increase, programs are stretched out. Weapons are usually ordered in numbers well below efficient production rates, to the detriment of the "industrial base." This only leads to further cost increases, the cycle repeats itself, and we find ourselves trapped in a Catch-22 situation. Tough decisions are not made, so the financial "bow wave" that always spills ahead is magnified. Attempts to improve efficiency, such as the current administration's multiyear procurement contracts, are very helpful, but do not get to the fundamental problems of planning and resources.

The lack of discipline in the budget system prevents making the very tough choices of deciding what to do and what not to do. Instead, strong constituencies in the Pentagon, Congress, and industry support individual programs, while the need for overall defense effectiveness and efficiency is not adequately addressed.

Pentagon leadership finds it virtually impossible to spend the time necessary to impose discipline on the budget process. Cycles overlap, and, as in 1982, we usually find Congress considering a last-minute multibillion-dollar supplemental appropriation at the end of one fiscal year and unable to agree on the budget before the start of the next fiscal year. At the same time, the Pentagon is struggling with the next five-year defense plan and the subsequent budget submission. This constantly immerses the leadership in confusing external struggles for public and congressional support and in bewildering internal disputes over resources and turf.

The same pressures burden the service leaders as they attempt to cope with managing procurement programs, recruiting and training the forces, and maintaining discipline and esprit. Chiefs are judged by their peers and services on their success in obtaining funding for their own major systems and on protecting service interests in the three afternoons a week they spend in meetings of the Joint Chiefs of Staff. Furthermore, a service chief, who is a service advocate while wearing one hat and supposedly an impartial judge of competing requirements while wearing the other as a member of the Joint Chiefs of Staff, has a fundamental conflict of interest.

To sum up, our defense establishment suffers serious deficiencies, including the following:

1. Strategy is so all-encompassing that it means all things to all men.
2. Leaders are inevitably captives of the urgent, and long-range planning is too often neglected.
3. Authority and responsibility are badly diffused.
4. Rigorous examination of requirements and alternatives is not made.
5. Discipline is lacking in the budget process.
6. Tough decisions are avoided.
7. Accountability for decisions or performance is woefully inadequate.
8. Leadership, often inexperienced, is forced to spend too much time on refereeing an intramural scramble for resources.
9. A serious conflict of interest faces our senior military leaders.
10. The combat effectiveness of the fighting force—the end product—does not receive enough attention.

Before too much criticism is heaped on the current administration, let me point out that these problems have been with us for decades and that there are no easy solutions.

What all this adds up to is that it is an uphill struggle for anyone—including a secretary of defense—to gain real control of our defense establishment. An earlier study on defense organization stated that everyone was responsible for everything and no one was specifically responsible for anything. The top leadership is too often at the mercy of long-entrenched bureaucracies. It is ironic that the services have, with considerable help from outside constituencies, been able to defeat attempts to bring order out of chaos by arguing that a source of alternative military advice for the president and secretary of defense runs the risk of undermining civilian control.

There has for some time been an imbalance in the degree of control that our civilian leadership exercises over operational and other defense matters. In operational matters, it is pervasive. An order cannot go out of Washington to move a ship or other combat unit or to take any other specific operational action without the specific approval and initialing of the directive by the secretary of defense. At times, defense secretaries and their staffs have been involved in the most minute details of operations.

In other areas, civilian influence is more often apparent than real. Defense secretaries are given very little comprehensive advice on alternative strategies or systems. In an attempt to fill the void, defense secretaries have often turned to civilian analysts for such advice. Such consultants can provide a useful service, but they cannot make up for the absence of alternative advice from experienced, serving military officers. That the Joint Chiefs of Staff, a committee beholden to the interests of the services, has not been able to provide such advice during its existence is amply documented in scores of studies over many years.

Civilian accountability within the Defense Department is undermined further by the rapid turnover or the inexperience of the senior leadership. In the thirty-five years since the department was founded, there have been fifteen secretaries of defense, and there have been nineteen deputy secretaries of defense in the thirty-three years since the establishment of that position. A recent study revealed that the civilian policy makers in the Defense Department stay on the job an average of only twenty-eight months.

Little of what I have said is new. Reams of paper have been used since World War II to describe these same deficiencies. President Eisenhower, who knew well both sides of the civilian-military equation, tried to resolve the basic problem, but the effects of his efforts were limited. Others have also tried, but with even less success. The bureaucratic resistance to change is enormous and is reinforced by many allies of the services—in Congress and elsewhere—who are bent on keeping the past enthroned. Civilian defense leaders have been reluctant to push hard for changes, either because they thought they could not succeed or because they did not want to expend the necessary political capital, which they believed was better spent on gaining support for the defense budget. Many have feared that raising basic organizational issues might distract attention from the budget and give ammunition to opponents, who would use admissions of organizational inefficiency to argue for further budget cuts. Yet, since the public already believes that all is not right with the Department of Defense, bold reforms would not only increase our defense effectiveness but would strengthen public support as well.

That the balance of influence within the defense establishment is oriented too much toward the individual services has been a constant theme of many past studies of defense organization. In 1982, a special study group of retired senior officers found it necessary to report that "a certain amount of service independence is healthy and desirable, but the balance now favors the parochial interests of the services too much and the larger needs of the nation's defenses too little."

It is commonly accepted that one result of this imbalance is a constant bickering among the services. This is not the case. On the contrary, interactions among the services usually result in "negotiated treaties," which minimize controversy by avoiding challenges to service interests. Such a truce has its good points, for it is counterproductive for the services to attack each other. But the lack of adequate questioning by military professionals results in gaps and unwarranted duplications in our defense capabilities. What is lacking is a counterbalancing system, one that involves officers not so beholden to their services, who can objectively examine strategy, roles, missions, weapons systems, war planning, and other contentious issues to offset the influence of the individual services.

President Eisenhower tried to resolve this problem in 1958 by removing the services from the operational chain of command. In essence, two separate lines of authority were created under the secretary of defense: an operational line and an administrative line. The operational line runs from the president, through the secretary of defense, to the combat commands—those theater or functional commands headed by the Eisenhowers, the Nimitzes, the MacArthurs of the future. The Joint Chiefs of Staff are not directly in this line of command but do, through the Joint Staff, provide the secretary oversight of the combat commands and pass his orders to them. The administrative line runs to the service departments responsible for recruiting, training, procurement, and a myriad of other tasks necessary to develop the forces assigned to the combat commands.

President Eisenhower intended that the operational side would assist the secretary of defense in developing strategy, operational plans and weapons, and force-level requirements based on the needs of "truly unified commands." The Joint Chiefs of Staff and the Joint Staff were to be the secretary's military staff in this effort. The services would remain the providers of the forces needed by the combatant commands but would not determine what to provide or how those forces would be employed. But President Eisenhower did not achieve what he wanted. The scales of influence are still tipped too far in favor of the services and against the combat commanders.

Although the combat commanders now brief the Defense Resources Board and have every opportunity to communicate with the secretary of defense and the chiefs, virtually their only power is that of persuasion. The services control most of the money and the personnel assignments and promotions of their people wherever assigned, including in the Office of the Secretary of Defense, the Joint Staff, and the United Command Staffs. Officers who perform duty outside their own services generally do less well than those assigned to duty in their service, especially when it comes to promotion to general or admiral. The chiefs of staff of the services almost always have had duty on service staffs in Washington but almost never on the Joint Staff. Few incentives exist for an officer assigned to joint duty to do more than punch his or her ticket and then get back into a service assignment. I cannot stress this point too strongly: He who controls dollars, promotions, and assignments controls the organization—and the services so control, especially with regard to personnel actions.

A most recent critique of defense problems was contained in a book published in 1982 called *U.S. Defense Planning*, written by John M. Collins of the Library of Congress. This study reveals some new deficiencies as well as pointing out the old ones. "Interests, objectives, policies, commitments, strategic concepts and force postures often fail to complement each other" and "Preoccupation with present problems leaves little time to contemplate those coming down the pike" are but two of many such conclusions.

Yet it is very difficult to break out of the Department of Defense's organizational maze. Many have struggled vainly within the system to make improvements in the balance between the operational and administrative lines. Solutions to some of the basic interservice problems are heralded every few years but to this date have not addressed the fundamental causes. To provide a balance, the services must share some of their authority, but they have proved to be consistently unwilling to do so. A service chief has a constituency which, if convinced that he is not fighting hard enough for what the service sees as its fair share of defense missions and resources, can destroy the chief's effectiveness.

Only the chairman of the Joint Chiefs of Staff is unconstrained by a service constituency, but he is in a particularly difficult position. His influence stems from his ability to persuade all his colleagues on the Joint Chiefs of Staff to agree on a course of action, and any disagreement requires by law a report to the secretary of defense. A chairman jeopardizes his effectiveness if, early in his tour, he creates dissension within the corporate body by trying to force the services to share some of their authority.

By the summer of 1980, after serving as chairman of the Joint Chiefs of Staff for two years, I had become convinced that we could not begin to overcome our defense problems without a basic restructuring of military responsibility. In the early fall, I discussed the problem with Secretary of Defense Harold Brown and found that he shared my concerns. Although he was soon to leave office, he has remained a staunch supporter of organizational change. My first conversation with Caspar W. Weinberger, just before he assumed the office, was also promising. He indicated a receptiveness to any ideas that would improve defense decision making and management. Soon thereafter I commissioned the group of retired senior officers mentioned earlier to examine the issues thoroughly and to interview and incorporate the views of the chiefs, the combat commanders, Joint Staff personnel, and many others.

At the same time, I studied the organizational arrangements in other countries, East and West. The Soviet Union has a highly centralized system with a general staff numbering in the thousands, but it also has many bureaucratic problems common to an authoritarian system. There are quite a few Western democracies with a centralized system that works well. For example, the Norwegians have a chief of defense who has great authority and control over the services and is considered a positive link in maintaining democratic control. At the other end of the spectrum, there are countries that keep their services well apart and in competition with each other. Iran under the shah and Argentina with its junta made up of the three service heads are examples of such competitive systems. Our system falls more toward the competitive than the centralized end of the spectrum.

In trying to determine where our system should be on this scale, I had long discussions with my British counterpart, Admiral of the Fleet Sir Terence Lewin, chief of the Defense Staff of the United Kingdom. Our system is an outgrowth of the British World War II system, and Sir Terence and I concluded that our respective organizational arrangements were not outmoded. We saw almost identical problems in our two military systems and came to very similar conclusions about what was needed. Despite strong opposition from two of the British services, Sir Terence was able to secure quick approval to act on his conclusions from Prime Minister Margaret Thatcher. The major change—providing a military counterbalance to the separate services—was implemented in 1982 and contributed to British success in the Falklands dispute.

Early in 1982, I aired certain proposals publicly in the winter issue of *Directors and Boards* magazine. General Edward C. Meyer, chief of staff of the army, soon published an article containing similar criticisms and recommended even greater changes in military organization.

This past summer, the House Armed Services Subcommittee on Investigations, under the chairmanship of Representative Richard C. White of Texas, held extensive hearings on the issue. The witnesses in support of major changes outnumbered the opponents by almost three to one. I was particularly impressed that all of the former secretaries and deputy secretaries of defense who testified supported at least as much change as I recommended, and most advocated even more.

It is no secret that the greatest opposition to any change came from the Department of the Navy, just as it did in 1947 and has ever since. I believe I understand, even though I cannot agree with the reasons. The Department of the Navy is the most strategically independent of the services—it has its own army, navy, and air force. It would prefer to be given a mission, retain complete control over all the assets, and be left alone.

The army is and always has been the most supportive of the services in cross-service activities and the strongest advocate of organizational changes that would improve unity of effort. Its reasons, too, are understandable—and I agree with them. The army is the least strategically independent service. It depends on the air force for much firepower and on the air force and navy for mobility; the army can, in fact, do very little in isolation and hence is particularly short-changed by a lack of integration and cooperation among the services.

The air force has some missions requiring the cooperation of the other services, and some that it can pursue independently. Not surprisingly, air force officers generally have been more ambivalent about change.

Given these circumstances, we cannot expect the services to agree on profound changes no matter how badly needed, for the changes inevitably would result in the services' giving up some of their sovereignty.

The bill drafted and then passed in the House avoided the issues on which the services are most sensitive; the bill contains some good provisions, but they are insufficient to correct the basic ills of the system. It is to be hoped that the Senate will hold in-depth hearings, for public airing of the issues is essential in obtaining widespread understanding and support. There is always great reluctance in Washington to take on entrenched bureaucracies in the absence of some consensus for change.

Since I dealt only with military organization in my initial proposals, some misinterpreted them as calling for an all-powerful chairman of the Joint Chiefs of Staff. That is definitely not my intent. On the contrary, my proposals are designed to provide the secretary of defense more balanced military advice and staff support in order to *strengthen* civilian control. I believe we must provide a proper balance between the services and the joint system—the administrative and operational lines of authority and responsibility. So long as the leadership of the operational side remains within the control of the four services, individual service interests—which are oriented to independent capabilities—will continue to dominate the military advice offered to the secretary of defense.

In broad outline, this is what I believe what must be done:

To eliminate service domination of the channels of military advice to the secretary and the president, the chairman of the Joint Chiefs of Staff—rather than the five-man committee of the Chiefs—should represent the operational side, while the service chiefs should continue to represent the administrative side of our military organization. The chairman would receive advice from both the service chiefs and the combat commanders in preparing his recommendation to the secretary of defense. Furthermore, there should be a provision for a direct appeal to the secretary of defense or the president, as appropriate, if a service chief disagreed with the chairman on a *joint* matter and felt strongly about the differences. The influence of the combat commanders on operational matters should be increased to equal that of the service chiefs.

To ensure that he can meet his responsibility to the secretary and the president, the chairman should be authorized to have a deputy chairman, and the Joint Staff should be assigned to the chairman rather than to the corporate body of the Joint Chiefs. The service chiefs and their staffs (most of which dwarf the Joint Staff) would still have access to the Joint Staff but would not have a de facto veto of all proposals which subordinated service interests to greater cross-service effectiveness.

Systems analysts should be transferred from the Office of the Secretary of Defense to the chairman's office to insure a good balance of civilian and military perspectives on alternatives offered to the secretary. As a related action, many of the more than five hundred military officers assigned to the Office of the Secretary of Defense should be reassigned back to their services as the Joint Staff becomes oriented to the entire system rather than service dominated.

Discipline should be imposed on the guidance-program-budget cycle. Not only should there be a requirement for an independent cost analysis of every major program, but greater reliance should be placed on the results. Until the system proves it can plan and execute in a disciplined way, a substantial percentage of dollars in the five-year program should be reserved for unexpected cost growth or contingency operations. This would force some tough decisions at the beginning of the cycle which would avoid wasting money and provide greater effectiveness in the long run by not allowing programs to start that cannot be supported even under the most optimistic budget projections.

Administrative matters should be decentralized to the services, with their leadership, military and civilian, being held more accountable for performance. Fixing responsibility for defensewide advice more clearly on a joint system not dominated by the services would allow the service chiefs and their staffs to spend much more time on running their services.

Substantial changes should be made in military personnel policies so that officers could develop a broader vision than that of their own service and could be better prepared for both service and interservice assignments. We should begin by encouraging and allowing a substantial number of graduates from one service academy to volunteer for transfer to another service immediately upon graduation. The air force benefited a great deal in its early days by receiving officers from both West Point and Annapolis—officers with basic understanding of the other services. And two- or three-year assignments of officers to another service should become more common.

The professional education system should be changed to stress the joint needs in defense by providing the National Defense University limited oversight of part of the curriculum of the Service War Colleges.

We should reexamine the retirement system, which provides great incentives for officers to serve for twenty years, but very few incentives for the best to stay longer. We still lose too many of our best officers at the peak of their capabilities. The joint system should be given some limited influence in the promotion and assignment of officers so that joint duty could become more attractive and rewarding for the best.

Finally, the congressional restrictions on tenure of assignment on the Joint Staff should be removed so that we do not continue to experience a 100 percent turnover in a little over two years. Collectively, the above should provide opportunities for greater stability and experience in officer assignments and, thus, the opportunity for better accountability of performance.

I do not claim that my proposals will solve all of our defense problems, but these or similar major changes can set us on the right course. Congressional action is needed on these organizational issues—the most important defense problem facing our nation. Additional money is badly needed for defense, but without major realignment, we will neither achieve the necessary capability nor spend the money as wisely as we should. The critical question is whether we will show the wisdom to do as the British did, or whether we will muddle along as we have in the past until some crisis or disaster awakens us to the need for change.

17

TOWARD A STRONGER
DEFENSE ESTABLISHMENT

Paul F. Gorman

General Gorman's focus is to explain why top-down reform measures,
such as the various JCS reform proposals, are generally disregarded. Not
unlike Clark in chapter 15, Gorman views cultural differences among the
services as the fundamental problem—one that can be remedied only
through JCS reorganization. He, like Jones, disagrees with those who
charge that the effect of JCS reform will be to reduce civilian control of the
military.

In April 1982, the chief of staff of the U.S. Army, General Edward C.
Meyer, became the first chief of staff since George C. Marshall to advocate a
national military authority above the army, beyond veto by his service. General Meyer noted some twenty studies on restructuring the high command
over a period of thirty-eight years. And his list was by no means exhaustive.
Reform of the civil-military interface is an aspect of military reform which
has probably had more prestigious and persistent advocacy than any other,
and yet General Meyer, like so many other senior military leaders who have
sought reorganization, is probably doomed to being ignored. Why is it that
repeatedly throughout the history of the United States proposals for top-down
reform have so often been disregarded or, if adopted at all, so adulterated as
to vitiate the purpose of the reformers?

The usual explanations hold that proposals like General Meyer's, or those
of General Jones, seem to foster a stronger military at the expense of civil

authority and to add superstructure without improving substance. In short, Congress should not be expected to accede to a most un-American shift in policy, one that renders civilian control more problematic and that assures more brass, but no more bang-for-the-buck.

These charges can be answered by drawing on past reports and studies. Let us, however, first review the current scene. As before on occasions since 1900, senior officers, both serving and retired, among them the most prestigious in the military profession, have gone public with a series of proposals designed to enhance the quality and continuity of the military advice to their civilian secretary for his pivotal decisions on defense policy and on resource allocation. They point out that the secretary is serviced for these purposes mainly by bureaucracies, which, albeit staffed by fellow military professionals, are insulated one from another and which compete fiercely for missions and money. They argue that however patriotic and well motivated each leader of a vertical conduit to the secretary may be, the wants and needs of his own bureaucracy are inevitably in tension with overall military requirements. Hence, the secretary would be better served by a reorganization providing for a supervening horizontal military staff free to monitor and critique all plans and undertakings and thus to influence the readiness of the armed forces as a whole. They hold that this staff should be headed by one senior military officer designated as the principal military adviser to the secretary and the president. This reorganization would, therefore, provide for the well-founded military analyses that the secretary requires to decide on issues of efficiency that cut across the several compartments within his department, or on the opportunities and risks entailed in deciding what forces to maintain ready for war.

To portray the currently proposed reforms as augmenting the role of the chairman or strengthening the authority of the Joint Chiefs of Staff is to obscure the essential principles espoused by General Meyer and General Jones, which are consistent with those of virtually every other reformer of defense organization back to Elihu Root and Alfred Thayer Mahan at the turn of the century: it is the civilian secretary, not the military head of staff, who is the intended beneficiary. The reformers have argued that civilian control would be better assured both by virtue of a better-advised secretary and by adding checks and balances to the military bureaucracies. Military options adduced for the secretary would be more numerous and more sharply delineated. Most importantly, these changes would assure that the nation would, by being better prepared to wage war, be more likely to preserve peace.

To illuminate these issues in the present controversy, it is useful to revisit those earlier controversies that arose late in the presidency of Theodore Roosevelt when prominent naval officers, including Admirals Steven B. Luce and Alfred T. Mahan, aided and abetted by a group of more junior officers, among them Commander William S. Sims, petitioned the president to bring about a reorganization of the Navy Department. Mahan perceived military administration as "embracing opposites"—as reconciling the different perspectives, on the one hand, of military professionals who have to train, maintain, and lead the force, and, on the other, of civilian leaders who by law superintend them, and of politicians who represent the people for whose security the force is raised and supported. Mahan held that existing organizations were unbalanced toward the civil.

Roosevelt finally acted, and on 25 February 1909, in a special message to the Senate, he set forth general principles for naval organization, followed shortly thereafter by specific legislative recommendations.[2] His report stated that the Office of the Secretary was executive in nature, and that law should preserve that official's full authority and responsibility, but that the division between the civil and military functions of the department should be recognized and more clearly defined. While the existing organization, which dated back to laws of 1842, provided for the peacetime administration of the department, there were no comparable provisions in statute for preparation for war or operations therein. The problem was exactly that the eight existing bureaus within the Department of the Navy, however well suited for civil administration or for mollifying politicians, were an impediment to the prosecution of war. Roosevelt stated that "independent authority, with undivided responsibility, though in principle proper, suffers historically from intrinsic inability to cooperate where a number of such independent units are present. The marshals of the first Napoleon—especially in Spain—in the absence of the Emperor, offer a familiar illustration. The bureau system as at present constituted by law contains no remedy for this inherent defect."

The report concluded that while it clearly was the responsibility of the secretary to coordinate the work of the bureaus, his tenure of office was short, and his military knowledge inevitably limited; hence, a reorganization was required to provide military continuity, as well as "knowledge and experience, digested formally," from a body designed to provide "the weightiest and most instructed counsel," a group "equipped not with advice merely, but with reasons." Here the hand of Admiral Mahan is especially evident. Mahan had written the president in January 1909 that the secretary of the navy needed a full-time, knowledgeable military staff with mastery of all information, domestic and foreign, that bore on naval policy, and that "the only means by which such consecutive knowledge can be maintained is by a corporate body continuous in existence and gradual in change. That we call a General Staff."

Such a body should be endowed with coherence and force by fixing upon its head sole responsibility for advice rendered to the secretary, "solemnly charged that in all he recommends he is sowing for a future he himself may have to reap." Further, since the purpose of the navy is war, that body "should be taken entirely from the class to which belongs the conduct of war, and upon whom will fall, in war, the responsibility for the use of the instruments and for the results of the measures which they recommend." Hence, a staff of naval officers should be maintained to provide the secretary "a clear understanding and firm grasp of leading military considerations. Possessed of these he may without great difficulty weigh the recommendations of his technical assistants, decide for himself, and depend on them for technical execution of that which he approves."[4] Thus, such a staff would help, not hinder, the secretary and would shed new light on technical issues, not obfuscate them.

The National Security Act of 1947, as amended in 1949, 1953, and 1958, establishes a secretary of defense with intradepartmental challenges not unlike those of the secretary of the navy in Roosevelt's era. In some respects, at least, he is in an even weaker position. After all, secretaries of the navy then had to contend only with eight semiautonomous bureaus. Today the secretary of defense has to cope with three military departments, our services, and a plethora of independent defense agencies, with his sole military advice coming from a committee, the Joint Chiefs of Staff, which has a Joint Staff that is less a general staff than an interservice matchmaking service.

The deficiencies of these latter organizations have been well documented in the Report of the Blue Ribbon Defense Panel of 1970, the Ignatius and Steadman reports of 1978, the Brehm Report of 1980, and the 1982 Brehm-Kerwin study for the chairman of the Joint Chiefs of Staff. What needs to be stressed is that divisions within the Department of Defense today are far more dysfunctional than were the divisions within the Department of the Navy at the turn of the century. After all, those navy bureaus were headed by naval officers, each of whom, in one sense or another, was pursuing the needs of his service. Today the secretary of defense has to accommodate service differences so deep and so divisive as to warrant reference to them as "cultural." By the latter term I mean that corpus of ideas, suppositions, traditions, customs, prejudices, and obstinacies which distinguishes one of the uniformed services from another. These cultural differences go beyond distinctive weapons systems, dress, forms of speech, and life style to dictate functional asymmetries among the services in their approach to command control and doctrine, and in their attitudes toward the functions of staffs for planning and operations. More importantly, since members of the JCS are products of their culture par excellence, much that has been deplored as disjointed in the Joint Staff can best be understood as cultural clash.

Let us look for a moment at some comparisons. Array in your mind, if you will, the four services side by side, starting on the left with the navy, then the air force, then the marines and on the right the army. One might select strategic mobility as a category of comparison and observe that the four services, so arrayed, are in proper order from left to right with respect to their intrinsic capabilities for force projection and sustainment: the navy has the greatest strategic independence, while the army is wholly dependent on other services for strategic mobility. Similarly, one might observe that the base operations of the navy and the air force are more like large-scale industrial undertakings, while those of the marines and the army are closer to cottage industries. But for our purposes here, which are to inquire into doctrine and into higher-echelon staff functions, we must probe more deeply.

I would suggest that to illuminate more surely the asymmetries among the services we might use the foregoing scale to compare four members of the JCS in chrysalis. Let's take four three-star commanders, each from a different service, operating afield. Each of these would dispose of a quite different number of movable subordinate entities, which differ in number by an order of magnitude. By "movable subordinate entities" we mean groupings of personnel and materiel responsive to a single human intelligence: ships, planes, tank crews, infantry squads, supply detachments, survey parties, and the like. The navy three-star would probably have at his disposal something on the order of 10^1 to 10^2 movable subordinate entities. The comparable air force three-star would have perhaps 10^2 to 10^3 movable subordinate entities, the marine some 10^3 to 10^4, and their army counterpart, a corps commander, would have 10^4 to 10^5 movable subordinate entities. These numbers are tyrannical, but probably less so than the communication systems and command mechanisms that would be available to each. The navy commander would have the most assured communications, the army commander the least. The navy commander would be dealing on the average with relatively high-ranking officers, and the average rank of subordinate leaders of the movable subordinate entities would decline as one proceeded across the array from navy to air force to marines to army. The navy commander's information concerning his subordinates would be quite precise and real-time, that of the army leader vague and slow-arriving. The navy commander would have, as a concomitant of all of the foregoing, the greatest tactical flexibility, the army commander the least. The navy command principle would be centralization, while that of the army commander would perforce be decentralization. The air force would be much closer to the navy in all these respects, the marines closer to the army.

These cultural realities dictate very different attitudes toward doctrine. For marine and army forces afield, doctrine is important for cohesion of effort; in the best sense of the term, it is consensus on how to fight. A consensus powerful enough to concert action amid the chaos and uncertainty of land combat, to facilitate decentralized yet complementary operations, must be nurtured by years of careful training.[5] Moreover, land force doctrine focuses mainly on human behavior, while that for air and sea warfare centers on weapons system performance. Changes of navy and air force doctrine are more readily absorbed by those cultures, and usually stem from the infusion of new materiel. Marine and army doctrine, however, can undergo transformation without major changes in equipment—the last several versions of the FM 100-5 are a case in point. No responsible leader of any service would disagree with the proposition that weapons system development should flow from preferred operating doctrine, but as a practical matter, without outside influence this is less likely to occur in the navy or air force, and more likely in the Marine Corps or army.

As for planning, the classic function of higher-echelon staffs, the navy commander would be interested mainly in orchestrating deployment schedules, determining load-out criteria, and maintaining readiness for a surge to high operating tempo. Once a ship is loaded for combat, in general, it matters little where it is then sent, one part of the hydrosphere being like another. The air force commander would have his staff pay serious attention to *de*ployment, but would probably regard *em*ployment as a matter of make-it-up-as-you-go-along, since one segment of aerospace is like another, and a targeted Soviet column on a road presents about the same problem for suppression and strike whether in central Europe or anywhere in Asia. The marine commander would want the staff to concentrate heavily on *de*ployment planning, especially for amphibious assault. Both the marine and the army commanders would want staffs to dig deeply into all aspects of *em*ployment to anticipate proper force mix and logistics, since their units would have to contend with all the clutter of the earth's land surface and would have to deal with all the variables and uncertainties induced by climate or enemy. And the army commander would feel the need for detailed advance planning even more than the marine, since he would want to prepare for sustained combat on land, and usually would have to provide most of the theater logistic infrastructure. These attitudes and convictions constitute part of the mental baggage each of these commanders would carry into the "tank" were he subsequently to serve on the JCS.

It is only natural, then, that manifestations of these cultural differences often dominate JCS recommendations and actions. Moreover, since each chief of service carries heavy personal responsibilities for research, development, and procurement, he often finds his own service's interests at odds with joint interests. These tensions occur not only within the JCS itself, but engender counterpart tensions in the Unified Commands and throughout the multi-layered Joint Staff structure where joint issues are addressed. But they occur within the JCS especially because four of the five members are charged with the responsibility to maintain the traditions, esprit, morale, and capabilities of their services—they are temple dogs, personal guardians of their culture. Such tensions spill over to the combat commands and within Pentagon staffs because officers assigned to joint billets come from and return to the culture that conditions them before joint duty and that exercises complete control over their subsequent promotions and assignments. An officer champions at hazard to his career causes that lead to greater joint effectiveness at the expense of the institutional interests of his own service. These have been cited persistently as flaws in the system:

JCS Special Committee, 1945:

Even in areas where unity of command has been established, complete integration of effort has not yet been achieved because we are still struggling with inconsistencies, lack of understanding, jealousies and duplications which exist in all theaters of operations.[6]

President Eisenhower, 1958:

I know well, from years of military life, the constant concern of service leaders for the adequacy of their respective programs, each of which is intended to strengthen the Nation's defense. . . . But service responsibilities and activities must always be only the branches, not the central trunk of the national security tree. The present organization fails to apply this truth.

While at time human failure and misdirected zeal have been responsible for duplications, inefficiencies, and publicized disputes, the truth is that most of the service rivalries that have troubled us in recent years have been made inevitable by the laws that govern our defense organization.[7]

The Symington Report, 1960:

The predominance of Service influence in the formulation of defense planning and the performance of military missions must be corrected. At present, defense planning represents at best a series of compromised positions among the military services. . . . Nor can the Joint Staff become fully effective in developing the basis for clear military judgments unless the present degree of influence exercised by separate Service thinking is sharply reduced.

In short, there is a clear need for defense interest rather than particular service interest.[8]

The Steadman Report, 1978:

The nature of the [JCS] organization virtually precludes effective addressal of those issues involving allocation of resources among the Services, such as budget levels, force structures, and procurement of new weapons systems—except to agree that they should be increased without consideration of resource constraints.[9]

The CJCS Special Study Group, 1982:

A certain amount of Service independence is healthy and desirable, but the balance now favors the parochial interests of the Services too much and the larger needs of the nation's defenses too little.[10]

In sum, to ignore Generals Meyer and Jones is to leave the secretary of defense without advisory recourse against the service bureaucracies.

But what about the danger of incipient militarism and presumptions that more numerous and influential generals will lead to four-star featherbedding, to more overhead without an iota of added military efficiency? Many Americans and their political leaders seem disinclined to believe that American military professionals are corporately capable of providing cogent advice on key military matters. This view is not based on disdain such as that of H. G. Wells, who opined that "the professional military mind is by necessity an inferior, unimaginative mind; no man of high intellectual quality would willingly imprison his gifts in such a calling." Rather, it reflects a conviction that military conservatism frequently inhibits proper choices among weapons systems, force structures, strategies, and tactics, so that reform, if it be needed, must come from the civil leadership or the Congress. Alfred Thayer Mahan himself stated that no military service can or should undertake to reform itself, but must seek assistance from outside. As Roman naval authorities continued to build oar-powered ships long after conversion to sail was indicated, so the U.S. Navy persisted with sail long after the era of steam had arrived. The U.S. Army spurned the machine guns of Gatling, Browning, Maxim, and Lewis and ignored Christie's tank, forcing those American inventors to sell abroad; and the army obstinately preserved large horse cavalry formations up until World War II, long after their operational relevance had diminished. Public receptivity to present debates over doctrine for AirLand battle, over force structure for strategic mobility, or over the kind and amount of ships for the navy indicates that many Americans believe that such matters are altogether too important to be left to any military staff.

Coupled with inherent suspicion of military conservatism is our atavistic fear of military domination. This takes the form of staunch opposition to a general staff, out of conviction that such a body, if empowered to arrange for the means of national security policy, would be *ipso facto* in a position to determine its ends. Congress has often acted to preclude the creation of any such staff. Just prior to World War I, the redoubtable Josephus Daniels attacked the naval reform movement that succeeded the Roosevelt proposals, emasculating legislation that would have established a general staff within the Department of the Navy by accusing sponsors of trying to "Prussianize" the navy. Today, the law of the land provides that "the Joint Staff shall not operate or be organized as an overall armed forces general staff and shall have no executive authority."[11]

The time has come to reconsider that legislation and the underlying prejudices that prompted it. Over the past twelve years, no official study of defense reorganization expresses doubts concerning the desirability of competent military advice; indeed, by identifying the absence of incisive military advice for the secretary as a shortcoming, they endorse its usefulness. Moreover, none of these studies anticipate an uncontrolled military, a step toward militarism. As General Jones has put it aptly, he is not trying to set up a man on horseback, only to provide a remedy for five men on a camel.

The principal reason for moving beyond a national command advised by a committee of chiefs of services is that however useful that arrangement may be for justifying force structure and procurement funds for modernization, it is patently not useful for prosecuting war. The payoff for defense organization is readiness for war. The armed services, qua services, do not fight wars, any more than the bureaus of the old navy fought wars. By law, the president, through the secretary of defense, with the advice and assistance of the JCS, establishes combat commands to perform military missions and prescribes the force structure of those commands. The military departments assign forces from the services to these combat commands for stated missions, and any force so assigned is to be under its full operational command. Moreover, as President Eisenhower—who of all presidents was most in a position to know—stated in his message to Congress on 3 April 1958:

> Separate ground, sea, and air warfare is gone forever. If ever again we should be involved in war, we will fight it in all elements, with all services, as one single concentrated effort. Peacetime preparatory and organizational activity must conform to this fact. Strategic and tactical planning must be completely unified, combat forces organized into unified commands, each equipped with the most efficient weapons systems that science can develop, singly led and prepared to fight as one, regardless of service. The accomplishment of this result is the basic function of the Secretary of Defense, advised and assisted by the Joint Chiefs of Staff and operating under the supervision of the Commander in Chief.

Eisenhower noted that as of 1958, a decade after Truman's reorganization,

> the [unified] commander's authority over these [service] commands is short of the full command required for maximum efficiency. . . . When military responsibility is unclear, civilian control is uncertain.[12]

Once more, of course, the changes envisaged by a reform-minded president fell short of his expectations. The revisions of the law in 1958 which ensued did not significantly ameliorate service divisions or put the combat commands in any better position to discharge their responsibilities. The 1978 Steadman report found that "most CINCs [commanders in chief] have limited power to influence the capability of the forces assigned to them . . . the Service and the components thus have the major influence on both the structure and readiness of the forces for which the CINC is responsible."[13] The most recent study, by the chairman's Special Study Group, concluded that "the military organizations given the responsibility for the planning and execution of joint activities— notably the JCS, the Joint Staff . . . and the various Unified Command headquarters—simply do not have the authority, stature, trained personnel, or support needed to carry out their jobs effectively."[14]

General Jones has advanced five recommendations:

1. The chairman, rather than the Joint Chiefs of Staff as a body, should be designated the principal military adviser to the president, the secretary of defense, and the National Security Council.
2. The secretary of defense and the president would continue to seek the corporate advice of the Joint Chiefs of Staff on subjects they deem appropriate.

3. Each service chief would have the right to submit his individual views and recommendations directly to the secretary of defense, and to the president as appropriate, on any joint issue on which that chief had particularly strong feelings.
4. A deputy chairman of the four-star rank should be authorized to assist in carrying out the chairman's responsibilities.
5. The Joint Staff should be made responsible directly to the chairman rather than to the Joint Chiefs of Staff as a body.

In addition, he has advocated incentives for officers to seek Joint Staff duty and educational reforms designed to help officers transcend service cultures.[15]

What would be different were these proposals adopted? General Jones believes that we would at least attain what President Eisenhower sought in his reorganization of 1958. To use Eisenhower's words of twenty-six years ago:

Strategic planning will be unified. . . . The Joint Chiefs of Staff will be provided professional military assistance required for efficient strategic planning and operational control. The control and supervision of the Secretary of Defense over military research and development will be strengthened . . . the new weapons and other defense undertakings are so costly as to heavily burden our entire economy. We must achieve the utmost military efficiency in order to generate maximum power from the resources we have available.[16]

General Jones looked for improved efficiency in the Department of Defense by

1. furnishing the secretary the responsible, crisp, timely, responsive military advice he seldom now receives
2. putting military strategy ahead of doctrine, and doctrine ahead of weapons systems, instead of the inverse, as is now the practice
3. giving the CINCs of the combat commands the effective voice in Defense decisions they now lack
4. preserving service views within the JCS, but balancing these with joint perspectives
5. assuring more time for each chief, freed from nitty-gritty joint affairs, to shepherd manning, training, provisioning, and weapon systems development within his own service

But perhaps the best explanation of what such proposals would accomplish was written seventy-five years ago in President Roosevelt's report to the Senate:

The requirement of war is the true standard of efficiency in an administrative military system. . . . Success in war and victory in battle can be assured only by that constant preparedness and that superior fighting efficiency which logically result from placing the control and responsibility in time of peace upon the same individuals and the same agencies that must control in time of war. There would be no shock or change of method in expanding from a state of peace to a state of war. This is not militarism; it is a simple business based upon the fact that success in war is the only return the people and the nation can get from the investment of many [billions] in the building and maintenance of a great [defense establishment].[17]

NOTES

1. Gen. Edward C. Meyer, "The JCS—How Much Reform is Needed?" *Armed Forces Journal 119* (April 1982): 82–90.

2. 60th Cong., 2d Sess., S. Docs. 740, 743.

3. *Congressional Record,* 60th Cong., 2d Sess., 43, pt. 4:3109 (S. Doc. 740).

4. *Letters and Papers of Alfred Thayer Mahan,* ed. Robert Seager II and Doris D. Maguire (Annapolis, Md.: Naval Institute Press, 1975), 3:275–77.

5. Title 10, U.S. Code §141(C) (1980): "The Joint Chiefs of Staff shall . . . (5) formulate policies for the joint training of the armed services; (6) formulate policies for coordinating the military education of members of the armed services."

6. Senate Committee on Military Affairs, *Hearings on S. 84 and S. 1482: Department of the Armed Forces; Department of Military Security,* 79th Cong., 1st Sess., 411–39.

7. *Congressional Record,* 85th Cong., 2d Sess., 104, pt. 5:6260 (H. Doc. 366).

8. House Committee on Armed Services, Investigations Subcommittee, *Hearings on Reorganization Proposals for the Joint Chiefs of Staff (H.R. 6828, Joint Chiefs of Staff Reorganization Act of 1982),* 97th Cong., 2d Sess., 636.

9. Ibid., p. 907.

10. Ibid., p. 750.

11. Title 10, U.S. Code § 143 (1980).

12. *Congressional Record,* 85th Cong., 2d Sess., 104, pt. 5:6259, 6261.

13. House Committee on Armed Services, Investigations Subcommittee, *Hearings on Reorganization Proposals for the Joint Chiefs of Staff,* p. 888.

14. Ibid., p. 750.

15. See chap. 16, "What's Wrong with the Defense Establishment?"

16. *Congressional Record,* 85th Cong., 2d Sess., 104, pt. 5:6259.

17. *Congressional Record,* 60th Cong., 2d Sess., 43, pt. 4:3109.

18

JCS REFORM: A COMMENTARY

Philip A. Odeen

Odeen sees the momentum for JCS reorganization growing, but success is far from certain. Because the political costs are high, reform proposals are most likely to be accepted at the start of an administration or when an unforeseen event provides strong impetus for change. He is concerned that reform alternatives don't go far enough to remedy the problems of the present system which he outlines. Odeen introduces the idea of a general staff, a much more radical reorganization than those discussed by others, but cautions that it carries an even greater political price tag.

The lack of action on JCS reform may be surprising, given the broad agreement that improvements are badly needed. Indeed, there are few issues where the consensus has been broader. In addition to the preceding chapters by Jones and Gorman, journalists have written favorably about the need for change, former DOD officials strongly back a strengthened JCS, and a string of active duty and retired senior military officers have either proposed specific reforms or supported the ideas of their colleagues.

Despite the lack of reform action, it is important that serious consideration is given to all reform ideas and proposals. Only in this way can reform be implemented when the appropriate political climate evolves. In this spirit, two questions are examined in this chapter. Do the reorganization proposals of General Jones and others go far enough to correct the agreed-upon deficiencies in the current organization? Given the high political costs and difficulty in adopting any proposal, have all alternatives been examined sufficiently so that when the climate is conducive for change the debate is mature enough to produce effective reorganization?

This chapter will develop these questions by examining the prospects for reorganization, the linkage between JCS reorganization and military reform, and the various considerations that need to be taken into account when proposing JCS reform.

THE MILITARY ADVICE VACUUM

Speaking of this problem as a vacuum may seem to be a misnomer. A vacuum denotes a void, and there is no void as far as advice from the military is concerned. There is a plethora of advice; unfortunately, most of it is of little value because of its vagueness, lowest-common-denominator nature, or lack of focus. What we face is a void of trenchant, decision-relevant, and timely advice in areas where senior defense officials need high-quality support that can best be given by professional military men.

Not surprisingly, this vacuum has sometimes been filled, at least in part, by advice from civilians. The McNamara defense management revolution in the 1960s was in no small part the result of shoddy cross-service coordination, poor or nonexistent analytic support for military department budgets, programs, and weapons choices, and the failure of the services and JCS to do long-range planning. These shortcomings gave the RANDs and CNAs their clout and helped spawn a host of "Beltway Bandits." All of these phenomena might well have occurred even with an effective central military staff. But the size and scope of these civilian organizations providing military analysis and advice would clearly have been reduced.

There are four primary areas where the current system for providing professional military input is clearly lacking.

1. *Developing solid and meaningful defense policies and strategies as a basis for the program and budget process.* A coherent, balanced defense effort must be based on sound strategic thinking and clear strategic priorities. Today's JCS structure is unable to provide this. The complex bureaucratic process makes it virtually impossible to develop crisp, concise policy papers. The committee structure, with each service essentially having a veto, makes it very difficult to set priorities or challenge service policy thrusts. As a result, the policies and strategies that emerge are generally compromised and of little help in making program and budget choices. The Joint Strategic Objectives Plan (JSOP) was almost legendary in its lack of reality or value, and its replacement (since 1978), the Joint Strategic Planning Document (JSPD), is not much better. But repeated efforts to provide more meaningful strategic input over the past fifteen years have foundered on the structural flaws of the JCS system. It is institutionally incapable of providing relevant and cogent advice.

2. *Providing advice to the secretary of defense on force structure and weapons requirements.* A huge gap exists between our strategy and policy (in part because they are so poorly formulated) and requirements for forces (wings, divisions, and ships) and specific weapons systems. Sound requirements analysis is a difficult and subjective task, but it must be done if our forces are to be capable of meeting our security needs. An important aspect of the needed military advice is cross-service needs, for example, airlift for army forces or air defense artillery for air force bases. Innovative thinking about ways one service can assist another in meeting its requirements is also essential. For example, it is possible to employ air force aircraft against Soviet naval forces.

3. *Helping senior defense officials make resource allocation decisions.* The most far-ranging decisions made by the secretary of defense revolve around the Five Year Defense Plan (FYDP) and the annual defense budget. Once the dollars are allocated, our strategic options are significantly constrained and our capabilities largely determined. Today this is done without meaningful cross-cutting military advice to help him make decisions on priorities. The secretary primarily receives single service views which, although of value, are biased and narrowly focused. The Joint Chiefs, as a body, are incapable of giving effective advice on the allocation of resources among the services. The Joint Staff simply lacks the analytical capabilities for program review. Melvin R. Laird, secretary of defense during the Nixon administration, made a valiant effort to bring the Joint Chiefs into the budget process and failed, despite the sympathy of most military leaders. Because there are inevitably winners and losers when such questions are addressed, the committee structure of the Joint Chiefs simply bogs down. Also, the laws greatly limit the ability of the chairman to voice his views independently.

4. *Planning for contingencies and conflicts.* The current planning effort often focuses on the wrong country, using the wrong scenario and the wrong forces. JCS reform is not a necessary precondition to fixing this problem. What is needed is greater priority and some limited, but high-level, interaction with senior officials (from the State Department and the National Security Council as well as the Office of the Secretary of Defense) to ensure that the political and diplomatic considerations are sound. But until we have a stronger military staff structure, such essential planning is unlikely to receive the priority it deserves.

Civilian officials in the United States have a far greater involvement in all four of the above areas than do their counterparts in other nations (for example, the United Kingdom, France, or Germany). Attributing this to the American fetish for civilian control is erroneous. Rather, it is a direct consequence of the failure of our system to provide sound, relevant advice by senior military officers. Like nature, defense management abhors a vacuum. When military advice is not provided, civilian advice fills the gap.

PROSPECTS FOR JCS REFORM

Prospects for early action on any of the JCS reform proposals are not bright. The navy's strong opposition, buttressed by supporters in Congress, is one factor. Another factor is the apparent lack of urgency for reform. Most of the problems cited are ones of omission, not commission, opportunities lost rather than specific failures. One cannot point to any specific disaster as having been caused by the current structure. Concerns about poor planning and budgetary advice, or potential problems of command during a crisis, have not been sufficient to galvanize either the executive or the legislative branch into action. Postwar administrations must shoulder at least some of the blame for the lack of action: they failed to seize the opportunity and push for meaningful improvements in the JCS structure.

While opportunities may have been lost, the issue will not go away. The breadth of support and the concern on the part of so many defense experts will keep the question alive; reform is almost certain to come. A major review of the defense management structure or a second push by another chairman or secretary of defense may be the catalyst. Another possibility is a military disaster or major planning failure, which, based on history, is more likely to be the triggering event.

JCS REFORM AND MILITARY REFORM

The connection between a stronger military staff system and military reform is perhaps tenuous. Most military reform issues are by nature the responsibility of the services, since they design and buy weapons and develop tactical concepts. Thus, it is unlikely that a more powerful chairman or even a general staff would play a major part in tackling the kind of issues discussed in this book.

Yet, there is a tie, a not insubstantial one. An effective military staff is likely to be the focal point of debate of major issues facing the secretary of defense and his key subordinates. The secretary will turn to and rely on his military advisers if he receives timely and relevant help. The availability of such military advice may encourage senior civilians to take on issues such as military reform. Without experienced military support these issues are likely to be ignored or left to the whims of service politics.

Although painful to address, the issues raised by the military reformers are crucial to the long-term effectiveness of our military forces and the ability to defend our national interest. As France discovered in 1940, a government must ensure that its military establishment addresses fundamental issues of strategy and that its weapons are suitable to fight the next, not the last, war. The lack of effective military advice seriously reduces the chance our civilian leadership will face up to such questions.

An effective military staff would also play a much broader role within the national security process. In the same way the staff would be helpful to the secretary of defense on issues like military reform, it would play a major role in the interagency process. An effective, responsive military staff organization would quickly find itself in the middle of questions handled by the National Security Council.

Issues addressed within the NSC system frequently have major military aspects. The dearth of useful military advice is a significant problem for the NSC staff in managing the process. Today's cumbersome JCS system is not able to participate in a way that adds much value to the analysis supporting presidential decisions. As a result, the Office of the Secretary of Defense is forced to provide much of the military input, even in areas that clearly should be the province of the professional military.

CONSIDERATIONS AFFECTING REFORM

To highlight some of the considerations affecting JCS reform, it may be useful to compare and contrast the Jones proposal with yet another proposal for reform; that is, the call for an American general staff. There are many who argue that the solutions proposed by both Jones and Meyer are not radical enough to redress the shortcomings of the current system. Instead, they advocate a general staff headed by a single senior officer, in the chain of command between the unified/specified commands and the secretary of defense, with direct responsibility for policy planning and operational matters. Both the Jones and general staff proposals would make the Joint Staff responsible directly to the chairman rather than to the Joint Chiefs of Staff as a body. Under the current system and in the Jones reorganization proposal, a tour of duty on the Joint Staff is limited to a maximum of three years. In contrast, the general staff proposal establishes a career staff. All personnel actions affecting these permanent staff officers, including evaluations and promotions, would be the sole responsibility of the general staff.

There are many who advocate this position in order to sever parochial service control over Joint Staff members. Yet, before determining the practicality of such a radical departure from our traditional military organizational pattern, at least three issues should be addressed.

First, what can be learned from the experience of other nations? Historians may have dissected the German general staff in great detail, but the lessons are not well understood in defense circles, let alone in Congress. As many have pointed out, the Germans did not have a true joint military staff during the Hitler period. Instead, Germany had an Army general staff, with the navy and air force operating largely independently. German experience in earlier periods may be more instructive, but the types of joint combat operations we plan for today were rare prior to World War II. The recent Falklands crisis may be a better source of guidance in that the British strengthened the position of the chief of the Defense Staff shortly before the crisis erupted. Some real world experience would be a valuable addition to the debate over how best to reorganize the JCS. This type of research would seem to be an area of particular interest for the War Colleges and other military institutions.

Second, we need to analyze how much more effective a full general staff system would be than the more limited JCS proposals made by Generals Jones and Meyer. Opponents of reorganization are quick to point out that any move to strengthen the role of the chairman, especially the establishment of a general staff, would decrease civilian control of the military. The uniquely American fear of the appearance of a "man on a horseback" makes it difficult to enact any change that appears to decrease civilian control over the military policy-making process. A chairman that speaks for the service chiefs, limiting the CINC's access to the secretary of defense, and a professional general staff are changes that would appear to limit that control. Civilian control resembles Justice Stewart's view of obscenity—you can't define it, but you know what it is when you see it. It is debatable whether any of these changes would actually decrease civilian control; in fact, many argue just the reverse. Nonetheless, many perceive that such measures would move the military away from that timeless principle.

The political cost of pushing through a radical change would be high. Before that cost is incurred, we must be sure it is warranted. Each of the shortcomings identified by the critics should be analyzed to identify the added value a general staff would provide. It may well be that a strengthened chairman of the JCS could overcome a major portion of the problems that have been cited while avoiding the high political cost of a general staff system.

Third, the practicalities of any JCS proposal must be thoroughly vetted. Senior military officers are only some of the players in the complicated national security process. Changes in the role of the military must harmonize with the other key participants and must be supported by an effective staff organization. To test any new concept, a well-thought-through proposal is needed, one that lays out the specifics. What responsibilities would the new organization have? How would it relate to the services and OSD? How large should it be? How would the individual members of the staff be selected, trained, and promoted? Would the chairman be chosen only after coming up through the ranks of the general staff? What about seemingly qualified and experienced senior officers from the individual services? Should permanent staff members be periodically sent back to their parent service so they do not become out of touch with problems in the field? Such questions are crucial to determining how practical any reorganization proposal would be, given the peculiarities of the American system.

Reform of the JCS is essential if we are to have a responsive and well-planned military establishment. Few people question the need for reform, but many doubt the need to proceed as far as a general staff. Much more analysis will be needed to determine the efficacy of the various proposals. We should build the intellectual capital we will need to make sound choices for JCS reform in order to be ready when the next opportunity for change presents itself.

President Eisenhower once drew a distinction between problems that were important and those that were critical, stating that "critical issues are seldom important and important issues are seldom critical." Critical issues are the type that demand attention because of tight (although arbitrary) deadlines or political/bureaucratic pressures for a decision; yet all too often these seemingly pressing problems matter little in the grand scheme of things.

Important issues often lack the same urgency. While most people might admit the need to address such questions, there is seldom a pressing requirement to focus on them now—they can wait until later. Reform of the JCS is just such an issue. In the long term it could make a substantial difference to the United States—indeed, our survival could well depend on the adequacy of our military advice and leadership.

VII

THE OUTLOOK FOR DEFENSE REFORM

The military reform movement has been detailed, at least in many of its most important aspects, in the preceding parts of this book. Issues have been identified and contending arguments have been posed.

It is useful, however, to step back from this level of discussion to compare and critique the arguments, to comment on important issues not raised, to attempt to respond to Professor Huntington's charge that the reform movement is intrinsically unable to transcend its current disjointedness and achieve conceptual coherence, and, finally, to assess the short and long run impact of military reform. These are the tasks of the chapters in this final part.

McKitrick and Chiarelli address the first three of these tasks in their appraisal chapter. More than simply recounting the principal issues and corresponding arguments, they raise fundamental questions and provide, where possible, a set of evaluative criteria for reference in assessing the rigor and validity of reform contentions. Equally important, these criteria are valuable for use by defense officials as they consider difficult policy choices including, but not limited to, reform proposals.

After discussing the strengths and weaknesses of the reform movement, Lind examines probable future directions of reformism. Impressed with the continuing existence and influence of the Congressional Reform Caucus, Lind argues that the caucus's political clout will serve to generate circumstances in which military reform will sustain itself, with or without assistance from extramilitary community actors.

Both Fallows and Clark examine the role of the public reform debate. Both agree that public debate can enlighten Americans' understanding of the unique characteristics of military operations and resource requirements. As a result, both argue, public political pressures can hold military policy makers accountable for provision of the most effective (qualitative) and most efficient (quantitative) military. Under these circumstances, far different from traditional public concern for "too little, or too much" defense, self-sustaining military reform is possible.

Clark, however, disagrees sharply with Fallows over culpability for defense deficiencies and responsibility for reform. After indicting the military as responsible for many of the deficiencies targeted by reformers, Fallows paradoxically calls on the military to lead the public debate for reform. Clark, in contrast, distributes both responsibilities much more broadly across the entire range of military policy actors.

The military reform movement is far-ranging, if somewhat disjointed. Consequently, the reform debate is unevenly developed across issue areas ranging, for example, from sophisticated doctrinal arguments to data-intensive accusations on procurement issues. One purpose of this book is to develop the reform impulse at a higher, more comprehensive, and more even level of quality.

While the editors agree that the reform debate can play a major role in catalyzing self-sustaining reform, it is also clear that debate tends to dichotomize issues and polarize arguments. Such simplifications retard reform and devolve into criticism. This final section attempts to bring balance and analytical objectivity to bear in hopes of promoting public curiosity, open-mindedness, skepticism, impartial interest, and tolerance in continuing debates over defense reform.

19

DEFENSE REFORM: AN APPRAISAL

Jeffrey S. McKitrick and Peter W. Chiarelli

McKitrick and Chiarelli comment on issues as organized in the major sections of this book. Their appraisal recaps key reform points, suggests criteria by which the debate can be evaluated, critiques the major arguments in the debate, introduces points not treated previously by the authors, and integrates the issues into a coherent commentary on conventional U.S. military affairs.

The purposes of this volume are threefold: (1) to present the central elements of the defense reform debate through the arguments presented by its protagonists; (2) to analyze the quality, rigor, and focus of the debate; and (3) to assess the reform debate's significance for the U.S. defense posture. In order to achieve the third purpose, we have introduced extra agenda considerations that aid in judging the implications of these issues for the long run.

The preceding chapters and editorial commentary have fulfilled, we hope, the first purpose. In addition, we have attempted to develop the larger contexts of defense policy and policy processes in which these issues, debates, and politics will continue to play.

In this chapter we identify questions that should be asked when evaluating the competing arguments. The intellectual exercise of formulating tentative answers may serve either to confirm existing policies or to suggest more appropriate alternative approaches. Answers may suggest specific criteria that are more useful for evaluating proposed or existing policies.

Throughout our appraisal we make explicit some of the not-so-apparent implications of current policy and various reform proposals. Many established policies and purported solutions look good on paper or when isolated and evaluated independent of real world considerations.

We have not attempted to identify or provide answers to all these difficult questions. Instead, this appraisal is designed to sharpen the debate by evaluating competing arguments.

Admittedly, this is a critical appraisal. We hope that readers will not interpret our treatment as unduly harsh but, rather, as an honest attempt to improve the quality of the debate. This appraisal, like the preceding chapters, attempts to interrelate and integrate the various reform issues so that they can be understood, analyzed, and evaluated within the context of the established defense policy-making process. The organization of this appraisal differs from the book in that we have elected to comment on only four of the five parts in the following order: The Organization of Defense Policy Making, Force Structure Issues, Modernization and Weapons Acquisition Issues, and Doctrinal Issues.

THE ORGANIZATION
OF DEFENSE POLICY MAKING

The National Security Act of 1947 was one of the most far-reaching attempts in recent history to improve the quality of defense policy by reforming the defense organization. The act, and its various amendments, established the air force as a separate service, combined the military departments into a single Department of Defense, and created the organization of the Joint Chiefs of Staff. These changes, and others, clarified the roles of the military services, improved planning through integration, allocated resources more efficiently, and enhanced the capability to conduct large-scale joint operations.

These same goals provide the impetus for current calls to reform the defense establishment. Yet, while the goals may be the same as in 1947, the reasons for the reform initiatives are different. The National Security Act was aimed at capitalizing on and institutionalizing the planning and operational procedures that had led to victory in World War II. Today's initiatives are spurred, however, not by success, but by perceived failure. The ten-year conflict in Vietnam—at a cost of over fifty thousand American lives and one hundred fifty billion dollars—was certainly seen by some as a failure of the U.S. defense establishment. Iran's seizure of the American embassy and the holding hostage of fifty-two American citizens for 444 days seemed proof of U.S. impotence. And the botched Iranian rescue attempt offered further proof that the American military establishment was incapable of coping with even small tasks (especially when compared with the successful Israeli raid on Entebbe). If the defense establishment could not handle "half wars" and raids, how could it hope to win "the big one"? It is not only past failure that has sparked reform initiatives in this area, but also the specter of future failure.

Further, the economic conditions of 1947 differed greatly from those of today. World War II transformed a depressed, stagnant American economy into a large, vibrant, growing one—an economy relatively untouched by the adverse aspects of war. In an expanding economy such as the United States enjoyed in the 1940s, choices between guns and butter were easier. By the 1970s, however, the picture had changed. The collapse of the Western international monetary system was compounded by the actions of the OPEC cartel in 1973. By the late 1970s, the United States was experiencing double-digit inflation; and by the early 1980s, double-digit unemployment. In this type of economic environment, resource allocation choices are more significant and more highly politicized.

The roles of the military services have also changed since 1947. Prior to 1947, the Department of War and Department of the Navy were cabinet-level organizations with a high degree of autonomy in their planning, programming, and operations. The National Security Act sought to change this situation by simultaneously diversifying (by adding the air force as a new service) and integrating (by forming DOD and OJCS) the defense establishment. Subsequent amendments to the act have served to reduce further the individual autonomy of the services by subordinating them even more to the Office of the Secretary of Defense. While in theory the Joint Chiefs of Staff provide the strategic guidance and service integration for defense policy, in reality, as an institution, the JCS plays a very limited role in these areas.

Those advocating reform in the organization of defense policy making must, therefore, take note of two considerations. First, the National Security Act resulted in a major reorganization of the defense community. Any proposals for further modifications will have to deal with the implications of the proposal for changes in the act, the bureaucratic and legal obstacles to change, and the political feasibility of enacting such changes. Second, reform advocates must be aware of different incentives for change in 1947 and today. Change that builds on success can be quite different from change that attempts to forestall failure.

Reform proposals dealing with defense organization generally rest on two assumptions. First, it is assumed the policy deficiencies are in some way a result of organizational deficiencies. Thus, if organizational deficiencies can be identified and eliminated, policy deficiencies will be remedied. This may or may not be the case. Policy deficiencies may be a result of other factors such as resource constraints, and hence, may only be partially correctable by making organizational changes. Even if policy deficiencies are related to organizational deficiencies, organizational solutions may only result in creating new policy deficiencies.

The second assumption is that there is some unique, inherent value in military advice and that efforts must be made to inject that advice more fully into the policy-making process. This also may or may not be true. It is possible that advice from military leaders may be valuable because of the individual rendering the advice rather than the fact that he or she is in the military.

In their chapter on defense budgeting, Clark and Fagan argue that even though the defense budget has not changed much in constant terms, changes of emphasis within the defense budget have occurred. Current trends toward greater emphasis on investment spending, they argue, are perverse for at least two reasons. First, such an emphasis constrains future defense choices, and second, it undermines operational readiness. However, it is worth noting that investment spending is a long process encompassing the research, development, production, procurement, and deployment stages. Surely, in case of future conflict, it would be better to have such a lengthy process behind you as a base from which to expand. Repair parts, fuel, and ammunition can be manufactured and delivered to a new battlefield faster than planes, tanks, and ships. Thus, an emphasis on investment spending at the expense of war stocks is not necessarily the strategic mismatch it appears to be at first glance. It may be better to have a more modern, less ready force than a less modern, more ready force if faced with the prospects of a world war.

If, however, increased investment spending comes at the expense of funds for fuel, parts, and ammunition to be used in training, the resulting readiness shortfall may be more serious. Training deficiencies cannot be overcome as quickly as inadequacies in war stocks, and the greater time involved results in a longer period of vulnerability for forces engaged in the initial battles of a future conflict.

If increased investment spending comes at the expense of manpower dollars, there are other adverse results. The United States could arguably have as good a standing force as it currently has at a lower cost by eliminating its "up or out" personnel policies and emulating the British system, which allows a soldier to make a career of the service without the necessity of being promoted. But in case of war, and a sixfold expansion of our armed forces, what would happen to all of our soldiers? If they were smart soldiers, they could be promoted to NCOs and could provide the cadre necessary for an effective, expanded force. If they were not smart soldiers, we would have to train NCOs for the large force. Given the resources necessary to develop NCOs versus training soldiers, the authors provide for an effective, mobilized force in a shorter period of time.

With respect to Reed's chapter on Congress, two points need to be made. First, however one interprets Congress's greater assertiveness in the foreign policy area, there is little evidence that Congress desires to replace the executive branch as the formulator of defense policy. Therefore, imputations that the Military Reform Caucus (or any other group) might enable Congress to do this seem to overstate the case. Second, Reed seems to ascribe too much rationality to the entire Department of Defense budgeting process. While

PPBS was designed to provide a rational framework for defense decision making, in actuality it has become a highly bureaucratized and politicized process. Thus, the creation of a similar capability on the part of Congress may simply be a case of creating a similarly undisciplined process. As Reed notes, there is little likelihood that Congress will ever take such a step. While Reed's use of dichotomies such as strategy-structure and equilibrium-disequilibrium may be heuristically useful, in reality there are no such clear distinctions, and attempts to explain events in such terms may obfuscate more than they clarify.

More importantly, Reed's thesis founders on the key questions of who and what the congressional reform movement is. He is often unclear as to whether particular comments refer to the congressional Military Reform Caucus or to Congress as a whole. There is significant difference in the amount of influence each wields. Nor does Reed explain the absence from the Military Reform Caucus of individuals such as Senators Nunn, Tower, and (the recently deceased) Jackson who have figured prominently in congressional action on defense issues.

As to what the reform movement in Congress is, Reed variously describes it as an attempt to assert influence over, innovate, shape, formulate, or build a consensus on defense issues. While at various times the congressional movement may adopt one or more of these varied objectives, such a diverse and chameleon-like approach causes one to wonder what its real purpose is.

Further, there appear to be other explanations, as good if not better than the one put forward by Reed, as to why the Congressional Military Reform Caucus has sprung up. Quite simply, it is good politics to be associated with a group that presumes to offer better defense at a lower price. No politician will ever get in trouble with his constituents for espousing such clearly desirable aims. And Reed pays little attention to another explanation, which is that some congressmen may have joined the group either as a way to promote their personal goals or as a way to protect the particular interests of their constituency. Congress is, after all, the national representation of regional and local interests.

Jones, in his critique of the defense establishment, claims that the current organization is inefficient and ineffective. These deficiencies derive, in his view, from overwhelming service influence in the process and an inability of the Office of the Secretary of Defense and the Joint Chiefs of Staff to control the parochial nature of service interests. While his criticism of the JCS is well founded, it is difficult to believe that OSD with its large and experienced staff and final authority over the defense budget is unable to exert influence over the programming and budgeting process. Additionally, Jones's proposal rests on the assumption noted earlier that military advice is inherently unique and valuable. If, however, military advice is valuable, but not unique, the same type of advice can be gained from sources other than the Joint Chiefs of Staff. If military advice is unique, but not valuable, then no amount of reorganization will make it more useful.

Gorman correctly points out that reform efforts have historically identified the lack of high-quality military advice as an area of concern and have focused on reorganization as the solution to this problem. Like Jones, he assumes that military advice is inherently unique and valuable. Yet Gorman also correctly points out that past efforts to rectify deficiencies in this area have failed. He argues that these failures were caused by cultural differences among the services and civilian reluctance to concentrate enough power in a single military body to overcome these differences. But perhaps the record of failure in this area is evidence that despite its inefficiencies, the system is adequate to meet the political and military needs of the nation. Perhaps all that needs to be done is to make those marginal adjustments necessary in any large organization to keep it up to date.

Odeen asserts that there are at least four areas of military policy where existing deficiencies exist of such magnitude as to dictate change. Yet it is not clear that reorganization is the only, nor even the most desirable, way to correct those deficiencies. Odeen allows that historical, political, and practical considerations must be factored in to any analysis in order to determine what, if any, reorganization needs be done.

Clark, in his chapter on interservice rivalry, points out that service rivalry can lead to innovation. But is innovation necessarily good? Surely at times consistency and continuity of effort are at least as good, if not better. Additionally, according to Clark's model, not all services will be innovating simultaneously. Therefore, at least some will be resisting reform. Besides acting as an obstacle to reform, might not such resistance be dysfunctional in terms of developing an integrated, joint military policy? Finally, one can conclude from Clark's chapter that innovativeness should be stimulated by the civilian leadership's manipulating the defense budget. But in a system where the many strains and stresses on the budget already result in a feast or famine approach to defense, such a conclusion is likely to be infeasible, incalculable, or counterproductive. A more useful approach would focus on redefining the services' roles and missions in an effort to obtain greater integration and cohesiveness of effort.

FORCE STRUCTURE ISSUES

The structure of our armed forces is one of the more visible aspects of the ongoing debate over defense policy. At the same time, other issues—weapons acquisition and doctrine, for example—intersect the issue of force structure. And how our forces are configured determines to a great extent what capabilities the U.S. has to meet existing threats to our national security interests. Force structures display an aspect of permanence not necessarily evident, at least to the same degree, in other defense policy choices. Due to the long lead times required to field new equipment, such capabilities can seldom be changed rapidly enough to meet changes in threats or interests.

The possibility of changing threats or interests then places a premium on designing flexibility into our forces so they may be more quickly reconfigured to meet those changes. Even existing threats may be so diverse that they necessitate a force structure with sufficient flexibility to respond to a wide range of scenarios. There is a danger, however, in allowing flexibility to become the sole criterion in force planning at the expense of adequate battlefield capability in any particular region.

There is an additional problem in designing forces to meet current or anticipated threats. Those threats may vary in degrees of likelihood and severity of consequence, and structuring forces to meet the most likely threats may leave the U.S. ill-equipped to meet the most severe. Forces designed to meet the most likely and the most severe threats equally may result in the U.S. being ill-prepared to adequately meet either threat.

Unfortunately, force structure issues are often inadequately addressed for at least two reasons. First, such issues are frequently framed in overly simple ways that fail to account for the numerous and complex missions and required capabilities of U.S. forces, which require different weapons systems and force structures. Second, force structure proposals often focus on a single service or component of a service and thus fail to assess the trade-offs in other services required to adopt that particular proposal. This single-service focus also fails to recognize that the services do not fight as services, but rather operate jointly in commands designed to fight an integrated battle in a particular theater.

Many of the current participants in the defense reform debate fall into these two traps as well as an additional one. Changes in areas other than force structures are often advocated without recognizing that such proposals have force structure implications; current force structures, therefore, can act as a constraint on the feasibility of such proposals.

How should one evaluate force structure proposals? The following criteria, at a minimum, should be used:

1. The threat to U.S. national interests, both current and anticipated. The threat should be analyzed for likelihood of occurrence and severity of consequence.
2. The U.S. strategy for meeting current and anticipated threats.
3. The flexibility dilemma. When does specialization of forces lead to a decreased ability to meet a variety of threats, and when does increased flexibility lead to a decreased ability to meet a particular threat?
4. Structural focus. Proposals should focus on the multiservice operational (unified) commands rather than on the individual services.
5. Total force package comparisons. The costs and benefits of total force packages (multiservice) should be used to evaluate force structure proposals.
6. Political implications. The political ramifications, both domestic and international, should be considered in force structure proposals.
7. Resource constraints. The fiscal, manpower, and economic constraints operative in defense planning and programming should be evaluated.

How well did the authors in this section address these criteria? Canby poses the problem as if it were simply a case of the United States and its allies being outnumbered in total divisions by the Warsaw Pact (in Europe) and North Korea (in northeast Asia). In doing so he focuses only on the current, most severe threat. His solution is to devote more resources to the army and to emphasize light (cheaper) divisions in order to equalize the number of divisions on both sides.

However, Canby's characterization of the problem may be incorrect. A simple comparison of numbers of divisions is a flawed approach, since Warsaw Pact divisions are only two-thirds the size of U.S. divisions. Even if the size differential were somehow included in the calculations, one would still end up with a rather inexact comparison. It is, after all, not numbers in a particular theater that matter as much as battlefield capabilities, something extremely difficult to assess outside of combat. Further, Canby does not address the political and military strategy this restructured force is to follow to meet the threat he has identified.

Canby's prescriptions do not allow sufficient flexibility to meet other, more diverse threats to national interest. Even if one concedes that his Jaeger infantry could be nearly as effective as armor forces in the urban sprawl of Europe or the mountains of Korea (a point that has yet to be definitely shown), of what utility are Jaeger infantry under other conditions? Would they prove to be as useful in the desert or open terrain? It seems hardly likely. And if not, what has his proposal cost in terms of time necessary to deploy new armor forces should those requirements exist?

By focusing on the services rather than the operational commands, Canby overlooks the vital roles performed by the other services (for example, tactical support by the air force) in achieving military success in a particular theater.

He also fails to compare the force packages required. Canby's proposal may result in less resources for the navy and the air force, which could have just as detrimental an effect on military operations as could inadequate ground forces.

In his proposal, Canby fails to recognize adequately that nations maintain various types of forces for a number of political reasons. International prestige and influence, along with national freedom of action (by avoiding over-reliance on allies), are some very good reasons why a country would want to maintain a variety of independent forces. Such reasoning was apparently a part of the British and French decisions to develop and maintain nuclear forces independently of the United States. Therefore, Canby's solution may not be politically feasible.

Ground forces are more manpower-intensive than naval and air forces. Yet, Canby does not adequately address how the additional ground combat units would be manned. Nor does he factor in the additional support and maintenance units, in terms of manpower and equipment, which would be required to support the additional divisions. When those costs are considered, his proposal may not be fiscally feasible.

By focusing on Soviet armor forces Mayer falls prey to the likelihood fallacy. While a Soviet invasion of Europe may be the most serious of possible contingencies, it is also the least likely for a number of reasons, not the least of which is the possession of nuclear weapons by the superpowers. A more likely threat may be a local conflict or insurgency. Mayer asserts that three light divisions is a number adequate to the task but fails to tell why he thinks so. He does not address what strategy his light or heavy forces would follow.

His recommendation for a mix of light and heavy forces implies awareness of the flexibility dilemma, yet Mayer does not provide us any insights into his thinking in this area and why it led to the specific proposal he makes.

Mayer's case for more armored divisions to counter Soviet armored divisions presumes that the best weapon against a tank is another tank. This is not necessarily the case. Precision-guided munitions delivered from tactical aircraft or artillery and antitank guided missiles offer alternatives to meeting a threat from armor. Interdiction against Soviet logistic areas may, by cutting off their fuel supply, reduce the number of Soviet armor forces available at the front. Had Mayer looked at multiservice operational commands rather than focusing on the services, he might have avoided this problem.

Mayer's recommendation for additional heavy forces to counter the Soviet heavy threat contains rather precise cost data showing that light forces are not much cheaper than heavy forces. But what is the total force package cost comparison? His proposal would call for more strategic sealift to deploy his heavy forces, but he has not calculated what that sealift would cost. And if the costs are such that the United States has fewer, albeit more capable, units, might not that reduce the areas where the United States could use military force to meet its interests? A military unit can only be one place at one time. If it is committed to the jungles of Vietnam (or El Salvador), how much degradation is caused in United States capabilities in Europe?

Finally, Mayer does not look in detail at the political and resource constraints that might affect his proposal. For example, a reduction in the number of light divisions in the U.S. force structure might be seen as a decline in the newly expressed U.S. commitment to deter aggression outside of Europe, with a consequent reduction in U.S. influence in those regions.

Record dismisses the Soviet threat as a primary determinant of U.S. force structure and advocates concentrating on Third World threats. He thus advocates increased emphasis on naval forces. Yet in his justification for additional carrier battle groups he claims that fifteen is not adequate and that several more are needed. Specifically, he asserts that at least six carrier battle groups are needed to prevail in the Indian Ocean and the Norwegian Sea. Besides the fact that Record provides no basis for such an assertion, one has to ask what naval forces these battle groups will be fighting in those areas.

While Record does not say so, it is clear that he is focusing on the Soviets. So while on the one hand he dismisses the Soviet threat to justify a switch to a maritime strategy, on the other hand he assumes a Soviet threat to justify an increase in the number of carrier battle groups.

Record concedes that the U.S. has interests in Europe, but recommends meeting those by withdrawing ground forces because of what he sees to be a lack of effort by our allies. But alliance maintenance has always been a difficult task, and withdrawal of U.S. ground forces may raise serious questions about U.S. commitment to the defense of Europe. If Europe were attacked, Record presumably would advocate going to its assistance, since his proposal leaves U.S. sea and air forces dedicated to its protection. But if that is the case, would it not be better to leave ground forces there to better conduct a successful defense? The task of fighting our way back into Europe would clearly be a more challenging task than defending with forces already in place.

It would appear that Record's proposed force structure would give greater flexibility to the U.S. capability to meet different kinds of threats in different locations. But what does it sacrifice in terms of meeting those threats effectively?

Record's proposed shift to a six hundred to eight hundred-ship navy and increased amphibious forces carries its own critique. He admits that such a force would provide little inland power projection capability, yet dismisses that fact by pointing out that much of the Third World has large coastal areas. Yet the battle, if it occurs, will have to take place at more than just the fringes of Eurasia. Power projection inland may prove critical. Additionally, there are Third World areas where seaborne forces will do no good whatsoever, such as the entire interiors of the African and Asian continents. And there are non-Third World areas where inland power projection is necessary, such as Europe.

Finally, Record does not provide adequate figures to assist in a determination of fiscal feasibility. How many more carrier task forces are required? What will they cost? What costs are required to provide the support infrastructure required by those additional task forces?

Those arguing for or against reform in other areas such as doctrine and weapons systems acquisition often fail to take into account whether their positions are feasible with current force structures. And if not, what force structures are required? Can maneuver warfare be done with today's force? If not, what changes are required? What will it cost in terms of time and money to effect those changes? Might it not be faster, cheaper, and less risky simply to expand the current structure?

What of striving for smaller, cheaper forces in an effort to enhance combat reliability and sustainability? Will that not require more forces to make up for the possible degradation in firepower and battlefield mobility of those forces? And if so, how will those forces be manned under the all-volunteer force? On the other side of the question, might not an over-reliance on high technology mean that fewer systems are bought, resulting in smaller forces and hence fewer places where the United States can simultaneously bring its military power to bear?

These questions and more remain unanswered by those espousing reform on all sides of the force structure issue. Until they are resolved, force structure is likely to be determined weapon-by-weapon and service-by-service. The cost of such an approach is measured by the erosion of purposeful coherence and consistency.

MODERNIZATION AND WEAPONS ACQUISITION ISSUES

Critics and supporters of the weapons procurement system have echoed both Perry and Sprey in discounting as rhetoric the phrase "quantity versus quality" when it is used to describe their differences. Yet that dichotomy seems valid, more times than not, when their actions, proposals, and solutions are examined. Unfortunately, because both sides have framed their arguments to attract the largest portion of the uninformed public, the analytical quality of the debate has suffered. By often couching their arguments in simplistic, questionable, single-factor analysis, both sides have in fact polarized the debate, leading to the conclusion that what is required is an either/or decision specifying quantity or quality. For the debate to advance to a point where more meaningful evaluation of the reformer's proposals and current programs can be accomplished, both sides must expand their analysis to address an entire set of critical issues.

There are a number of comparisons that should be addressed in evaluating procurement decisions. Simply comparing the performance characteristics of individual weapons systems is not sufficient. Rather, those concerned with weapons acquisition policies should apply a consistent set of cost and benefit criteria in evaluating those systems.

When evaluating the benefits that any weapon will bring to a service's inventory, at a minimum, the following should be considered.

Weapons should be evaluated as they will be deployed, and all supporting systems should be included.   Because weapons are sent to fight in platoons, battle groups, or wings, comparisons should be made under battlefield conditions. For example, the M1 (Abrams) tank was designed to fight as part of a combined arms team with supporting systems that enhance its effectiveness. Tests to compare the Abrams and the M60—a tank it will *supplement,* not replace—should be conducted with platoons of tanks, under conditions closely resembling those that would exist during actual combat and that include the participation of critical supporting systems. The high-speed mobility of the M1 can only be appreciated if it is deployed in combined arms operations with an infantry carrier that can keep up with the Abrams moving cross-country. Other examples are the false evaluations of a Nimitz-class aircraft carrier without its aircraft and escort ships, or formations of fighter aircraft without a supporting AWACS (Airborne Warning and Control System).

Different weapons systems, designed for the same mission, cannot be assumed to have equal capabilities. Too often cost comparison estimates assume equal capabilities. If an analyst stresses the lower cost of any weapon when compared to its counterpart, the capabilities of each system should be evaluated. For example, in evaluating antitank weapons, factors such as overall PK (Probability of Kill) rates, PK at different ranges (individual minimum and maximum effective ranges), and PK during periods of limited visibility should be taken into account. The 106-mm recoilless rifle (M40A2) sells for a fraction of the cost of its replacement, the TOW (tube-launched, optically-tracked, wire-guided) missile. Many reformers argue that the older, cheaper, battle-tested 106-mm should never have been replaced by the TOW. To support their claim they cite a similar PK at ranges under 1000 meters. Even if analysts accept this equal capability, and many would not, it is important to know that only the TOW can engage targets from 1000–3750 meters. Furthermore, the TOW alone has a passive sight, which allows it to kill tanks at night and during periods of limited visibility.

Proponents of a particular weapon often promise dramatic savings if the system they support is purchased. Historically, cost estimates have proven unreliable when compared to the actual cost of the fielded weapon. When evaluating cost comparisons the following criteria should be examined.

Cost comparisons are incomplete without factoring in the expense of support systems, maintenance, and spare parts. If support systems are required for a weapon to perform up to maximum capabilities, the cost of the entire package must be considered when evaluating cost-effectiveness. Different systems require differing levels and amounts of maintenance. Additionally, similar weapons may have dissimilar operating costs. An often cited advantage of modern fighter aircraft is that they utilize integrated circuits, making them easily repaired by simply replacing a plug-in module. Yet the cost of the module and the skill level of the technician making the repair on both the plane and the "black box" may have a significant impact on the overall cost of maintaining that weapon in the force.

Cost estimates must take into account the special conditions that operate within the defense marketplace. There is limited competition among defense contractors in the early stages of the weapons procurement process. The critical difference in the defense marketplace is that because the government is contracting for goods for which it is the sole consumer, it must assume the cost of all stages of development. If a program is canceled or scaled down at any point in the development cycle, the military assumes all costs. The consumer looking to buy an electronic calculator can shop around, compare prices, and delay his purchase until any defects are corrected.

Therefore, even though the government is a monopsonistic buyer, the economic forces that have pushed down the price of an electronic calculator are not duplicated in the defense sector. Dr. Perry's assertion that the "selective application of electronics is the key to limiting defense cost" rests on a misleading comparison. He bases that claim on the fact that electronics is the one area of the consumer economy that has shown a substantial price decline in the last twenty years. However, an important reason for these price reductions, not addressed by Perry, is the highly competitive nature of the consumer electronics market. The unique characteristics of the weapons acquisition process and the questionable ability of any bureaucracy to maximize its return on investment render Perry's assertion problematic.

The opportunity does exist for the government to benefit from the diminishing cost and lower prices of consumer products that have military applications. However, because of the dissimilar nature of the defense and civilian markets, cost estimates of military systems utilizing technology pioneered in the civilian sector should not assume equal savings. Further, it should be understood that the military is required to develop and purchase systems and components that have no application and, therefore, no demand in the civilian sector; for example, tanks and nuclear attack submarines. As a consequence, the cost of such weapons will be higher than for equipment, such as aircraft navigational systems, for which there is a demand outside the armed forces.

Procurement decisions must take into account the personnel required to operate different types of weapons systems. Most approaches to weapons design present force planners with difficult personnel problems. Although Sprey dislikes the use of the "quantity or quality" dichotomy, he states that the army could buy three M60s for one M1. To a budget-conscious Congress and public, such claims are extremely persuasive and seem to support the reform contention that the use of proven technology will yield a larger force for the same amount of money. They become less dramatic when the following questions are posed: Where do we get the four armor crewmen and support personnel required for each additional tank added to the inventory? Can the all-volunteer force support such an increase? What is the cost of training, maintaining, and paying these additional soldiers? When the answers to these questions are evaluated, the simple logic of this reform argument becomes less evident. Thus, evaluations of weapons systems must integrate capabilities and cost.

Comparisons must be made at similar stages in each weapon's procurement cycle. One of the primary targets of the reform movement is the army's new main battle tank, the M1. Sprey begins his critique of the M1 by comparing its operational mobility with that of its twenty-year-old predecessor, the M60. Sprey rates the older, battle-tested M60 superior in this category. He bases his evaluation on the higher maintenance rate of the M1, documenting his conclusion with data extracted from the Operational Test II

(OT II) for the Abrams tank. The problem with this type of comparison is that it presupposes that a new system still in operational testing will compare favorably with one that has been fielded for over twenty years. If Sprey had compared these tanks at similar stages in their development (OT II or OT III), he would have discovered that the M1 had a higher operational rate than the M60.

Comparisons should include trainability considerations. Perry is correct in pointing out that advances in microelectronics technology have a "corollary benefit beyond enhanced weapons performance characteristics and reduced production costs: training of weapons operators on simulators." The use of simulators may prove to be a double-edged sword. They are a relatively inexpensive and effective training tool for teaching gunnery skills, but they are just that—simulators. At best they generate test conditions associated with firing a weapons system. There is a danger that if the high cost of electronically guided munitions requires trainers to become overly reliant on the use of simulators as substitutes for live firings, crew proficiency may suffer.

There is no segment of the reform debate where the public posturing of both sides has caused greater polarization. They seem intent on talking past one another, advancing solutions that will only exacerbate other, sometimes more serious, problems. Nonetheless, both the reformers and the defenders of the status quo have identified deficiencies in the weapons acquisition process. Granted, there are a multitude of structural and bureaucratic obstacles to overcome if deficiencies are to be corrected. However, the systematic use of the suggested criteria may assist in correcting these deficiencies and improving the weapons acquisition process.

DOCTRINAL ISSUES

Although the defense reform movement is more accurately characterized as wide-ranging and disjointed, a number of key issues are discernible. One of these revolves around the question of what sort of doctrine is the most appropriate guide to the operational aspects of the armed forces. Reformers and establishmentarians have engaged in fierce doctrinal disputes over issues such as the degree of offensive orientation, the importance of linear formations, centralized command and control versus battlefield initiative, and the roles of political objectives, terrain, and enemy combat formations in orienting military operations.

What if, however, this debate is a false one? For example, what if there is no real discussion, but, instead, only acrimonious polylogue caused by serious conceptual confusion and imprecision? Or, if the debate represents substantive disagreement over precise concepts, what is the utility of framing arguments in terms of polar ideals (for example, firepower-attrition versus maneuver doctrines) that are fundamentally without empirical content?

These questions lead to more serious concerns about the substantive content of the doctrinal debate. Is the debate over appropriate operational techniques and skills (in which the basic question is *how* to do), or is it over operational methodology (in which the basic question is how to decide *what* to do)? Or does the debate mix both elements? Different implications derive from answers to these questions, suggesting that little is to be gained from continued theological debate and polylogue. Perhaps reformers should focus on efforts to shape the infrastructure of the services in order to promote those factors that facilitate the implementation of historically successful precepts on which all agree: for example, initiative, flexibility, orientation on enemy weaknesses, synergistic combinations of maneuver and firepower, and speed of execution.

Before further developing these ideas, it is useful to examine the content of doctrine itself. Definitions abound. The joint service definition of doctrine speaks of the "fundamental principle by which the military forces or elements thereof guide their actions in support of national objectives. It is authoritative, but requires judgment in application."[1]

While military strategy relates the application of total military capabilities to national political purposes, and "soldier skills" refers to individual military skills, military doctrine focuses on how specific services and joint forces operate to train, deploy, and conduct military operations. As such, military doctrine should be embodied in a comprehensive and coherent set of statements which answer questions such as these:

1. Against what threats should the employment of our forces be shaped? Should our doctrine focus on the most likely or the most serious threats?
2. At what echelon of our force structure should the execution of our doctrine focus?
3. What general concepts should guide the employment of our forces? Should those concepts be primarily offensive or defensive in orientation?
4. How should we allocate our forces?
5. How should our fire support be used in conjunction with the employment of ground forces?
6. What role, if any, should special weapons, including chemical and nuclear systems, play in our operational scheme?

In addition to informing operational thinking, doctrine guides training. Units should train as they expect to fight. Therefore, training should reflect thinking about such questions and should be realistic in terms of terrain, pace, duration, and levels of confusion. Moreover, training must emphasize joint operations. Thus, we can identify the value of doctrine in many ways:

1. It provides prescribed routines for handling simple tasks.
2. It identifies key assumptions and concepts to provide a common basis for understanding operational thinking.
3. It provides a point of reference from which commanders can adapt as appropriate to the situation.

4. It provides a conceptual vehicle for debate, discussion, and evolutionary change.
5. It provides a vehicle for achieving the primacy of integrated, joint operations and forces over the more parochial concerns of the services.
6. It provides a model for training reservists and mobilized forces unable to train sufficiently to develop innovative approaches.

At the same time, however, military doctrine carries a number of risks. These derive from the basic doctrinal dilemma: doctrine must be explicit and specific to achieve useful empirical content; to the degree that this occurs, however, dogmatism and doctrinal righteousness too often prevail. Efforts to avoid this pitfall often result in doctrine that is so abstract as to be of no value in the field. Generally, however, doctrine errs on the first count and thus is misinterpreted and operationalized into prescriptive formulae, templates, and "school solutions" that inhibit flexible thinking and repress innovative approaches. As a result, operational rigidity, predictability, and dogmatism stimulate dissent and criticism within and outside the military.

Certainly most would agree that dogma is bad, and that dogmatic doctrine is especially undesirable. Doctrine may be criticized, then, for its dogmatism, apart from any substantive objection.

As a result, a number of reasons may explain the severe criticism of the army's "active defense" doctrine, enunciated in the 1976 version of FM 100-5, *Operations*. First, active defense doctrine was indicted because it was perceived by critics as didactically assuming a "meet the enemy force where it is strongest," defensive orientation in which "battle calculus" was used to assess relative movement and attrition rates as the basis for distributing forces on the battlefield. Second, it was condemned because of objections to the attrition concept and firepower exchange ratio analysis used to operationalize this concept. While one can take exception with the latter issue, to be fair, it must be noted that the active defense represented step-level changes from traditional thinking, for example, acceptance of risk, rejection of linearity, reliance on extensive battlefield movement and maneuver. Viewed in this light, the active defense represents a significant departure from traditional precepts and may be credited with having helped continue a constructive doctrinal evolution.

If doctrine is viewed as offering guidance on how to think, the doctrinal debate vaporizes in the face of two fundamental precepts: (1) "be smart!" and (2) be adaptive in applying techniques to the particular circumstances of a given situation. The "doctrine is methodology" perspective admits of no doctrinal debate because few would argue with these two precepts.

In contrast, doctrine can be viewed as the embodiment of "how to do" techniques and skills. In this case, the doctrinal debate is seen as focusing on the relative merits of alternative frameworks. If this is the case, reformers are seen as arguing over how to evaluate and identify the best prescriptive framework: firepower-attrition or maneuver, for example. This view collapses with equal ease, however, because no one views doctrine in so narrow a way as to exclude methodological considerations.

Finally, doctrine can be viewed as properly dealing with guidelines for both the selection and execution of techniques. Although most observers are likely to be most comfortable with this broader definition of doctrine, the implications for the doctrinal debate are clear: extensive confusion and ultimate acceptance of the fact that the debate dissolves into admonitions to be smart and adaptive.

If, then, doctrine as a conceptual framework says too much to be meaningfully discerning, or too little to transcend the obvious, we are left with little basis for legitimately conducting and analyzing the debate. If we are unable to clarify the nature of doctrine, and require all protagonists to speak to the same concepts with the same rigorous standards and levels of empirical content, there is little to be gained from continuing to argue over the merits of alleged doctrinal alternatives: for example, maneuver versus firepower-attrition.

Instead, two constructive tasks suggest themselves. First, we should recognize and applaud the fact that the reform debate has successfully focused attention on important assumptions and thinking and has successfully influenced the evolution of operational precepts in the armed forces in the 1980s. Moreover, reformers have provided the impetus for continued doctrinal evolution. This acclaim is qualified by cautioning that the debate may have prompted little that was new; indeed, successful combat leaders have always espoused the ideas of maneuver warfare. Rather, the debate has usefully challenged fixed assumptions and doctrinal righteousness to help create a command climate and professional milieu in which innovativeness is encouraged in training, contingency planning, techniques, and exercises.

Second, it may well be more useful to note the parallel conceptual directions of the ideas espoused by Lind and Wass de Czege and to concern ourselves briefly with suggestions for implementing systemic reforms within the services that are critical to the effective institutionalization, practice, and development of these ideas. It is not useful merely to debate theoretical constructs or enough to adopt a particular system of thought. Far more important is identifying and advocating reforms that will facilitate the practice of proven successful techniques and fresh thinking. Leaders should be developed who have the requisites for fast, innovative, and intelligent selection and adaptation of these techniques: intelligence, character, integrity, education, flexibility, experience, and initiative.

Possible reforms may include:

1. The use of brevet promotions to reward outstanding performance and thinking by "frocking" an officer with a temporary promotion and assignment to a combat leadership billet. This practice rewards such desirable behavior without challenging promotion, pay, and officer grade/end strength constraints.

2. The continued development of cohort units in which personnel are stabilized in order to promote cohesiveness and operational readiness.
3. Expanded investment in large training areas in which joint, large-scale exercises can be conducted under extended and realistic circumstances. The army's National Training Center and the air force's Operation Red Flag represent the invaluable quality of training in force-on-force exercises. Such programs should be expanded and structured with joint forces.
4. Increased emphasis would be given to joint deployment exercises in which forces are confronted with extended and realistic requirements for mobility, battlefield operations, and logistics.
5. Training exercises must emphasize realistic scenarios that require constant change and are ill-suited to set solutions.
6. Measures need be taken to create a command climate in which flexibility, innovativeness, initiative, and failure are encouraged. Such measures include stabilized command tours (to include general and flag officer billets) and increased emphasis on training exercises based on learning, evaluation, and development, rather than as tests of commanders.
7. Officer education and training must aim at developing leaders who know techniques and, more importantly, are experienced in facing new and tough operational situations requiring flexible adaptation of techniques. Particularly useful are historical case studies, education in military art and history, war games and simulations for unit leaders and staffs, and professional examinations as part of promotion selection processes.

CONCLUSION

The debate does not stop here. There are no easy answers to the questions posed in this and preceding chapters. It is a frustrating fact that the more these issues are studied the greater the problems appear, while the solutions seem less evident. If frustration breeds helplessness, there is a danger that the problems will grow even greater and the consequences become more serious. B. H. Liddell Hart attested to the universality of this precept for all reform movements when he wrote, "Helplessness induces hopelessness, and history attests that loss of hope and not loss of lives is what decides the issue of war."[2] We offer this appraisal not to promote a feeling of helplessness but to move those concerned with these issues from the ranks of what Lupfer calls the critics to what we hope will be a nation of reformers.

NOTES

1. *Dictionary of United States Army Terms* (Headquarters, Department of the Army, 1969), p. 160 (suppl., 1974).
2. B. H. Liddell Hart, *The Real War, 1914–1918.* (Boston: Little, Brown & Co., 1930), p. 472.

20

DEFENSE REFORM:
A REAPPRAISAL

William S. Lind

Lind evaluates the successes and failures of the military reform movement and considers its future directions. He believes that postwar American military performance and the recent large defense budgets will make reform critiques, proposals, and solutions even more appealing in the future. According to Lind, the most fundamental goal of the reformers is to make continuing reform a self-generating process within the services, thus putting civilian reformers out of business.

The most surprising and improbable fact about the military reform movement is that there *is* a military reform movement. In a political environment dominated by Political Action Committees (PACs), highly paid professional lobbyists, and well-entrenched special interests, and in a military where orthodoxy, bureaucratic gamesmanship, and "farm defending" have long been the norm, a totally atypical element has emerged. The civilian component of the reform movement is, at its core, just a handful of people. None of them is prestigious by the usual Washington standards. They have no money, they are not supported by PACs, they can deliver no votes. In style, which counts for a great deal among the courtiers of Washington, they are outsiders who wear turtlenecks instead of pinstripes, are seldom seen on the plush links of the Congressional Country Club, and think more about what they are saying than to whom they are talking.

No astute Washington observer would predict such a group could be influential—yet, it has been. The reformers have badly shaken the "business as usual" defense establishment. They have gained the support of more than fifty members of Congress. Armed with little but ideas, they have taken on opponents rich in both money and influence, and they are winning. It is wildly improbable.

Why has it happened? Three fundamental reasons are Vietnam, the Mayaguez incident, and the abortive hostage rescue attempt. Three times in the last two decades, U.S. forces have gone into combat. Three times, they have failed. In Vietnam, the reputedly most powerful nation on earth was defeated by a fifth-rate power. In part, it was defeated for political reasons. But in part, the failure was military, and if many soldiers claim our forces did well, many others realize they did not. Vietnam was followed by a Pyrrhic victory in recapturing the Mayaguez, which in turn was followed by national humiliation in the Iranian desert.

Defeats have consequences. One consequence of our defeats was growing doubt among politicians, the press, and the public about the competence of the American military. The defense establishment ignored these doubts or, when they could not, tried to deflect them with patriotic bluster, the privileges of rank, and the claim to special expertise on defense issues.

In so doing, they created a vacuum that reformers have moved to fill. Reformers argue that we need a stronger military, but that the strength of a military must be gauged by its ability to win in combat, not by how much money it costs. They say that to be pro-defense one must oppose the failures associated with the "business as usual" crowd.

The Reagan administration's defense program has added fuel to the fire lit by our recent military performance. By boosting defense spending during a severe recession while cutting the budget back in other areas, the administration not only put the defense establishment on the skyline, it unintentionally insisted it wear a black hat. While the public generally believes we need a strong defense, it also harbors longstanding suspicions of the defense establishment. The sight of Pentagon officials joining weapons contractors in a budgetary feeding frenzy while unemployment lines lengthen has caused politicians, press, and the public to give the reformers a hearing.

Two of the reform movement's central themes have proven particularly timely. The first is the need to set proper priorities among people, readiness, and procurement. The reformers argue that a correct balance puts people first, readiness almost coequal, and procurement last. The Reagan program, in contrast, raises procurement as a percentage of the defense budget from 27 percent in 1981 to 39 percent in 1987, and drops readiness (operations and maintenance) from 33 percent to only 25 percent over the same period. It also denies any military pay raise in FY 1984. The inevitable result will be a three-fold crisis:

1. A procurement crisis, generated by major cost overruns, in which we will

increasingly find ourselves unable to purchase the weapons the defense establishment has planned

2. A readiness crisis resulting from having proportionally fewer dollars to support each weapon at a time when new, more complex weapons, which require increased maintenance and training, are entering the inventory

3. A personnel retention crisis caused by a pattern of placing the burden of defense budget reductions on military pay and allowances

Each crisis is likely to hit at about the same time, roughly within the next three to five years. Each is likely to demand the expenditure of billions of dollars beyond what is projected in the administration's five-year defense plan. With public resentment of defense spending growing rapidly, and with federal deficits likely to be even higher than they are now, the money will not be there. The only way to pay the bills will be with cuts in the force structure.

A wide section of civilian opinion—much wider than those who identify themselves as military reformers—sees this pot of sludge waiting at the end of the Reagan rainbow. These people fear the long-term implications if a massive spending binge ends up providing a smaller, weaker military. And they see that the administration's massive increase in procurement spending is the engine driving the train.

This tends to make them open to the reform movement because the reformers have an alternative to current procurement policy. Others may call for procuring fewer weapons or for better management in the Pentagon. But the reformers offer a different way to think about what kinds of weapons we need, a way that can lead to more effective weapons in greater numbers at reduced cost.

This is the second timely reform criticism of "business as usual": the criticism that in weapons design and procurement, the choice is not "quality versus quantity." Rather, "In most major weapons, the real choice we face is between a few complex, unreliable, ponderous and ineffective weapons systems and numerous simple, small, agile and effective systems. In other words, the choice is actually 'complexity' versus 'quality *and* quantity,' and the dilemma is that the 'business as usual' establishment prefers the 'complexity' side."[1]

The press in particular has been interested in the reformers' procurement ideas. Massive cost overruns in weapons programs, personnel carriers with armor that vaporizes and burns when hit, F-18s that flunk operational tests and F-15s that don't do nearly as well against F-5s as promised are all good press material. Since many of the revelations about problems in new weapons have come from reformers, the press has beaten a small path to their door.

But the appeal of military reform to civilians goes beyond immediate reactions to the Reagan defense program. Not only politicians but also the population at large understands the price we pay in dollars and in national security for our failure to develop a post-Vietnam national consensus on defense policy. Whatever one administration does is undone by its successor.

Even relatively minor initiatives are caught up in endless congressional wrangles. Weapons programs live in a world of stop-and-go budgeting, cost overruns, and extensive delays before the troops see the new equipment. While our global adversaries plod along at a relatively steady (if sometimes exaggerated) pace, all the frailties they usually ascribe to "bourgeois democracy" are seen at their worst in the conduct of our defense policy.

The foregoing concerns just one wing of the military reform movement: the civilian wing. Of equal importance are the reformers inside the military. Who are they? They come from all four services, although they are most numerous in the army and the marines—the services that most directly experienced the frustration in Southeast Asia. They range from lieutenants through generals. Some openly proclaim their reform views in military journals; others work more quietly.

What do they do? First, they develop the ideas that constitute reform—ideas about maneuver warfare, unit cohesion, ways to design effective weapons, changes in military education, restructuring the JCS, and so on. While civilian reformers have played a role in exploring these and other reform concepts, they have generally done so while working closely with people inside the military, people who have the service and combat experience civilian reformers often lack. Much of the credit for these ideas that has gone to civilians in fact belongs to people in the military.

Second, they make reform happen. Civilians can talk about maneuver warfare; only uniformed reformers can use it in exercises, relate it to fire support and logistics procedures, tie it into war plans, and integrate it with training—in sum, make it something we can *do* instead of something we just talk about. The same is true in other areas. Civilians can discuss the need for JCS reform, but the discussion cannot lead to action until members of the JCS call for it—as some have. Civilians can suggest ways to define quality in weapons, but reformers in the services can write the specifications and conduct the competitions so that correct criteria are the basis of actual judgments and choices.

Third, uniformed reformers apply pressure for reform to the services' own "business as usual" elements. They help service and OSD leadership understand that reform is not just a political phenomenon but also a substantive one, and that there are valid and compelling military arguments for the changes the civilian reformers advocate. To the degree that leadership wants to retain its subordinates' respect, it must address these arguments, and it must do so openly and fairly. There is no question that much of the reform now evident in the marines and the army results not from external pressure but from internal initiatives.

Fourth, and perhaps most important, the uniformed reformers work to overcome the divisiveness that plagues our national security policy. They share the politicians' and public's awareness of the high price we pay for our lack of consensus. They realize no new consensus can be built on requests for ever-larger defense budgets that push aside questions about how the money is spent by saying, "We're the experts." A new consensus can only be built on a new partnership, on genuine and open dialogue, and on efforts to rebuild mutual trust between military and civilians concerned with defense issues. The uniformed reformers work to create that dialogue and trust—often in the face of hostility from "business as usual" elements within their own services.

Does military reform offer the basis for a new national defense consensus? It may. Both civilian and uniformed reformers have the creation of a new and enduring consensus as one of their foremost goals. Only reform addresses both of the public's attitudes about defense: its desire for a strong defense and its skepticism about the Pentagon. The reformers realize that a consensus can only be built around a military that can win in combat, doesn't break the national treasury, and gives a dollar's defense for a dollar in taxes.

One sign military reform may offer a basis for political consensus is the support it attracts from conservatives. It is perhaps not surprising that a movement critical of "business as usual" in defense has attracted substantial liberal support. It may surprise some to realize that it has at least as much support among conservatives. Conservative support can be explained on several grounds. Some conservatives identify strongly with the reformers' focus on winning in combat. Others see that defense traditionalism—raising the budget and giving the Pentagon whatever it wants—cannot serve as the basis for a new defense consensus, while reform possibly can.

Many conservatives share the reform movement's skepticism about bureaucracies and the effects of bureaucratic behavior. In the past, conservatives have tended to see uniformed bureaucrats as somehow different from civilian bureaucrats. Now, more and more of them are coming to realize that all bureaucracies behave similarly, in that all tend to make their decisions on intra-institutional rather than external market criteria. As Senator Gary Hart wrote, "In industry, bureaucratic behavior leads to bankruptcies like that of Penn Central. In government, it leads to massive waste. In war, it leads to defeats such as Austria's humiliation by Prussia in 1866, and France's collapse in 1940."[2] Conservatives are beginning to see the same parallels.

Whatever the reasons for the extensive conservative participation in the reform movement, its significance for the prospects of achieving real reform is profound. The defense establishment's political base in Congress, among the press, and in the public is conservative. If enough conservatives demand military reform, the services must deliver it. They cannot turn to the left for political support of "business as usual" in the face of conservative demands for change.

Where does the reform movement go from here? It still faces an uphill fight. In Congress, reformers are still outnumbered by both traditionalists and antidefense types. The reform movement lacks resources and even minimal institutionalization. Understanding of the intellectual content of reform is spotty, even among nominal reformers.

Several specific weaknesses in the reform movement need to be addressed promptly.

First, while the movement has had some success in the marines, the army, and even the air force (for example, the F-16), it has had little effect on the navy. Because of its geography, the United States is inherently a sea power. The best United States Army, Marine Corps, and Air Force have little strategic meaning if a hostile power can control the sea. A potentially hostile power, the Soviet Union, has built a navy that can challenge us for control of the sea, and it seems inclined to do so should conflict occur.

Individual reformers, civilian and uniformed, have raised a number of specific issues relating to the navy, but the reform movement has yet to come to grips with such central problems as America's lack of a credible naval strategy and application of the Boyd Theory and concepts of maneuver warfare to the naval environment. Reformers must develop reform ideas that can offer a comprehensive alternative to current naval policies, concepts, and practices.

Second, communications within the reform movement, especially between civilian and uniformed reformers, must be improved. Today, there is a spiderweb of contacts, channels, and "samizdat" distribution of documents between the two wings of the movement. Much has been accomplished through this system, despite its somewhat random nature. But a more regular, institutionalized method of communication is clearly required. One possibility is a new military journal, written explicitly from a reform perspective and oriented toward the officer corps.

Third, civilian reformers must become more willing to support reforms initiated by the services themselves. Many have been conditioned by years of political and institutional guerrilla warfare to be highly suspicious of anything initiated by the services. Too often, such suspicion has been justified. Most bureaucracies, when pressured to change, try to change appearances rather than substance, and the military is adept at that practice. In the army and the marines, however, some genuine change now seems to be taking place. While civilian reformers have generally been supportive of the marines, they have tended to dismiss even genuine change by the army as merely cosmetic.

In fact, the army is now making some real progress. The new FM 100-5 is a major improvement over its predecessor, and while few are likely to become skilled practitioners of maneuver warfare just by reading it, it does legitimize many of the reformers' doctrinal arguments. General Edward C. Meyer's moves toward a regimental system seem to embody a genuine commitment to improve unit cohesion. The army and the reformers are still at loggerheads on most equipment issues, but if a genuine dialogue has developed on doctrinal issues (and it has), it may be possible to create one on hardware questions as well.

Most important, the atmosphere within the army is changing. Until quite recently, army officers with reform sympathies risked being labeled heretics.

Now, this is less and less the case. Questions that had long been off limits can now be raised and debated openly within the army, including hard questions such as tactical competence and officer integrity. A new spirit is discernible, one that allows juniors to make suggestions and have them seriously considered by their superiors, that permits unit commanders to talk to civilian theorists and draw on their ideas, and, perhaps most important, that gives winning in combat priority over bureaucratic behavior. As a result, the nature of the army's problem is changing. It is becoming less an attitude problem and more an information problem.

In fact, the civilian wing of the reform movement is already succeeding at what may be its most fundamental long-term goal: making reform a continuing, self-generating process *inside* the services. The goal of the civilian reformers must be to put themselves out of business. Military reform is, by the nature of the military art, a never-ending process. No solution to a military problem is timeless. A reformed American military is not one that takes the ideas of the current reform movement and builds a rigid new structure upon them, but one that develops within itself an enduring capability for imaginative change, for self-renewal. That can only happen if reform is internalized, if it becomes the property of the services themselves. A successful civilian reformer is, ultimately, one who has made his own efforts irrelevant.

Will the military reform movement succeed? It will either succeed in reforming the military before we suffer a major defeat, or it will succeed after one. The reformers' goal is, of course, the former. History suggests it is possible; Fisher's reforms of the Royal Navy early in this century occurred without a British defeat. But history also suggests that reform without defeat is the exception, not the rule. Most great military reforms, like the Scharnhorst reforms in Prussia, have only been possible after a military disaster destroyed the credibility of the "business as usual" defense establishment.

Can we be Fishers instead of Scharnhorsts? The only possible answer is yes, because we must be. Our responsibility to the nation and to those who will fight on the next battlefield makes reform without defeat a necessity.

NOTES

1. From the briefing of the Congressional Military Reform Caucus.
2. Sen. Gary Hart, "What's Wrong with The Military," *New York Times Magazine,* 14 February 1982.

21

PUBLIC PERCEPTION, POLITICAL ACTION, AND PUBLIC POLICY

James Fallows

Fallows contends that the public perceives its only choices concerning military spending as being "more" or "less." The resulting peaks and valleys in the defense budget, Fallows argues, have a very negative impact on the long-term national security of this country. To reverse this trend, he recommends that the military take the lead in opening up the debate in order to educate the public about defense issues. He believes that an educated public will become the national constituency required to counteract defense parochialism, thereby ensuring steady-state levels of sufficient defense spending.

In the years since the Soviet invasion of Afghanistan, some things about American defense policy have changed dramatically. Most obviously, the United States has committed itself to spend more money on the military. The real change in this direction took place during the last year of the Carter administration. However different the Reagan administration may sound in its rationales and its rhetoric, its "rearmament" plans are essentially continuations of the trend President Carter set with the military budgets he proposed in 1980.

But other things have changed very little. Among the most important is the nature of public discussion about defense. With a few significant exceptions, political debate about the military still boils down to "more" from the right wing and "less" from the left, as it has for at least ten years. During the first two years of the Reagan administration, "more" had its day. Then it was time for "less" again.

Behind both views is a conception of military force and the military budget as mere symbols of larger ideological struggles. To many on the left, the military is a potential peril that will be put to wrongful use if allowed to prosper, and whose surplus should be wrung out and applied to worthier ends. To many on the right, an increase in the military budget can symbolize, all by itself, a renewed commitment to freedom around the world and order at home. Neither side seems particularly interested in the tasks that military forces might have to undertake or the tools they would have to use.

My impression is that many members of the professional military community on the whole accept this situation. To some extent, they have no choice. Among the sacrifices soldiers agree to make for their country is muting the full expression of their political views.

But the military community, broadly defined, includes many people who are not so constrained: retired officers and the numerous civilian authorities on defense. They, too, often seem to feel that the most they can ask of the outside world is that it leave them alone. They may think there is no point in trying to involve the general public in the nuances of their profession. The nation's history, after all, shows no signs of Prussian reverence for martial values. They may know that while it would be logical to define our international interests first and only then develop our military strategies, things rarely happen in so neat a fashion in American politics. Many of them deal with classified information and come to believe that only the handful of people who are similarly informed can sensibly consider military options. And at times like the early eighties, when things seemed to be going their way in terms of public support and funding for military projects, they are naturally inclined to leave well enough alone and not to burden the public with arguments that might confuse its view.

For all these reasons, it is easy to understand why military politics usually proceed on two levels: one of expert discussion within the military community, and another of slogans, accusations, and promises made by politicians and public commentators. Those on the outside are held at arms's length by their lack of expert knowledge. Those on the inside see little reason to invite the others in—and, in the case of active-duty soldiers, they are aware of the constitutional limits on their involvement in political discussions.

Understandable though it may be, I believe this pattern has its dangers, much as the general reluctance to deal with the rising costs of domestic entitlement programs, such as Medicare, is politically understandable but economically disastrous. In the case of the military debate, the greatest danger is to the American force itself.

As long as the public believes that the only consequential choice for the military is the choice between "more" and "less," the military will be subject to the boom and bust cycles of funding and of political support that have been its bane for thirty years. Viewed as one long block of time, the last three decades might seem an era of remarkable constancy in military spending. Outlays for the military, adjusted for inflation, were almost the same at the beginning of the eighties as they had been thirty years before. But at any given moment during that period, the budget was swept up in a rapid rise or fall. Politicians, reflecting public sentiment, have started pumping up the budget when it seemed neglected, or when the government has needed to pay for wars. With depressing predictability, they have then cut it back when the bills came due. "The peaks and valleys for the Defense Department budget are the worst things that can happen as far as the long-term national security of this country," Melvin Laird, Richard Nixon's first secretary of defense, has said.[1] From quartermasters to chiefs of staff, military men have understood the damage Laird described. When President Reagan announced his determination to start a military build-up while cutting tax rates at the same time, he started the budget toward the peaks again. The valleys will inevitably follow.

The "more versus less" mentality poses another, more serious threat to the military: a repetition of the general pattern of the war in Vietnam, in which politicians committed military force to a role beyond its authorized means. No one doubts that the American military could have "won" against the North Vietnamese forces and the Viet Cong, but it apparently could not be done within the limits that American politicians imposed or at a cost the American public was willing to pay. At the root of that disaster lay a misunderstanding of the special nature and requirements of a military force. Political leaders—and, it must be recalled, many military officials—spoke as if military force could be applied in small doses, and adjusted up and down, as with a rheostat.

Later, as American forces were being withdrawn from Vietnam, the volunteer army was begun. The principal motive for its creation was, of course, a desire to reduce the political cost of the war; but the public justifications were put in the language of economists and personnel managers, rather than that of leaders responsible for convincing men to make the unique sacrifices of combat.

There is little evidence that the special realities of military life are more clearly part of the public debate now than they were ten years ago. And so, as the pressure inevitably mounts to squeeze money from the Pentagon, it will most likely be done in ways that seem sensible and efficient, from the perspective of civilian budgeteers and private industry, but that may ignore the irrational, inefficient ingredients of military effectiveness. A regimental system, to use one example, will probably look less efficient, on a cost-per-man-year basis, than rotating and replacing soldiers individually. It is easy to imagine the speeches that will be given and the editorials written about this instance of military waste, even though the human bonds and loyalties developed in a regiment may be one of the most effective supplements to our military force.

It would seem, then, that the military community has a greater interest than anyone else in seeing that the public fully understands the nature of its tasks and the rules of its life. The effort to understand these special military realities lies at the heart of the arguments about military reform. Whether they are for or against a particular weapon or interpretation of military history, people inside the community have recently debated these issues with great passion. Why, then, has so little of that concern with military realities percolated to the outside world?

One reason is that some of these issues can be resolved only inside the community. The general public will never participate in a debate over the operational implications of attrition versus maneuver warfare. Politicians may express concern about professional standards within the military, but only soldiers themselves can create a climate in which proper professional ethics are rewarded.

Another reason is that many other groups share responsibility for making the defense debate what it is today. Example number one is Congress, which proves day after day that particular interests (the air force base in my district, the electronics supplier that employs one thousand of my constituents) are far stronger than general ideas such as military reform. To choose only one illustration of many, Congressman Addabbo (D., N.Y.) has become known as a scourge of the Pentagon because of his opposition to several weapons projects. At other times, however, against the air force's desire to stop buying the A-10 aircraft, Congressman Addabbo has succeeded in getting money for a small A-10 production run put back in the budget. The specific merits of the A-10 are not the issue here; my point is that one politician's intervention meant that this airplane, once known for its inexpensive effectiveness, has soared in unit cost and will continue to be purchased. It need hardly be mentioned that many of Congressman Addabbo's constituents work at the plant where the A-10s are built. Perversely, Addabbo's success with the A-10 advanced the interests of the groups that most oppose the airplane. By making the A-10 look more expensive, it made its bureaucratic rivals—the Apache helicopter for ground support, and the F-15 for general emphasis in the Tac Air budget—look like better buys. Similarly, liberal Californian politicians, who are generally suspicious of new strategic projects, have made a point of supporting the B-1 bomber, which is manufactured north of Los Angeles.

Unfortunately, complaining about Congress is like complaining about the weather. Congress acts the way it does because there have always been divided interests in the nation, and the national legislature was established to give them voice. But the balance between particular and general interests can be affected by the climate of political ideas. Thus, in his first year in office, President Reagan could convince congressmen to do what they naturally resist: accept changes that hurt some of their constituents. They did so because of the president's contention that larger interests—national economic recovery, reining the growth of public spending—were thereby served. But by the end of the president's second year, when the notion that everyone would share in the sacrifice had been destroyed, so was the president's ability to lure congressmen away from their concentration on the particular. The lesson for military policies is that without a clear, persuasive explanation of the general goal, the particular interests will always dominate. This is another reason why arguments about military reform should be carried to the general public.

Besides Congress, the press has borne great responsibility for keeping military discussions at the "more versus less" level. In my view, the major newspapers and news services have grown far more discerning in their coverage in the last few years, far less willing to view military questions purely as disagreements between liberals and conservatives. Still, the typical newspaper presents its readers either with exposés about slothful generals and wasteful boondoggles or with unquestioning rehashes of the latest official claim. Television usually offers an even more starkly simplified view.

Yet another reason some military men are reluctant to take their case to the public is that they fear what the public will choose. In this they resemble many liberal activists, who would prefer to convince a federal judge that school children should be bussed or antipollution equipment should be installed than to make their case to the legislature or the public. For example, one prominent senior officer contended that exposing the public to doubts and disagreements about military policy would inevitably weaken support for the military and for America's international commitments. In my view, this is a fundamental misunderstanding of the nature of an electorate. It assumes that the public can never grasp the complications of an issue, that it will instead be pacified by a facade of official consensus. Still, it is a view some in the military community hold.

But when all these explanations have been noted, is there still some responsibility that falls on the military community itself—something more its members could have done to combat the "more versus less" mentality? I believe there is, especially in the period since the military build-up began and the military reform arguments grew more intense.

Obviously there are delicate distinctions involved here. I am not suggesting that men and women in uniform should have been moving directly into political debate or working the talk-show circuits. But it is also perfectly obvious that military professionals, in uniform and out, know how to send the signals they want to the general public. Certain generals and admirals are frequently quoted in newspapers and on television. Certain colonels write regularly for civilian publications. Almost any officer interested in policy debates knows that the arguments in professional journals often spill over to affect press coverage. Civilian "defense intellectuals" and DOD officials freely plunge into political discussion.

In short, although the constraints of civilian control must be respected, members of the defense community who want to affect the debate can and have done so. The tone they set can have a tremendous effect on the way the other participants—press, Congress, the public—perceive the issues at stake. My contention is that at least since the beginning of the Carter-Reagan defense build-up, the military influence has too often brought out the worst in the other participants rather than the best—that is, has too often concealed the real meaning of choices rather than explained them.

For example, consider the strange history of the phrase "window of vulnerability," which has played so large a part in the case for the MX missile. As used by Ronald Reagan in his days as a candidate, it retained its original, Committee-on-the-Present-Danger connotation. It referred to the hypothetical possibility of a Soviet first strike that would destroy America's Minuteman missiles. Barring the actual strike, it referred to the dangerous political imbalance that would result if both sides knew the United States was vulnerable.

Soon after the administration took office, it proposed the first of several basing schemes that plainly offered no solution to this problem (putting the MX missiles in "hardened" Titan silos). The problem itself was therefore redefined. From that point on, when the president, the secretary of defense, and their associates said "window of vulnerability," what they meant was the world-wide line-up of Soviet and American forces. This is a legitimate subject for them to discuss, but it is very different from what they had been passionately arguing to the public for the previous several years. If frank language encourages honest political choice, this development could hardly be welcome. The civilian leadership was most responsible for the semantic lightfootedness, but there were few signals of dissent from within the military.

There is a second illustration, far graver in its consequences. It is the calculated disingenuousness with which civilian and military leaders have discussed the realities of military budgeting.

What was really at stake as Congress decided on military proposals in the summer and fall of 1982 was not that year's federal deficit or that year's military posture. It was, instead, the spending trend for much of the eighties. The biggest increases in the Fiscal Year 1983 budget were not for outlays—money spent that year—but for budget authority, the money committed for later in the decade. In deciding on the budget for 1983, Congress foreclosed the most important choices about military budgets in 1986 and 1987. The reason, of course, was that the long-term commitments to buy new equipment, especially ships, would claim much of the money that would be available later in the decade.

Most professional observers understood this perfectly; most members of the public did not. Some of them, of course, would have ignored the issue even if it had been included in the halftime activities at the Super Bowl. But others were misled because the administration and its allies did so little to explain the lasting consequences of the decisions made in 1982. For example, during the summer of 1982, when Congress awoke to the possibility of nearly endless federal deficits, the administration and many military experts argued that there was no point in looking to the Pentagon for an answer. Because so little of the money was going to be spent right away—$165 million for two nuclear-powered aircraft carriers, for example—canceling big procurement projects would make virtually no dent in a federal deficit of $100 billion or more. Columnist George Will summed up the administrations's reasoning in an article at that time. He listed the aircraft carriers and other big-ticket items, such as the B-1 bomber and the MX missile, and then calculated what a pathetically small difference it would make *in the immediate deficit* even if every one of them were cancelled. Similar reasoning was frequently heard.

What made it so disingenuous was that politicians and economists were not worried about the immediate deficit. The deficits for 1982 and 1983 were immense, but deficits always soared in recession years. The economists were panicked, instead, by the fear that huge deficits would persist in 1985 and 1986, even if the economy recovered. That was exactly when the full $6.8 billion cost of the aircraft carriers and the corresponding costs for other big projects would be payable.

In arguing for the aircraft carriers and other projects, military and civilian officials seemed to feel that they were seizing their own "window of opportunity," locking in purchases that a fickle public could not cancel later on. But this temporary victory came at a price: the trouble it ensured for the men who would have to use and maintain the tanks and missiles and ships later in the decade. If the history of modern military budgets demonstrates anything, it is that planners chronically underestimate the final price of each new weapon, although they chronically overestimate the amount of money that will be theirs to spend. The result is to force last-minute cuts in the few areas that can be reduced—namely, the operations and maintenance budget, payroll, training accounts, and other ingredients of military readiness.

The first harbinger of this pattern was seen early in 1983, when President Reagan proposed a pay freeze for public employees, including the military. The air force chief of staff, General Gabriel, responded that it would make more military sense to cancel certain weapons projects than to start down the long road of whittling away the operations accounts. As we move farther along that road in the eighties, arguments like General Gabriel's will become moot: the time to choose between procurement and operations will have passed. Perhaps this is the outcome that Congress and the public would have chosen if they had fully understood its consequences. My guess is that they would have taken a different course if the realities of military budgeting had been more honestly explained. Congress, the press, and the civilian political leadership could each have done more to highlight the question; but so too could the professional military.

A third illustration is the debate about selecting weapons for the modern American military. Here, of course, I have my own bias. In my reporting, I found myself persuaded by the argument generally associated with the military reform movement. I attempted to convey some of those arguments in my book, *National Defense;* as those arguments have been praised and attacked, so have I been. In rendering testimony on this point, therefore, I am hardly objective. But precisely because of my own involvement, I have a sense of the gulf between the thinking that goes into the military reform analysis and the interpretations made by its antagonists.

To its adherents, the reform analysis of military equipment involves the proper matching of machinery to the human and technical circumstances of combat. This view emphasizes above all else that a combination of tactics, human qualities, and machinery has historically distinguished effective from ineffective combat forces.

This view is usually summed up by its opponents as "quality versus quantity." In the eyes of its adherents, who differ substantially in their overall world views, that is simply not the choice. The fairer distinction is one suggested by Senator Hart, when he said that sometimes there is a conflict between different *kinds* of quality: the purely technical versus the strategic and military. In certain cases, from the machine gun to the nuclear-powered ballistic missile submarine, the two kinds of quality coincide. In other cases, they do not. It is on the connection between these kinds of quality that the movement concentrates.

The military reform view may also be caricatured as an antitechnology or low-tech mentality, but this is an even cruder approximation of its content. All members of the movement have emphasized the value of technological breakthroughs that serve the rules of combat. Most often, these break-throughs simplify mechanical processes or speed up a combatant's ability to respond. The radios that Guderian gave his Panzer Divisions in World War II are one illustration; guidance systems that home in on infrared or radio energy sources are another. The question is whether a specific technical breakthrough is appropriately matched to the realities in which it will be employed—the human realities of confused and fearful troops, the logistic realities of clogged and disrupted supply lines, the tactical realities of unpredictable behavior by an adaptable enemy, even the economic realities of budgetary uncertainty.

If there is a general pattern this group has tried to suggest, it is that complex weaponry is, on the whole, worse suited to these realities than simpler pieces of equipment. Thus, when William Perry says again and again that complexity, not technology, is the enemy of military effectiveness, he is not rebutting the reformers' position, as he imagines himself to be doing. He is instead confirming their central tenet.

What, then, is the disagreement between the two sides of this debate? To begin with, it is over the standards that will tell us which technologies are most likely to meet the test of combat, and which are likely to complicate and fail. Here the most obvious difference between the sides is the degree of skepticism they bring to drawing-board claims. Surveying a history of previous failures—for example, the ineffectiveness of strategic bombing in World War II, or of radar-guided missiles in Vietnam—some people, especially designers and procurement officers, see nothing more disturbing than the failed flights before the Wright brothers. They discount the mistakes, say they have learned the essential lessons, are sure that the great breakthrough is at hand.

Their predictions are, by definition, impossible to disprove. But another group of people is impressed by the long-time pattern of peacetime military bureaucracies. When not subject to the tests of combat, they have often promoted projects that fit their own standards and convenience but have had to be discarded as ineffective when warfare actually began. (For example, the unreliable torpedoes that plagued several navies at the start of World War II.) They have often proven too optimistic, and rarely too skeptical, in their estimates of how well a weapon would work and how much it would cost to build. Knowing this, the military reform group considers that a rigorous, realistic, independent testing system is at least as important as design bureaus that come up with new ideas. Whenever possible, they emphasize shoot-offs and fly-offs as the way to select weapons, not estimates and extrapolations of what a new system "should" be able to do.

Behind that difference of outlook often lies a difference in bureaucratic interest. That is, the people who are most optimistic about new and complex weapons are often the people with a stake in building or buying them. It would be amazing if this were not so. The best way to understand the federal government—or any large organization—is usually to see its policies as the result of competing bureaucratic interests. The arguments made for the most complex weapons are invariably couched in terms of loyalty to the fighting man. ("We don't want to send American boys out in anything but the best. . . .") But in peacetime procurement, it is hard to tell where the fighting man's interests begin and the budget's interests end.

Even in wartime it can be hard to tell. If the sole interest of the army's ordnance bureaus had been to send American boys out with the best, would the history of the M-16 rifle in Vietnam have been what it was? Would there have been so much tampering and so many destructive modifications to the original, superbly reliable design? Is that story so different, in its fundamentals, from the more recent history of the F-100 engine, in which the air force, faced with performance problems at a politically inopportune time, altered the tuning of the engine without telling the pilots?

It could, perhaps, be argued that the rifle and the airplane engine were inhouse questions of no consequence to the public—until the public began using the altered rifle in Vietnam. But the clearest illustration of bureaucratic interests affecting public argument is the military response to warfare in Lebanon and the Falkland Islands.

These battles offered exactly the kinds of real, combat evidence that can be invaluable in determining the proper selection of tactics, machines, and men. But as the very first results came in, before there was a chance to evaluate the evidence carefully or even be sure that the apparent results were the truth, American military authorities were already declaring a conclusive victory for their side. The battle they seemed to have in mind was the political battle over the defense budget.

After the sinking of the *Sheffield* by an Exocet missile, the secretary of the navy flew hurriedly back to the country to support the case for large aircraft carriers. And with equal haste, the opponents of big carriers declared them obsolete. Immediately after the Israeli Air Force's victory over the Syrians, one prominent U.S. Air Force general was quoted as saying that you don't hear much from the low-tech crowd any more; in their briefings, civilian officials put out the line that the superiority of all American weapons in all circumstances had been confirmed.

Simply as a question of appearances, these conclusions seemed too rushed to be judicious. As further evidence about the engagements came to light, they also seemed questionable on the merits. Some American equipment had performed well (for example, the Sidewinder missile, the F-15 and -16 fighter planes), and others had not (for example, the M113 armored personnel carrier). But the most important implications of the engagements could not be shoehorned so easily into the high tech versus low tech or quality versus quantity arguments.

To begin with, it was hard to contend that differences in machinery caused the difference in result. To put it more plainly, did anyone (except perhaps the Syrians) imagine that if the Syrians and Israelis had swapped equipment, the Syrians would have won? Tactics, skill, commitment, surprise—these seemed to demand a place near the top of any list of lessons of the Middle East warfare. Why were they generally missing from the instant analyses offered to the public by military experts? I suggest it is because they were seen as either damaging or irrelevant to the political argument for more defense spending. The sinking of the *Sheffield* was presented as an unanswerable ratification of precision-guided weapons. But did it not also illustrate the vulnerability of a ship or other platform that beamed out tremendous radio energy to control its own armaments—thereby allowing enemy missiles to home in on it? And does this not complicate the question of which of the new munitions could successfully be used in combat? The British made effective use of their nuclear-powered attack submarines, but the Argentines apparently penetrated British anti-submarine warfare defenses with their smaller, modern diesel-electric. Did this clearly prove either the high tech or low tech case, or did it indicate the need for more careful evaluations of effective strategies? Unreliable fuses on their torpedoes and bombs probably hampered the Argentines more than any single piece of British equipment. Why did this not merit mention in background briefings by the generals and policy makers?

In short, if these episodes of combat, like others before them, carried complicated implications that could only be understood after careful assessment, why were military officials so quick to respond and so eager to focus on the supposed ratification of high tech? To judge solely by appearances, the reason was that many of them had come to view these wars as sales tools rather than as evidence to be mined for its every lesson, no matter how inconvenient.

Consider the contrast of two other aspects of the defense debate, where the public has joined more fully in considering the essential issues. I mention them not because I endorse the decision so far reached in either case but because they differ in one important way from the questions of budgeting and weapons I have just discussed.

One is the draft. In democratic politics, no legislator has anything to gain by supporting conscription. The enemies he makes will outweigh, in their bitterness, the admirers he wins. Therefore, as a practical matter, politicians will not seriously consider the draft as long as unemployment remains so high and the immediate threat to American security so low. Even so, in the last two or three years the draft has been debated, and it seems to me that all sides of the argument have been aired. The American public has heard the numerical analyses of the American force, the demographic predictions about future recruitment, the libertarian opposition to compulsory service, the sociological and political fears about an unrepresentative force, and the military judgments about the practical effects of the volunteer philosophy. Whether you agree or disagree with the decision to support the volunteer force, you cannot complain that the relevant arguments have gone unstated.

The other subject is nuclear weapons policy. Here, to a greater extent even than with the draft, emotions run high. On one side are groups who feel that human survival is so threatened that extraordinary protests must be made. On the other are groups equally concerned about the imbalances of military power that, in their view, imperil America's security, and the world's. Each group may find the other's assumptions outrageous and its policies suicidal. But in the course of this debate, arguments have been made and answered, as they should be in a democracy.

What do these two cases have in common? For one, they involve a human element that people can instantly grasp. Everyone can imagine himself or his children being taken off to boot camp, or see his city beneath a mushroom cloud. In contrast, no one outside the military cares about the Aegis system or BVR radar.

But there is another similarity: these are not fundamentally budgetary questions. Yes, several big-budget items hang on the nuclear policy America chooses, and those battles—over the MX missile and B-1 bomber—were fought with the ferocity customary for large procurement projects. But nuclear strategy raises other questions that are political and philosophical rather than budgetary, and the draft affects only the manpower and training budgets. Is this why the military establishment found it easier to speak frankly with the public on these questions than on the many others in which specific budget items were at stake?

It should be obvious that I think the answer is yes. I do not thereby imply that military officers are negligent or corrupt. More than most of the rest of us, they feel the weight of their responsibility for the nation's safety. But they need help in discharging that responsibility. Unless politicians understand the special realities of the military task, they will not give soldiers the tools they need—and may assign them duties they cannot carry out. Unless the public also understands, it will not support politicians who defend the military's interest. Unless the press understands, it cannot shape the way the military's future is discussed.

For better or worse, despite constitutional provisions, the professional military inevitably shapes each of those understandings. The soldier's job will be easier if he more honestly shares with his countrymen the nature of his task.

NOTE

1. Quoted in the *Washington Post*, 30 November 1982.

22

THE OUTLOOK

Asa A. Clark IV

This concluding chapter summarizes the genesis and import of the military reform movement. The gap between often astute reform analysis and largely ineffective implementation of reform precepts is explained by "bureaucratic particularism and incrementalist policy making." Arguing that vibrant and informed public debate is essential to generate political pressures for reforms appropriate for the best military, Clark discusses specific roles in the policy community which will help spark and sustain the reform debate and, by extension, reform itself.

In the Foreword to this volume, Samuel P. Huntington praises the military reform movement for raising the right questions, properly focusing attention on areas of concern in military affairs, and sparking public debate with zeal and contentiousness. But where is the reform movement headed? How will it proceed? Can it be sustained?

Some observers perceive the reform movement as ephemeral, both in terms of political clout and political life expectancy. They argue, therefore, that the movement is an irrelevant and passing phenomenon.

This chapter, however, argues the proposition that military reform is not emphemeral, but rather is fundamentally important and presents significant opportunities for long-run mitigation of pervasive problems in the defense establishment. Specifically, it is only through vigorous public debate that sufficient political pressures can be generated to compel a robust peacetime U.S. military posture. Only under the continuous influence of such political pressures can qualitative innovativeness be catalyzed and exploited to ease, both in the short and long run, tough trade-offs among readiness, modernization, deployability, and sustainability.

Before proceeding to these fundamental questions, two misconceptions must be laid to rest. The first rejects the efficacy and the very existence of a military reform movement. This view stands on a variety of arguments, one of which is that no corporate or cohesive group of reformists, sharing some level of consensus regarding a specific set of issues, can be identified. Rather, many diverse actors, motivated by diverse interests, advocate diverse positions on diverse issues. Moreover, few (if any) reformers attempt to interrelate positions on the myriad of micro-issues into a comprehensive, coherent framework for assessing and revising U.S. military policy. The results are disjointedness and incoherence—hardly the stuff of political movements.

Another argument is that there is no reform movement; rather, only a coterie of self-serving, politically motivated individuals seeking to generate personal impact. Still another is that the movement offers nothing substantively new. Stripped of rhetoric, reformist arguments are revealed as truisms that work in focused wartime environments but are obscured in peacetime bureaucratism.

Although there is room for disagreement over the effectiveness of the reform movement's influence on military policy, the movement clearly exists and continues to operate. In addition to the public writings and speeches of reform luminaries, the movement's primary workings continue to be reflected in the conferences, meetings, briefings, and "maneuver warfare boards" of its diverse membership.

The second misconception rests on perceptions that the reform movement is a novel and short-lived phenomenon. As Lupfer reminds us, however, innovativeness and reform impulses are represented in a long tradition of military reform: for example, Scharnhorst, Douhet, Ashworth, Mitchell, Rickover, and Root. Because this reform dynamic inheres in the military, it is important to understand how to employ these impulses to the advantage of U.S. military policy.

As stated previously, this book is aimed at advancing the public's and policy makers' levels of understanding of military policy. Accordingly, the book presents arguments relating to the central issues in the military reform movement's agenda. It attempts to analyze those arguments and to assess the long-run and more qualitative implications of these issues. These purposes are now achieved, if incompletely.

More importantly, the book aims to advance the public's and policy makers' levels of understanding of how to exploit—continually and constructively—the reformist impulse to the advantage of the effectiveness of U.S. military policy. It is to this end that this chapter is devoted.

ROOTS OF REFORM: SPONTANEOUS PUBLIC CONCERN OR POLITICAL ORCHESTRATION?

To answer these questions, it is necessary to examine the sources of the ongoing reform movement. Because these have been discussed earlier, they are only briefly recapped here. The sources are loosely categorized as *systemic* and *orchestrated*.

Systemic Sources. The reform movement is in part a natural outgrowth of a number of factors, one of which is intrinsic reformist tendencies within the military (for example, the extensive debate within the army over the political and military feasibility of the 1976 "active defense" tactical doctrine for defending central Europe).

Not only the military but also the general public has shown concern for the overall U.S. defense posture. Public concern has been provoked by sustained Soviet build-ups in conventional, theater, and strategic forces; the poor recent U.S. military combat track record in Vietnam, the Son Tay and Mayaguez incidents, and the "Desert One" rescue raid into Iran; and continued reports of severe deficiencies in the armed forces (for example, racial problems on U.S. Navy combat ships, drug use, weapons procurement cost overruns, production delays, and performance failures; high emigration rates of skilled technical personnel).

Recently there has been increased policy and public focus on conventional forces issues, caused by heightened perceived importance of conventional forces balances for stable deterrence in a strategic circumstance of U.S.-Soviet nuclear parity. In addition, there are heightened public anxieties generated by perceptions of the erosion of U.S. global power in a more complex and interdependent world, and reinforced by uncertainties regarding U.S. interests, threats to these interests, and the efficacy of U.S. military force vis-à-vis these threats.

Other systemic sources of the reform movement are a resurgence of American assertiveness and conservatism in reaction to the spiritual calamities of Vietnam, Watergate, and Iran; the public allure of reformist promises of more defense for fewer dollars in a period of economic malaise, budget deficits, and high defense spending; and continuing congressional assertiveness in policy-making roles vis-à-vis the executive branch.

Finally, because the military reform movement is, quite simply, good politics, it is not surprising that a substantial number of senators and congressmen have attached themselves to the reform movement by joining the Congressional Reform Caucus. In addition to exercising their substantive concern for these issues, caucus members are able to enjoy the benefits of simultaneous advocacy of pro-defense and pro-economy positions, while quietly working to maintain defense spending in their own states or districts. As a result, the Congressional Military Reform Caucus has attracted membership and support sufficient to focus publicity, lead the defense debate, and exert influence to a not insignificant degree. Consequently, the public reform movement continues to flourish, in large part, because of the participation and leadership of congressional reformers.

The military reform movement, therefore, represents a spontaneous, if disjointed, response to a complex environment of mutually reinforcing trends and circumstances. In this perspective, assessment of future directions of reform properly derives from examination of the degrees of overlap and incongruence, both short and long term, among patterns of these various systemic factors.

Orchestrated Sources.   Another view, however, holds that the military reform movement reflects, in large measure, the carefully orchestrated efforts of a systematic reform campaign. Serving as the catalyst and cadre for the movement is a small group of dedicated reformers who desire "to create a broad, enduring national consensus in favor of a stronger defense . . . and to build a military which cannot only deter war, but, if conflict does occur, can win at the conventional level."[1]

Described in the introduction to part 1, these reform leaders pursue ends by working to sustain an effective military reform movement ("a loose alliance of members of Congress, defense analysts, and military officers") and a vibrant public military reform debate.

The tactics of the leadership core are sophisticated, comprehensive, and inherently political. One focus of these tactics is the military, particularly the junior and mid-career officer corps. On the presumption that the younger officers are not yet so socialized as to be incapable of change and critical self-examination, the reform movement promotes doctrinal innovativeness in the field through writings, conferences, and especially in the form of so-called "maneuver warfare boards." Reform arguments in this realm are theoretical and rational, and they explicitly target substantive concerns of the officer corps across the services. In this effort they are helped, of course, by the fact that many military officers (junior *and* senior) view themselves as properly in the vanguard of military reform. This role conception is reinforced by the ethics of military professionalism and a continuing climate of unit doctrinal experimentation.

A second focus of reform tactics is the civilian sector—both within the defense community and with respect to the larger public. Here tactics aim to exploit public concern for defense effectiveness, efficient procurement, and fiscal economy. For example, frequently cited critiques of defense procurement capitalize politically on the public's interest in these visible and easily understood issues. Arguments are attuned to create and shape an extensive political climate in which intensive pressures are continually exerted on policy makers. In this way, the reformist cadre intends to get the attention of policy makers and either to make them receptive to military reform precepts or to replace them.

Once the appropriate political climate is created, the reform impetus can be sustained and expanded into important substantive issue areas other than weapons procurement and aggregate spending. At this point, both avenues of this reform "double envelopment" campaign continue to exploit the influence generated by public defense debate-induced political pressures on policy makers in order to implement the substantive precepts of the military reform agenda.

From this second perspective, then, the military reform movement is viewed as the result of a purposive and comprehensive political campaign, waged in multiple arenas and guided by a core of reformists. Therefore, assessment of the reform movement's future directions properly focuses on examination of the vitality and sustainability of the public defense debate, the political pressures generated by the debate, and the relative responsiveness of central policy makers to such pressures.

Clearly, the reform movement is best understood as a consequence of forces present in *both* views. Accordingly, this assessment should follow the methodologies suggested by both perspectives. However, the environmental set of systemic factors must be taken as a given because they are exogenous to the reform movement. Therefore, assessment of the success of military reform is best derived through application of the second view: examination of political pressures generated by public debate and of policy makers' receptivity to reform arguments in the context of these political pressures.

EFFECTS OF REFORM

Results of the reform movement's efforts are manifest in a plethora of published argumentation and reform advocacy, in substantial experimentation and innovativeness in tactical doctrine and force structure by the army and marines, in the greater attention paid to fresh analytical thinking about long-held assertions in military organization and operations, and in the increasing sharpness of defense debate. Reformers are unable, however, to point to much evidence that their arguments and recommendations have been successfully adopted.

A number of explanations suggest themselves. The observation may be wrong and, in fact, military reform may proceed, but in ways that are undramatic and not visible to the public.

Alternatively, invoking the "reform is a political campaign" explanation suggested by the second perspective discussed above, the reform movement is seen as still in the preliminary phase of stimulating, sharpening, and focusing debate-induced political pressures. Conclusions that limited success portends failure are premature until the reform debate has gained sufficient momentum to create the political climate necessary for receptiveness to systemic reform.

Or perhaps the reform movement is more peripheral than inherent, and more noise than substance. Although the reform movement continues to successfully stimulate critical attention to defense issues, this "fire and smoke" publicity is unlikely ever to exert meaningful reform pressures on the military establishment.

While all three explanations are partially true, the third is the most interesting. Central to this explanation is the fundamental degree to which military policy—a vital instrument serving the public interest of providing the common defense—is dominated by particular interests. Although the reform movement continues to provoke and evoke innovative and critical analyses of military questions, implementation of remedial and innovative measures too often founders on the shoals of bureaucratic particularism and incrementalist policy making.

"STRUCTURAL PARTICULARISM"
IN THE MILITARY ESTABLISHMENT

The lack or slowness of response of the military establishment to reform initiatives, whether generated internally or imposed externally, is well known and has been extensively discussed.[2] This inertia is explained, in large part, by inherent characteristics of military policy. We can identify a number of such characteristics subsumed under the rubric of "structural particularism":

1. Important elements of military policy are difficult to understand because they are substantively arcane, politically invisible, and empirically nonoperational.
2. Because military policy is multidimensional—its components include strategy, doctrine, force structure, organization and C³I (command, control, communications, and intelligence), hardware, resource management, and so forth—policy making is extremely complex and confounded by high issue density and interdependence, uncertainty, time compression and extrapolation, and problems of coordination and integration.
3. Policy making is shared among many actors (individuals, organizations, interest groups, industries, agencies, communities) whose policy roles vary through different phases of the policy process.
4. Military policy involves committing scarce resources to functions whose actual impact on military effectiveness is difficult to evaluate.
5. Because national security objectives are diffuse and difficult to operationalize, and because many intervening organizational frames of reference compete for attention, the objectives of military policy become increasily fractionated. Consequently, parochialism corrupts the rationality and coherence of military policy making.

One consequence, among many others, of these policy characteristics is an incongruence between ideals—a professional military ethic to be innovative, skeptical, and positivist—and institutions, in the form of institutional rigidity and resistance to innovative change or reform. This tension has undermined, and will continue to undermine, the effectiveness of U.S. military policy.

A second consequence of the characteristics is conservatism and resistance to change. It is worth noting that these obstacles to change in the military are not merely inherent but irremediable as well; they spring from the very characteristics that define military organizations everywhere. This is not to assert the impossibility of change in the military, only the difficulty of achieving it. It is equally true, however, that some militaries historically have evidenced greater resistance to change than others. For a variety of reasons, some cultural, some perhaps even accidental, certain militaries have occasionally displayed an inordinate lack of receptivity to proposals for change.

This point was never more cogently stated than in C. S. Forester's book *The General*. Forester chided the British general staff for their tendency to rely on traditional solutions to new technological challenges, that is, massive frontal assaults against entrenched German machine gun positions. Forester described the deliberations of the British general staff in these terms:

> In some ways it was like the debate among a group of savages as to how to extract a screw from a piece of wood. Accustomed only to nails, they had made one effort to pull out the screw by main force, and now that it had failed they were devising methods of applying more force still, of obtaining more efficient pincers, of using levers and fulcrums so that more men could bring their strength to bear. They could hardly be blamed for not guessing that by rotating the screw it would come out after the exertion of far less effort; it would be a notion so different from anything they had ever encountered that they would laugh at the man who suggested it.[3]

The lesson here for all of the participants in the military reform debate is the need to be receptive to new ideas, the importance of a genuine willingness to listen to proposals for change from whatever quarter they may arise. As Forester so eloquently notes, even seemingly intractable problems may sometimes have simple solutions. While the state may possess a monopoly of control over the military, national security is the collective responsibility of both the military and civilian segments of society. That implies a mutual obligation to, among other things, listen to new ideas sincerely advanced and examine them with the intellectual honesty they deserve.

Despite the inherent difficulties of changing the military, and the uncertainty of our times, a recognition of these difficulties should not dilute the importance of reform. For something so costly and so serious, a better way must always be sought, but it must be sought with the understanding of the limits of change. The military is both always difficult to change and always in need of change for the better. True change for the better can only be achieved through appreciation of the inherent limitations to change, a factual basis for recommendations, a logical and consistent approach, and a willingness to accept the consequences.

In this context, the reform movement and the continuing defense debate are vitally important. By educating and mobilizing public interest, the reform movement's contribution to U.S. national defense lies in creating a political climate in which policy makers are held accountable for all aspects of defense: short- and long-run, quantitative and qualitative. The value of the public debate is to activate a national political constituency for the common defense. Specifically, the military reform movement, including its congressional wing, the Military Reform Caucus, plays a potentially critical role in educating the public and mobilizing a national constituency that serves to hold defense policy makers accountable to the public interest, rather than hostage to pork-barrel politics and the organizational thickets of structural particularism.

Mobilizing public debate and political interest is difficult; sustaining them is even more difficult. Nonetheless, to the degree that the reform movement succeeds in igniting such debate, at least two benefits obtain. First, the bureaucratism and parochial interest serving that are endemic to defense policy making are subordinated to the transcendant common defense, in great part, by the political climate created through public accountability. Second, in acting as the public interest constituency, the reform movement serves to protect and encourage those intangible, less visible, but critical qualitative facets of military policy which otherwise, because they are unprotected by constituents outside the military, are condemned to relative fiscal neglect.

DEFENSE DEBATES

As noted earlier, military reform debate is part of an American tradition of sustained and vigorous defense debate. Recent examples of this tradition include the debates over military unification (1940s), the building of the hydrogen bomb (1950s), Vietnam (1960s), arms control approaches (1970s), and MX deployment (early 1980s).

In addition to a longstanding tradition of vigor, American defense debates have tended to reflect a variety of emotional world views. For example, those holding the "internalist" world view conceive the chief threat to be unconstrained American militarism and argue, therefore, for defense cutbacks, funding priority for social programs, and constraints on the executive's military policy discretion. In contrast, those holding the "externalist" perspective view the USSR (or Communism, or a variety of Soviet surrogates) to be the primary threat to security and argue, accordingly, for a strong defense, a preemptive global interventionist foreign policy, and executive policy discretion.

Too often defense debates fail to consider systematically what sort of military strategy is appropriate to support a foreign policy approach derived from a particular world view. Instead, public debates tend either to focus on a particular discrete issue—because it is visible, identifiable, and understand-

able (for example, C5A cost overruns, ABM deployment, or military conscription)—or, as is the case more generally, to fixate on aggregate economy
and efficiency issues: for example, guns versus butter budget priorities, the
level of overall defense spending, waste and mismanagement within the
DOD.

While these are important concerns, they represent only small slices of
military policy as a whole and, more importantly, fail to even begin to
address the tough questions of how one constructs a paradigm for developing
and evaluating overall defense policy or military strategy.

A number of consequences generally result from typical public defense
debates:

1. Military policy issues are usually framed in terms of *inputs* and competing
   claims for these inputs. Public perceptions of military policy, then, are often
   collapsed into concern for the distributive consequences: budget dollars, jobs,
   production contracts, wages—the stuff of particular interests and domestic
   politics. Insufficient attention is paid to questions regarding what sorts of
   policy *outputs* provide the capabilities necessary for the best military policy—
   the stuff of national interests and foreign policy.
2. Priorities tend to shift from long-range to short-term considerations.
3. American cultural proclivities to employ managerial efficiency criteria—which
   do not readily recognize many unique features of combat and battlefield confusion—are reinforced by the public's fixation with aggregate quantitative considerations of economy and efficiency.
4. These debates often reinforce general suspicion of and biases against the military establishment.

Although public debates over Vietnam, nuclear strategy and arms control,
and NATO force modernization have grappled with fundamental policy
assumptions and objectives, few debates have transcended the dysfunctional
consequences noted above in order to serve as a constructive force for comprehensive and coherent consideration of ways to improve military policy and
provision of the common defense.

This is the charge of today's military reform movement. Just as reformers
intend to work for better military policy in the public interest the triumph of
the common defense over structural particularism—so this chapter argues the
importance of reformers serving as a constructive force by sparking and
focusing the public defense debate.

ROLES IN THE REFORM DEBATE

As discussed earlier, defense debates too often serve to reinforce negative
public perceptions of the military as an institution and suspicion of military
policy. Correspondingly, many of these critics lay the burden of reform on
the military. This anthology has attempted to support, among other things, an
alternative assertion that the responsibility for bad military policy is wide-

spread and includes the OSD, Congress, defense industries, the media, and others.

If these various actors are equally responsible for deficient military policy, the military cannot be charged with chief responsibility for reform or for leading the reform debate. Rather, all key military policy actors must exercise meaningful roles. Because this eventuality is quite unlikely—akin, perhaps, to asking the commercial nuclear power industry to regulate and reform itself—we must look instead for constructive measures to recommend to key policy players who are likely to play leading roles in guiding the public debate to develop and sustain the military reform impulse. Although not exhaustive, a number of observations are briefly discussed to suggest ways in which holders of key roles can stimulate constructive debate and build public political pressures for policy accountability and reform receptivity.

The President and the Executive Office. The president is the key; as the paramount opinion shaper and chief executive, only he can lead an enlightened debate, clarify the issues, focus the arguments, direct critical examination of assumptions and implications, and persuade the military community to examine reform precepts (and other proposals) that would enhance military policy.

It is a fact, however, that limited time and expertise as well as political constraints make it difficult for the president to effectively articulate comprehensive considerations about complex, qualitative issues. Moreover, the president wants to avoid unnecessary political confrontations and perceptions of micro-managing in the defense sector. Therefore, the president's role is best defined as leading the defense debate at a general, but comprehensive and enlightened, level, and publicly committing the force of his office to moving the military policy community to critically evaluate, adopt, and implement constructive reform measures.

The Congress. As discussed by Reed in chapter 14, the Congressional Reform Caucus plays important roles vis-à-vis military reform: education of congressmen and senators, articulation of reform precepts as an "alternative defense analysis institution," criticism and oversight of administration policies, and acting as catalyst of the public debate. These roles are aided to the degree that recognized congressional defense policy experts join in redirecting issue-specific controversy to broader, more comprehensive public debate.

The implications of the Supreme Court's 1983 decision to strike down the legislative veto as unconstitutional will likely remain unclear for decades. Nonetheless, it is likely that broader, public interest defense perspectives will prevail over the particularism of "iron triangle" policy making as these issue-specific sub-governments are absorbed into fuller legislative and executive participation.

The Office of the Secretary of Defense.   Because of perceptions that he is obsessed with only two themes—foreign threats, and the necessity of increased defense spending (both of which serve to fixate public attention on superficial, aggregate, quantitative issues)—the secretary of defense faces a traditional public credibility problem. Nevertheless, the OSD must play the lead role in substantively articulating the unique characteristics of military policy and a comprehensive, strategy-based framework for guiding this policy. Starting with clear conceptions of a U.S. national political strategy, the secretary must articulate the elements of a coherent military strategy and show how, in the short and long run, the various components of military policy are derived and interrelated. In addition, justifications must explicitly identify the opportunity costs of not supporting proposed military policy in terms of foregone capabilities or further constraints on strategic flexibility.

On the hardware side, OSD should consider creating an autonomous test and evaluation board, independent of the services, the Defense Advanced Research Projects Agency (DARPA), and the Office of the Undersecretary of Defense for Research and Engineering (OUSDRE) to serve as an ombudsman for research, development, and acquisition matters and to provide independent review and evaluation of projects to the secretary. In addition to serving as a disinterested third party in hardware evaluation, the board could monitor interservice coordination and joint systems integration. This latter function would be invaluable, especially in areas such as strategic mobility and C³I.

The Military.   Reform of the Joint Chiefs of Staff has been discussed in preceding chapters. Although the variety of reform proposals is far-ranging, strengthening the Joint Staff independently of the services is viewed as of fundamental importance. In contrast to public fears that such reforms disrupt civilian control of the military, control is enhanced to the degree that the JCS and Joint Staff achieve independence from the services, are the chain of command link between the president/OSD and the services, and are free to exercise authority and countervailing influence over particularistic elements among the services. In addition to providing an alternative source of military expertise, a reformed JCS serves to impose planning and operational jointness on autonomous services and fragmented military policy. Peacetime military policy becomes the result of policy processes and relationships that would obtain in wartime, with the unified and specified commands serving as the operational foci, as coordinated by the JCS and directed by OSD and the president.

Fully cognizant of the danger of violating constitutional precepts and the legacy of civil-military relations, the military should pursue activist roles aimed at informing the debate and encouraging consideration of fresh ideas. Such measures might include:

1. continued emphasis on congressional testimony (particularly by representatives of a reformed JCS);
2. increased participation in interdepartmental coordination and policy groups;
3. stronger congressional liaison efforts;
4. greater emphasis on critical analysis in military publications and encouragement of publication by military officers;
5. expanded use of public affairs resources, Recruiting Command personnel, ROTC personnel, and military installations to explain the features of military operations and policy.

The Media. Media treatment of defense issues in general, and coverage of the reform impulse in particular, can substantially move public attention beyond traditional superficialities to reinforce constructive reform pressures. Greater in-depth and objective treatment of issues is necessary. The media must constantly strive to uphold the highest standards of the journalistic profession: For example, thorough research, extensive interviews to gain insights on all perspectives, more emphasis on larger contexts (less on micro-issues). In addition to examining the uniqueness of the military and the consequent appropriateness of managerial efficiency criteria for evaluating military policy issues, the media can educate the public on key qualitative issues that are less well known.

CONCLUSION

Secure in the knowledge that the reform impulse inheres in the military policy community, reformers must always continue to advocate self-criticism and innovativeness in military policy and policy processes. Moreover, reformers must continue to stimulate public debate in order to create an informed public constituency that will hold the military policy community accountable.

The reform movement is dedicated to achieving the best possible military. Necessary analysis of needed reforms is forthcoming in the reform movement. What is *not* forthcoming are policy responses and implementation of reform measures. This continuing gap is explained, in large measure, by the persistence of pervasive structural particularism in military policy making.

Successful reform implementation requires debate, analysis, and response by key policy-making actors. This will occur to the degree that vigorous public debate continues. This debate is important in raising the salience and public understanding of military policy issues. Only an interested and enlightened public can generate sufficient pressure on policy makers for political accountability to ensure that public interests of defense prevail over particular interests so that the best military policy is attainable.

Assessment of "whither military reform?" can be viewed in the short and long run. The short-run prognosis reflects answers to questions for each issue area (for example, doctrine, procurement): Who are the reformers? Who are the key policy makers? To what degree is there overlap? What is the propensity for reform of these policy makers? To what extent are they sensitive to public debate and accountability? How many actors are key to this policy sector? To what extent do vested and countervailing interests mitigate against reform?

Short-term evaluation of reform success, using these criteria, is problematic and yields a mixed picture. Referring to the general policy sectors along which this anthology is organized, one can forecast the likelihood of successful reform during the 1980s as:

Doctrine	High
Procurement	Poor
Force Structure	Low
JCS Reorganization	Fair

The utility of such speculation is clearly questionable. Far more important is the long-run outlook for military reform. Here the central question focuses on the degree to which inveterate, inherent reformist tensions within the military policy community are able to exert continuous reform pressures and successfully develop a policy climate in which critical review, public accountability, innovativeness, and dedication to an ethic of selfless commitment to the best military are encouraged and self-perpetuated.

In his classic work, *The Common Defense*, Huntington observes that

> the greater the opposition to innovation within the executive, the more prolonged is the discussion within the executive, the more extensive are the efforts of the proponents of innovation to arouse support outside the executive, and, hence, the more extensive is the public debate of the issue stimulated by the proponents of innovation before the Administration makes its decision.[4]

This hypothesis expresses the dynamic and vital role of the reform debate. The military reform movement's long-run outlook, as defined above, will reflect the vigor, constancy, and quality of the ongoing public debate. This volume is dedicated to sustaining and sharpening this debate in order that the long-run movement toward reform continues to be fulfilled.

NOTES

1. Sen. Gary Hart, mimeographed letter accompanying "A Military Reform Budget for FY 1984," dated 14 March 1983.
2. See chap. 15, Asa A. Clark IV, "Interservice Rivalry and Military Reform"; chap.

16, David C. Jones, "What's Wrong with the Defense Establishment?"; chap. 17, Paul F. Gorman, "Toward a Stronger Defense Establishment."

3. C. S. Forester, *The General* (New York: Penguin Books, 1936), p. 173.

4. Samuel P. Huntington, *The Common Defense* (New York: Columbia University Press, 1966), p. 291.

CONTRIBUTORS

RICHARD K. BETTS is a senior fellow in Foreign Policy Studies at the Brookings Institution. He received B.A., M.A., and Ph.D., degrees in government from Harvard University, where he served on the faculty in 1975–76 before coming to Brookings. He is the author of *Soldiers, Statesmen, and Cold War Crises*, which won the Harold D. Lasswell Award for the best book on civil-military relations in 1977 and 1978, and coauthor of *The Irony of Vietnam: The System Worked* (1979), which won the 1980 Woodrow Wilson Prize for the best book in political science. In addition to two other books, Betts has also published over two dozen articles on nuclear policy, strategic intelligence, conventional forces and strategy, arms trade, and other subjects in *International Security, World Politics, Orbis, Foreign Policy, International Studies Quarterly, Survival, Political Science Quarterly, Asian Survey, Washington Quarterly,* other journals, and edited volumes. He also serves on the editorial boards of *Orbis, Journal of Strategic Studies,* and *Atlantic Quarterly* and is a consultant to the National Intelligence Council and Central Intelligence Agency.

STEVEN L. CANBY is a Washington-based defense consultant with C&L Associates. He is a graduate of the United States Military Academy and received a Ph.D. degree from Harvard University. He has written numerous studies on military strategy and tactics, military organization, and defense manpower and is adjunct professor in the National Security Studies Program at Georgetown University.

Major PETER W. CHIARELLI, an armor officer, is assistant professor of international relations and Soviet studies at the United States Military Academy, West Point. He is an associate author of *American National Security: Policy and Process* (Johns Hopkins University Press, 1981).

Lieutenant Colonel ASA A. CLARK IV is an infantry officer and associate professor of international relations at the United States Military Academy, West Point. Clark received a Ph.D. degree in international relations from the University of Denver and is the coeditor of *Conventional Deterrence in NATO* (forthcoming, Spring 1984).

Lieutenant Colonel THOMAS W. FAGAN is an armor officer and associate professor of economics at the United States Military Academy, West Point. As director of the Office of Economic and Manpower Analysis, West Point, Fagan advises the army staff on manpower questions.

JAMES FALLOWS is Washington editor for the *Atlantic* and author of *National Defense* (1981), which won an American Book Award in 1982. He has written for numerous magazines since 1972 and was, for the first two years of the Carter administration, the president's speechwriter. Fallows studied American history at Harvard and economics at Oxford, as a Rhodes Scholar.

NEWT GINGRICH is a Republican Congressman from the 6th Congressional District of Georgia. Congressman Gingrich has published numerous articles on the issues of the day, with special emphasis on defense and foreign policy. He is currently at work on a study of the reforms needed to ensure the long-term survival of the United States. In the House, Congressman Gingrich is a member of the Military Reform Caucus.

General PAUL F. GORMAN, United States Army, is the commander in chief, United States Southern Command, and as such commands all U.S. armed forces stationed or training in Latin America. His previous assignment was assistant to the chairman of the Joint Chiefs of Staff. General Gorman is a veteran of both the Korean and Vietnam conflicts, and his numerous assignments include service on the U.S. Delegation Staff, United States/Vietnam Talks, Paris.

General DAVID C. JONES, United States Air Force, Retired, served as chairman of the Joint Chiefs of Staff from June 1978 to June 1982. General Jones's article "Why the Joint Chiefs of Staff Must Change" (Hay Associates' magazine, *Directors and Boards,* February 1982) was influential in sparking the current debate over JCS reform.

ROBERT W. KOMER, undersecretary of defense for policy from 1979 to 1981, is a visiting professor at George Mason University and George Washington

University. He has written numerous articles on defense issues including "Maritime Strategy vs. Coalition Defense" (*Foreign Affairs*, Summer 1982).

WILLIAM S. LIND serves as Senator Gary Hart's legislative assistant for armed services and as president of the Military Reform Institute. Besides being the primary architect of maneuver warfare as defined by the reform caucus, he has written numerous articles on military topics for the *Marine Corps Gazette, Military Review, Air University Review, Naval Institute Proceedings*, and *Harper's*.

Major TIMOTHY T. LUPFER is an armor officer in the United States Army and formerly assistant professor of military history at the United States Military Academy, West Point. Lupfer is a Rhodes Scholar and wrote a highly acclaimed study entitled *The Dynamics of Doctrine: The Changes in German Tactical Doctrine during the First World War* (U.S. Army Command and General Staff College, Leavenworth Paper no. 4, July 1981).

JOHN D. MAYER, JR. is a principal analyst with the National Security and International Affairs Division of the Congressional Budget Office. He was assigned to the Office of the Assistant Secretary of Defense (Program Analysis and Evaluation) prior to assuming his current position. His publications include "Rapid Deployment Forces: Policy and Budgetary Implications" (Congressional Budget Office, 1983).

Major JEFFREY S. MCKITRICK, an infantry officer, is assistant professor of national security studies at the United States Military Academy, West Point. He recently wrote an article entitled "A Military Look at Military Reform" (*Comparative Strategy,* 1983).

PHILIP A. ODEEN is regional managing partner for a management consulting firm in Washington, D.C. Past positions include director, Program Analysis, National Security Council for Dr. Henry Kissinger. Recipient of a Fulbright Scholarship, Odeen has published a number of studies including "Domestic Factors in U.S. Defense Policy," in *America's Security in the 1980s* (Adelphi Papers no. 173, International Institute for Strategic Studies, London, Spring 1982).

Lieutenant Colonel JOHN M. OSETH is a military intelligence officer in the United States Army and formerly assistant professor of American foreign policy at the United States Military Academy, West Point. Oseth has a law degree and a doctorate in political science, both from Columbia University. He has published several articles on military and intelligence affairs.

WILLIAM J. PERRY, undersecretary of defense for research and engineering from 1977 to 1980, is an executive in an investment banking firm in San Francisco. Perry received his Ph.D. degree in mathematics from Pennsylvania State University and is currently a member of the Advisory Council and a visiting scholar at Stanford University. His numerous publications include

"Technological Prospects" in *Rethinking the U.S. Strategic Posture* (Ballenger, 1982).

JEFFREY RECORD is a senior fellow at the Institute for Foreign Policy Analysis. He was formerly legislative assistant for national security affairs to Senator Sam Nunn, and a research associate on the Brookings Institution's Defense Analysis Staff. He is the author or coauthor of numerous books on military affairs, including *Sizing Up the Soviet Army* (1975); *U.S. Nuclear Weapons in Europe: Issues and Alternatives* (1974); and *Where Does the Marine Corps Go from Here?* (1976). His most recent major works, *Force Reductions in Europe: Starting Over; The Rapid Deployment Force and U.S. Military Intervention in the Persian Gulf; NATO's Theater Nuclear Force Modernization Program: The Real Issues;* and *U.S. Strategy at the Cross-roads: Two Views;* were published by the Institution in 1980, 1981, and 1982.

Major JAMES W. REED is an infantry officer, United States Army, and formerly assistant professor of international politics at the United States Military Academy, West Point. He is an associate author of *American National Security: Policy and Process* (The Johns Hopkins University Press, 1981).

PIERRE SPREY, a prominent member of the military reform movement, is a defense consultant in Washington, D.C. Since 1968, he has been deeply involved in the genesis of key weapons for increasing the size and effectiveness of U.S. forces while decreasing their cost; weapons that include the F-16 fighter, A-10 close combat air support aircraft, GAU-8 30-mm cannon, and the M48A5 tank.

Colonel HUBA WASS DE CZEGE is an infantry officer in the United States Army. He is currently assigned to the army's Command and General Staff School at Fort Leavenworth, Kansas, where he served as one of the primary authors of the army's new field manual, FM 100-5, *Operations*.

INDEX

The Johns Hopkins University Press

The Defense Reform Debate

This book was composed in Times Roman text
and Optima display type by BG Composition
Inc., from a design by Cynthia W. Hotvedt.
It was printed on S. D. Warren's 50-lb.
Sebago Eggshell paper and bound in Joanna
Arrestox A by The Maple Press Company.